Hybridity: Law, Culture and Development

This book explores recent developments in the concept of hybridity through a multi-disciplinary perspective, bringing ideas about legal plurality together with the fields of peace, development and cultural studies. Analysing the concepts of hybridity and hybridization, their history, their application in law and legal studies, and their implications for thinking and rethinking legal plurality, the book shows how the concept of hybridity can contribute to an understanding of the processes that occur when different normative or legal orders or frameworks confront each other.

Nicolas Lemay-Hébert is based in the International Development Department, University of Birmingham, UK, and **Rosa Freedman** in the Law Department, at the University of Reading, UK.

Law, Development and Globalization
Series Editor – Julio Faundez
University of Warwick

During the past decades, a substantial transformation of law and legal institutions in developing countries has taken place. Whether prompted by market-based policies or the international human rights movement, by the relentless advance of the process of globalization or the successive waves of democratization, no area of law has been left untouched. The aim of this series is to promote cross-disciplinary dialogue and cooperation among scholars and development practitioners interested in understanding the theoretical and practical implications of the momentous legal changes taking place in developing countries.

Titles in the series:

Justice Reform and Development: Rethinking Donor Assistance to Developing and Transitional Countries
Linn Hammergren

Law and Society in Latin America
Cesar Rodriguez Garavito

Policing and the Politics of Order-Making
Peter Albrecht and Helene Maria Kyed

Violence Against Women in Legally Plural Settings: Experiences and Lessons from the Andes
Anna Barrera Vivero

Forthcoming titles in the series:

Multinational Integration, Cultural Identity and Regional Self-Government
Roberto Toniatti and Jens Woelk (eds)

Hybridity: Law, Culture and Development

Edited by Nicolas Lemay-Hébert and Rosa Freedman

Routledge
Taylor & Francis Group
LONDON AND NEW YORK

First published 2017
by Routledge
2 Park Square, Milton Park, Abingdon, Oxon, OX14 4RN

and by Routledge
711 Third Avenue, New York, NY 10017

First issued in paperback 2018

Routledge is an imprint of the Taylor & Francis Group, an informa business

British Library Cataloguing in Publication Data
A catalogue record for this book is available from the British Library

Library of Congress Cataloging-in-Publication Data
Names: Hybridity: Exploring Power, Social Structures, and Institutions Beyond the Liberal West (Conference) (2014 : Birmingham, England) | Freedman, Rosa, editor. | Lemay-Hébert, Nicolas, editor. | University of Birmingham. Institute of Advanced Studies, organizer.
Title: Hybridity : law, culture and development / Rosa Freedman and Nicolas Lemay-Hébert.
Description: Abingdon, Oxon ; New York, NY : Routledge, 2017. | Series: Law, development and globalization | "This edited collection is the result of a workshop organised in March 2014 at the University of Birmingham's Institute for Advanced Studies, entitled: Hybridity: Exploring Power, Social Structures, and Institutions Beyond the Liberal West.—ECIP introduction. | Includes bibliographical references and index.
Identifiers: LCCN 2016057091| ISBN 9781138673427 (hbk) | ISBN 9781315561950 (ebk)
Subjects: LCSH: Legal polycentricity—Congresses. | Law and globalization—Congresses.
Classification: LCC K236 .H93 2017 | DDC 340.9—dc23
LC record available at https://lccn.loc.gov/2016057091

ISBN 13: 978-1-138-33359-8 (pbk)
ISBN 13: 978-1-138-67342-7 (hbk)

Typeset in ITC New Baskerville Std
by Swales & Willis Ltd, Exeter, Devon, UK

Contents

Contributors

Christina Baghdady completed her studies in International Politics and Policy (BA Hons) at the University of Liverpool; and her MA in International Relations (Security Studies) at the University of Birmingham. Her research interests are in MENA region related issues; in particular the role of Religion in Egypt and its impact on social, political and economic development pre and post the Arab Uprising.

Kim Barker is a Lecturer in Law at Wolverhampton Law School. Her research focuses on the regulation of online behaviour and communities, but also spans intellectual and digital properties, particularly in the context of comics and games. Her current research focuses on online misogyny, and the absence of regulation in this area. Her most recent publication is 'Virtual Spaces and Virtual Layers - Governing the Ungovernable?' in the *Information & Communications Technology Law* (2016).

Danielle Beswick is Senior Lecturer, International Development Department, University of Birmingham. Her research focuses on post conflict statebuilding, the international relations of Africa, and African peacekeeping. She has undertaken research funded by the British Academy and the UK Economic and Social Research Council, including a current ESRC seminar series on UK Africa relations. Danielle has published articles in peer-reviewed journals including *African Affairs, Third World Quarterly* and *Development and Change.*

Fiona de Londras is Professor of Global Legal Studies at the University of Birmingham. She has published widely on counter-terrorism, constitutionalism and human rights, including the books *Critical Debates on Counter-Terrorism Judicial Review* (CUP; with Fergal F. Davis) and *The Impact, Legitimacy and Effectiveness of EU Counter-Terrorism* (Routledge; with Josephine Doody).

Sam Fowles is a PhD candidate at Queen Mary University of London. His research focuses on human rights, legal theory and public international law. Sam regularly advises MPs and NGOs on legal issues.

Rosa Freedman is Professor of Law and Global Development, University of Reading. Her research focuses on the intersection of international law and international relations, with a particular focus on the United Nations, human rights, and peacekeeping. She has published two monographs, *Failing to Protect: The UN and the Politicization of Human Rights* (Hurst; OUP, 2014) and *The United Nations Human Rights Council: A Critique and Early Assessment* (Routledge, 2013), as well as many articles and book chapters. She frequently appears in international and national media, works closely with the UN and with state governments, and sits on the advisory boards of international NGOs.

Eric Heinze is Professor of Law at Queen Mary, University of London. His books include *Hate Speech and Democratic Citizenship, The Concept of Injustice, The Logic of Constitutional Rights, The Logic of Liberal Rights, The Logic of Equality, Sexual Orientation: A Human Right,* and *Of Innocence and Autonomy: Children, Sex and Human Rights.* His chapters and articles include pieces in *Oxford Journal of Legal Studies, Harvard Human Rights Journal, Modern Law Review, Ratio Juris, Legal Studies, Michigan Journal of International Law,* and *Journal of Social & Legal Studies.*

Ruth Houghton is a Graduate Teaching Assistant at Durham Law School. She has previously worked as a research assistant for projects on the United Nations Human Rights Council, the International Labour Organisation, and non-justiciability in international law. Her doctoral research focuses on Global Constitutionalism and the norm of democracy.

Paul Jackson is Professor of African Politics, International Development Department, University of Birmingham, and research fellow in the Centre for African Studies, University of the Free State. He is the author of several articles and books and his research focusses on security sector reform, decentralisation and post-conflict reconstruction. He is also the co-editor of the *Routledge Studies in Security and Development* book series. His most recent publications include editing the *Elgar Handbook of Security and Development* (Edward Elgar, 2015) and *Securing Sierra Leone, 1997–2013: Defence, Diplomacy and Development in Action* (Royal United Services Institute Whitehall Papers No. 82, 2015).

Mark Kirkham is a doctoral candidate in international development at the Department of International Development, University of Northampton (UK). In addition, he is an associate lecturer in International Development at the University of Northampton. His research interests include hybrid statebuilding and how the military engages with international civilian organizations during the process of post-conflict peacebuilding.

Nicolas Lemay-Hébert is Senior Lecturer, International Development Department, University of Birmingham. He is the co-editor of the *Journal* *of Intervention and Statebuilding* and the *Routledge Studies in Intervention and Statebuilding*. His research focuses on narratives of resistance to international interventions, the political economy of interventions, and statebuilding and peacebuilding issues. His most recent publication is *Semantics of Statebuilding: Language, Meanings and Sovereignty* (London: Routledge, 2016).

Philipp Lottholz is a Doctoral Researcher at International Development Department, University of Birmingham. In his research, he looks at processes of hybridisation, contestation and hegemony in community security and peacebuilding in Kyrgyzstan, which he tries to understand against the backdrop of post-liberal statebuilding in post-Soviet Central Asia. His empirical focus is on the role of civil society actors in police reform, youth politics and local crime prevention. Philipp's research interests include peace- and statebuilding, political sociology, post-Soviet/post-Socialist studies and post-decolonial International Relations.

Phillip Myers is a doctoral candidate and Teaching Associate at University of Birmingham in the Department of Classics, Ancient History, and Archaeology. His doctoral research focuses on the hybridity and acculturation in the ancient world, specifically examining the Republican and pre-Roman period in Spain. His research interests extend also to economic and political history and the development of ancient imperialisms.

Louisa Riches is Principal Lecturer, Leeds Law School, Leeds Beckett University. Louisa is currently undertaking a PhD at the University of Leeds, titled 'A critical appraisal of the function of the United Nations Universal Periodic Review in relation to states in crisis' and has given related conference papers in the UK and overseas. More broadly, her research focuses on matters relating to rights and equality with her most recent publication being L. Riches and S. Gardiner, 'Racism and Homophobia in English Football', (July 2016) *International Journal of Discrimination Law*. Louisa is the book review editor for *European Journal of Current Legal Issues*.

Gareth Sears is a Senior Lecturer in Roman History at the University of Birmingham. He works on Roman period Africa and on late antiquity more generally. He has directed archaeological fieldwork at Cyrene, Libya and in and around Split, Croatia. He is the author of *The Cities of Roman Africa* (History Press 2011), co-author of *The City in the Roman West c. 250 BC–c. AD 250* (CUP 2011) and co-editor of *Written Space in the Latin West* (Bloomsbury 2013).

Gëzim Visoka is a Lecturer in Peace and Conflict Studies at Dublin City University in Ireland. Dr Visoka's research focuses on post-conflict peacebuilding, and his most recent books are *Peace Figuration after International Intervention* (Routledge, 2016) and *Shaping Peace in Kosovo* (Palgrave Macmillan, 2016). Dr Visoka has published seven book chapters and fourteen articles in peer-reviewed journals, including: *Journal of Common Market Studies, Foreign Policy Analysis, International Peacekeeping, Civil Wars, Journal of Intervention and Statebuilding,* and *Peacebuilding.*

Ben Warwick is a Lecturer in Law at the University of Birmingham (UK). He is Co-Coordinator of the CRN on Economic and Social Rights at the Law and Society Association. He researches the system(s) of protection for socio-economic rights, with a particular focus on how these rights interact with resource questions. He has published on these topics in journals such as *International and Comparative Law Quarterly.*

George Wilson is a PhD candidate in law at the School of Law, University of Leeds. His doctoral research explores minimum wages and collectively agreed pay, specifically, how changes in industrial relations systems affect their operation. This has influenced a recent research project on regulatory hybridity and new modes of governance, that was funded by the Worldwide Universities Network and undertaken at the University of Wisconsin-Madison, USA.

Jon Yorke is Professor of Human Rights and the Director of the Centre for Human Rights at Birmingham City University. His research focuses on the protection of human rights within the multi-lateral fora, and the global movement for the abolition of the death penalty. He is the editor of *The Right to Life and the Value of Life: Orientations in Law, Politics and Ethics* (London: Routledge, 2010) and is the co-editor of the Routledge Series *Controversies in American Constitutional Law.*

Introduction

Chapter 1

Critical hybridity

Exploring cultural, legal and political pluralism

Nicolas Lemay-Hébert and Rosa Freedman

Hybridity has emerged as one of the all-purpose theoretical lenses, meant to reflect the everyday complexity of a world that remains primarily seen through highly compartmentalised lenses. Migrating from the cultural and postcolonial fields, hybridity considerations have now permeated many disciplines, including peace and conflict studies, international development, and law. Closely associated with postmodern preoccupations, hybridity theorists question the untenable dualism of the human–nature distinction, understanding it instead as hybrid networks of human and non-human elements,[1] but also of the other binaries sometimes mobilised by researchers to simplify categorisations, including the (widely used) 'modern–traditional', 'international–local' or 'us–them' binaries. However, despite waves of theorisation of the concept, the general feeling is still that 'hybridity is almost a good idea, but not quite'.[2]

This edited book's main objective is to create a space for a conversation to take place inside disciplines as well as across them, with the final aim of creating bridges between different accounts and perspectives of hybridity and hybridisation.[3] Contributors to this book come from different fields, including culture and literary studies, classics, law, development, and peace and conflict studies. Actually, most of the contributors to this book would probably dispute this traditional pigeon-holing of associating one scholar with a particular field – as most have made an intellectual journey across different disciplines or are aiming to do so. However, we do not pretend to a pure 'trans-disciplinary' approach here,[4] as most contributions revolve around the fields of peace and conflict studies and international law, mirroring the editors' *discipline de provenance.* Similarly, the aim of the book is certainly not to reach an 'all-purpose, final definition of hybridity'[5] that would encompass and at the same time transcend disciplinary boundaries, but rather to make the connections between the various approaches to hybridity both salient and intelligible. As Peter Burke noted, hybridity has attracted growing interest in a number of disciplines, but scholars in one discipline are rarely aware of what is happening in the others.[6]

This book further aims to steer the discussion away from the celebratory conception of hybridity by meshing it with considerations of power structures and relations. Jan Nederveen Pieterse rightly points out that the most conspicuous shortcoming of hybridity is that it is seen as the triumph of neoliberal multiculturalism, which leads some hybridity scholars to skip over questions of power and inequality.[7] There is indeed a form of vacuousness in the general 'hybridist post-national talk',[8] reproducing discourses of globalisation and cosmopolitanianism, and celebrating the 'creolization of the world'.[9] Along the line of Marwan Kraidy's work, we believe that it is imperative to situate every analysis of hybridity in a specific context where the conditions that shape hybridity/hybridities are addressed.[10] Hybridity is not parity[11] – a sort of revenge of the subaltern or the 'weak' against the powerful boundary-creating forces at play; on the contrary, it is hegemonically constructed in the interest of dominant societal actors.[12] It does not imply a 'peaceful coexistence of the vis-à-vis, but rather a violent hierarchy',[13] hierarchy that needs to be identified in order to be overturned.

Hybridity, culture and postcolonial studies

Following older themes of syncretism in anthropology and creolisation in linguistics, hybridity has increasingly become a prominent theme in cultural and postcolonial studies. On the micro level, hybridisation has been associated with the study of the breaking up of racial, national, linguistic or other identity binaries, as well as revealing connectors and influences across 'national' borders, in the process refuting the 'boundedness' and 'essentialism' of the modern episteme. The complexity of individuals' identities and their own personal route has hence been highlighted. On the macro level, hybridity is seen as a way to analyse the impact of globalisation, sometimes with direct connection with the 'reactive nationalisms or ethnicities' in the Balkans and Africa.[14] The common starting point of all of these approaches is the focus on the wide register of multiple identity, cross-over, pick-n-mix, boundary-crossing experiences and styles.[15]

However, hybridity studies have a specific connection with racial studies that cannot be denied. Hybridity is generally understood as the 'impurification of standard or canonized forms'.[16] For Joshua Lund, 'to theorize hybridity is to operate within a discourse of race'.[17] More precisely, it is the Eurocentrically articulated theory of race which determines the modern intelligibility of hybridity. Hence, for Lund, hybridology needs to be linked to considerations of the 'coloniality of power', which is not currently done in the common work on creolisation and *mestizaje*. This is what brings certain authors to say that hybridity is more than 'just another form of syncretism'.[18]

Finally, hybridity is inherently linked with the work of Homi Bhabha, for whom hybridity is a third space, 'a difference "within", an "in-between" reality'.[19] It is a space of translation, 'where the construction of a political object that is new, *neither the one nor the other*, properly alienates our political expectations, and changes, as it must, the very forms of our recognition of the moment of politics'.[20] For Bhabha, hybridity is not necessarily a third term that resolves the tension between two cultures, but rather holds the tension of the opposition and explores the spaces in-between fixed identities through their continuous reiterations.[21] Most authors included in this collection make an explicit reference to the work of Bhabha when conceptualising hybridity and hybridisation.

Hybridity in development, peace and conflict studies

Recent practical and theoretical failures of liberal interventionist practices have led to a growing interest in so-called 'liberal-local' hybrid forms of peace which 'intellectually enables an engagement with the lives of ordinary people, in their own everyday rather than in a static and distant state context'.[22] Studies on hybridity have led to a new wave of insightful contributions on spaces of interventions, moving away from the unhelpful binaries of 'local' vs 'international', 'bottom-up' vs 'top-down', 'modern' vs 'traditional', 'internal' vs 'external', 'centre' vs 'periphery', or 'Western' vs 'Non-Western'. This scholarship represents a changing landscape, but there are (at least) two main, and complementary, strands that have emerged in the last few years. The first one focuses on the interplay between international and local practices, norms and institutions,[23] as a way to emphasise local agency in its interaction with outside forces,[24] and/or to engage with local actors beyond the nation-state.[25] The second strand of scholarship is more focused on transcending universalising theories to include the plurality of social orders.[26] As such, it is not focusing on the international–local interface as much as on the complexity of the societal orders in postcolonial and post-conflict societies. The first approach is a direct challenge to liberal institutionalism and its ordering of the world through specific interventions, and suggests looking at the complex creations that emerge out of interventions (hybrid forms of peace as an end-result, hybrid peace governance as means of intervention or simply hybridisation as a process). The second one challenges (neo-)Weberian notions of the state as a lens through which we generate knowledge about these postcolonial and post-conflict societies.[27] The starting point of this scholarship is not the necessity to fix fragile or failed states – which is the most common starting point of liberal interventionism[28] – but the actual diversity of governance arrangements across the world and the need to apprehend this complexity. Concerns about state capacity give place to considerations about societal cohesion,[29] which in turn enables us to go beyond the reification of specific concepts like the 'state', 'institutions' and 'social contract', among others.

This scholarship has faced an 'anti-hybridity backlash' of its own, with scholars demanding the jettisoning of the local–international binaries for their homogenisation and simplification of the 'international'[30] and bundling together of local actors.[31] On this last point, Jenny Peterson reflects on the blatant absence of power considerations in specific hybridity contributions, which has led to overlooking power differentials at the local level, for instance.[32] This is also an issue that has been raised by a number of contributions in this collection (see Beswick and Jackson for instance). Some also question the programmatic agenda behind hybridity studies, considering it a problem-solving tool reproducing the Eurocentrism, dualisms and hierarchies inherent to the liberal interventionism literature.[33] The prescriptive assumptions of some of the hybridity scholarship are also lambasted by recent work on the subject.[34]

While there is much debate on the capacity of the hybridity scholarship to go beyond the international–local binary (despite the claims of this scholarship), there is less attention to the virtual, intangible 'third space', as discussed by Bhabha, among others. Lisa Smirl has contributed to this in the field of humanitarian interventions, mobilising the anthropological concept of 'liminality' as an in-between space,[35] but more work on this would need to be done to apprehend the complexity of hybridisation processes. Also, if we follow Canclini in that the object of study is not hybridity but the actual processes of hybridisation,[36] this would lead us to develop more empirical discussions on how hybridisation actually occurs in post-conflict or postcolonial societies, 'making it useful for interpreting relations of meaning that are reconstructed through mixing'.[37]

Hybridity and legal pluralism

Legal discussions have played a prominent role in the burgeoning academic discussions on possible 'hybrid forms of peace'. Mirroring the hybrid forms of peace discussion, the legal pluralism debate also revolves around, on the one hand, a distinction between potential alternative models that could deal with the failure of state-centric approaches or existing 'national' structures of equality and justice, and on the other hand the practical analysis of hybridisation practices. For instance, some advocate in cultural studies a legal pluralism that would 'countenance a coexistence of jurisdictional systems for different cultural and religious traditions and accept varieties of institutional design for societies with strong ethnic, cultural, and linguistic cleavages'.[38] Others look at the justice sector as a prime area of focus of hybridisation practices in post-conflict settings. The failures and limitations of the top-down justice and reconciliation agenda promoted by international courts (precisely the International Criminal Tribunal for Ex-Yugoslavia, the International Criminal Tribunal for Rwanda and the International Criminal Court) have led to a variety of *hybrid tribunals*, where both the institution and the applicable law consist of a mix of international and domestic. These institutions have been analysed in great detail and in a variety of cases, including Sierra Leone,[39] Cambodia,[40] Timor-Leste,[41] Bosnia and Herzegovina[42] and Kosovo.[43] Wider implications for hybrid models of justice have also been explored in Afghanistan,[44] Ethiopia,[45] Rwanda,[46] Sierra Leone[47] and Timor-Leste[48] among other cases. Whether some of these experiments have constituted genuine attempts at promoting alternative frameworks for peace building built around everyday practices or have been yet another way for international actors to co-opt local actors and practices to further their own peacebuilding agendas is still a question under debate.[49]

More generally, the study of interactions between the multiple legal orders – from the very local level to the global level, and from customary law, to indigenous law, religious law or law connected to specific cultural group – enables us to look at the competing claims of authority in what is generally understood as legal pluralism. This opens up perspectives for the analysis of the power relations in specific societies – how and why individuals and groups within a society select specific legal authorities and orders over others, and how specific individuals and groups pursue specific state-building agendas linked to particular legal traditions.[50] Legal pluralism as a sub-field of socio-legal studies has been quite vibrant in the last thirty years, nevertheless there is a growing consensus that 'legal pluralism' is better conceptualised as 'normative pluralism' to indicate the wider conception of 'law' prevalent in most of these approaches.[51] Some scholars also aim to redefine the legal pluralism agenda as an agenda about *critical* legal pluralism following postmodern and social constructivist theories, looking at how narrating subjects treat law rather than treating society and subjects as 'real entities' that law can treat.[52] Not unlike hybridity, legal pluralism is understood as a 'common historical condition',[53] a feature which makes the two phenomena hard to analyse without entering into a wider sociological study of socio-legal or socio-political order.

Outline of the book

This edited collection offers a mix of analytical and empirical takes on hybridity and hybridisation. Whilst some do use hybridity to unpack complexity, most adopt a critical perspective, connecting hybridisation processes with underpinning power structures and relations. Taken together, these contributions point towards the main different avenues the hybridity agenda can take in the next couple of years.

Part I, 'Localising hybridity', offers insights into how hybridity can be more than a descriptive lens and become an analytical lens, highlighting how it gains relevance through a critical approach. Through a review of the transitology and the statebuilding literatures, *Philipp Lottholz* underlines the importance of an ontological understanding of hybridity; of what precisely is being hybridised. For Lottholz, despite the recent hype, hybridity is not more than a concept or a 'lens', as it is not exactly helpful in answering the 'bigger' questions about power, peace or development in domestic and international political contexts. This should be done through a critical inquiry into disputes over the value, meaning and content of peace, development and human rights in different cultural contexts with a focus on the 'hybrid subjectivities' which are, according to Lottholz, already an empirical reality in today's globalised and interconnected world. In the next chapter, *Rosa Freedman* and *Philipp Lottholz* analyse how the international law arena can be seen as what Bhabha calls a 'Third Space'. They argue that hybridity in international human rights law is produced as states from the Global South resist traditional notions of rights but use the existing human rights system to put forward their own ideologies that challenge the dominant framework. Through a discursive hybridity framework based on the work of Mikhail Bakhtin, they show that the recent emergence of Third Generation or 'hybrid human rights' can be seen as reflecting the *heteroglossia* – the multiplicity of different norms, values and cultural frameworks – characterising the negotiations at human rights bodies. For *Fiona de Londras,* the hybrid nature of terrorism and counter-terrorism as mechanisms of resistance within asymmetrical power relationships illustrates the critical usefulness of conceptualising counter-terrorism as a hybrid phenomenon. She further sheds light on how these phenomena are operating in between the spaces and categories usually employed in social or political analysis and are thus neither legal, nor extra-legal; neither public nor private; neither national nor international. *Ruth Houghton* develops the claim that hybridity can be at the same time empirical and critical, descriptive and analytical. Through her study of NGO participation at the United Nations Human Rights Council (UNHRC), Houghton demonstrates that hybridity can be used in an empirical sense to collect evidence of the plurality of actors in international decision-making, but also that hybridity has a more critical aspect that can be used to unpack the power dynamics between different actors at the UNHRC, and to disentangle prior hybridisation practices within the organisation (see Visoka in the conclusion who makes this point).

Part II, 'Hybridity in history and culture' discusses hybridity and hybridisation with a strong focus on empires, colonisation and 'Romanisation'. *Gareth Sears* comes to the conclusion that 'Romanisation' and 'hybridity' theories might be a good descriptive tool to understand how people in North African Roman territories created the spaces of cult to the god Ba'al Hammon/Saturn – both physical and conceptual; although, as he argues, it does not provide enough analytical traction to understand the process at play, at least not in its current framing in the classics discipline. There is a need to examine the motives of those creating, perpetuating and (sub)consciously hybridising the cults; to understand the context of hybridisation and the interests of the main actors. In a similar fashion, *Philip Myers* takes us on a journey into the interrelations between Iberian and eastern Mediterranean cultures – which created *de facto* hybrid cultures – and shows how this hybridity has been analysed and debated by modern scholars. Myers argues that the ancient world of the Mediterranean was neither 'Romanised' nor 'orientalised', but began to follow along a general cultural trend towards a very broad cultural homogeneity, where local cultures became hybridised rather than losing their substance. In his fascinating take on William Shakespeare's *The Tempest* and *Cymbeline, Eric Heinze* searches for insights into legal hybridity emerging during the early phases of European colonialism and the seventeenth-century politics of absolute sovereignty. Through the study of Shakespeare, Heinze manages to highlight how the notion of hybridity can equally help us recognise imbalance and coercion within colonial dynamics while emphasising the transformations along the entire spectrum of those dynamics. Hybridity certainly arises through imposition and coercion, argues the author, but also proceeds through strategic self-interest or indeed through ambient and diffuse assimilation. Thanks to his ability to juggle between socio-legal and cultural studies, the author also rests the case that interdisciplinarity is key to grasp the complex nature of the current discussions on hybridity. *Mark Kirkham* builds on the work of Kraidy, especially his contribution on critical transculturalism, to analyse the role of the 'state' in the Ottoman Empire. As the author points out, Ottoman sultans have shown an ability to play the mediator or referee role – discussed by Kraidy through critical transculturalism – in managing the different communities included in the empire, thus creating an ancient kind of multiculturalism sustained through a set of institutions and policies. 'Based on this analysis and a review of different perspectives on the significance of this model, Kirkham argues that this practice could potentially be of interests to contemporary statebuilders, despite the obvious pitfalls of anachronistic interpretation of this historical moment.

Part III, 'New developments in hybridity and legal pluralism', includes four contributions on hybridity from a legal perspective. *Louisa Riches* analyses the Universal Periodic Review through the lens of normative pluralism, a theoretical framework which enables the author to analyse the UPR's agenda of protection and promotion of universal rights and freedoms without furthering cultural difference and tensions. The normative pluralist approach also accommodates state-centrism (a key feature of contemporary international law) whilst also allowing for contributions from non-state actors, and offers a more analytical take on the issue compared to the legal pluralism lens which takes stock of the coexistence, overlap or interplay of different legal systems. In this context, the hybridity lens is understood as a means to assist with understanding the dynamic nature of the institution, with reference to the development of multiple hybrid and normative (legal and non-legal) structures, as each country selects which recommendations to accept and (more importantly) to implement. *Jon Yorke* inquires whether the European Union and the Council of Europe can be identified as 'hybridiser(s)' of abolitionism, promoting abolitionism by way of gradually hybridising practices and discourses both within European institutions themselves and in partner countries. Through the dialogue between Jacques Derrida and Elisabeth Roudinesco on this issue, Yorke analyses how the 'classical' theory of sovereignty stands in contradistinction to the global movement for abolition; how the idea of reasserting sovereignty without capital punishment was introduced in Europe and is now being promoted globally. In his chapter, *Ben Warwick* looks at how greater nuance can be added to descriptions of socio-economic rights realisation and suggests that hybridity can overcome linear and essentialist features of some of the mainstream approaches in human rights analysis. *Kim Barker* and *Christina Baghdady* examine the building of 'cyber communities' during and after the Arab Spring. For the authors, it is possible to perceive digital connections as forms of communities, and indeed, groups with shared connections, values and norms. These communities are hybrid in form, with close connections to similar processes of creolisation (or 'cybridity'). The authors approach this issue through the regulatory perspective, wondering how new regulations can better take into account the issues in the virtual and the non-virtual worlds. This is obviously quite a sensitive issue, especially in the context of the Arab Spring and the new practices of securitisation emerging in the region.

The contributions included in Part IV, 'Hybrid approaches to peace, development and justice', reveal structural processes at play in specific case studies – whether it is rural West Africa, human rights abuses in southern and central Africa or post-genocide Rwanda – in the process underlining the conditions that shape hybridity(ies). *Danielle Beswick* analyses the case of hybrid statebuilding in Rwanda – a polity at the intersection between local and international actors pursuing their own specific agendas, conditioned by their own histories and their previous interactions with each other, and in the process shaping up the hybrid 'third space', that is, the Rwandan state. Beswick borrows from the work of Roger Mac Ginty to underscore the agency of local actors, looking at hybrid peacebuilding processes that have developed after the genocide (through the local transitional justice system), but also to underscore that the 'hybrid forms of peace' created can lead to the strengthening of the position of specific 'local' elites. She then questions who specifically gain from such hybrid solutions. This is also an issue raised by *Paul Jackson*, who analyses power structures at the local level, and the different ways local actors use their positionalities to further their own agenda. Jackson does this through a study of the relationship between local power, decentralised authority and justice in the West African countryside through the lens of hybridity, underscoring the fact that local authorities are neither fully formal nor informal or, indeed, traditional or modern. *Sam Fowles* uses hybridity as a tool for deconstruction of human rights abuses, analysing the structural causes of abuse of children accused of witchcraft in southern and central Africa. In doing so, Fowles explicitly uses and questions Bhabha's conception of dichotic hybridity, in which the resistance of a subaltern culture to a dominant culture creates new cultural phenomena. He analyses the various influences and structures at play, including African folk traditions, American charismatic Christianity and capitalism, all of which inform the belief in and abuse of 'child witches'. Finally, in his chapter, *George Wilson* discusses the transformative potential of hybridisation through a critical account of hybridity, building on the work of Kraidy, among others. He offers a unique perspective on peace and development studies by linking the recent debates on hybridity in this field with those in the fields of law and 'new' governance.

In the conclusion to this edited collection, *Gëzim Visoka* offers his thoughts on the current state of the hybridity discussion, with a specific focus on peace and conflict studies. Taking stock of the critique the hybridity scholarship has faced recently, Visoka suggests (1) engaging in more systematic and empirical analysis of hybridisation processes; and (2) avoiding the prescriptive and normative bias that is sometimes present in the work on hybridity. He further offers three possible alternatives for expanding the epistemological perspectives on hybridity, building on the work of Zygmunt Bauman on liquidity, Gilles Deleuze on assemblage and Norbert Elias on figuration.

This edited collection is the result of a workshop organised in March 2014 at the University of Birmingham's Institute for Advanced Studies, 'Hybridity: Exploring Power, Social Structures, and Institutions Beyond the Liberal West'. Most of the contributions included in this book come from papers presented in the workshop. We would like to thank all the contributors, but also Sue Gilligan and Sarah Jeffery from the IAS, and Philipp Lottholz and Mattias Hjort for assistance in the final editing and preparation of the manuscript for publication.

Notes

1 Anders Blok and Torben Elgaard Jensen (2011) *Bruno Latour: Hybrid Thoughts in a Hybrid World* (Abingdon: Routledge).
2 Marwan Kraidy (2012) *Hybridity, of the Cultural Logic of Globalization* (Philadelphia, PA: Temple University Press), p. vi.
3 For a similar project, see Philipp Stockhammer (2012) 'Questioning Hybridity', in P. Stockhammer (ed.), *Conceptualizing Cultural Hybridization: A Transdisciplinary Approach* (Berlin: Springer-Verlag), 1–3.
4 Michael Shapiro (2012) *Studies in Trans-Disciplinary Method: After the Aesthetic Turn* (London: Routledge).
5 Kraidy, *Hybridity*, p. vi.
6 Peter Burke (2009) *Cultural Hybridity* (London: Polity), 5.

7 Jan Nederveen Pieterse (2001) 'Hybridity, So What? The Anti-Hybridity Backlash and the Riddles of Recognition', *Theory, Culture and Society* 18(2–3): 224. See also Anjali Prabhu (2007) *Hybridity: Limits, Transformations, Prospects* (Albany, NY: SUNY Press); Visoka in Ch. 18 in this volume.

8 Gayatri Spivak (1999) *A Critique of Postcolonial Reason: Toward a History of the Vanishing Present* (Cambridge, MA: Harvard University Press), 361. See also: Aijaz Ahmad (1992) *In Theory: Classes, Nations, Literatures* (London: Verso), 68–9.

9 Burke, *Cultural Hybridity*, 115.

10 Kraidy, *Hybridity*, p. vi. See also Amar Acheraïou (2011) *Questioning Hybridity, Postcolonialism and Globalization* (Basingstoke: Palgrave), 1.

11 Peter McLaren (1997) *Revolutionary Multiculturalism: Pedagogies of Dissent for the New Millennium* (Boulder, CO: Westview Press), 10.

12 Kraidy, *Hybridity*, 67.

13 Jacques Derrida (1981) *Positions* (London: Athlone Press), 41.

14 Homi Bhabha (1994) *The Location of Culture* (London: Routledge), 6–7; Burke, *Cultural Hybridity*, 7–8.

15 Pieterse, 'Hybridity, So What?' 221.

16 Joshua Lund (2006) *The Impure Imagination: Towards a Critical Hybridity in Latin American Writing* (Minneapolis, MN: University of Minnesota Press).

17 Ibid. 3.

18 Simone Drichel (2008) 'The Time of Hybridity', *Philosophy & Social Criticism* 34:6, 605.

19 Bhabha, *Location of Culture*, 19.

20 Ibid. 37.

21 Drichel, 'Time of Hybridity', 605.

22 Oliver Richmond (2009) 'Becoming Liberal, Unbecoming Liberalism: Liberal-Local Hybridity via the Everyday as a Response to the Paradoxes of Liberal Peacebuilding', *Journal of Intervention and Statebuilding* 3(3): 333.

23 Oliver Richmond and Audra Mitchell (2012) 'Introduction: Towards a Post-Liberal Peace: Exploring Hybridity via Everyday Forms of Resistance, Agency and Autonomy', in O. Richmond and A. Mitchell (eds), *Hybrid Forms of Peace: From Everyday Agency to Post-Liberalism* (Basingstoke: Palgrave), 1–38; Roger Mac Ginty (2010) 'Hybrid Peace: The Interaction between Top-Down and Bottom-Up Peace', *Security Dialogue* 41(4): 391–412.

24 See Mac Ginty, 'Hybrid Peace', or Roberto Belloni (2012) 'Hybrid Peace Governance: Its Emergence and Significance', *Global Governance* 18: 21–38.

25 See Francesco Colona and Rivke Jaffe (2016) 'Hybrid Governance Arrangements', *European Journal of Development Research* 28(2): 175–83. This is also a concern that is reflected in the legal scholarship on hybridity.

26 Volker Boege, Anne Brown, Kevin Clements and A. Nolan (2009) 'On Hybrid Political Orders and Emerging States: What is Failing – States in the Global South or Research and Politics in the West?', *Berghof Handbook Dialogue Series* 8: 15–35; David Roberts (2008) 'Hybrid Polities and Indigenous Pluralities: Advanced Lessons in Statebuilding from Cambodia', *Journal of Intervention and Statebuilding* 2(1): 63–86; Peter Albrecht and Louise Wiuff Moe (2015) 'The Simultaneity of Authority in Hybrid Orders', *Peacebuilding* 3(1): 1–16.

27 Roger Mac Ginty and Oliver Richmond (2016) 'The Fallacy of Constructing Hybrid Political Orders: A Reappraisal of the Hybrid Turn in Peacebuilding', *International Peacekeeping* 23(2), 1–2; Philipp Lottholz and Nicolas Lemay-Hébert (2016) 'Re-Reading Weber, Reconceptualising State-Building: From Neo-Weberian to Post-Weberian Approaches to State, Legitimacy and State-Building', *Cambridge Review of International Affairs* (online first).

28 Sonja Grimm, Nicolas Lemay-Hébert and Olivier Nay (2014) 'Fragile States: Introducing a Political Concept', *Third World Quarterly* 35(2): 197–209.
29 Nicolas Lemay-Hébert (2014) 'The Semantics of Statebuilding and Nationbuilding: Looking beyond Neo-Weberian Approaches', in Nicolas Lemay-Hébert, Nicholas Onuf, Vojin Rakic and Petar Bojanic (eds), *Semantics of Statebuilding: Language, Meanings and Sovereignty* (London: Routledge), 89–105.
30 A project described as quixotic, looking for liberal 'windmills' on hybrid donkeys and postliberal mares. Dominik Zaum (2012) 'Beyond the "Liberal Peace"', *Global Governance: A Review of Multilateralism and International Organizations* 18(1): 130.
31 Lee Jones and Shahar Hameiri, 'Beyond Hybridity to the Politics of Scale: International Intervention and "Local" Politics', *Development and Change* (forthcoming). See also the response to this anti-hybridity backlash from two of the main scholars on hybridity in peace and conflict studies: Oliver Richmond and Roger Mac Ginty (2015) 'Where Now for the Critique of the Liberal Peace?', *Cooperation and Conflict* 50(2): 171–89.
32 Jenny Peterson, 'A Conceptual Unpacking of Hybridity: Accounting for Notions of Power, Politics and Progress in Analyses of Aid-Driven Interfaces', *Journal of Peacebuilding and Development* 7(2): 14.
33 Suthaharan Nadarajah and David Rampton (2015) 'The Limits of Hybridity and the Crisis of Liberal Peace', *Review of International Studies* 41(1): 49–72. This argument is challenged by Visoka in this volume.
34 Gearoid Millar (2014) 'Disaggregating Hybridity: Why Hybrid Institutions Do Not Produce Predictable Experiences of Peace', *Journal of Peace Research* 51(4): 501–14; Gezim Visoka (2012) 'Three Levels of Hybridisation Practices in Post-Conflict Kosovo', *Journal of Peacebuilding and Development* 7(2): 23–36. Contributions such as Kirkman's in this volume can certainly be located in the 'prescriptive' category.
35 Lisa Smirl (2012) 'The State we aren't in: Liminal Subjectivity in Aid Worker Auto-biographies', in Bliesemann de Guevara (ed.), *State Building and State Formation* (London: Routledge), 230–45; John Heathershaw (2016) 'Who are the "International Community"? Development Professionals and Liminal Subjectivity', *Journal of Intervention and Statebuilding* 10(1): 77–96.
36 Nestor Garcia Canclini (1995) *Hybrid Cultures: Strategies for Entering and Leaving Modernity* (Minneapolis, MN: University of Minnesota Press), p. xxvii.
37 Ibid., p. xxix.
38 Seyla Benhabib (2002) *The Claims of Culture: Equality and Diversity in the Global Era* (Princeton, NJ: Princeton University Press), 19.
39 David Cohen (2007) '"Hybrid" Justice in East Timor, Sierra Leone and Cambodia: "Lessons Learned" and Prospects for the Future', *Stanford Journal of International Law* 43(1): 1–38; Chandra Lekha Sriram (2006) 'Wrong-Sizing International Justice? The Hybrid Tribunal of Sierra Leone', *Fordham International Law Journal* 29(3): 472–506.
40 Cohen, '"Hybrid" Justice in East Timor'; Laura Dickinson (2003) 'The Promise of Hybrid Courts', *American Journal of International Law* 97(2): 295–310; Helen Horsington (2004) 'The Cambodian Khmer Rouge Tribunal: The Promise of a Hybrid Tribunal', *Melbourne Journal of International Law* 5(2): 462–82; Olga Martin-Ortega and Johanna Herman (2012) 'Hybrid Tribunals: Interaction and Resistance in Bosnia and Herzegovina and Cambodia', in Oliver Richmond and Audra Mitchell (eds), *Hybrid Forms of Peace: From Everyday Agency to Post-Liberalism* (Basingstoke: Palgrave), 73–87.
41 Cohen, '"Hybrid" Justice in East Timor'; Dickinson, 'Promise'.

42 Martin-Ortega and Herman, 'Hybrid Tribunals'.
43 Dickinson, 'Promise'; Laura Dickinson (2002) 'The Relationship between Hybrid Courts and International Courts: The Case of Kosovo', *New England Law Review* 37: 1059–72.
44 Ali Wardak and Humayun Hamidzada (2012) 'The Search for Legitimate Rule, Justice and a Durable Peace: Hybrid Models of Governance in Afghanistan', *Journal of Peacebuilding and Development* 7(2): 79–88.
45 Bruce Baker (2013) 'Where Formal and Informal Justice Meet: Ethiopia's Justice Pluralism', *African Journal of International and Comparative Law* 21(2): 202–18.
46 Phil Clark (2014) 'Negotiating Reconciliation in Rwanda: Popular Challenges to the Official Discourse of Post-Genocide National Unity', *Journal of Intervention and Statebuilding* 8(4): 303–20.
47 Lisa Denney (2014) *Justice and Security Reform: Development Agencies and Informal Institutions in Sierra Leone* (London: Routledge); Paul Jackson (2011) 'Decentralised Power and Traditional Authorities: How Power Determines Access to Justice in Sierra Leone', *Journal of Legal Pluralism and Unofficial Law* 43(63): 207–30.
48 Cynthia Horne (2014) 'Reconstructing "Traditional" Justice from the Outside in: Transitional Justice in Aceh and East Timor', *Journal of Peacebuilding and Development* 9(2): 17–32.
49 Chandra Lekha Sriram (2012) 'Post-Conflict Justice and Hybridity in Peacebuilding: Resistance or Cooptation?', in Oliver Richmond and Audra Mitchell (eds), *Hybrid Forms of Peace: From Everyday Agency to Post-Liberalism* (Basingstoke: Palgrave), 58–72. See also Nicolas Lemay-Hébert and Stefanie Kappler, (2016) 'What Attachment to Peace? Normative and Material Dimensions of Peacebuilding', *Review of International Studies* 42(5): 895–914.
50 For a study of the conflict between Weberian, national system of justice and traditional systems of justice in Timor-Leste, see: Nicolas Lemay-Hébert (2011) 'The "Empty Shell" Approach: The Setup Process of International Administrations in Timor-Leste and Kosovo, its Consequences and Lessons', *International Studies Perspectives* 12(2): 188–209.
51 Brian Tamanaha (2008) 'Understanding Legal Pluralism: Past to Present, Local to Global', *Sydney Law Review* 30: 395–6.
52 Martha-Marie Kleinhans and Roderick Macdonald (1997), 'What is Critical Legal Pluralism?', *Canadian Journal of Law and Society* 12: 46. See also: Victor M. Muniz-Fraticelli (2014) *The Structure of Pluralism* (Oxford: Oxford University Press).
53 Tamanaha, 'Understanding Legal Pluralism', 376.

Part I

Localising hybridity

Chapter 2

Nothing more than a conceptual lens?

Situating hybridity in social inquiry

Philipp Lottholz

Abstract

In this chapter I will argue that it is not the use of hybridity per se that will decide if an analytical puzzle or policy problem can be solved, but that this question depends on the positioning of social researchers and decision makers. By reviewing transitology, institutionalist statebuilding and critical peacebuilding literatures, I will show how hybridity is applied both in Western-centrist and evolutionary thinking and ideas of potentially more emancipatory 'hybrid' and 'post-liberal forms of peace'. The subsequent exploration of applications of hybridity in analyses of situations of protracted crisis and 'governance without government' highlights how the application of hybrid solutions can lead to violence, marginalisation and other regressive outcomes despite such emancipatory potential. On this basis, the importance of an ontological understanding of hybridity, i.e. on *what* is being hybridised or hybrid, is discussed in the third section in order to argue that it is the realm of ideas that should be given more attention in hybridity research. The usefulness of the concept of 'hybrid subjectivities' will be exemplified by briefly reviewing the case of political transition in post-Soviet Central Asia and the hybridisation processes that occur in this environment characterised by multiple informational spaces, subjectivities and worldviews.

Introduction: a clear view on hybridity in social inquiry

If '[w]e are all hybrids',[1] and if everything is hybrid, then how can hybridity help us to understand the world? This is a reasonable concern and only one among the many raised by those critical, sceptical or reserved vis-à-vis the concept of hybridity. While many of such views rest on initial or emotive judgements rather than balanced considerations, the views of those who celebrate hybridity either as solution to problems of oppression and marginalisation, or at least a space of resistance against inherently imperfect power, hierarchy and empire,[2] seem equally wishful and dreamy, at least from a critical theory perspective.[3] This chapter endeavours to give an overview of the different applications of hybridity at the intersection between peace and conflict studies and political science and International Relations (IR), and, further, to sketch out a critical and inter-disciplinary approach to using hybridity, which takes into account the criticisms made of past proponents of hybridity.

In order to offer a somewhat 'sober' view on the possible role of hybridity in social inquiry, I argue that hybridity is not anything more than a concept or 'lens', as it is not helpful in answering the 'bigger' questions about power, peace or development in domestic and international political contexts. Thus, when it comes to social or (socio-)legal inquiry, hybridity *per se* does not provide answers to the question about how to settle disputes over the value, meaning and content of peace, development and human rights in different cultural contexts. All of the above require scholarship to take some position – implicitly or explicitly – within the different debates of the philosophy of knowledge.[4] Thus, where hybridity seems to transcend positivist/interpretivist, universalist/relativist and critical/problem-solving binaries,[5] it usually merely replicates or reframes them. By illustrating such cases, this contribution offers a critical reading of hybridity in order to draw attention to its limits. Given the complexity of the global environment, I will argue that a prime dimension for social inquiry should be the conceptual or ideational realm of hybridisation, because people's ideas, subjectivities and understandings of the world, not to say 'ontologies', are perhaps most accessible and influential in the trajectories of peaceful social development. This illustrates the importance of the often neglected or insufficiently addressed question: 'What is actually being hybrid, or hybridised?' It is thus argued that only by addressing the concern about the ontology of hybridity, or social inquiry for that matter, is it possible to clearly position research and manage the expectations put into it and in concepts such as hybridity. As a way of addressing this concern, I offer the idea of exploring the complexity of social processes through the concept of 'hybrid subjectivities' that can help account for the ambivalence and fluidity characterising the stances of the subjects of social change.

The chapter is divided into three sections. First, I show how in democratisation and political transformation (or 'transitology') literature hybridity has been applied with associations of impurity, backwardness and failure to democratise, which mirrors the scientism and white/European supremacy of racial biology. It will be shown how the corresponding orthodoxy of liberal democracy and statebuilding – problematic given its Eurocentric and scientist connotations – were criticised and provided with an alternative by scholars looking at hybrid political orders and the possibility of accommodating the needs and values of populations in non-Western and non-developed countries. Second, I will present a critical view of hybrid modes of social and political order that resonate with some critical contributions in this volume. By reviewing cases where institutional hybridity leads to marginalisation, exclusion and structural and physical violence, I will illustrate that hybridity cannot be taken for granted as a solution to problems of social order and post-conflict reconstruction. The following section then shows how hybridity can be applied to try and make sense of social process in the complex and non-linear global environment. It will be argued that, while political science and other frameworks in peace and conflict studies inevitably face problems given this complexity, what critical social inquiry can do is to bring local subjectivities into the scope of analysis. By inquiring into the ways people think about, see and act in the world, as well as the trajectories that influence these individual life-worlds, it is possible to shed light on processes of peace- and statebuilding and political transition. The conclusion highlights the critical importance of a non-essentialist, subjectivist and non-linear approach to social inquiry in a pluri-ontological world.

Hybridity and transitology: exposing scientism and teleological thinking

Adopting a hybrid lens in the research on the emergence, consolidation and transformation of political order is a worthwhile undertaking but, as this contribution argues, is predetermined by the stance that the research assumes towards 'bigger' questions. After showing how political science and peace and conflict scholars interested in political transition and statebuilding are implicitly or explicitly basing their research on the assumption of superiority of Western liberal-democratic political order, I will indicate how this thinking has been challenged by research on hybrid political order in the South Pacific.

To limit the actual complexity and fluidity of the different players, it makes sense to distinguish two broad strands of literature that have confronted the issue of hybridity in different ways, but have both taken the inevitable spread, predominance, desirability and corresponding need to enforce the building of liberal-democratic states after a 'Western' template to be a natural fact. Scholars interested in political transformation and democratisation have been focusing on the so-called 'third wave' of democratisation, i.e. mostly countries situated in Latin America and the former Eastern bloc. Such 'transitology' scholars have dominated the discourse on post-Cold War socio-political and economic transitions.[6] Most importantly, they seem to have embraced liberal democracy as the only legitimate form of political order, thus espousing Francis Fukuyama's 'end of history' thesis, i.e. the idea that liberal-capitalist democracy has proven to be the only viable form of political order on the globe.[7] Apparently convinced of the evolutionary force that would put all countries on the trajectory towards liberal democracy, this strand of scholarship was preoccupied with understanding the emergence, resilience, 'durability' and general nature of authoritarian or otherwise non-democratic political regimes well into the third decade after the collapse of communism.[8] Kristian Petrov captures this Hegelian determinism in defining this kind of research as 'teleological transitology', which he defines as 'transition research in which regime change appears as purposeful, preordained and therefore predictable, virtually unstoppable, and impelled by a future goal'.[9]

From this position, hybridity is seen as an attribute of regimes pointing to their impurity or failure to develop a fully 'democratic' modus operandi. Steven Levitsky and Lucan Way's concept of 'competitive authoritarianism' is a case in point, as it tries to rationalise the way in which authoritarian regimes engage in democratic reforms in order to increase domestic and international legitimacy. Based on earlier democratisation literature they offer four conditions that make up a 'procedural minimum' definition of democracy:

> 1) free, fair and competitive elections; 2) full adult suffrage; 3) broad protection of civil liberties, including freedom of speech, press and association; and 4) the absence of nonelected 'tutelary' authorities (e.g., militaries, monarchies, or religious bodies) that limit elected officials' power to govern.[10]

In an attempt to refine their model, they add the condition that there has to be 'a *reasonably* level playing field between incumbents and opposition'.[11] The idea that their model can work if the playing field between opposition and government is just *reasonably* level points to a general shortcoming. By adopting analytical categories such as 'level playing field', 'opposition' or 'civil liberty' these analyses try to apply a grid of political analysis – based on ideas of how political and social order emerged in Western countries – to other contexts. This approach is limited if not flawed as it is based on the assumption of universal drive towards democratisation and a universal logic according to which such processes occur or can be made to occur. In other words, whether they are 'competitive authoritarianism' or other attempts to grapple with the problem of non-democratic, 'hybrid', regimes do not appear to matter, because the literature on hybrid regimes and its variations applies a universal logic that disregards cultural variations in the practices of collective decision-making and perceptions of what is a legitimate social or political order. As Stewart and colleagues[12] have suggested, transitology scholars did not take into account the possibility that hybridity in the sense of incomplete transition towards democracy might indeed be a *hardly*, if at all, *eradicable condition*. As I will show below, such hybridity can equally be seen as result of cultural difference in the building up and operation of mechanisms and institutions of social ordering.

Another group that seems to be convinced of the liberal democratic 'end game' comprises institutionalist statebuilding scholars, who invest their academic efforts in inquiring what makes states stable and viable and, conversely, why some other states fail, become fragile and conflict-prone.[13] Basing their line of argument on Helman and Ratner's seminal article titled 'Saving Failed States',[14] the scholars contend that states should be assessed in terms of their capability to deliver public goods and services,[15] effectiveness to execute government policies[16] and that, in order to build up a liberal-democratic polity it might be necessary to impose some institutions in a top-down manner with military power.[17] Numerous scholars have criticised this version of a 'liberal peace' and its different hegemonic and imperial implications,[18] and for its focus on institutions as such as opposed to state–society relations, social cohesion and the importance of domestic politics.[19] Thus, Hameiri[20] concluded that the failure is more with the neo-institutionalist 'failed state' paradigm as such, rather than with the states examined. Rather than focusing on if not 'fetishising' supposed 'Weberian' institutions as the essence and criterion for legitimate statehood, scholarship in IR, political science and beyond should face up to the necessity of doing more culturally sensitive research on social orders and the development of a '*post*-Weberian' approach to understanding statebuilding and state formation processes.[21]

An alternative application of hybridity, based on an alternative world-view, is offered by a group around the German scholars Kevin Clements and Volker Boege. Echoing the critics of neo-institutionalist statebuilding and 'failed state' analysis,[22] they argue that social order should not be preconceived by an evolutionary logic of graduation to liberal democracy but that, on the contrary, statebuilding should be reconsidered by taking into account the 'strength, resilience and persistence of custom and tradition both as a source of identity and as a means of organising social, economic and political systems'.[23] Examining different cases on the Solomon Islands, in Melanesia and Bougainville (all in South-East Asia), their seminal 2007 article concludes that customary forms of social order can be viable or even more suitable in sustaining peace, and that such forms of social order need not be at odds with modern, Weberian state institutions but might be compatible, or even work in complementarity, with the latter. This research has arguably created a touchstone and an 'aura of hope' for scholars of peace and conflict studies and beyond.[24] Richmond, for instance, proposed the idea of a 'post-liberal peace', in which the Western-centric precepts of a liberal-democratic peace are negotiable and commensurable with non-Western, traditional forms of social organisation.[25] This debate not only framed 'post-liberal' or 'hybrid' forms of peace as emancipatory alternatives to the 'liberal peace', but also as empirically observable patterns resulting from resistance on the part of the subjects of international intervention. As Mac Ginty argued, the 'liberal peace' is *de facto* being subverted and resisted against by its implementers and recipient populations at large, all of which engage in different covert and perhaps even unconscious forms of resistance and non-compliance.[26]

This literature illustrates how hybridity can be a useful concept to understand the emergence and consolidation of peace in (post-conflict) transitional orders. It is apparent, however, that it is not the application of hybridity *per se* that informs the contribution of this group of scholars, but their critical stance vis-à-vis the teleological understanding of global development and statebuilding processes espoused by transitology and statebuilding scholars of the two decades following the Cold War. Hybridity was only used by this group of scholars as a lens to uncover and criticise the failures and inherent contradictions of political transformation and post-conflict reconstruction programmes and to show how arrangements alternative to the Western version of statebuilding can be viable. Any use of hybridity other than as such a critical lens, as I argue, is associated with risks and problems. To illustrate this I will show in the next section how the application of hybridity in research and political programming can incur uncertainty and even lead to dire and violent outcomes.

From hybrid order to 'hybrid violence': ambiguous implications of hybridity in practice

This section will illustrate the negative potential exposed by hybridity applied in the research on and design of political orders. The added value of the concept of hybrid political orders and the potential of combining customary, non-Western forms of order with Western-style, 'Weberian' state institutions is critically reviewed and the dangers of underestimating the ambiguities are problematised. The section opens with a discussion of the important but often blurred distinction between research that appreciates and sees potential in hybridity and, on the other hand, approaches that advocate hybrid solutions to complex problems and thus are confronted with failure following their application. In a second step, I will review different relativist approaches in order to illustrate how they risk the consolidation of regimes of 'hybrid violence'.[27]

Indeed, as its proponents admit, hybrid forms of peace and political order need not be benign, but might be 'malevolent' and lead to marginalisation and human rights abuses.[28] Hence, while hybridity helps us to take into account the historical and social complexities of different national contexts, it does not help in understanding some problems that are determined by more structural and global trajectories. It is becoming more and more obvious that social inquiry faces a fundamental problem concerning its basis of existence and modus operandi: how should researchers position themselves vis-à-vis policy and institutional actors (who decide about or directly provide crucial funding) if the possibility of delivering reliable analyses requires significant investments of time and money and, further, giving funders and policy-makers predictions and recommendations is often required? Scholars using hybridity frameworks have not been exempt from such trajectories, finds Gearoid Millar, who divides hybridity literature into a 'descriptive' and a 'prescriptive' group, where the latter 'assumes that administering hybrid institutions will foster predictable peace-promoting experiences among local people', while the former retain a merely analytical ambition of understanding phenomena of hybridity.[29] Making predictions about future developments and recommendations for policy design appears problematic, though, for multiple reasons. I will show this with regard to what Millar calls 'predictive' hybridity literature, in order to substantiate the point that hybridity is mostly, if not only, useful as an analytical lens for a critical or 'descriptive' approach but lends itself as apparatus for predictions and policy-instructions in as little extent as most other social scientific concepts and theories.

The scholars prescribing the use of hybrid arrangements in establishing and maintaining social order can be subsumed under a wider strand of literature advocating a relativist or pragmatist approach to situations of protracted conflict and crisis. Raeymaekers, Menkhaus and Vlassenroot, for instance, argue that the protracted crises in African countries such as South Sudan or Democratic Republic of Congo (DRC) are not merely an instance of chaos and anarchy, but also offer a lot of opportunities for different sets of non-state actors.[30] Thus, a certain measure of order and service provision would have been sustained by the latter on a community level, leading them to argue that 'governance without government' is possible and probably the best available solution.[31] Similarly, Smits and Wright note that, where non-state actors have the stronger reach than state institutions themselves, they might indeed be the only source of stability.[32] An instructive proof of this possibility is the case of Somaliland, where the regional government has taken over the monopoly of violence and successfully built a state *de facto* independent of the central government of Somalia and functioning while not acknowledged by the international community at large.[33]

Given such positive examples of a hybrid approach to establishing the monopoly of violence, Sukanya Podder discusses the role of non-state armed groups (NSAGs) in post-conflict settings and argues that they are seen too exclusively as spoilers and might under certain conditions generate the social legitimacy to establish and stabilise peace settlements.[34] While her 'entry points' provide a seemingly straightforward way of incorporating local solutions in establishing order and peace, the possibility of 'key variables underpinning the transition of rebel groups into constructive political roles'[35] appears to be limited to the extent that the criteria for identifying 'socially legitimate' NSAGs are not the same across different social contexts. Whether it is possible to establish any reliable information on whether and how NSAGs transform into socially legitimate and non-violent actors seems to come down to a question of worldview and, ultimately, epistemology. As many would argue, it would require in-depth research into the life worlds of communities in order to approximate knowledge about such processes; and the scenario of reducing such complex and contingent trajectories to 'a set of variables' appears ambitious if not dangerous when considering the following cases.[36]

The spectrum of authors advocating the application of hybrid forms of governance, cooperation with 'spoilers' and attempts to transform and reintegrate them extends into a realist approach that has also been labelled as 'neo-trusteeship' or 'hybrid authority'.[37] These approaches have been shown to be conceptually deficient,[38] as they lead to warlordism[39] and other regressive outcomes. Similar to other critical analyses,[40] Kate Meagher scrutinises the positive potential of hybrid security governance and the integration of non-state armed groups in the cases of the RCD-ML (Rally for Congolese Democracy – Movement for Liberation) in Eastern DRC and the 'Bakassi Boys' in Eastern Nigeria.[41] In the former case she finds that what appears locally grounded and legitimate with the population is more of a projection of regional economic interests and ethnic manipulation and coercion if not outright violence on the local level. Thus, the order and stability the RCD-ML sustains in Eastern Congo, as well as its taking over of 'state-like' functions in the education and transport sector, conceal the fact that overall the livelihoods in the provinces under this local 'monopoly of violence' have deteriorated and much of the mining activity and infrastructure provision is realised with the help of forced labour and under threat of armed violence.[42]

As the RCD-ML refuses to integrate its fiscal structures with the DRC's central apparatus and its armed forces are partly kept independent from the DRC's army, it manages to maintain a parallel security and economic structure which is often complicit if not actively participating in violent crimes committed in its own territory. This is a parallel to the Bakassi Boys, a network of vigilante groups in Eastern Nigeria which, after its initial establishment in 1998, took over criminal prosecution and tax collection functions from 'Nigeria's dysfunctional policing and justice institutions' in two federal states. After failing to obtain undisputed legal status and being captured by local political elites, however, the network became associated with 'political thuggery and partisan killings merged with acts of kidnapping and wanton violence', meaning that this initially hopeful case of popular vigilantism ended up 'reproducing rather than challenging predatory and unaccountable modes of governance'.[43] While such analysis illustrates well the slippery slope between hybrid authority and 'hybrid violence',[44] Jana Hönke's book on transnational hybrid security governance deepens this integration of local perspectives and regional/global 'assemblages' to show how in the case of mining sites in South Africa, and Katanga, Eastern DRC, the 'regimes of practice' of security firms reproduce global hegemonic structures as they superordinate corporate interests over livelihood and humanitarian concerns of the local population.[45]

Not least the contributions to this volume, first and foremost those by Beswick and Jackson, illustrate how local and hybrid solutions to complex problems are not necessarily an improvement vis-à-vis top-down liberal peacebuilding. In particular, traditional and customary justice systems can marginalise certain groups or individuals (see Jackson's chapter). Approaches that are labelled 'indigenous', and thus enjoy greater legitimacy vis-à-vis international peacebuiding actors, can also serve to marginalise and mute voices and positions that have a right to be heard in post-conflict contexts (see Beswick's chapter). Especially the authoritarian features of states that emerged from conflict, involving the transformation of armed groups into political parties, such as in Rwanda, Angola or Cambodia paint a rather bleak picture for the future of hybrid approaches to conflict resolution. As argued by Jonathan Fisher in a recent forum article, researchers can be susceptible to a 'Potemkin village' effect of taking the things they see and hear from their respondents as representative and disregard the hidden silences, violence and oppression that such a façade may be covering (as in today's Rwanda, in his particular case).[46] The only way to resolve this informational deadlock of research is a focus on people's worldviews and understandings from a multi-angle perspective, involving individuals from different backgrounds and affiliations. In the following section, I will show how uncertainty does not only pertain to predictions and policy recommendations but is part of a wider concern with the complexity and non-linearity the current global order can be seen to be characterised by.

'Hybrid subjectivities' as a way to tackle ontological challenges of a non-linear world

This section has two main purposes. First, I will show how the discussions around the concept of hybridity in political science, IR and beyond are reflective of a more fundamental concern with the claims to truth and validity that 'social scientists' are making. It will thus be shown that non-essentialist, inductive concepts of hybridity are key if we understand the world as one of non-linear processes, where emerging complexity renders classical research and policy frameworks that are based on linear and evolutionary conceptions of knowledge ineffective. Second, and based on this radically reflective stance, I will argue that the 'conceptual' realm and the hybridisation and diffusion processes occurring in it are a very, if not the most, promising avenue to explore in research on peace and conflict and beyond. Drawing on literature presenting research from post-Soviet Central Asia, I will indicate how the refocusing on what I call 'hybrid subjectivities' has already happened and can be pursued further.

Why do hybrid solutions in zones of shared sovereignty or legal pluralism bear so much danger? This is not, as I argue, due to inherent characteristics and structures of societies, but much more because of the increasingly complex nature of the international system, the non-linearity, ungovernability – indeed unknowability – of social and political developments in the current world. To the latter point, David Chandler has introduced into peace and conflict studies the idea of conceiving of the international system as a non-linear system, which cannot be understood by reductionist and linear 'scientific' approaches, let alone governed by the corresponding 'neoliberal' approaches to policy.[47] Drawing on different works in chaos, complexity and systems theories,[48] he argues that the current global environment can be seen as characterised by 'emergent complexity', which is self-perpetuating and in a process of constant flux.[49] The assumption made in evolutionary theory, and especially liberal internationalism, that it is possible to 'make things work' by finding out the ways to do it, i.e. finding the hidden variables or biases, or the hybridities that distort the process, is thus rendered obsolete:

> The problematic of a complex emergent order is not that of knowing more, 'filling in the gaps' of knowledge, but an ontological problem, i.e. the problem exists at the level of what is to be known (it is not linear and law-bound) rather than at the level of how we might know the underlying reality.[50]

Chandler employs ex-US Secretary of Defense Donald Rumsfeld's allegory of the 'unknown unknowns', designating factors, which influence events unexpectedly and are impossible to know beforehand. Contrary to the 'neoliberal episteme's' implicit assumption that it is possible to know (all) the 'unknowns' that influence events, requiring science to advance methodology to such a degree that these 'unknowns' can be uncovered, Chandler posits that emergent complexity demands the development of approaches that can accommodate the emergence of new unforeseen factors and variables that turn out to play a role in the process.[51]

The approach to deal with such complexity is then not a classic, technocratic and knowledge-based one, but a *resilience* approach envisaging the creation of mechanisms and capabilities on local and individual levels for dealing with the plethora of issues the world brings up. Resilience, with its 'flat' ontology that is interested in the 'everyday life' of the subject as a source of approaches for sustainable development,[52] thus is akin to Richmond's and Mac Ginty's ideas of looking at the 'everyday' and indigenous practices of building peace and political orders.[53] But, while acknowledging their critique vis-à-vis liberal, linear understandings of intervention and transformation, Chandler also argues that 'post-liberal' and 'hybrid peace' approaches deepen the voluntaristic understanding of liberal frameworks, as the locus decisive for post-conflict transformation is merely shifted from governmental institutions and national elites to the so-called 'local' level.[54] This critique might not be entirely justified given these scholars' awareness of the messiness and ambiguities of the potential for peace and conflict transformation in the social milieu and scale referred to as 'local' in the early hybrid peace literature. The concern from which the critique emanates is very relevant, however. Rather than conceiving 'everyday' and 'local' perspectives and actors as a source or driver of peace, this refocusing enables an analysis of how peace is enacted among populations, which is of itself more valuable than accounts of peace and post-conflict transition that are based on elite-level and aggregate data, which offer little insight and presuppose the transferability of meaning both across and within contexts.

This conceptual step foregrounds the configuration of the critical, interdisciplinary research agenda for hybridity that I seek to outline here. Such an approach would put local subjectivities at the centre of the analysis for two crucial reasons. First, putting subjectivities or the worldviews of people first makes it possible to question whether and how these subjects lend themselves to the overall interrogation in the first place. Put simply, the overarching questions and terms of engagement of one's research might not be shared by people in the focus of this research. Given the increasing challenge that emerging complexity and the looming of 'unknown unknowns' posit to social research, this engagement with the subjects of research appears to be a minimal and very feasible step to be taken. Anthropologist Martin Hoolbraad captures this difference in ontologies in the following phrase:

> [T]he difference between [. . .] analyst and [. . .] subject lies not in the different perspectives each may take upon the world (their respective 'world-views' or even 'cultures') but rather in the ways in which either of them may come to define what may count as a world [. . .] in the first place.[55]

Secondly, inquiry into subjectivities would allow a substantial study of hybridisation processes in what Millar calls the conceptual – or ideational – realm of hybridity. More than discourse and practice, this metaphysical realm can be seen as the main site of intervention and resistance towards it, both in explicit and subconscious ways.[56] It is a constant filter through which real-world action is mediated with the respective context or what Miller, with reference to Bourdieu, calls a deeply historical, socially embedded and inter-subjectively constructed 'self-evident and natural order which goes without saying'.[57] Furthermore, it is clear that such local subjectivities are not only rooted in local history and sociality, but that they will inevitably be affected by global processes to greater or lesser extent, too. Chandler invokes Althusser's conception of ideological embeddedness of the subject, which emphasises how 'Ideological State Apparatuses' shape people's subjectivities and worldviews, as they transfer the influence of multiple global material and ideational forces into people's everyday lives.[58] Thus, what is seen as a 'local' and somewhat authentic or 'pure' subject needs to be problematised in terms of its 'always-already' global condition and insertion into mechanisms of ordering, hierarchy, mobilisation and action.[59] This 'embeddedness' is concealed through the institutions and frameworks of territorial and political governance, culture and, ultimately, language that are habitually used to 'categorise', 'map' and 'order' the world, both by 'ordinary people' and researchers.[60] Taking 'hybrid subjectivities' as a departure point for social inquiry would be a way of accommodating this complexity and multifariousness characterising analytical premises that are often presented as simple and straightforward, or the most reasonable.

Perhaps one of the global regions where ideological embeddedness is most apparent, but also most ignored, are the post-Socialist countries of the former Soviet Union and Central and Eastern Europe. The sluggishness and failure of, or even popular resistance against, democratic transformations in these countries poses a paradox to many scholars, especially the 'transitologists' above. A way to resolve this paradox is a new focus on the subjectivities observable in these post-Socialist countries, and the concurring attempt to understand the ways in which authoritarian governments legitimise themselves. Anna Matveeva's 2009 article titled 'Legitimising Central Asian Authoritarianism' provides a valuable entry point from a political science perspective, as she argues that relative stability and effective law enforcement may already be enough to justify authoritarian rule in the eyes of the people of a given state.[61] Other scholars have developed perspectives from other disciplinary angles in order to shed light on the worldviews of people conferring legitimacy to the hybrid democracies, if not outright authoritarian regimes, of Central Asia. Tommaso Trevisani's 'Ethnography of Consent in Uzbek Authoritarianism',[62] for instance, provides different examples how threats to one's own livelihood and the stabilisation of one's own situation are being rationalised in both historical perspective and with regard to the current emergence of a strong Islamic movement in Central Asia. Respondents' statements such as 'We are in Asia here, not in Europe. Democracy does not work here'[63] highlight the disillusionment with the transition period that serve as justifications for being acquiescent of an authoritarian regime that oppresses opposing opinions in sometimes very obvious ways. Approaching the issue from a literary perspective, Marcel Cornis-Pope reviews the identity struggles of authors in the post-communist period and thus provides an insight into how post-communist regimes can garner legitimacy by offering a sense of belonging to people trying to cope with the sense of loss characterising their 'psychodrama of identity in a post-1989 world'.[64]

Inquiry into the subjectivities and worldviews informing transition processes need not merely reveal details about resistance against democratisation, transition and intervention. On the contrary, the sources and mechanisms of support for such projects are equally elucidated. Christopher Schwartz, for instance, has done research on how people in Central Asia dealt with the collapse of the Soviet Union in 1991 and finds that a significant proportion of what one would call 'ordinary' people embraced democracy and free markets as a given in the way they saw their country should develop, and took it for granted that 'people are now more market-oriented'.[65] Other works point out the paradoxical way in which democratisation and liberalisation have been adopted for reform agendas in Central Asian countries, and how much of the 'old' knowledge and practices were discarded, while Western, 'modern', and 'civilised' knowledge was embraced as new orthodoxy.[66] There appears to be an urgent need to inquire into how subjects of transition and global integration understand – or, indeed, *anticipate* – political reform, peace- and statebuilding and development programming according to the Western, 'liberal peace' blueprint.[67] Merging the knowledge on such 'hyper-liberal' worldviews and their traditional, neo-authoritarian counterparts would help to better understand the tensions and potentials for political or violent conflict, both within Central Asia and beyond. It would further enable an empirically grounded analysis of hybridisation processes in both the conceptual realm and the practice of reform and transition. Such analysis has already been presented in insightful legal and political ethnographies, especially in the case of Kyrgyzstan. Aksana Ismailbekova, for instance, showed how a local election committee combined democratic electoral standards with culturally grounded moral principles in their running of the election station and distribution of unused ballots.[68] Judith Beyer, on the other hand, explains how so-called *aksakal* (elder) courts apply their faint knowledge of the Kyrgyz law with the help of their own conception of appropriateness and social norms, in the process hybridising, if not subverting, the laws and the principles of equality and protection on which they are based.[69]

While this survey of literatures on social change in post-Soviet Central Asia was very brief, it was helpful to indicate the benefits of realising a research agenda on 'hybrid subjectivities'. First, the view on the subject as globally embedded offers a way forward from the currently prevailing focus of local–international interaction, which seem to unwittingly construct subjectivities without problematising sufficiently their exposure to and interlinkages with global discursive and material trajectories. By tackling the way in which local subjectivities are embedded in and influenced by global imaginaries and ideological forces, it is possible to bring back in 'the "big picture", universalist meta-narratives, and critical sociological understandings'.[70] Second, such a refocusing on subjectivities would also enable a discussion of the ambiguity and uncertainty and conflict potential inherent in so-called hybrid social formations. An instructive case is Goode and Stroupe's conceptualisation of nationalist practices and discourse as 'constructivism for the masses', in which they tackle the problem that '[p]ractices that legitimate authoritarian rule in one social context may become ironic or subversive in others' and are thus situated on a continuum of forms of resistance which requires in-depth and context-specific study.[71] This hints at a third point, which concerns the potential differences in ontologies between researchers and researched. That is, the reasons for one and the same action or utterance having different meanings from different people's perspectives might not be mere difference in cultural interpretation, but might stem from a different understanding of the world as such on the part of researchers and subjects, respectively. Such a more fundamental understanding of difference would equip research to capture the drivers of social processes more accurately and avoid the voluntaristic and linear tendencies of traditional social science research.

Conclusion: towards a pluri-ontological understanding of hybridity

This chapter has attempted to indicate how hybridity is applied in political science, peace and conflict literatures and how the further development of the research agenda on 'hybrid subjectivities' offers a promising avenue to be both mindful of the limits of hybridity and social inquiry more generally. I have pointed out how the transitology literature used hybridity implicitly or explicitly as an attribute associated with impurity and incompleteness of political transitions towards democracy and, in a similar vein, how the institutionalist statebuilding literature nurtured the idea that 'state failure' and 'fragility' can be addressed if countries work towards certain institutional, service delivery and democratic governance standards. The concept of hybrid political orders proposed by Clements, Boege and others – based on the idea of combining state and non-state, modern and traditional, formal and informal structures and actors in establishing social orders – was presented as a viable alternative to such essentialist, Western-centric and positivist views. Hybridity has thus created an 'aura of hope' in peace and conflict studies, especially among a group of critical scholars that synthesised political science/IR approaches with ethnographic and anthropological elements. Still, it was made clear that hybridity might be helpful as a tool to understand and shed critical light on certain processes, but not in overcoming the limits of predicting social outcomes and design policies accordingly. To illustrate this critical point, I have reviewed literature about cases where hybridity is applied within pragmatist approaches to design policy solutions or inquire the desirability of hybrid solutions to situations of protracted crises and 'governance without government'. While these situations seemed to be not all that bleak, and to even provide opportunities for new approaches of ordering society, as Raeymaekers *et al.*, alongside other authors, argue, there appears to be a certain danger in what Jenny Peterson calls 'hybrid programming'.[72] Hybrid governance arrangements can lead to outright violence or, when viewed in a macro perspective, to the instantiation of hybrid transnational security regimes that superordinate corporate and other particular economic interests over collective livelihoods and human security concerns.

Finally, I have offered a reflection on the more fundamental ramifications of these discussions for the validity and analytical authority of hybridity approaches and social inquiry in general. Based on the growing realisation that social research, let alone making predictions and policy recommendations, is rendered increasingly difficult given the emergent complexity of the current global environment and the equally growing sense of urgency to act and – on part of social scientists – instruct policy decisions, I have argued that social research should make a sincere effort to inquire into the subjectivities of the very people it seeks to do research on. This would be, as I have argued, the most feasible and appropriate reaction to the concerns with the increasing hardship of producing reliable social research, but also a move towards studying 'conceptual hybridisation' which appears very timely. Inquiring into 'hybrid subjectivities', as I have shown for the case of Central Asia, can help to shed light on the largely ignored factors of political transition and the failure or lack thereof. Based on such thinking, authors such as Matveeva were able to formulate alternatives to the Western-centric inquiry about the time it would take for post-Soviet authoritarian regimes to collapse, and to ask how they actually manage to maintain legitimacy in the eye of economic and political turmoil.

Such engagement appears to be highly needed in a world where accusations and alienation between different countries go hand in hand with their increased political and cultural differentiation. Only by investigating the hybridisation of, or resistance against, homogenising trajectories such as democratisation and political and economic standardisation in the ideational realm, is it possible to develop a sufficient understanding of the hybridisation empirically observable by the already consolidated disciplines and their methodological apparatuses. On a critical note, the idea of '*hybrid* subjectivities' of course presupposes that these are made up of different distinguishable elements, which would indicate a unified ontology including a clearly delineated conceptual and discursive field. In keeping with the 'pluri-ontological' approach proposed here and with a 'dialogist' perspective on social phenomena,[73] I would qualify this hybridity of subjectivities as one rooted in the fact that in a world of multiple coexisting ontologies, even a subjectivity can only be unified and clearly defined through black letters on white paper. More accurately, such a monistic picture could only be one representation of an ontologically hybrid and thus multiple subjectivity, the exploration of which should be one goal for critical social inquiry.

Notes

The author would like to thank the German Academic Exchange Service (DAAD) Doctoral Scholarship and the University of Birmingham School of Government and Society Doctoral Research Bursary for funding the research that was done for this chapter. Further thanks are expressed to Nicolas Lemay-Hébert and Fabian Burkhardt for valuable comments.

1 Roger Mac Ginty (2011) International Peacebuilding and Local Resistance: Hybrid Forms of Peace (Basingstoke: Palgrave Macmillan), 1.
2 Such 'hopeful' applications can mostly be traced back to Homi Bhabha's (1994) major work *The Location of Culture* (London: Routledge) and include Keith Nurse (1999) 'Globalization and Trinidad Carnival: Diaspora, Hybridity and Identity in Global Culture', *Cultural Studies* 13(4): 661–90; among others.
3 See for instance Pnina Werbner (2001) 'The Limits of Cultural Hybridity: On Ritual Monsters, Poetic Licence and Contested Postcolonial Purifications', *Journal of the Royal Anthropological Institute* 7(1): 133–52; Jonathan Friedman (1999) 'The Hybridization of Roots and the Abhorrence of the Bush', in Mike Featherstone and Scott Lash (eds), *Spaces of Culture: City, Nation, World* (London: Sage), 230–56; for an overview of critiques of hybridity see Jan N. Pieterse (2001) 'Hybridity, So What? The Anti-Hybridity Backlash and the Riddles of Recognition', *Theory, Culture and Society* 18(2–3): 219–45.
4 This point is further discussed in Philipp Lottholz (2015) 'Exploring the Boundaries of Knowledge via Hybridity', *Journal of Intervention and Statebuilding* 10(1): 136–42, 136, see also Werbner, 'Limits of Cultural Hybridity', 150.
5 A good introduction into the conflict of universalism and relativism form a socio-legal perspective is provided by Ronald Cohen (1989) 'Human Rights and Cultural Relativism: The Need for a New Approach', *American Anthropologist* NS 91(4): 1014–17; on critical vs problem-solving perspectives in peacebuilding see Michael Pugh (2013) 'The Problem-Solving and Critical Paradigms', in Roger Mac Ginty (ed.), *Routledge Handbook of Peacebuilding* (Abingdon: Routledge), 11–24.
6 Some of the most instructive works are: Steven Levitsky and Lucan A. Way (2010) *Competitive Authoritarianism: Hybrid Regimes After the Cold War* (Cambridge: Cambridge University Press); Kathleen Collins (2006) *Clan Politics and Regime Transition in Central Asia* (New York: Cambridge University Press); Thomas Carothers (1999) *Aiding Democracy Abroad: The Learning Curve* (Washington, DC: Carnegie Endowment for International Peace); for a critical view see Thomas Carothers (2002) 'The End of the Transition Paradigm', *Journal of Democracy* 13(1): 5–21; for an analysis of transitology's discursive dominance and inroads into policy see Rudolf L. Tőkés (2000) '"Transitology": Global Dreams and Postcommunist Realities', *Central Europe Review* 2(10), http://www.ce-review.org/00/10/tokes10.html (accessed May 2016).
7 Francis Fukuyama (1992) *The End of History and the Last Man* (New York: Simon & Schuster).
8 See for instance Valery J. Bunce and Sharon L. Wolchik (2011) *Defeating Authoritarian Leaders in Postcommunist Countries* (Cambridge: Cambridge University Press); Guillermo O'Donnell and Philippe C. Schmitter (2013) *Transitions from Authoritarian Rule: Tentative Conclusions about Uncertain Democracies*, 4th edn (1st edn 1986) (Baltimore, MD: Johns Hopkins University Press).
9 'The Concept of Transition in Transition: Comparing the Post-Communist Use of the Concept of Transition with that Found in Soviet Ideology', *Baltic Worlds* 7(1): 29–41, 30.

10 Levitsky and Way, *Competitive Authoritarianism*, 6.
11 Ibid., emphasis added.
12 Susan Stewart, Margarete Klein, Andrea Schmitz and Hans-Henning Schröder (eds) (2012) *Presidents, Oligarchs and Bureaucrats: Forms of Rule in Post-Soviet Space* (Farnham: Ashgate), 3.
13 See Nicolas Lemay-Hébert (2013) 'Rethinking Weberian Approaches to Statebuilding', in David Chandler (ed.), *Routledge Handbook of International Statebuilding* (London: Routledge), 3–14, 4 ff.
14 Gerald B. Helman and Steven R. Ratner (1992–3) 'Saving Failed States', *Foreign Policy* (Winter): 3–20.
15 Robert I. Rotberg (2004) 'The Failure and Collapse of Nation-States', in Robert I. Rotberg (ed.), *When States Fail: Causes and Consequences* (Princeton, NJ: Princeton University Press), 1–50.
16 Francis Fukuyama (2004) *State-Building: Governance and World Order in the 21st Century* (Ithaca, NY: Cornell University Press).
17 Roland Paris (2004) *At War's End: Building Peace After Civil Conflict* (Cambridge: Cambridge University Press).
18 For instance Mark Duffield (2007) *Development, Security and Unending War: Governing the World of Peoples* (Cambridge: Polity); Roger Mac Ginty and Oliver P. Richmond (eds), (2009) *The Liberal Peace and Post-War Reconstruction: Myth or Reality?* (London: Routledge).
19 Nicolas Lemay-Hébert (2009) 'Statebuilding without Nation-Building? Legitimacy, State Failure and the Limits of the Institutionalist Approach', *Journal of Intervention and Statebuilding* 3(1): 21–45; Shahar Hameiri (2010) *Regulating Statehood: State Building and the Transformation of the Global Order* (Basingstoke: Palgrave Macmillan).
20 Shahar Hameiri (2007) 'Failed States or a Failed Paradigm? State Capacity and the Limits of Institutionalism', *Journal of International Relations and Development* 10(2): 122–49.
21 Philipp Lottholz and Nicolas Lemay-Hébert (2016) 'Re-Reading Weber, Reconceptualising State-Building: From Neo-Weberian to Post-Weberian Approaches to State, Legitimacy and State-Building', *Cambridge Review of International Affairs* (online first).
22 See Volker Boege, Anne M. Brown and Kevin P. Clements (2009) 'Hybrid Political Orders, Not Fragile States', *Peace Review* 21(1): 13–21.
23 Kevin P. Clements, Volker Boege, Anne Brown, Wendy Foley and Anna Nolan (2007) 'State Building Reconsidered: The Role of Hybridity in the Formation of Political Order', *Political Science* 59(1): 45–56, 46.
24 Jenny H. Peterson (2012) 'A Conceptual Unpacking of Hybridity: Accounting for Notions of Power, Politics and Progress in Analyses of Aid-Driven Interfaces', *Journal of Peacebuilding and Development* 7(2): 9–22, 16; for instructive examples on hybridity in peace and conflict studies literature see Mac Ginty, *International Peacebuilding*; Oliver P. Richmond and Audra Mitchell (eds) (2011) *Hybrid Forms of Peace: From Everyday Forms of Peace to Post-Liberalism* (Basingstoke: Palgrave Macmillan). See also Visoka in this collection for a more in-depth discussion.
25 Oliver P. Richmond (2011) *A Post-Liberal Peace* (Basingstoke: Palgrave Macmillan).
26 Mac Ginty, *International Peacebuilding*, 84 ff.
27 Keith Krause (2012) 'Hybrid Violence: Locating the Use of Force in Postconflict Settings', *Global Governance* 18(1): 39–56.
28 Richmond, *A Post-Liberal Peace*, 136; Mac Ginty, *International Peacebuilding*, 28; Roger Mac Ginty and Oliver P. Richmond (2016) 'The Fallacy of Constructing Hybrid Political Orders: A Reappraisal of the Hybrid Turn in Peacebuilding', *International Peacekeeping* 23(2): 219–39.

29 Gearoid Millar (2014) 'Disaggregating Hybridity: Why Hybrid Institutions do Not Produce Predictable Experiences of Peace', *Journal of Peace Research* 501–14, 502.
30 Timothy Raeymaekers, Ken Menkhaus and Koen Vlassenroot (2008) 'State and Non-State Regulation in African Protracted Crises: Governance without Government?', *Africa Focus* 21(2): 7–21, 8.
31 Ibid., see also Ken Menkhaus (2006–7) 'Governance without Government in Somalia: Spoilers, State Building, and the Politics of Coping', *International Security* (Winter) 31(3): 74–106.
32 Rosan Smits and Deborah Wright (2012) *Engagement with Non-State Actors in Fragile States: Narrowing Definitions, Broadening Scope*, Conflict Research Unit Report (The Hague: Clingendael Institute), 4.
33 Marleen Renders (2012) *Consider Somaliland: State-Building with Traditional Leaders and Institutions* (Leiden: Brill).
34 Sukanya Podder (2013) 'Non-State Armed Groups and Stability: Reconsidering Legitimacy and Inclusion', *Contemporary Security Policy* 34(1): 16–39, 31.
35 Ibid. 34.
36 See Kate Meagher (2012) 'The Strength of Weak States? Non-State Security Forces and Hybrid Governance in Africa', *Development and Change* 43(5): 1073–1101.
37 James D. Fearon and David D. Laitin (2004) 'Neotrusteeship and the Problem of Weak States', *International Security* 28(4): 5–43; Marleen Renders and Ulf Terlinden (2010) 'Negotiating Statehood in a Hybrid Political Order: The Case of Somaliland', *Development and Change* 41(4): 723–46. For examples of this approach see Ali Wardak and Humayun Hamidzada (2012) 'The Search for Legitimate Rule, Justice and a Durable Peace: Hybrid Models of Governance in Afghanistan', *Journal of Peacebuilding and Development* 7(2): 79–88; Timothy Raeymaekers (2010) 'Protection for Sale: War and the transformation of Regulation on the Congo–Ugandan Border', *Development and Change* 41(4): 563–87; Raeymaekers *et al.*, 'State and Non-State Regulation'; Menkhaus, 'Governance without government'; Helen Horsington (2004) 'Cambodian Khmer Rouge Tribunal: The Promise of a Hybrid Tribunal', *Melbourne Journal of International Law* 5: 462–85. For an overview see Millar, 'Disaggregating hybridity', 12.
38 Richard Caplan (2007) 'From Collapsing States to Neo-Trusteeship: The Limits to Solving the Problem of "Precarious Statehood" in the 21st Century', *Third World Quarterly* 28(2): 231–44.
39 As in the Afghan case; see Heather Marquette (2011) 'Donors, State Building and Corruption: Lessons from Afghanistan and the Implications for Aid Policy', *Third World Quarterly* 32(10): 1871–90.
40 Jonathan Goodhand and Oliver Walton (2009) 'The Limits of Liberal Peacebuilding? International Engagement in the Sri Lankan Peace Process', *Journal of Intervention and Statebuilding* 3(3): 303–23; Anna Leander (2004) 'Wars and the Un-Making of States: Taking Tilly Seriously in the Contemporary World', in Stefano Guzzini and Dietrich Jung (eds), *Contemporary Security Analysis and Copenhagen Peace Research* (London: Routledge), 69–80.
41 Meagher, 'Strength of Weak States?'
42 Ibid. 1085 ff.
43 Ibid. 1097.
44 Krause, 'Hybrid Violence'.
45 Jana Hönke (2013) *Transnational Companies and Security Governance: Hybrid Practices in a Postcolonial World* (London: Routledge).
46 Jonathan Fisher (2015) 'Writing about Rwanda since the Genocide: Knowledge, Power and "Truth"', *Journal of Intervention and Statebuilding* 9(1): 134–45.

47 David Chandler (2014) 'Beyond Neoliberalism: Resilience, the New Art of Governing Complexity', *Resilience* 2(1): 47–63; 'Resilience and the "Everyday": Beyond the Paradox of "Liberal Peace"', *Review of International Studies* 41: 27–48.
48 David Chandler (2013) 'Peacebuilding and the Politics of Non-Linearity: Rethinking "Hidden" Agency and "Resistance"', *Peacebuilding* 1(1): 17–32; 18 n. 1.
49 Chandler, 'Beyond Neoliberalism', 48.
50 Ibid. 50.
51 Ibid. 50–1.
52 Chandler, 'Resilience and the "Everyday"', 3–4.
53 Richmond, *A Post-Liberal Peace*; Richmond and Mitchell, *Hybrid Forms of Peace*; Mac Ginty, *International Peacebuilding*.
54 Chandler, 'Peacebuilding and the Politics of Non-Linearity', 24–5. See also Julian Graef, who labels this paradox as a one of 'liberal-local hybridity', a binary conceptualisation which ends up concealing the emancipatory potential of international actors, the negative potential of local actors, if not the very processes that determine (post-conflict) transitions in more significant ways than the interaction between the 'international' and the 'local'. See Julian Graef (2015) *Practicing Postliberal Peacebuilding: Legal Empowerment and Emergent Hybridity in Liberia* (Basingstoke: Palgrave Macmillan), 5, 31, 34 ff.
55 Martin Hoolbrad (2013) 'Turning a Corner: Preamble for "The Relative Native" by Eduardo Viveiros de Castro', tr. Julia Sauma and Martin Hoolbrad, *HAU: Journal of Ethnographic Theory* 3(3): 469–71, 470.
56 Millar, 'Disaggregating Hybridity', 505.
57 Pierre Bourdieu (1977) *Outline of a Theory of Practice* (Cambridge: Cambridge University Press), 166; cited in Millar, 'Disaggregating Hybridity', 505.
58 Chandler, 'Peacebuilding and the Politics of Non-Linearity', 25; Louis Althusser (2008) *On Ideology* (London: Verso), 1–60, 42.
59 Gurminder K. Bhambra (2015) *Connected Sociologies* (London: Bloomsbury), ch. 7.
60 To this end, Graef invokes the aspect of emergent hybridity, i.e. a more dynamic conceptualisation where the fluidity of meaning over time foreground 'an emergent ontology of uncertain and imminent becoming', instead of adopting analytical binaries like 'international vs local', which explain (ontological) complexity away; Graef, *Practicing Post-Liberal Peacebuilding*, 5, 31, 34.
61 Anna Matveeva (2009) 'Legitimising Central Asian Authoritarianism: Political Manipulation and Symbolic Power', *Europe-Asia Studies* 61(7): 1095–1121.
62 Tommaso Trevisani (2014) 'The Reshaping of Cities and Citizens in Uzbekistan: The Case of Namagan's "New Uzbeks"', in Madeleine Reeves, Johan Rasanayagam and Judith Beyer (eds), *Ethnographies of the State in Central Asia: Performing Politics* (Bloomington, IN: Indiana University Press), 243–260.
63 Ibid. 247.
64 Marcel Cornis-Pope (2012) 'Local and Global Frames in Recent Eastern European Literatures: Postcommunism, Postmodernism, and Postcoloniality', *Journal of Postcolonial Writing* 48(2): 143–54, 152.
65 Christopher Schwartz (2013) 'The Relics of 1991: Memories and Phenomenology of the Post-Soviet Generation', in Sevket Akyildiz and Richard Carlson (eds), *Social and Cultural Change in Central Asia: The Soviet Legacy* (London: Routledge), 188–200, 197.
66 Sarah Amsler (2007) *The Politics of Knowledge in Central Asia: Science between Marx and the Market* (London: Routledge), 4–5; see also Richard Carlson (2013) 'The Failure of Democratisation in Kazakhstan: The Role of International Investment and Civil Society in Impending Political Reform', in Akyildiz and Carlson, *Social and Cultural Change*, 127–44.

67 See also Petrov, 'Transition in Transition'.
68 Aksana Ismailbekova (2014) 'Performing Democracy: State-Making through patronage in Kyrgyzstan', in Reeves *et al.*, *Ethnographies of the State*, 78–98.
69 J. Beyer (2014) '"There is this law . . . ": Performing the State in the Kyrgyz Courts of Elders', in Reeves *et al.*, *Ethnographies of the State*, 98–123.
70 Chandler, 'Resilience and the "Everyday"', 48.
71 J. Paul Goode and David R. Stroup (2015) 'Everyday Nationalism: Constructivism for the Masses*', *Social Science Quarterly* 96(3): 717–39.
72 Peterson, 'Conceptual Unpacking', 50.
73 For a general introduction see Adriana Aubert and Martin Soler (2007) 'Dialogism: The Diagotic Turn in the Social Sciences', in Joe L. Kincheloe and Raymond A. Horn, Jr. (eds), *The Praeger Handbook of Education and Psychology*, (Westport, CT: Praeger), 521–529. The original work most instructive for this approach is Mikhail M. Bakhtin (1981) *The Dialogic Imagination: Four Essays by M. M. Bakhtin*, ed. Michael Holquist, tr. Caryl Emerson and Michael Holquist (Austin, TX: University of Texas Press); see next chapter (Freedman and Lottholz) for an application.

Chapter 3

Peace as a hybrid human right

A new way to realise human rights, or entrenching their systematic failure?

Rosa Freedman and Philipp Lottholz

Abstract

The Right to Peace is a recent example of the tension and disagreement that the attempts to codify third generation rights or 'hybrid' human rights arouse. States from the Global South utilise the human rights system to further their interests, but they face resistance from still-dominant Global North powers who adhere to other human rights ideologies. Resistance also occurs from different experts who claim that the introduction of non-traditional subject matters such as equity or democracy will serve to dilute the international human rights system rather than to improve the outcomes produced. To account for the change in international human rights legislation as a reflection of shifting dynamics in global politics, we deploy a discursive hybridity framework based on the work of the Russian philosopher and literary critic Mikhail Bakhtin. We show how the increasingly significant shifts in the body of human rights texts can be seen as reflecting the heteroglossia – the multiplicity of different norms, values and cultural frameworks – characterising the negotiations at human rights bodies. The right to peace and other hybrid human rights can therefore be seen as expression of 'dialogicality', but are equally marred by inconsistency, vagueness and diverging understandings among their promoters and by the corresponding implementation dilemmas.

Introduction

As with many other contributions in this volume, this chapter is concerned with the processes of semantic slippage and the transformation of ideas and institutions over time, all of which could be subsumed under the term 'conceptual hybridity'. While some contributors show that the creation of new, hybrid institutions or identities in conflict-prone contexts can lead to hidden exclusion or marginalisation (see Jackson's and Beswick's contributions), Yorke's analysis has developed the concept of 'hybridisation strategy' in order to examine the efforts of European lawmakers and human rights campaigners to promote the abolition of the death penalty worldwide. Using a similar approach, albeit in a different subject matter, we will examine the Right to Peace as an example of hybrid human rights. As Rosa Freedman has already shown in an earlier piece that conceptually foregrounds this chapter,[1] third generation or 'hybrid human rights', appear to create what Homi K. Bhabha calls a 'Third Space' – a space where the weak resists the dominant by adopting elements from dominant, hegemonic discourses and thus challenging dominant forces with their own devices. In this chapter, we will show how the Right to Peace can be seen to be such a Third Space, or, perhaps more appropriately, a *result* of international human rights legislation that has occurred in such a Third Space in the international human rights arena.

In this sense, we argue here that hybridity in international human rights law is produced – whether in the form of actual legislation, or negotiation practices in human rights bodies – when states from the Global South resist traditional notions of rights but use the existing human rights system to put forward their own ideologies that challenge the dominant framework. This enables their voices to be heard and, crucially, for them to bring into the arena their own norms and values that were not originally incorporated into the system. The overarching interest of our inquiry is therefore to show how the concept of 'peace' is used by different actors in order to contest Western hegemony and epistemic authority, and to influence the outcomes produced by the human rights system. We will also address the concerns about such a hybridisation strategy, which point to the potential dangers of believing in the possibility of promoting peace via its promotion as a human right.

The evolution of third generation or 'hybrid' human rights has to be seen against the backdrop of the dominant ideologies, which can be distinguished as Western civil and political rights (first generation rights), and Soviet notions of human rights, i.e. economic, social and cultural rights or second generation rights.[2] Unlike them, the Right to Peace is both individually and collectively focused, and stresses rights and responsibilities of individuals, groups and states. It further broadens the scope of human rights to include issues not traditionally considered to be part of that field. The Right to Peace also seeks to move the international human rights law system away from solely focusing on notions of state sovereignty and individual freedoms from state interference and towards a greater emphasis on states' responsibility for the global order. The Right to Peace and other third generation rights are thus maybe rooted in traditional understandings of 'rights', but to the same extent pose a challenge to these understandings as they expand international human rights law in different aspects. Critics insist that these rights are being developed largely *ad hoc* at the practical level and that they undermine the human rights system. This chapter does not aim to determine whether peace ought to be a human right. Instead, it provides a theoretical perspective on why and how the Right to Peace – alongside other third generation rights – is developing within the human rights system. Our main argument is that the promotion of the Right to Peace is part of a bigger process in which discourses and frameworks of meaning from the Global South are gradually being asserted vis-à-vis traditional, dominant approaches in the international human rights system. Through their sheer weight, actors from the Global South thus manage to shift the tide in human rights law bodies towards approaches that emphasise states', groups' and individuals' obligations in ensuring peace, rather than the justiciability of these different actors in case they fail to do so.

We begin our discussion by introducing the reader to the development and recent proliferation of third generation rights, and the way in which hybridity can be applied to understand this process. We then develop our framework for the analysis of hybrid human rights, before turning to our case study in which we assess how the Right to Peace has been promoted at the international, regional and national levels. We conclude the chapter with a discussion of whether the expansion of human rights law affected by the introduction and promotion of the Right to Peace (alongside other third generation rights) can be seen to dilute international human rights law or whether it may give effect to more desirable outcomes.

A discursive-contextual framework for understanding hybrid human rights

Hybridity is relatively underused as a theoretical lens through which to view events occurring at the international level, especially in the realm of human rights law. It has been applied in the analysis of peace- and statebuilding interventions and transitional justice.[3] Our approach builds upon but also extends the framework developed by Freedman[4] by adding a focus on the hybridity and 'dialogicality' of international human rights along the lines of Mikhail Bakhtin.

First, hybridity is a *theoretical lens* through which different social, political and legal processes may be viewed. It is in this sense by no means limited to the realm of identity in a biological sense, and the corresponding widespread application in racial, cultural and postcolonial studies.[5] Rather, hybridity can be seen as a condition of complexity and multifariousness of seemingly homogeneous and unified phenomena, whether it is a physical or biological object or creature, or whether a text, practice or social institution is concerned. In this regard, one very convincing approach to theorise hybridity, which has so far been little regarded beyond cultural studies, is that developed by the Russian philosopher and literary critic Mikhail Bakhtin. Like Homi Bhabha, whose work is the perhaps most authoritative conceptualisation so far,[6] Bakhtin reasons that hybridity may be used as a way of subverting or resisting hegemonic discourse while adopting the latter's main elements.[7] His notion of *heteroglossia* is relevant to international law as it emphasises the presence of multiple registers of meaning and values on which actors may draw in constructing their own discourse.[8] *Heteroglossia* implies a pluralist ontology that allows for many frames of meaning. Thus, Bakhtin's approach offers the possibility to assert values and norms within the international arena through their promotion in negotiations and gradual inclusion into legal text and implementation practices in international law. This leads to an extension of the somewhat two-dimensional conceptual apparatus of Bhabha, who offers mainly 'mimicry' and open contestation as strategies, into a conceptual device for understanding changes in globally dominating legal norms. Furthermore, Bakhtin makes an important link between discourse as hybrid phenomenon in and of itself and, on the other hand, the social, historical and otherwise context that predetermines and inevitably influences discourse. In Bakhtin's words:

> Directed toward its object, a word enters a dialogically agitated and tense environment of alien words, evaluations and accents, is woven into their complex interrelationships, merges with some, recoils from others . . . and all this may in an essential manner shape the word, may leave a trace in all its semantic layers, may complicate its expression and influence its entire stylistic profile. The living utterance, having taken meaning and shape at a particular historical moment in a socially specific environment, cannot fail to brush up against thousands of living dialogic threads, woven by socio-ideological consciousness around the given object of the utterance; it cannot fail to become an active participant in social dialogue.[9]

Bakhtin is insisting that utterances or discourse more generally are a product of their context and will therefore reflect shifts in the configurations of this context. This trajectory promises to be useful in the analysis of international law, especially the emergence of third generation or 'hybrid' human rights, which can clearly be seen as an expression of a changing landscape in global politics.

Based on the assumption of Bakhtinian *heteroglossia* or 'dialogicality' of discourse, it is further logical to imagine and try to analyse hybridisation as a *process* through which identities and cultures are forged, with a 'multiplicity of outcomes' that depend on 'complex and context-specific realities'.[10] Postcolonial scholarship has devoted attention to such processes occurring in formerly colonised societies. Our contribution will focus on hybridisation that takes place within the international arena (the international human rights law system in particular), and which can thus be qualified as more discursive, conceptual and semantic. International institutions, in terms of formal bodies and the place that they provide for like-minded states to meet within regional groups and political blocs, provide a platform for construction of hybrid norms that draw on the different registers and normative discourses of the respective participants.

Lastly, based on the consideration of hybridisation processes, it is possible to decompose the *products* of such processes into their constituent elements, at least to some extent. The products of such processes are, for instance, international criminal courts and tribunals in the sense that these are new institutions that are created, staffed and allocated a budget. Still, from the legal point of view, the actual essence of such *physical* institutions are the practices they perform (and which are also subject to and products of hybridisation) as well as the constituent instruments or legal texts that lead to their creation. More than statutes of institutions, it is of course the body of international human rights law that is of great interest for analysis through a hybridity lens.

This taxonomy of hybridity as *theoretical lens*, as *process*, and the hybrid nature of the products of international human rights legislation is our basis for understanding how hybridity operates at the international level. We will apply this approach first to international human rights law and then to the Right to Peace in order to explore how hybridity operates within and impacts upon the human rights system.

Revolution, resistance and hybridity: past trends in international human rights law

In order better to understand the meaning of currently emerging hybrid, or third generation, human rights, it is necessary to discuss movements of resistance that preceded today's more covert and gradual changes in international human rights law. During the creation and early years of modern international human rights law, many states were unable to present their norms and ideologies within international institutions.[11] Dominant global ideologies have been at the fore in the development of international human rights law ever since the Universal Declaration of Human Rights of 1948.[12] Thus, international human rights legislation was mostly dominated by Western legal frameworks (emphasising civil and political rights, or first generation rights), and by Soviet notions of rights (economic, social and cultural rights, or second generation rights). Until recently, decolonised and developing states, alongside allies from the Non-Aligned Movement,[13] have promoted a 'third generation' of rights. This terminology was first articulated by Karel Vasak in relation to collective rights or those rights which could only be realised 'by the combined efforts of individuals, states, public and private associations, and the international community'.[14] Initial efforts focused on ensuring rights directly stemming from colonial experiences and the process of decolonisation – most notably rights to self-determination, development and permanent sovereignty over resources. They are rooted in postcolonial ideas, such as those of Fanon who insists that imperialist culture, language and identity must be rejected in order to realise decolonised states' national interests.[15] States that had been formed in response to colonisation sought to assert rights to govern over themselves, as well as to economic and social development.[16]

Current legal, political and ideological battles within the international arena indicate an agency on the part of Global South states that is less reflective of oppositional stance expressed in the rights to self-governance and development but a gradual hybridisation of normative discourses. This demonstrates a more 'syncretic dynamic'[17] that unfolds between the former coloniser and the colonised, or the dominant and the dominated. It also means that countries from the Global South are being more strategic rather than confrontational; they are using the human rights system, based on the dominant ideology, to further their own interests and ideologies. Whereas earlier third generation rights introduced radical change into the individual-centred system so as to include collective rights, hybrid rights utilise the framework as it currently exists in order to promote previously unrepresented norms.[18] This more complex dynamic already signals how the rights created in these processes will probably be inconsistent in terms of how different actors will understand them.

In terms of the actors behind their emergence, hybrid rights are predominantly created and promoted by states from the Global South, particularly from Africa, Asia and Latin America. Hybrid rights focus on responsibilities and duties, which illustrate ideological differences that are particularly apparent when contrasting the African and European regional human rights systems.[19] Yet, rather than rejecting the individual-centred dominant human rights framework, those states seek to use it to promote their own human rights values. Countries bring their own norms into international fora – regional mechanisms and the United Nations – and form group identities within this international 'Third Space'. International institutions provide arenas within which states from the Global South can exercise collective power.[20] Individually or in sub-groups, countries that lack sufficient influence when alone unite to pursue collective aims through the creation and promotion of hybrid human rights. The heterogeneous identities within such blocs can be seen in the older alliances of the Non-Aligned Movement and the Group of 77[21] – whose allegiances originally stemmed from anti-imperialism and lack of alignment to the dominant powers – as well as in the more recently created Organisation of Islamic Cooperation and G7+.[22] All of those blocs span at least three of the five geographic regions, which enables formation of significant cross-regional alliances. Heterogeneity requires collective objectives to be based on a mosaic of norms, cultures, values and experiences.

Hybrid human rights and change in the international human rights system

The emergence of third generation or hybrid human rights can be seen as product of the shifting dynamics in the international human rights system. Third generation rights can be seen as hybrid because they transcend existing frameworks of human rights legislation and combine different elements from the latter to create new legal texts that are promoted through 'soft law' methods, which circumvents the need for custom or treaties to create international law.[23] These new methods of creating human rights and the substance of those rights stand in tension to the traditional human rights system, which is why some have questioned the usefulness and desirability of these new 'hybrid' rights. In order to elucidate this conflict, we will explore the three main ways in which hybrid rights challenge and impact upon the dominant international human rights law framework in terms of (a) substance, (b) subjects and (c) scope.

'Substance' refers to the content of a right. Hybrid rights are interdependent with other subject areas that fall outside of the human rights matrix. Traditional human rights regulate areas like labour and social justice, while more broadly conceived areas such as the environment or economics have so far remained peripheral. The impact of those broader areas upon human rights has long been understood, but the regulation of those areas has previously occurred through their own specialist arenas. Hybrid rights focus upon matters that are linked to human rights but would traditionally have been dealt with through other institutions, such as different UN bodies or other political forums. Bringing negotiation and policy-making processes on those topics into the human rights system demonstrates new ways of thinking about what constitutes a 'human right'. Further, this presents a reaction to the criticism that other institutions are weak or inadequate, insofar as human rights bodies then become new arenas for addressing shortcomings in those fields. Critics of hybrid rights, however, are more likely to insist that introducing these issues into human rights bodies undermines the existing system by overloading the system and diluting understandings of what constitutes a human right.

Hybrid rights challenge the dominant ideology on the substance of rights through increased focus on responsibilities and duties. Such rights move beyond individuals or groups, and focus also on responsibilities of states. Such a refocusing is reflective of human rights ideologies from the African continent, laid out for instance in the African Charter on Human and Peoples Rights.[24] One example of a hybrid human right is the right to a democratic and equitable international order. It is ambiguous in terms of rights and responsibilities,[25] which apparently stem from its incorporation of the polarised, and sometimes competing, ideologies from the Global North and South. The resolution creating a Special Procedures mandate includes certain rights but its emphasis is on duties, for example, the 'responsibility of the nations of the world for managing worldwide economic and social issues' (para. 3[p]), or the 'promotion of equitable access to benefits from the international distribution of wealth through enhanced international cooperation' (para. 3[n]). Such focus on broad and vague responsibilities makes it difficult for states to understand their obligations let alone for them to be held accountable for failing to uphold or give effect to those duties. In this sense, the right to a democratic and equitable international order does not have a tangible substance that can be protected, is immeasurable in terms of implementation and needs to be invoked in combination with other human rights. Still, by framing the right in this way it becomes part of the human rights discourse as do other third generation rights.

'Subjects' refers to who is bound by the human rights and to whom those obligations are owed. Third generation rights have expanded the subjects of human rights in terms of both the rights-holders and who owes the obligations. A main criticism of third generation rights is that, unlike traditional rights, it is difficult to identify who would constitute a victim if one of those rights is violated. Whereas previously almost all rights – civil and political, and economic and social – focused on individuals as rights-holders, collective rights promoted the idea of peoples' rights.[26] Hybrid rights take this idea further, focusing on states as an entity that may hold rights. These newer rights also expand traditional understandings of who is bound by obligations. Individuals and communities, as well as groups of states, may have obligations to uphold the rights of others. According to the Declaration on the Right to Development, for instance, '[a]ll human beings have a responsibility for development, individually and collectively'.[27] Moreover, the rights to international solidarity and to a democratic and equitable order are aimed as much at states as an entity and at groups of states as they are at collectives or groups of individuals. States are the primary rights-holders, with the idea being that realisation of those rights will then enable countries to ensure all other human rights for individuals under their control. As already indicated, this shift away from individuals being the sole rights-holders and the shift towards rights entailing corollary duties are in line with African ideologies on human rights.[28]

Within these hybrid rights that emphasis on the corollary nature of rights and duties is not only exercised via-à-vis individuals and states, but also states collectively, meaning that states are made responsible for human rights in other states. This builds on the foundations laid in the ICESCR[29] whereby parties are responsible for ensuring core minimum standards within countries where the maximum available resources have been exhausted and yet base-levels of rights remain elusive or unattainable.[30] Within hybrid rights a more expansive approach to responsibility is expressed through states being responsible for rights being realised within other states, as opposed to the narrower responsibility of violations being remedied. In addition, non-state actors are included as duty bearers, as well. The right to international solidarity seeks to encourage 'more international actors [. . .] to take initiatives towards international solidarity, and to practice it in international relations'.[31] This broad objective may lead to a range of international actors being bound by obligations that traditionally have only bound states.

'Scope' refers to where the rights apply and where a state is bound by obligations. Traditional rights place obligations upon states to respect, protect and fulfil the right.[32] Generally, the scope of those rights exists within territory where a state exercises control, with some degree of extraterritorial applicability.[33] By extending the substance and subjects, third generation rights also extend the scope of international human rights. They move beyond traditional territorial and extraterritorial application so there becomes a collective responsibility of all states to ensure that all countries are able to implement human rights. It is clear, then, that these processes, linked to the emergence and consolidation of third generation rights, have a transformative effect on the international human rights system. Having traced and contextualised the emergence of third generation rights and the challenge they pose to the international human rights system, we are now able to turn to the case study of the Right to Peace.

Hybridity and the Right to Peace: developments at the universal, regional and national levels

The relationship between peace and human rights is well-understood, with its importance for the realisation of other rights emphasised in key international instruments.[34] Yet, peace has traditionally been dealt with by security and political institutions rather than human rights bodies, and its development as a human right remains controversial. Attempts to bring it into the human rights system represent a crucial shift in how states view and promote peace.

The ideology underpinning peace as a human right presents a challenge to dominant frameworks insofar as it counters the widely used conceptualisation of peace as the 'absence of war'. Notions moving beyond pre-emptive militarisation and securitisation stem from non-Western ideologies of peace and represent other values and cultures. Latin American countries have been at the fore in promoting an ideology that prefers diplomatic and non-military solutions rather than military proliferation and securitisation. Those states have already developed and codified peace as a human right at the national and regional levels, as our analysis will show. In the international arena, they have been joined by some African and Asian countries and are at times supported by Nordic states.

In order to assess the prospects of introducing the Right to Peace into the international human rights law matrix, and to understand the impact that it might have, we will use and apply the hybridity framework developed above.

We will explore how peace is being promoted at the universal, regional and national levels, as well as the hybridisation processes occurring on each of these levels.

The Right to Peace at the universal level

Peace was first proposed as a human right in the 1978 Declaration on the Preparation of Societies for Life in Peace.[35] The Declaration, accepted by a majority of the General Assembly, stated that 'every nation and every human being . . . has the inherent right to life in peace'.[36] Six years later, the Declaration on the Right of Peoples to Peace[37] was adopted. It set out that 'the peoples of our planet have a sacred right to peace'.[38] Those documents, which are not legally binding, did not specify the substance, scope or subjects of the proposed right, but instead drew together general principles of peace that were already accepted, at least in theory, by all UN members. Subsequently, different attempts have been made to elaborate upon and develop these declarations. Many countries that were willing to support the declarations were reluctant to accept attempts to codify peace as a human right.

The next attempts to advance the Right to Peace were made in the 1990s. The Norwegian Institute of Human Rights attempted codification through the 1997 'Draft Oslo Declaration on the Human Right to Peace', which stated that peace is the ultimate aim of the UN system and that 'every human being has the right to peace'.[39] The consultation process with 117 states demonstrated that countries diverged in how they viewed peace, with some viewing it as a human right, a moral right or a human aspiration, respectively.[40] Although all states supported peace as a moral principle,[41] codification efforts failed because of a lack of consensus on it being a human right. States opposing the Right to Peace insisted 'that if peace becomes a right and is codified, using force will be more difficult'.[42] Bringing peace into the human rights system would thus enable states to breach international law with impunity by pointing to the Right to Peace to resist enforcement measures such as sanctions, no-fly zones and intervention. Such enforcement powers are used in situations where there are serious breaches of international law and blocking them by claiming that they violate the Right to Peace would remove one of the few tools held by the international community that can be used to encourage – or attempt to coerce – states to comply with international legal obligations. The divide in opinion was largely along the lines of the countries from the Global North and from the Global South. This division had become more entrenched and has presented a barrier to codification at every stage. Global North states have clear historical, social, economic and cultural reasons underpinning their votes, including a human rights ideology that focuses on individuals and justiciability, legal emphasis on state sovereignty and the right to self-defence, as well as political concerns about effectively maintaining international security. Thus, the failure in the 1990s in the attempts to achieve consensus on peace as a human right was not surprising to many observers.

Support for codification gained renewed momentum at the beginning of the twenty-first century when debates on war and peace re-emerged after terror attacks on 9 September 2001 and the invasion of Iraq in 2003. The momentum occurred at the UN, in particular the principal human rights bodies, first the Commission on Human Rights and later at its successor, the Human Rights Council. Global South countries have dominated both of those bodies and have used them to create and promote hybrid human rights.[43] The Commission[44] and the Council adopted resolutions on the right to peace. Voting on those resolutions, however, was far from unanimous and once again demonstrated the clear ideological divide on this issue between the Global North and South. Global South states sought to use the Commission to promote their own human rights ideologies that challenged the dominant framework, whereas Global North countries resisted those attempts. Those patterns continue at the Commission's successor body.

The Human Rights Council is currently the main vehicle for efforts to codify and enshrine a human right to peace. An expert workshop on the Right to Peace convened by the UN High Commissioner for Human Rights led to the adoption of Resolution 14/3,[45] which called for a draft declaration on the Right to Peace. Subsequently, the HRC adopted Resolution 20/15 establishing 'an open-ended intergovernmental working group with the mandate of progressively negotiating a draft United Nations declaration on the right to peace'.[46]

Twenty-two states sponsored Resolution 20/15: Algeria, Angola, Belarus, Bolivia, China, Congo, Costa Rica, Cuba, Democratic People's Republic of Korea, Djibouti, Dominican Republic, Ecuador, Egypt, Iran, Lebanon, Malaysia, Nicaragua, Palestine, Sri Lanka, Sudan, Syria, Venezuela and Viet Nam. They insisted that the human Right to Peace has a fundamental nature. Referring to the indivisibility of human rights, Syria argued that peace is inseparable from the right to life.[47] Sri Lanka emphasised that 'peace is a precondition for the enjoyment of all other human rights', while Venezuela criticised opponents of the resolution as seeking to 'reclaim the right to war'.[48] It is clear that states' intentions for sponsoring the resolution are diverse. Peace is part of national cultures and laws in Latin American countries such as Costa Rica and Nicaragua, which points to a clear ideological motivation for sponsoring the resolution. The reason for Cuba's and Venezuela's support for the resolution may be similarly value-based, although it might as well be a method for undermining dominance of the Global North in the international human rights system and would follow similar strategies on other matters at the Council by both of those states.[49] Syria and Sri Lanka used variations of postcolonial discourses pointing to terrorism – rather than imperialism – as an oppressing factor that the resolution would address. Sri Lanka thus claimed that it had been 'denied peace for over 3 decades due to a ruthless terrorist conflict'.[50] Neither of these two countries could legitimately claim that they would prioritise peace over currently ongoing counter-insurgency, security and stabilisation operations, not least owing to the internal conflicts and atrocities perpetrated by their governments at that time. A human right to peace, however, would have enabled them to resist international intervention in internal conflicts, as was emphasised by countries resisting this and earlier attempts to codify the right.

Thirty-four Human Rights Council members from Africa, the Middle East, Latin America and Asia voted in favour of the resolution. The US was the only country to vote against it, while abstentions were recorded from Austria, Belgium, Czech Republic, Hungary, India, Italy, Norway, Moldova, Poland, Romania, Spain and Switzerland. The European Union submitted a letter to the Inter-Governmental Working Group (IGWG) in which it set out six main reasons for its common position.[51] The link between peace and human rights was thus accepted, but the signatories insisted that there was no legal basis in international human rights law and that such a right could not be defined owing to its vague content. It was added that peace ought not to be dealt with in a human rights forum and that recognising it as a 'stand-alone' right would undermine the UN Charter, which legitimises reasons for the use of force.

The US criticised the failure to define peace in the resolution,[52] the inclusion of many issues unrelated to peace[53] and the bringing of the topic into human rights bodies rather than using more appropriate institutions to address those matters.[54] The Report of the Open-Ended Inter-Governmental Working Group on the Draft United Nations Declaration on the Right to Peace[55] set out that the US views were shared by other delegates. Opponents insist that peace is not a human right but 'rather a goal that could be best realized through the enforcement of existing identifiable and distinguishable human rights'.[56]

Despite this opposition, the majority of states sought to define peace in a holistic manner by looking at what is necessary to create conditions for its existence and protection[57] rather than by setting out clear parameters and definitions of the right. They included provisions to tackle poverty and other political and economic injustices in order to preserve peace and mitigate potentials for conflict while emphasising that it is a prerequisite for the implementation and realisation of all other human rights.[58] Voting patterns on the Right to Peace and on other third generation rights demonstrate that such claims do not fit with the dominant or traditional ideologies and frameworks on human rights.[59] It is precisely this resistance and challenge to the dominant framework that demonstrates the hybridisation of the international human rights canon that occurs alongside attempts to codify a human right to peace. Rather than Global North dominance, what we see is a multiplicity of normative discourses, many of which are in favour of a Right to Peace, which is reminiscent of Bakhtin's idea of *heteroglossia* and the hybridisation effected by it.

Regional level

The development of a Right to Peace has achieved far greater success within some regions than at the international level, which is mostly owing to the greater homogeneity at the regional level in terms of political, cultural, geographic and other ties.[60] Differences between states remain, but where there is a common ideology or cause it is more easily developed and enshrined at the regional than the international level.

The main efforts to codify a human Right to Peace have been made in Latin America, where hybrid ideologies are forged between states before being advanced within the international arena. Many of the countries concerned share common conceptions of and emphasis on peace, although there are key differences between states and not all countries view the advancement of peace as a high priority as compared with other subject matters. NGOs and civil society actors have been active in keeping peace within the spotlight and encouraging efforts to develop it into a human right. The Spanish Society for International Human Rights Law (SSIHRL) was at the fore of the initiative at the turn of the millennium, when it educated and influenced individuals, states and regions to support relevant UN resolutions and declarations.[61] It held conferences and consultations with international experts[62] in order to develop the Right to Peace. In 2006 it adopted the Luarca Declaration on the Human Right to Peace, with support from more than 500 civil society organisations and academic institutions. As a result, seven regional declarations have been adopted based on that text. At the regional level, civil society has increased the momentum for the discussion, development and codification of the Right to Peace; and it might be expected that those developments, in turn, will increase the promotion of the Right to Peace within UN human rights bodies.

The SSIHRL has encouraged states to consider the need to codify the human right to peace and has garnered support for the 'World Alliance for the Human Right to Peace'.[63] This is in keeping with its mission, which is to 'promote and implement the international human rights law values within Spain and other Spanish-speaking countries'.[64] Utilising the expertise provided by this and other civil society actors and the fora that they create, states have forged common understandings of the human right to peace. The regional group is then better equipped to collectively advance the right in international institutions. Using international human rights institutions and traditional ways for creating new rights, GRULAC (the Latin American and Caribbean Group) has advanced the Right to Peace. The regional level, therefore, is a place where potential is generated and consensus found, leading to the solidification of human rights ideology. This is a process of hybridisation and interaction of people and organisations from different cultural backgrounds, which might only be linked by language or historical, if not colonial ties.

Latin American countries were joined by some Nordic states in their efforts to promote the Right to Peace. Academics, institutions and civil society actors from Norway in particular have been closely involved with the advancement of the right to peace. Indeed, as set out above, Norway was central to codification efforts in the 1990s. However, within the international arena those countries tend to align with their European counterparts and have not supported recent Human Rights Council resolutions attempting to codify the Right to Peace, as set out above. This may be owing to pressure from other European states or to Norway disagreeing with the way the right was developing. This once again shows the importance of regional political dynamics and predominant human rights ideologies.

National level

At the national level, peace as a human right has been the subject of case law within countries that have enshrined the Right to Peace within national constitutions. Two case studies demonstrate how peace operates as a human right within national law. Costa Rica has promoted and protected the Right to Peace through legislation and litigation. In 1948, Costa Rica's President abolished the country's military and codified this change in Article 12 of the new constitution.[65] In 1997 a law was passed making peace education compulsory in public schools,[66] which indicates how deeply a culture and ideology of peace must be rooted in this society. Furthermore, Roberto Zamora Bolanos effectively established the concept of litigating on the Right to Peace and guaranteeing its domestic legal recognition. He successfully litigated against the Costa Rican government in order to protect the Right to Peace on two occasions. The first case focused on the government's support for the invasion of Iraq and the second dealt with the government's plans to extract and process nuclear materials.[67]

In 2003, Zamora sued Costa Rica's President and Minister of Foreign Affairs before the Constitutional Court for Costa Rica's inclusion in the 'Coalition of the Willing'. The Court ruled that joining the Coalition was against the constitution, international law and the UN system.[68] The Court held that the invasion contradicted the fundamental value of peace, which forms part of Costa Rica's identity,[69] leading to the country's exit from the Coalition in September 2004. It was not until Zamora's second suit, however, that the Court legally recognised the human right to peace. In 2006 Zamora challenged the Arms Decree on the grounds that granting permits for the extraction and manufacturing of nuclear material was unconstitutional.[70]

The Court unanimously sided with Zamora and annulled three sections of the Arms Decree. The court reasoned that these sections threatened the state's Right to Peace and the UN Declaration on the Right of Peoples to Peace.[71] It found that such nuclear activities 'were conceived and designed to encourage the negative value of war',[72] which directly conflicts with Costa Rica's culture of peace. The court in this case established that peace is more than just 'the absence of war, it must go beyond that, preventing and rejecting continuously all decision and act which might derive and end in such a circumstance'.[73] This shows how a human right to peace can be established and upheld if a country has enshrined it within its constitution. The case of Costa Rica shows what a codified Right to Peace could look like and gives us an insight into the supporters of the Right to Peace within the international human rights arena.

Japan is another country where similar case law exists. Article 9 of Japan's constitution enshrines the renunciation of war and the possession of war power.[74] The Constitution's preamble also recognises 'that all peoples of the world have the right to live in peace, free from fear and want'.[75] In the *Naganuma Case*,[76] it was ruled that removing a forest reserve from the register to construct a self-defence missile base was unconstitutional because it posed a risk of violating the Right to Peace for those around the base.[77] In March 2007, the Court discussed the state's involvement in sending military forces to Iraq. The District Court in Nagoya held that 'the right to live in peace is a fundamental right which underlies all other basic human rights and by virtue of which we can enjoy those rights'.[78] In *Mori v Japan*,[79] the Court had to decide on whether the right to live in peace was a 'concrete right' with legal standing from Article 9 of the Constitution and its preamble.[80] The High Court held that deploying troops does not itself violate the Right to Peace but nonetheless accepted the concreteness of the right in theory.[81] They also found a violation of Article 9 in relation to the Self Defence Force integrating their air transport activities with the use of force by Coalition forces.[82] Shortly after the decision, the District Court in Okayama reaffirmed the existence of the right in a similar Iraq deployment case, providing further guidance on the right's substance.[83]

The courts in Japan and Costa Rica have legally recognised a human right to peace and rejected the argument that peace is just an abstract concept or a political ideal. The human right to peace in those states is rooted in their histories and cultures and enshrined in their laws and legal systems. Those states have used the human rights matrix to protect and promote a right that stems from their own cultures, norms and values. It has become apparent how their human rights ideologies prioritise peace over security, stability and pre-emptive war; and espouse the state's or government's responsibility for a peaceful life of its citizens through non-engagement with armed conflict, rather than allowing engagement in, support of, or preparation for armed conflict under the condition of not harming citizens. Costa Rica and

Japan have then taken the outputs from these cases and utilised them in the regional and international arenas, acting together with other countries that seek to codify the human right to peace. Our preceding analysis has shown how this has led to the creation of regional and inter-regional alliances, which have successfully challenged dominant human rights ideologies and their individualistic and collectivist ontologies.

The Right to Peace, like other third generation rights, presents a hybrid of these previously dominant approaches and while combining them also attempts to shift the scope of rights towards the responsibility held by states to engage in actions that secure collective actions for making the international system more equitable and solidary. The obligations and concrete rights that have been codified into soft law, such as the right to a democratic and equitable international order or the right to international solidarity, are already achievements in and of themselves, as they are an expression of Bakhtinian *heteroglossia* and are characterised by dialogicality, i.e. the inclusion of multiple different voices within the international human rights arena. Whether codification of those rights and the Right to Peace is an effective way of making the international system more equitable or peaceful is a concern that goes beyond this discussion.

Concluding observations: expansion or dilution?

In this chapter we have used hybridity as a lens to explore the development of third generation rights, with particular attention on the emerging Right to Peace. Third generation rights challenge the dominant human rights framework by seeking to bring into the system ideas, norms and values that are not traditionally understood as having a place within the human rights matrix. With increasing globalisation and tectonic shifts in the geopolitical landscape, there is growing emphasis on bringing previously unrepresented cultures, norms and values into the international human rights system. Hybridity provides a theoretical lens for understanding the ideologies underpinning those rights, the processes through which they are created, and the rights themselves. In order to account for this interdependence of global politics and international human rights law as an example of the relationship between discourse and social context, we have looked at the promotion of third generation or 'hybrid' human rights through the lens provided by the Russian philosopher Mikhail Bakhtin who views text as inextricably linked with and produced by social context. To show how the international human rights arena is becoming ever more pluralistic and witnessing increasingly significant challenges towards Western dominance, we have focused on the proponents of the Right to Peace and the human rights ideologies they develop in their national context and cultivate on the regional level.

The failure to codify peace as a human right demonstrates, however, that the dominant framework is not easily challenged. Some states oppose the Right to Peace as a stand-alone right because it lacks a legal basis, and argue that peace is simply a political context in which other rights can be enjoyed. They insist that the link between human rights and peace could be made without a reference to it as a human right. Alston, echoing the position of some states,[84] is concerned that the precise content of the right has not yet reached enough certainty to guide the activities of states on the subject matter, although he concedes that the development of rights is an ongoing process and that the soft law on peace might lead to clarification of the right's scope.[85] De Zayas, however, insists that the right has a legal basis and is indispensable to other human rights.[86] He responds to criticisms by explaining that the right's broad scope and vague provisions are directly linked to the nature of peace. The right consists of positive elements 'which necessarily include[s] freedom of thought, conscience, opinion, expression, belief and religion'.[87] In order to fully guarantee international peace, it is necessary not only to protect negative aspects, such as avoiding war, but also positive provisions, such as encouraging freedom and education about peaceful alternatives to war.

On a critical note, the question that must be asked of each new third generation right is whether it is being advanced in order to make the international human rights system more effective, or whether it may end up undermining the existing work. Different countries are seeking to expand the system, some for idealist motivations and others for political objectives unrelated to human rights. In this sense, the dilemma at the heart of the idea of the Right to Peace is that the introduction and codification of this right may lead to outcomes that are worse than those produced by the current system. This dilemma is visible in the case of states with ambiguous motives for developing or supporting a new right to peace. Syria and Sri Lanka might have very different reasons for promoting the Right to Peace – for example, the desire to protect themselves from international efforts to curb the violence perpetrated by the governments within their territories – than Costa Rica and Japan, which are countries that have legally enshrined cultures and ideologies of peace. Hence, a key question our discussion raises is how to address hybrid coalitions where some actors are promoting new rights to undermine the system or to secure other political aims while others are pursuing codification for ideological and cultural reasons. Developing a human right to peace, then, is not without problems. As we have shown, using hybridity as a lens through which to view the ideologies underpinning the Right to Peace and the processes through which it is developing enables a better understanding of the right itself.

Notes

1 Rosa Freedman (2013) 'Third Generation Rights: Is there Room for Hybrid Constructs within International Human Rights Law', *Cambridge Journal of International and Comparative Law* 2(4): 935–59.
2 For a discussion of human rights terminology see Karel Vasak (1990) 'Les différentes catégories des droits de l'homme [The different categories of human rights]', in André Lapeyre, François de Tinguy and Karel Vasak (eds), *Les dimensions universelles des droits de l'homme* [The universal dimensions of human rights] (Brussels: Bruylant), 119–50.
3 For an overview see Freedman, 'Third Generation Rights', 942, as well as Freedman and Lemay-Hébert in the introduction to this volume.
4 Freedman, 'Third Generation Rights'.
5 See Robert J. C. Young (1995) *Colonial Desire: Hybridity in Theory, Culture and Race* (London: Routdledge) for an overview.
6 Homi K. Bhabha (1994) *The Location of Culture* (London: Routledge); see Freedman, 'Hybrid Human Rights', as well as Houghton's and Riches's contributions in this volume for an application in international law.
7 Mikhail M. Bakhtin (1981) *The Dialogic Imagination: Four Essays by M. M. Bakhtin*, ed. Michael Holquist, tr. Caryl Emerson and Michael Holquist (Austin, TX: University of Texas Press).
8 Ibid. 7, 67.
9 Mikhail M. Bakhtin (1981) 'Discourse in the Novel', in Bakhtin, *Dialogical imagination*, 259–422, 267–77.
10 Ibid.
11 Antony Anghie (2004) *Imperialism, Sovereignty and the Making of International Law* (Cambridge: Cambridge University Press).
12 General Assembly Resolution (GA Res.) 217A (III), 'Universal Declaration of Human Rights', 1948, UN Doc. A/810, 71.
13 The 'NAM' was formed at the Asian-African Conference, a political gathering held in Bandung, Indonesia, in April 1955. The conference was convened in part due to frustration of many newly independent countries unable to secure UN membership due to Cold War politics.
14 Vasak, 'Les différentes catégories'.
15 The most instructive work in this regard is Frantz Fanon (1968) *The Wretched of the Earth* (New York: Grove Press).
16 See GA Res 41/128, 'Declaration on the Right to Development', 4 December 1986, UN Doc. A/RES/41/128.
17 Albert J. Paolini (1999) *Navigating Modernity: Postcolonialism, Identity and International Relations* (Boulder, CO: Lynne Rienner), 54.
18 See Freedman, 'Third Generation Rights', 943 ff., on this distinction.
19 See generally B. Obinna Okere (1984) 'The Protection of Human Rights and the African Charter on Human and People's Rights: A Comparative Analysis with the European and American Systems', *Human Rights Quarterly* 6(2): 141–59.
20 Eric Heinze (2008) 'Even Handedness and the Politics of Human Rights', *Harvard Human Rights Journal* 21: 7–46.
21 G-77 was named at its creation in 1964, when 77 states jointly prepared for the UN Conference on Trade and Development. It worked in parallel with NAM, focusing on economic issues. On the relationship between NAM and G-77, see e.g. Thomas G. Weiss (2008) *What's Wrong with the United Nations and How to Fix it*, (Cambridge: Polity), 49.
22 G7+ was formed by a group of fragile and conflict-affected states in order to provide a mechanism for focusing on and engaging with peacebuilding and

statebuilding. The heterogeneous group brings together states and international actors in order to facilitate development and capacity-building.

23 Including UN resolutions and decisions, and creation of Special Procedures mandates.

24 The African Charter on Human and Peoples Rights was the first human rights treaty to set out responsibilities alongside rights, cf. U. Oji Umozurike (1983) 'The African Charter on Human and People's Rights', *American Journal of International Law* 78: 902–12.

25 HRC Res. 8/5, 'Promotion of a Democratic and Equitable International Order', 18 June 2008, UN Doc. A/HRC/RES/8/5. Another exemplary aspect is '[t]he promotion and consolidation of transparent, democratic, just and accountable international institutions in all areas of cooperation', at para. 3(g).

26 For a historical overview of collective, group and peoples' rights, see Ian Brownlie (1988) 'The Rights of Peoples in Modern International Law', in James Crawford (ed.), *The Rights of Peoples* (Oxford: Clarendon), 1–16.

27 GA Res. 41/128, 'Declaration on the Right to Development', 4 December 1986, UN Doc. A/RES/41/128, Article 2(2).

28 Okere, 'Protection of Human Rights'.

29 International Covenant on Economic, Social and Cultural Rights, article 2(1).

30 See for instance Limburg Principles on the Implementation of the ICESCR, 8 January 1987, UN Doc E/CN.4/1987/17, para. 30.

31 Human Rights Council (HRC) 4th Session, 'Report of the Independent Expert on Human Rights and International Solidarity, Rudi Muhammad Rizki', 7 February 2007, UN Doc. A/HRC/4/8, para. 4.

32 Philip Alston and Gerard Quinn (1987) 'The Nature and Scope of States Parties' Obligations under the International Covenant on Economic, Social and Cultural Rights', *Human Rights Quarterly* 9(2): 156–229.

33 See e.g. Human Rights Committee, 'General Comment No 31 (2004)', 26 May 2004, UN Doc. CCPR/C/21/Rev.1/Add.13.

34 See e.g. UN Charter Preamble and Article 1 in the Universal Declaration of Human Rights, 1948, UN Doc. A/810.

35 GA Res. 33/73, 'Declaration on the Preparation of Societies for Life in Peace', 15 December 1978, UN Doc. A/RES/33/73.

36 Ibid., Article 1.

37 GA Res 39/11, 'Right of Peoples to Peace', 12 November 1984, UN Doc. A/RES/39/11.

38 Ibid., Article 1.

39 Norwegian Institute of Human Rights in cooperation with UNESCO, 'The Human Right to Peace: Oslo Draft Declaration', 6–8 June 1997 – see General Conference, 29th session, Report by the Director-General, Paris 1997, Doc. 29 C/59, http://unesdoc.unesco.org/images/0011/001100/110027e.pdf (accessed April 2016).

40 HRC 14th Session, 'Report of the Office of the High Commissioner on the Outcome of the Expert Workshop on the Right of Peoples to Peace', 17 March 2010, UN Doc. A/HRC/14/38, para. 32.

41 Director-General of UNESCO, 'Report on the Result of the International Consultation of Governmental Experts on the Human Right to Peace delivered to Executive Board', 17 April 1998, UN Doc.154 EX/40.

42 Mikel Mancisidor and Cristina Linaje (2009) 'Declaración de Luarca sobre el Derecho Humano a la Paz: una explicación y una lectura desde Euskadi [The LUARCA declaration on the human right to peace: an explanation and a reading for the Basque region]', in *Hacia la Paz desde los Derechos Humanos: Reflexiones sobre el Derecho Humano a la Paz* [Making peace a human right: reflections on the human right to peace] (Etxea: UNESCO), 57–68.

43 See Freedman, 'Third Generation Rights'.
44 For instance Commission on Human Rights Resolutions 2002/71, 'Promotion of the Right of Peoples to Peace', 25 April 2002, UN Doc. E/CN.4/Res/2002/71; and 2005/56, 'Promotion of Peace as a Vital Requirement for the Full Enjoyment of All Human Rights by All', 20 April 2005, UN Doc. E/CN.4/RES/2005/56.
45 HRC Res 14/3, 'Promotion on the Right of Peoples to Peace', 17 June 2010, UN Doc. A/HRC/RES/14/3.
46 HRC Res 20/15, 'Promotion of the Right to Peace', 17 July 2012, UN Doc. A/HRC/RES/20/15.
47 See [no author], 'UN Hijacked by Cuba's "Right to Peace" |Farce', *UN Watch*, 22 February 2013, http://blog.unwatch.org/index.php/2013/02/22/week-long-session-to-promote-so-called-right-to-peace (accessed April 2016).
48 Ibid.
49 See Rosa Freedman (2013) *The United Nations Human Rights Council: A Critique and Early Assessment* (London: Routledge), ch. 7.
50 Statement by Sri Lanka, 18 February 2013. Although there is no official document number, all states' comments are available on the OHCHR website, 'First Session of the Open-Ended Intergovernmental Working Group on the Draft United Nations Declaration on the Right to Peace (18–21 February 2013)' http://www.ohchr.org/EN/HRBodies/HRC/RightPeace/Pages/WGDraftUNDeclarationontheRighttoPeace1stsession.aspx All statements have been compiled at http://www.ohchr.org/Documents/HRBodies/HRCouncil/WGRightPeace/StatesGeneralComments.pdf.
51 EU letter to the IGWG, 15 February 2013, http://www.ohchr.org/Documents/HRBodies/HRCouncil/WGRightPeace/StatesGeneralComments.pdf (accessed April 2016).
52 US letter to IGWG, 18 February 2013, http://www.ohchr.org/Documents/HRBodies/HRCouncil/WGRightPeace/StatesGeneralComments.pdf (accessed April 2016).
53 HRC 20th Session, 'Report of the HRC Advisory Committee on the Draft Declaration on the Right of Peoples to Peace: Statement by the US', 16 April 2012, UN Doc. A/HRC/20/31.
54 Ibid.
55 HRC 23rd Session, 'Report of the Open-Ended Inter-Governmental Working Group on the Draft United Nations Declaration on the Right to Peace', 26 April 2013, UN Doc. A/HRC/WG.13/1/2.
56 Ibid., para 21.
57 Alfred de Zayas (2011) 'Peace as a Human Right: The Jus Cogens Prohibition of Aggression', in Asbjørn Eide, Jakob T. Muller and Ineta Ziemle (eds), *Making Peoples Heard: Essays on Human Rights in Honour of Gudmundur Alfredsson* (Leiden: Brill), 27–42, 13.
58 Ibid.
59 Freedman, *United Nations Human Rights Council*, 951.
60 See Bruce M. Russett (1967) *International Regions and the International System: A Study in Political Ecology* (Chicago, IL: Rand-McNally).
61 HRC 17th Session, 'Progress Report of the Human Rights Council Advisory Committee on the Right of Peoples to Peace', 1 April 2011, UN Doc. A/HRC/17/39, 4.
62 Carlos Villán-Duran (2009) 'The Human Right to Peace: A Legislative Initiative from the Spanish Civil Society', *Spanish Yearbook of International Law* 15(1): 8.
63 Ibid. 11.
64 Spanish Society for International Human Rights Law, 'Our Vision', *AEDIDH*, http://aedidh.org/?q=node/214 (accessed April 2016).

65 Alex Sánchez, 'Costa Rica: An Army-less Nation in a Problem-Prone Region', *Council on Hemispheric Affairs*, 2 June 2011, http://www.coha.org/costa-rica-an-army-less-nation-in-a-problem-prone-region/. (accessed April 2016).
66 In 1997 Costa Rica created the Law on the Alternative Resolution of Conflicts and Promotion of Social Peace.
67 Ethan Katz and Matthew Lackey, 'Costa Rica as a Peaceful State: One Costa Rican Lawyer's Odyssey v. His Nation's Establishment', *Council on Hemispheric Affairs*, 19 March 2010, http://www.coha.org/costa-rica-as-a-peaceful-state-one-costa-rican-lawyer%E2%80%99s-odyssey-v-his-nation%E2%80%99s-establishment (accessed April 2016).
68 Benjamin A. Peters (2013) 'Security Without Deadly Violence', in Joám E. Pim (ed.), *Non-Killing, Security and the State* (Omaha, NE: Creighton University), 179–98, 188–90; concerning ruling 192–94.
69 Luis R. Zamora Bolaños, 'The Lowest Form of Military Aggression', *Americas Program*, 10 August 2010 http://www.cipamericas.org/archives/2885 (accessed April 2016).
70 Peters, 'Security Without Deadly Violence'.
71 Ibid. 189.
72 Alonso Mata, 'Court Cancels Three Sections of Arias' Arms Decree', *La Nación*, 7 November 2008.
73 Peters, 'Security Without Deadly Violence', 189.
74 Symposium on the Right to Peace, 'The Nagoya Declaration on the "Right of Peoples to Peace"', 3 December 2011, http://mail.aedidh.org/sites/default/files/Nagoya%20Declaration.pdf (accessed April 2016).
75 Preamble of the Japanese Constitution, 3 May 1947.
76 *Ito v Minister of Agriculture and Forestry* (Sapporo District Court), September 1973, 712 HANREI JIHO 24.
77 Ibid.
78 Ibid.
79 Nagoya High Court, *Mori v Japan*, 27 April 2008, Case Number: Heisei 19 (Ne) 58, Title: Appeal requesting injunction against the deployment of the self-defense forces to Iraq date of decision.
80 Hudson Hamilton (2010) 'Mori v Japan: The Nagoya High Court Recognises the Right to Live in Peace', *Pacific Rim Law and Policy Journal* 19(3): 549–63.
81 Nagoya High Court, *Mori v Japan*, 79, 22–25.
82 Hamilton, 'Mori v Japan', 550.
83 Unreported decision of the Okayama District Court, 24 February 2009, see Nagoya High Court, *Mori v Japan*.
84 Statement by Sri Lanka, see n. 50.
85 Henry J. Steiner, Philip Alston and Ryan Goodman (2007) *International Human Rights Law in Context: Law, Politics, Morals* (Oxford: Oxford University Press), 325, 326.
86 Alfred de Zayas,'The Individual Dimension of the Right to Peace', statement delivered to the Closed Expert Meeting on the Advisory Committee Declaration on the Right to Peace, Caux-Montreux, 26–27 Nov. 2012, www.ohchr.org/Documents/Issues/IntOrder/CauxStatement.doc (accessed April 2016).
87 Ibid.

Chapter 4

(Counter-)terrorism and hybridity

Fiona de Londras

Legal scholars have written much about different 'models' of counter-terrorism, with the 'criminal justice' and 'military' models dominating the discourse.[1] However, these models of counter-terrorism law, and its place within a broader ecosystem of counter-terrorism measures, policies and practices, fail to appreciate the breadth, complexity and drivers of counter-terrorism when viewed in the round. Indeed, this is indicative of legal scholarship on counter-terrorism, which tends (in contrast to some sociological scholarship in the field) to focus almost exclusively on doctrinal legal research, infrequently placing counter-terrorist law and policy within its broader context. In this, hybridity may be a helpful lens through which to view counter-terrorism law and practice; it may facilitate our understanding of counter-terrorism as a field of practice with multiple limbs and elements, indicating more fully the terrain on which critical engagement with terrorism and counter-terrorism ought to focus.

This chapter aims to illustrate the hybrid nature of terrorism and counter-terrorism as mechanisms of resistance within asymmetrical power relationships and, through considering its combination of measures and engaged actors, to illustrate the critical usefulness of conceptualising counter-terrorism as a hybrid phenomenon. In this respect, I outline the hybrid nature of terrorism (when understood as a phenomenon that challenges established power structures and domination) and counter-terrorism (as a phenomenon combining a broad mixture of approaches and instruments). Understanding counter-terrorism in particular as a hybrid phenomenon is useful for the proper analysis, identification, critique and understanding of both individual counter-terrorist measures (putting them in their broader policy and legal context) and for counter-terrorism *per se.*

Terrorism as hybridity

The concept of terrorism is mired with definitional controversy, not least because of the persistent lack of an international legally binding definition of the phenomenon that is universally accepted.[2] This results from long-standing and primarily political disagreements about whether resistance movements and state actions should be included within the concept, reflecting persistent discordance in the rhetorical commitment to countering terrorism and the practical, political contestation about what constitutes the legitimate use of force, 'legitimacy' being the bright line that divides terrorism from other forms of violence.[3]

Bearing that in mind, it is instructive – for the sake of convenience – to take as a starting point the definition of terrorism adopted (in non-binding form) by the United Nations General Assembly in its 1997 UN Declaration to Supplement the 1994 Declaration on Measures to Eliminate International Terrorism, annexed to UN General Assembly Resolution 51/210. Having reaffirmed that all UN member states condemn terrorism 'wherever and by whomsoever committed', the General Assembly went on to provide the following definition:

> Criminal acts intended or calculated to provoke a state of terror in the general public, a group of persons or particular persons for political purposes are in any circumstance unjustifiable, whatever the considerations of a political, philosophical, ideological, racial, ethnic, religious or any other nature that may be invoked to justify them.

For the purposes of considering terrorism and counter-terrorism as contemporary and hybrid practices, this offers an acceptable working definition. It suggests, at the very least, that terrorism might be categorised as hybrid as it challenges a form of (perceived or actual) domination (for which purposes the illegitimacy of the means of challenge is not determinative of its hybridity or otherwise), *and* because it pursues that challenge through a broad combination of means unbounded (generally) by analogous organisational, political, legal and legitimacy-related principles, structures and rules that (to varying levels of 'success') shape state action, including state *reaction* to terrorism. Although violence that falls within this definition is *prima facie* deemed 'illegitimate', it is clear that it is effectively a violence that is *purposive* that is captured here. 'Random' or 'senseless' violence does not generally fall into the category of terrorism as defined here; although we may deem the use of such violence illegitimate and criminal, we do not tend to consider it 'terroristic'.[4] Terrorist violence, however, is illegitimate for its targeting of civilians and/or its deployment in the place of (or sometimes in conjunction with) forms of political engagement for the purposes of achieving the aims that motivate it.

For some theorists it is the domination to which this violence seeks to respond that explains the abandonment of non-violent approaches. These theorists explain, rather than excuse, such violence as a response to repression and domination that seems otherwise immune to effective non-violent resistance. This emerges as an important narrative in both national and international terrorism. The use of violence by nationalist and republican groups in Northern Ireland, for example, has been characterised as a response to both unwanted occupation and the effective abandonment of the Catholic community by the state, if not its outright oppression.[5] In respect of contemporary terrorism at the international level – sometimes referred to as 'Islamist fundamentalism' – Jock Young has argued that this is a form of resistance to the seemingly limitless domination (political, economic and cultural) of 'the West' and resultant Occidentalism.[6] Importantly, this reflects a characterisation of terrorism as a form of rational political choice, as argued by Crenshaw in 1981.[7] Although research into the causes of terrorism tends to illustrate that a variety of different factors are relevant in different contexts,[8] this diversity does not preclude the identification of some core 'root' causes of terrorism. Terrorism research has long distinguished between preconditions (root causes) and precipitants (trigger causes) of terrorism.[9]

A comprehensive study of the existing research on the causes of terrorism has found that terrorism as resistance to dominance of some kind is a recurring theme.[10] In terms of this dominance, there appears to be a clear 'root causes' relationship between terrorism and a lack of democracy, civil liberties and the rule of law, high economic growth through rapid modernisation (especially in respect of 'ideological' terrorism), dictatorship and (ongoing or historical) occupation. All of these situations are related with asymmetrical power relationships in which terroristic violence, triggered by a particular event or trend at any given point, becomes a counter-hegemonic strategy. In that, terrorism is remarkably successful. This does not mean that terrorism succeeds in achieving the ultimate political or ideological objectives of the individual or group actors involved, but rather that it manages to shift power in some important ways.

Providing the public good of security is a core duty of the nation-state and, since the creation of major international institutions, the so-called 'international community'.[11] In addition, states consider themselves to have the monopoly on the infliction of legitimate violence within the boundaries of legality and justification laid down in domestic and international law. Once a terrorist campaign begins – and often before an attack has been perpetrated – states' responsibilities to their residents, their neighbouring states, their citizens abroad, their allies and the international community at large trigger a need to respond. The response here, whether it is legal, political, economic or otherwise, is counter-terrorism.

As a practice, counter-terrorism is both responsive and preventive: it both responds to a perceived and/or crystallised threat, and attempts to prevent the emergence of future threats and attacks. In the context of counter-terrorism, states and international institutions may have superior political and economic resources to those available to terrorists, but they are relatively disempowered vis-à-vis the terrorist threat: the hybridity of terrorism frustrates easily recognised categories, boundaries and understandings of the international and transnational system. This manifests itself in a number of ways.

First, terrorist organisations are likely to be significantly more adaptable than states are capable of being.[12] As states and international institutions introduce measures to disrupt terrorist activity, resourcing and communications, the groups in question tend to adapt their working practices to evade these measures. The state cannot, however, retreat from those measures. It will instead invest resources in their implementation and, often, legal and political resources in their (political and legal) defence and maintenance, as well as working to devise and implement more measures responding to terrorists' adaptation strategies. States are, thus, committed to investing significant political, human, economic and often diplomatic resources in these measures, while the more adaptable terrorist organisations at which they are aimed innovate around them. Not only does this strategically disadvantage the state when compared to terrorist organisations, but it also necessitates the investment of vast amounts of economic resources into counter-terrorism, creating second order impacts for social protection, welfare, international aid and other budget allocations at national level. This is in addition to the direct (micro- and macro-) economic impacts of terrorism and counter-terrorism, which are themselves strikingly significant.[13]

Secondly, terrorist organisations – where they have a clear structure – do not generally operate subject to the principles of transparency, accountability, lawfulness and deliberation that liberal democracies are founded on. Thus, terrorist policies, strategies and approaches may be devised and implemented with relative ease, while states will *generally* have to contend with expectations of justificatory deliberation, lawfulness, answerability and often be tested in their counter-terrorism by political and judicial review at national and international levels.[14] Although there are plentiful notorious examples of states introducing speedy and repressive 'panic-related' measures in response to particular terrorist attacks,[15] as the time from an attack extends greater demands for justification and lesser tolerance of security overreach tends to emerge. This is notwithstanding the perceived level and nature of a terrorist threat at any given time. Thus, although states may capitalise on a period of fear and panic, as panic subsides the environment becomes somewhat less receptive to repressive measures introduced with reduced deliberation. A great deal of counter-terrorism law and policy is made outside of this time period, when a more robust process is demanded.

This leads, finally, to a third aspect in which states are relatively disempowered in counter-terrorism: the demands of law. Terrorism does not comply with law: terrorist organisations are not bound by constitutions of the kind that limit governments, and they do not generally comply with international legal standards such as international humanitarian law.

States, in contrast, must and *generally do* comply with law. This does not mean that counter-terrorism never takes place outside of law: it is clear that it does. Neither does it mean that legal standards might not be subjected to deeply troubling overt or covert recalibration in counter-terrorist contexts.[16] However it does mean that states commit significant time and resources to establishing the legal permissibility of their desired counter-terrorist measures, including in judicial review. While there is a clear interest in keeping state actions within legal boundaries for reasons of legitimacy as well as for legal reasons relating to the integrity of the legal system and its constitutionalist resilience, it is at least arguable that approaches that are unlawful or the lawfulness of which is disputed, may serve important short-term security purposes that the state considers to warrant unlawful activity. Such activity, of course, brings with it more critiques and demands for accountability from civil society, responding to which consequently absorbs yet more of the state's legal, political and economic capital. The desirability of holding states to their legal limitations is not in dispute, however the implications of this are an important element of the hybridity of terrorism. While these exercises in legal accountability are ongoing, terrorist organisations devote themselves to devising and executing their own agendas, unburdened by the need for democratic and legal legitimacy.

The nature, as well as the success, of terrorism as a hybrid 'entity', and the desire of states to be effective in addressing it, more or less necessitates hybridity in counter-terrorism itself, to which this chapter now turns.

Hybrid counter-terrorism

I have already referred above to counter-terrorism as an 'ecosystem', a term intended to convey the great scale and diversity of measures, approaches, policies and instruments that comprise counter-terrorism and, thus, the nature of counter-terrorism as a dynamic and delicate enterprise. As an activity or practice, counter-terrorism defies us to arrive at a definition any more exacting than 'that which tends to *counter* terroristic activity'. In some ways, the circularity of this definition is reflective of the nature of terrorism itself, which is a broadly drawn and diverse set of activities aimed at disrupting dominant state power. Given the challenges involved in defining counter-terrorism, it is instructive to look at the counter-terrorist strategies adopted by national and international governance entities, and particularly those of states and international institutions, to counter terrorism; strategies that, taken together, indicate the hybridity of counter-terrorism itself.

In the main, these strategies split into a number of strands. The UN's Global Counter-Terrorism Strategy identified four areas of activity:

1 Measures to address the conditions conductive to the spread of terrorism.
2 Measures to prevent and combat terrorism.

3 Measures to build states' capacity to prevent and combat terrorism and to strengthen the role of the United Nations system in this regard.
4 Measures to ensure respect for human rights for all the rule of law as the fundamental basis of the fight against terrorism.[17]

At the European Union level the Counter-Terrorism Strategy focuses on four activities: prevent, protect, pursue and respond, which in turn are the out-working of the Union's strategic commitment '[t]o combat terrorism while respecting human rights, and make Europe safer, allowing its citizens to live in an area of freedom, security and justice'.[18] At a national level there is a similar trend. By means of example, the United Kingdom's counter-terrorism strategy, known as CONTEST, adopts a four-part strategy of pursue, prevent, protect and prepare.[19] These approaches at national, regional and international level indicate the contemporary nature of counter-terrorism as a hybrid activity that envelops and transcends the national and international, public and private, law and non-law.

Neither national nor international

Although international institutions have long had an interest in peace and security, the politics as well as the practicalities of counter-terrorism meant that, in the main, counter-terrorist law and policy were driven and implemented at state level prior to the autumn of 2001. This does not mean that there was no internationalised counter-terrorism prior to September 2001. The UN had adopted numerous international conventions on countering specific manifestations of terrorism (although ratification rates were low),[20] was implementing sanctions as a counter-terrorist measure against Al Qaida and its associates,[21] and had addressed terrorism at Security Council and General Assembly levels on various occasions. At European Union level an informal group known as the TREVI (Terrorism, Radicalism, Extremism and Violence International) group had been established in 1975 (following the Munich Olympics). This group comprised interior and justice ministers engaged in information exchange outside of the formal treaty structures of the European Union. However, counter-terrorism remained primarily a matter for states themselves to address.

Although this did not change utterly in 2001, one noticeable feature of the post-11 September 2001 *milieu* was the internationalisation of counter-terrorism through the involvement of supranational institutions and organisations. In large part, the elements of counter-terrorism that have been internationalised in this way are those that relate to the transnationalism of terrorism and terrorist activities themselves, as well as those that ease the burdens of negotiating national interests in much counter-terrorist interaction. The content and scope of Security Council Resolution 1373, passed shortly after the attacks on the Pentagon and World Trade Center, are indicative of this.

In an extraordinary step, this Resolution directed all member states of the United Nations to introduce laws preventing, suppressing and criminalising activities relating to terrorist fundraising,[22] freeze funds and assets of those involved in or associated with terrorism,[23] and prohibit material support for terrorism.[24] In addition, states were directed to refrain from supporting terrorist activity, '[t]ake the necessary steps to prevent the commission of terrorist acts' including through providing information to other states, provide assistance to other states in investigating and prosecuting terrorist financing or support, prevent the movement of terrorists through their borders and refuse safe haven to terrorist actors and activities.[25] States were 'called upon' to improve mechanisms of exchanging operational information on terrorism and terrorist activities, and broadly to enhance their cooperation in the field of counter-terrorism.[26] The Resolution went on to establish the Counter-Terrorism Committee with broad coordinating and capacity-enhancing functions, as well as functions relating to the implementation of counter-terrorist sanctions.[27] Although the United Nations' counter-terrorist infrastructure has developed significantly in the intervening years, Resolution 1373 set the ground conditions for a significant internationalisation of counter-terrorism, with the Security Council effectively acting as a proxy legislator for all member states as well as establishing counter-terrorist cooperation as an international good, if not an expectation of membership of the international community of states committed to the maintenance of peace and security.

As well as operating on a global level (i.e. UN level), one way of trying to address the perceived global terrorist threat is to club together in geographically close states; in other words to regionalise counter-terrorism to some extent. This has been evident in the EU, not just in intelligence sharing and coordination where club approaches long predate 2001, but also in more general counter-terrorism activities such as counter-radicalisation, disruption of financial and communications capacities and cross-border pursuit.

Prior to the attacks of 11 September 2001 the European Union had no autonomous counter-terrorism law and did not have a comprehensive approach to countering terrorism.[28] This was a product, primarily, of the continuing nationalism of criminal justice as a general matter in the European Union at the time. However, the emergence of a clear area of common justice and home affairs together with the attacks of 2001 and subsequent attacks on London and Madrid meant that counter-terrorism emerged as a significant activity within the EU over the next decade. In the time between September 2001 and July 2013 well over 200 measures were introduced under the counter-terrorism rubric of the European Union, eighty-eight of which were 'binding' law.[29] In that time period the EU introduced twenty-six action plans and strategy documents, twenty-five regulations, fifteen Directives, eleven Framework Decisions, twenty-five Decisions, one Joint Action, three Common Positions, eleven Recommendations, four

Resolutions, 111 Council Conclusions, and eight International Agreements in the counter-terrorism field.[30] These measures cover a wide range of activities, and might be broken into three broad categories: capitalising measures, terrorism-specific measures and terrorism-related measures.

Capitalising measures are measures that reflect policy choices predating major terrorist attacks but where the political impetus for implementing these policy choices was offered by the post-attack atmosphere, such as the European Arrest Warrant and the EU Data Retention Directive. In contrast, terrorism-specific measures are ones that were introduced in order to respond to a perceived risk from terrorism, rather than being general criminal justice measures. As the member states of the European Union retain the vast majority of counter-terrorist and security competence, these measures are, in truth, relatively sparse at the EU level and relate to matters in which a transnational approach is required. The primary example of this is the EU's system for the disruption of terrorist financing.[31] Terrorism-related measures are measures that are introduced in order to respond to general security concerns, including terrorism. As with capitalising measures, these are unlikely to be perceived as primarily or even largely 'counter-terrorist', although they have a clear counter-terrorist application and in some cases the justificatory rhetoric surrounding their introduction referred expressly to the threat from terrorism.

In the round, the combination of measures introduced by the EU since September 2001 indicates the emergence of the EU as an internal counter-terrorist space of the Union, notwithstanding the fact that the member states still maintain control over the vast majority of their own counter-terrorism policy, including domestic laws, international affairs (with the exception of CFSP elements of counter-terrorism) and so on. This is further reinforced by the emergence of a counter-terrorist infrastructure within the European Union, including the position of EU Counter-Terrorism Coordinator.[32]

The European Union is also, however, a significant external actor in counter-terrorism, taking a role in capacity building and in international reactions to terroristic activity. An excellent example is the recent meeting in Paris of a number of sub-Saharan states that are joining together to confront Boko Haram and the disruptive threat that it poses. In this the EU, as a highly developed supranational regional organisation with its own constitutional and legal system, offers an interesting model for what can go right – and what can go wrong – in the regionalisation of counter-terrorism. The EU also plays an important external role in counter-terrorism including in the generation of norms, practices and *best* practices through its participation in the coordination and capacity-building activities of the UN Counter-Terrorism Committee, its inclusion of counter-terrorism and security clauses in its international agreements, its engagement in security activities and capacity building with third countries and so on. Thus, the EU is both a significant norm generator (or at least modality-designer) internationally and transnationally *and* an exemplar of regionalised CT.

This positioning of counter-terrorism as something that is simultaneously national, regional, transnational and international illustrates the first way in which contemporary counter-terrorism can be conceptualised as hybrid; a characterisation that is made necessary by the hybrid capacity and nature of terrorism and its nature as a phenomenon with local nodes of activities and global ramifications.

Neither public nor private

Contemporary counter-terrorism can be accurately characterised as, to at least some extent, a partnership between public and private actors. I have previously typologised privatisation in counter-terrorism in terms of open privatisation, closed privatisation, statutory privatisation and non-contractual co-option.[33] Open privatisation takes place by means of out-sourcing undertaken through open contracts that are declared and can be scrutinised by the public and in open political discourse. Closed privatisation, on the other hand, comprises out-sourcing that is grounded in closed contracts, meaning contracts either the existence or the contents of which are not publicised and which are, consequently, not subject to public discussion and deliberation. Statutory privatisation takes place through placing obligations on private entities by means of legislation. Finally, non-contractual co-option takes place when non-state actors are 'co-opted' into counter-terrorism in an informal, networked manner without any clear outline of the parameters of the co-option or, indeed, publicisation of the fact of the cooperation, co-option and counter-terrorist activities of the non-state actor involved, or where they are involuntarily co-opted through the use of their capacities and resources by state actors.

These different kinds of privatisation are not abstractions; they are, rather, happening all around us all of the time. They are also often identifiable in both the national and international dimensions of countering terrorism, and illustrate the hybridisation of public and private activities into a complex counter-terrorist ecosystem.

The contractual engagement of private military companies in 'on the ground' counter-terrorism and of private security providers in the provision of 'secure solutions' to sites of physical intelligence-gathering are all examples of open privatisation in contemporary counter-terrorism. Private entities and profit-making companies are also involved in internationalised counter-terrorism, contributing to the review of existing measures and strategies and, both formally and informally, to the development of new measures and strategies whether as 'stakeholders' or as consultants.

As is to be expected, we know less about the prevalence of closed privatisation because, by its very nature, it is highly secretive. That said, some examples of such privatisation have come to light, not least in the context of extraordinary rendition. By means of (largely unsuccessful) litigation in the United States as well as investigations by NGOs, the Council of Europe and the European Union it has become clear that the practice of extraordinary rendition involved significant volumes of contractual engagement with aviation logistics, security and aviation services companies. These contracts are closed because their very existence is denied and, indeed, when companies suspected to have been involved are sued by victims of rendition the US government has used the very strong 'state secret' defence to prevent courts ordering their discovery, thus reinforcing the closed nature of these contracts.[34]

Statutory privatisation is widespread in the counter-terrorist context, and it seems that states are increasingly interested in extending it. This is well demonstrated by the creation of legislative requirements for telecommunications companies to retain communications data, which states may then access in statutorily outlined circumstances. The introduction of an obligation for all telecommunications companies to retain 'metadata' beyond the period of time required for business use was a prominent part of the EU's response to the London and Madrid bombings, although it had been on the political agenda (and rejected by the European Parliament) prior to that.[35] The controversial Data Retention Directive that was introduced in 2006 required companies to retain telecommunications metadata for a period of time between six and twenty-four months (with the exact retention period varying depending on each member state's implementing legislation), so that this data could then be accessed by the state in the investigation of serious crimes including terrorism. The Directive imposed significant financial burdens on these companies, as well as raising very significant civil liberties concerns, and was eventually struck down by the Court of Justice of the European Union in April 2014.[36] Notwithstanding that Court's finding that blanket surveillance of this kind is a disproportionate interference with individual rights, the United Kingdom introduced such data retention in the summer of 2014[37] and in August of that same year the Australian Attorney General announced the intention of the government there to do the same.

Non-contractual co-option is the fourth and final type of privatisation to consider in the context of counter-terrorism. There are at least three interesting ways in which such privatisation takes place in contemporary counter-terrorism. First, rather than use statutory instruments which are burdensome and time-consuming, it is not unusual for the state to simply 'ask' a private company to 'lend a hand' and these requests are routinely acceded to; here formal and informal networks between individual security and private actors, as well as inter-entity cooperation, may operate to create possibilities for such hybridised approaches to counter-terrorist praxis. So, for example, where there is a thread on an internet forum that 'seems' radicalising or seems to be sharing information about bomb-making or encouraging so-called 'Nike terrorism' ('just do it') service providers might be made aware of it by the state and asked to remove it without any legal instrument – like a court order – being acquired to *force* them to do so; similarly search engines might be asked to filter content from their search results (i.e. to have some things not appear) or to super-weight some results over others. This is not an entirely idiosyncratic approach to the regulation of 'harmful' materials online: in the United Kingdom, for example, such regulation takes place by means of a hybrid of criminal law (in the form of online possession offences) and cooperation of this kind between the state and internet service providers.

A second form of non-contractual co-option is the involuntary engagement of the resources or capacities of private entities – especially corporations – by intelligence and security services. This ranges from sentiment analysis to the use of court orders to secure commercially collected information. Sentiment analysis is an increasingly prominent part of contemporary counter-terrorism, and effectively comprises the constant surveillance and assessment of 'sentiments' as expressed on open online forums such as Twitter or Facebook. In contrast to this, involuntary co-option by means of court orders or other instruments of legal compulsion creates legal imperatives for corporations to hand over information that might be of use to intelligence or security services such as telephone records: an activity undertaken in significant volumes in the United States by means of FISA warrants and so-called "NSA letters'. Also falling within the category of non-contractual co-option is the involvement of communities in counter-terrorism. Such involvement is a core part of counter-radicalisation which, in turn, is a fundamental element of states' preventative counter-terrorism strategies. However, community involvement is not limited to counter-radicalisation strategies, but has also become part of counter-terrorist policing, often with significant deleterious impacts on societal cohesion.[38]

Neither legal nor extra-legal

Countering terrorism does not take place by law alone. Rather it extends beyond the promulgation and implementation of laws, as already indicated to some extent by the references above to internet governance, counter-terrorist capacity-building and counter-radicalisation. To characterise counter-terrorism as being neither legal nor extra-legal is to allude to two different traits of counter-terrorism: first, the use of instruments and modalities beyond law for the purposes of countering terrorism, and second engagement in activities that do not have a clear legal grounding in the name of counter-terrorism.

Effectively countering terrorism involves efforts to try to stabilise and moderate situations of instability, conflict and insecurity as well as targeting specific terrorist activities. In this respect, there is only a limited amount that legal instruments have the capacity to achieve. Rather, non-legal instruments and approaches are employed. This is reflected in the shift in contemporary times to a concentration on human security on an international level. This shift, which can be problematised as a manifestation of 'securitisation',[39] involves the deployment of resources in the attempt to stabilise broader conditions in which it is believed insecurity and radicalisation might flourish, including the provision of basic socio-economic goods such as education, food, shelter and healthcare. Although such securitisation raises serious questions as to the growth of the 'security agenda' as well as the reshaping of rights as matters of broader security,[40] the devotion of international and national energies to these efforts is an important example of counter-terrorism beyond law. Similarly, counter-radicalisation – already mentioned above – focuses on using non-legal measures to moderate the conditions in which terrorism is thought capable of flourishing. Beyond this, diplomacy, international politics and geopolitics, investment in technology and (military and non-military) intervention for the purposes of stabilisation are all key parts of a contemporary counter-terrorism that goes well beyond law.

Going beyond law, however, can also mean engaging in approaches that are not clearly grounded in law. Termed 'extra-legal' by Oren Gross,[41] this can include *but also goes beyond* 'unlawful' activities. Certainly, some activities that have been labeled 'counter-terrorism' both since and before 2001 are clearly unlawful, including torture. Others, however, fall into a different space: that of legal uncertainty. In this conceptual space, states do what they consider to be 'necessary' regardless of whether there is a clear legal grounding underpinning them. In many cases, lawfulness is disputed and, reflecting the comments above about states' general fidelity to law, governments will frequently go to substantial lengths in the attempt to establish lawfulness where this is disputed (a set of claims and counter-claims sometimes termed 'lawfare'). Prominent examples of this include the activities of the National Security Agency and other US agencies that were spectacularly revealed by Chelsea (formerly Bradley) Manning and Edward Snowden.

All of this reinforces the fact that countering terrorism has become a hybrid activity, combining the legal and non-legal in an attempt to both prevent terrorism and respond to terroristic violence, plots and activities as they emerge.

Conclusions

In counter-terrorism, as in all other fields, law does not exist in isolation. Rather, it results from, shapes, and is shaped by its broader societal and operational context. However, for lawyers working in counter-terrorism (including the author) there is a tendency to focus on legal instruments and to assess the scale, nature, success, effectiveness and deficiencies of counter-terrorism as matters purely of legal analysis. This results not only from the volatility of the legal landscape and the challenges of staying abreast of legal arguments and measures, but also the practical challenges of becoming familiar with the counter-terrorist terrain; an activity that realistically requires sustained engagement with the community of counter-terrorist practitioners at national, international, public and private levels. In spite of these limitations, however, the nature of counter-terrorism as a response to terrorism, itself a hybrid phenomenon, makes such a limited horizon challenging for those whose interest is in critically evaluating the true scale and shape of counter-terrorism, its (societal, operational and legal) impacts, and its effectiveness.

The application of a hybridity lens to this exercise holds some potential for our shaping of legal and interdisciplinary scholarship and research on ecosystemic counter-terrorism by expanding the horizons, as well as ensuring the appropriate contextualisation, of legal analysis. Given the persistent, adaptable and challenging nature of both terrorism and counter-terrorism, such a comprehensive approach to understanding these related phenomena is vital. Without a textured and comprehensive understanding of terrorism and its dynamics, we can neither identify nor critically analyse the shape, scale and scope of *counter*-terrorism, its impacts and its effectiveness. Law is only a small part of counter-terrorism which, as outlined above, is properly understood as a broadly based, multi-part and multi-actor ecosystemic activity happening on and across multiple scales. An alertness to the hybrid nature of counter-terrorism allows us to identify the context in which particular laws operate, to analyse those laws within that context, and to avoid the lawyerly impulse to totalise 'law'. This does not mean that all counter-terrorism *law* research needs to be cross- or multi-disciplinary, but rather that even doctrinal legal research into such laws will benefit from taking context into account in order to understand the working, limits, reach and success of such laws (including proposed legal responses to terrorism).

Notes

1 See e.g. for an overview, Robert Chesney and Jack Goldsmith (2008) 'Terrorism and the Convergence of Criminal and Military Detention Models', *Stanford Law Review* 60(4): 1079–1133, 1079.

2 For a good overview see Ben Saul (2006) *Defining Terrorism in International Law* (Oxford: Oxford University Press).

3 On legitimacy, violence and terrorism see Laura Donohue (2005) 'Terrorism and the Counter-Terrorist Discourse', in Victor V. Ramraj, Michael Hor, and Kent Roach (eds), *Global Anti-Terrorism Law and Policy* (Cambridge: Cambridge University Press), 13–36.

4 Legal definitions of terrorism often specify that a prescribed list of criminal activities are terrorist where there are done with the purpose, aim or intention of achieving a certain end. See e.g. UN Security Council Resolution 1566 (2004) and the Terrorism Act 2000 (United Kingdom).

5 See generally Richard English (2003) *Armed Struggle: The History of the IRA* (London: Palgrave Macmillan); and Joseph Ruane and Jennifer Todd (1996) *The Dynamics of Conflict in Northern Ireland: Power, Conflict and Emancipation* (Cambridge: Cambridge University Press).
6 Jock Young (2007) *The Vertigo of Late Modernity* (London: Sage).
7 Martha Crenshaw (1981) 'The Causes of Terrorism', *Comparative Politics* 13(4): 379–99, 379.
8 For an excellent overview see 'Exploring Root and Trigger Causes of Terrorism' (2008) *Transnational Terrorism, Security and the Rule of Law,* http://www.transnationalterrorism.eu/tekst/publications/Root%20and%20Trigger.pdf (accessed January 2016).
9 Crenshaw, 'Causes of Terrorism'. See also Jeffrey I. Ross (1993) 'Structural Causes of Oppositional Political Terrorism: Towards a Causal Model', *Journal of Peace Research* 30(3): 317–29.
10 'Exploring Root and Trigger Causes'.
11 This is evident from the first line of the Charter of the United Nations, which provides 'We the Peoples of the United Nations determined to save succeeding generations from the scourge of war', as well as from the powers conferred on the Security Council to maintain international peace and security by Chapters VI and VII of the Charter.
12 This is not to suggest that all terrorist organisations demonstrate adaptability; rather some level of organisational sophistication and capacity for learning is likely required. See e.g. Calvert Jones (2006) 'Al-Qaida's Innovative Improvisers: Learning in a Diffuse Transnational Network', *Cambridge Review of International Affairs* 19(4): 555–69.
13 On the economics of terrorism and counter-terrorism see Friedrich Schneider, Tilman Brück and Daniel Meierrieks (2010) *The Economics of Terrorism and Counter-Terrorism: A Survey (Part II)*, CESifo Working Paper Public Finance, 3012 (Munich: CESifo).
14 I have previously identified these as 'legitimacy factors' in counter-terrorism. See Fiona de Londras (2011) 'Can Counter-Terrorist Internment ever be Legitimate?', *Human Rights Quarterly* 33(3): 593–619.
15 By 'panic-related' I mean measures that are driven by, respond to and are introduced in the context of 'manufactured' (or 'moral') panic, 'bottom-up' (or genuine) panic, or a combination of the two. See Fiona de Londras (2011) *Detention in the 'War on Terrorism': Can Human Rights Fight Back?* (Cambridge: Cambridge University Press), ch. 1.
16 See Helen Fenwick and Gavin Phillipson (2011) 'Covert Derogations and Judicial Deference: Redefining Liberty and Due Process Rights in Counter-terrorism Law and Beyond', *McGill Law Journal* 56(4): 863–918; Helen Fenwick (2014) 'Post 9/11 UK Counter-Terrorism Cases in the European Court of Human Rights: A 'Dialogic' Approach to Rights' Protection or Appeasement of National Authorities?' in Fergal F. Davis and Fiona de Londras (eds), *Critical Debates on Counter-Terrorism Judicial Review* (Cambridge: Cambridge University Press), 302–23.
17 'Plan of Action', Annex to General Assembly Resolution 60/288 of 8 September 2006.
18 Council of the European Union (2005) *European Union Counter-Terrorism Strategy*, http://register.consilium.europa.eu/doc/srv?l= EN&f=ST%2014469%20 2005%20REV%204 (accessed June 2016).
19 HM Government (2011) *CONTEST: The United Kingdom's Strategy for Countering Terrorism*, https://www.gov.uk/government/uploads/system/uploads/attachment_data/file/97995/strategy-contest.pdf (accessed June 2016).

20 Conventions deposited with the Secretary-General of the UN: Convention on the Prevention and Punishment of Crimes against Internationally Protected Persons, Including Diplomatic Agents, adopted by the General Assembly of the United Nations on 14 December 1973; International Convention against the Taking of Hostages, adopted by the General Assembly of the United Nations on 17 December 1979; International Convention for the Suppression of Terrorist Bombings, adopted by the General Assembly of the United Nations on 15 December 1997; International Convention for the Suppression of the Financing of Terrorism, adopted by the General Assembly of the United Nations on 9 December 1999. Conventions deposited with other depositaries: Convention on Offences and Certain Other Acts Committed on Board Aircraft, signed at Tokyo on 14 September 1963. (Deposited with the Secretary-General of the International Civil Aviation Organisation); Convention for the Suppression of Unlawful Seizure of Aircraft, signed at The Hague on 16 December 1970 (deposited with the Governments of the Russian Federation, the United Kingdom and the United States of America); Convention for the Suppression of Unlawful Acts against the Safety of Civil Aviation, signed at Montreal on 23 September 1971 (deposited with the Governments of the Russian Federation, the United Kingdom and the United States of America); Convention on the Physical Protection of Nuclear Material, signed at Vienna on 3 March 1980 (deposited with the Director-General of the International Atomic Energy Agency); Protocol on the Suppression of Unlawful Acts of Violence at Airports Serving International Civil Aviation, supplementary to the Convention for the Suppression of Unlawful Acts against the Safety of Civil Aviation, signed at Montreal on 24 February 1988 (deposited with the Governments of the Russian Federation, the United Kingdom and the United States of America and with the Secretary-General of the International Civil Aviation Organisation); Convention for the Suppression of Unlawful Acts against the Safety of Maritime Navigation, done at Rome on 10 March 1988 (deposited with the Secretary-General of the International Maritime Organisation); Protocol for the Suppression of Unlawful Acts against the Safety of Fixed Platforms Located on the Continental Shelf, done at Rome on 10 March 1988 (deposited with the Secretary-General of the International Maritime Organisation); Convention on the Marking of Plastic Explosives for the Purpose of Detection, signed at Montreal on 1 March 1991 (deposited with the Secretary-General of the International Civil Aviation Organisation).

21 Security Council Resolutions 1267 and 1269, both of 1999.

22 Operative Paragraph 1(a), (b), (c), SC Resolution 1373 (2001).

23 Operative Paragraph 1(d), SC Resolution 1373 (2001).

24 Operative Paragraph 1(e), SC Resolution 1373 (2001).

25 Operative Paragraph 2, SC Resolution 1373 (2001).

26 Operative Paragraph 3, SC Resolution 1373 (2001).

27 Operative Paragraph 6, SC Resolution 1373 (2001).

28 See generally Cian C. Murphy (2012) *EU Counter-Terrorism, Pre-emption and the Rule of Law* (Oxford: Hart Publishing).

29 Ben Hayes and Chris Jones (2013) *Catalogue of EU Counter-Terrorism Measures Adopted since 11 September 2001*, SECILE Consortium, http://secile.eu/wp-content/uploads/2013/12/Catalogue-of-EU-Counter-Terrorism-Measures1.pdf (accessed June 2014).

30 Ibid.

31 Council Implementing Regulation (EU) No. 1285/2009 of 22 December 2009 implementing Article 2(3) of Regulation (EC) No. 2580/2001 on specific restrictive measures directed against certain persons and entities with a view to

combating terrorism and repealing Regulation (EC) No. 501/2009; Council Regulation (EU) No. 1286/2009 of 22 December 2009 amending Regulation (EC) No. 881/2002 imposing certain specific restrictive measures directed against certain persons and entities associated with Osama bin Laden, the Al-Qaida network and the Taliban; Council Decision 2009/1004/CFSP of 22 December 2009 updating the list of persons, groups and entities subject to Article 2, 3 and 4 of Common Position 2001/931/CFSP on the application of specific measures to combat terrorism; Directive 2005/60/EC of the European Parliament and of the Council of 26 October 2005 on the Prevention of the Use of the Financial System for the Purpose of Money Laundering and Terrorist Financing. OJ L 309, 25 November 2005.

32 For an overview see Josephine Doody (2015) 'The Institutional Framework of EU Counter-Terrorism', in Fiona de Londras and Josephine Doody (eds), *The Impact, Legitimacy and Effectiveness of EU Counter-Terrorism* (London: Routledge), 40–61.

33 Fiona de Londras (2013) 'Privatised Counter-Terrorist Surveillance: Constitutionalism Undermined', in George Williams, Fergal F. Davis and Nicola McGarrity (eds), *Surveillance, Counter-Terrorism and Comparative Constitutionalism* (London: Routledge), 59–72.

34 On privatisation in extraordinary rendition see Fiona de Londras (2011) 'Privatized Sovereign Performance: Regulating in the "Gap" between Security and Rights?', *Journal of Law and Society* 38(1): 96–118.

35 See Ben Hayes and Chris Jones (2013) *The EU Data Retention Directive: A Case Study in the Legitimacy and Effectiveness of EU Counter-Terrorism Policy*, SECILE Consortium, http://secile.eu/wp-content/uploads/2013/11/Data-Retention-Directive-in-Europe-A-Case-Study.pdf (accessed January 2016).

36 Joined Cases C-293/12 and C-594/12, Judgment of the Grand Chamber, 8 April 2014.

37 Data Retention and Investigatory Powers Act 2014.

38 See Clive Walker (2011) 'The Paradox of Global Terrorism and Community-Based Security Policing', in Ralph Henham and Mark Findlay (eds), *Exploring the Boundaries of International Criminal Justice* (Farnham: Ashgate), 253–74.

39 That critique is disputed, however. For an overview see Rita Floyd (2007) 'Human Security and the Copenhagen School's Securitization Approach: Conceptualizing Human Security as a Securitizing Move', *Human Security Journal* 5(37): 38–49.

40 See e.g. Liora Lazarus (2007) 'Mapping the Right to Security', in ed. Liora Lazarus and Benjamin J. Goold (eds), *Security and Human Rights* (Oxford: Hart Publishing), 325–46.

41 Oren Gross (2003) 'Chaos and Rules: Should Responses to Violent Crises Always Be Constitutional?', *Yale Law Journal* 112(5): 1011–1134. For a refinement and defence of the extra-legal measures model see also Oren Gross (2009) 'Extra-Legality and the Ethic of Political Responsibility', in Victor V. Ramraj (ed.), *Emergencies and the Limits of Legality* (Cambridge: Cambridge University Press), 60–94.

Chapter 5

Hybrid processes for hybrid outcomes

NGO participation at the United Nations Human Rights Council

Ruth Houghton

Introduction

The Serpentine Bar is at the Palais des Nations in Geneva, just outside Room XX, which is known as the Human Rights and Alliance of Civilisations Room and is where the United Nations Human Rights Council (UNHRC) meets. Between 8 and 26 September 2014, representatives from approximately 279 non-governmental organisations (NGOs) mingled in the bar with state delegates from an estimated 175 UN Member States and two non-Member States at the 27th UNHRC Council Session.[1] At the entrance to the open-plan bar is the NGO Welcome Stand, which has an array of leaflets covering campaigns, events and forthcoming seminars, displayed for delegates to see. Nearby are the side rooms, where NGOs hold side-events and panel discussions.

Watching NGO representatives prepare for oral submissions to the UNHRC, advertise side-events, discuss proceedings and resolutions with each other and with states, it is easy to see why NGOs are considered important actors in international decision-making.[2] Witnessing the activities of NGO representatives puts into doubt the idea that states are the only influential actors in the international system, and the UN particularly. The participation of NGOs in international decision-making is not a recent phenomenon, as the UN Charter in 1945 provided for the involvement of NGOs at the Economic and Social Council (ECOSOC) and its subsidiary bodies.[3] There has been an increase in the number of NGOs participating in international organisations (IOs),[4] but questions remain about the role and significance of NGOs in international decision-making.[5]

Previously this question has been addressed using legal analysis of the institutions and the mechanisms for participation.[6] Focus on the legal instruments tends to find a limited role for NGOs as states are the 'ultimate law-makers'.[7] This chapter seeks to address the question using hybridity as a lens to explore the role of NGOs at the UNHRC. First, hybridity can be used to show international decision-making is no longer the prerogative of states, but that there is a plethora of actors participating at the international level.

Second, hybridity can be used to consider the more nuanced power dynamics between these different actors.

Hybridity can be divided into two different claims: empirical and critical.[8] The empirical aspect of hybridity highlights that 'hybridization happens' in the first place, and, more specifically, where it occurs,[9] that is, where hybrids can be seen and where hybrids are created. In this sense, hybridity challenges the perceived state-centricity of international decision-making by showing the hybrid nature of decision-making given the plurality of actors.[10] Second, hybridity can be used as a critical lens to explore the power relations between different actors in international bodies.[11] It can help to move away from a focus on legal instruments to discuss how different actors are treated at the UNHRC, and it gives rise to a consideration of whether NGOs 'compete with other actors in a dynamic marketplace of ideas',[12] or whether they sit on the peripheries of decision-making.[13] The legal, doctrinal and linguistic analysis already undertaken by scholars in international law overlooks questions about where NGOs are acting and their interactions with states in informal settings.[14] Using hybridity helps to uncover a more nuanced picture of the relationship and further questions state dominance in international decision-making.

In this chapter, hybridity is first used in the empirical sense to explore the types of actors in international decision-making and in particular, at the UNHRC. Consideration of the hybrid nature of the UNHRC and NGOs will question the narrative that states are the only actors in international decision-making. Hybridity will then be used as a critical lens to explore the relationship between states and NGOs at the UNHRC.

Challenging the state-centric accounts of international decision-making

The Peace of Westphalia in 1648 placed state sovereignty and equality between states as central principles of international law.[15] States, as the original subjects of international law, 'were the sole law-making power'.[16] However, this narrative of state-centricity in international decision-making does not accurately reflect the reality of global governance. The NGOs at the Serpentine Bar are seen lobbying, pressuring governments to adopt or modify resolutions, as well as running awareness campaigns that bring local issues into the debate. NGOs also play an important role in the implementation of human rights policies and monitoring the compliance of states.[17] Furthermore, there is a plethora of non-state actors such as transnational corporations, civil society actors and particular political elites, which are influencing international law and international decision-making.[18]

International legal scholarship has traditionally dealt with the issues of actors in international law through the concept of 'legal personality', which distinguishes between subjects and objects of international law.[19]

States were the subjects of international law, whilst individuals and non-state actors had object status.[20] Scholars such as Rosalyn Higgins and Robert McCorquodale have challenged this bifurcation as it fails to acknowledge the multiple actors who have influence in international decision-making. They prefer to speak of 'actors' or 'participants'.[21]

The legal personality discourse is accompanied by a doctrinal focus on international legal instruments.[22] According to the constitutive documents of international bodies, states are the dominant actors and non-state actors have a limited role.[23] In international relations scholarship, there has been a move to quantify the participation of transnational actors (TNAs), which includes non-state actors, at IOs.[24] Thomas Sommerer and Jonas Tallberg draw a distinction between 'access' and 'participation'.[25] For them, 'access consists of the institutional mechanisms whereby TNAs may take part in the policy process of an IO'.[26] This access may 'be granted either by the member states of an IO or by international bureaucracies servicing the IO'.[27] In contrast, 'participation denotes TNAs' presence in these institutional venues'.[28] In highlighting 'formal access' this discussion reiterates a focus on legal instruments and, whilst it considers access to spaces such as 'the gallery of decision-making bodies',[29] it overlooks the more informal spaces where non-state actors can have influence.

Hybridity can be used to explore the 'presence' and participation of non-state actors at IOs. To explore the role of 'participation', the membership of IOs can be considered. However, focusing on membership status alone provides for only a narrow understanding of hybrid organisations. The work of Homi Bhabha and specifically his idea of the 'Third Space' can highlight broader understandings of hybrid organisations.[30] The 'Third Space', as he understood it, can be metaphorical, but it can also be a specific place; a 'place of invention' where binary distinctions are dissolved.[31] Distinctions between national and international or local and global,[32] and between subject and object, can be challenged in this 'Third Space', as it creates spaces for participation that are not constrained by criteria such as membership.[33] Thus, the acts of participation or interactions that happen within the 'Third Space' are also considered. In this respect, hybrid organisations or bodies challenge the categories used to define actors in international decision-making as they provide spaces for participation.

This two-part framework of membership and participation can be applied to IOs and NGOs to highlight the plurality and complexity of the actors involved in international decision-making. The hybridisation processes highlight the spaces for participation of actors that are otherwise omitted in a state-centric narrative. There are multiple levels of hybridisation to be explored in the processes of international decision-making, such as the hybridisation of the IOs and international bodies and the continuing hybridisation process facilitated by the involvement of NGOs.

International organisations

The state-centricity, or the idea that states are the sole subjects in international law and international decision-making, is challenged by the role of IOs.[34] International law already identifies IOs, such as the UN, as subjects of international law and confers to them rights and responsibilities, which implies that international law is not a monoculture of states.[35] Whilst it should be noted that IOs are still created by states and have state membership,[36] some of these organisations can be classified as hybrid organisations because of their membership.[37] In a hybrid IO, 'both private transnational actors (NGOs, parties, or companies) and governments or governmental agencies are admitted as members', which means they have 'full rights or participation in policy-making, including the right to vote on the final decisions'.[38] These hybrid IOs facilitate the participation of non-state actors through membership criteria.

Beyond this 'hybrid' membership, and looking more broadly at the question of participation, other IOs and bodies can be conceptualised as being hybrid in other ways. For example, the International Labour Organisation has states as members, but its Constitution states that each member state sends a tripartite delegation made up of two government delegates, and a representative of employers and workers.[39] Further, it is possible to understand IOs as sites or spaces[40] with 'a designated arena where various governmental and nongovernmental participants compete and cooperate'.[41] There is a mix of actors that attend the meetings of these international bodies, such as NGOs and other civil society actors, whether as invitees, lobbyists or protestors.[42] Besides being hybrid organisations merely because of the mixture in membership, IOs are hybrid through informal acts of participation; they witness the influence of and engagement with a plurality of actors. In the next section, the hybridity framework of membership and participation will be used to consider whether the UNHRC is a hybrid international body.

United Nations Human Rights Council

The UNHRC is the principal human rights body of the UN. There are three Council Sessions a year, with the option to hold Special Sessions, and the process of Universal Periodic Review considers the human rights records of forty-eight states a year. The UNHRC is a 'forum for dialogue',[43] it provides a necessary space for information sharing on international human rights and, importantly, this dialogue involves not just states, but also NGOs.[44] The membership in the UNHRC consists only of UN Member States.[45] NGOs and other civil society actors do not have membership at the UNHRC, so under a narrower definition of a hybrid IO based on membership, the UNHRC would not be seen as hybrid. However, the extent of participation provided for in the UNHRC mandate exposes multiple instances and mechanisms of hybridisation.

The UNHRC can be described as a hybrid body because of the involvement of 'States that are not members of the Council, the specialized agencies, other intergovernmental organizations and national human rights institutions', as well as individuals as Special Rapporteurs or Independent Experts and the participation of NGOs.[46] The participation of NGOs is provided in Article 71 of the UN Charter, which states that ECOSOC 'may make suitable arrangements for consultation with non-governmental organisations'.[47] The arrangements were set out in ECOSOC Resolution 1996/31 and subsequently adopted by the UNHRC,[48] meaning that NGOs have to apply for consultative status before they can participate at the UNHRC. There are two main types of consultative status that can be granted: general and special. General consultative status means 'organizations that are concerned with most of the activities of the Council', while special consultative status applies to 'organizations that have a special competence in, and are concerned specifically with, only a few of the fields of activity covered by the Council'.[49] An NGO has either general consultative status or special consultative status, according to its expertise, and this consultative status allows written and oral submissions by the NGOs.[50]

The involvement of NGOs is further buttressed through the procedures and processes set out in the UNHRC Institution-Building Package. This states that participation should include 'all relevant stakeholders, including non-governmental organizations and national human rights institutions'.[51] Indeed, emphasis is placed on NGOs because of their important role in the protection of human rights as stated in the preamble of the UNHRC mandate, which '[acknowledges] that non-governmental organizations play an important role at the national, regional and international levels, in the promotion and protection of human rights'.[52]

In this sense, the UNHRC can be seen as a hybrid IO because of its mechanisms for NGO participation. The UNHRC has previously been conceptualised as a 'Third Space', as it provides for interaction between states.[53] Yet, the UNHRC also facilitates 'non-linear and multi-directional'[54] interactions between diverse NGOs[55] and between NGOs and other actors including individuals, state delegates and political elites. It is thus not just a 'Third Space' for states, but for a plurality of actors. In the next section, hybridity is used to highlight how this hybridisation facilitates participation of other, often excluded, actors.

Non-governmental organisations

Focusing on the hybrid outcome, such as a hybrid organisation, a hybrid government or regime,[56] overlooks the hybrid nature of the actors involved in the hybridisation processes. This is an important aspect because of the spaces these hybrids create for increased participation.[57] This section considers the extent to which NGOs at the UNHRC encourage acts of informal participation. The hybrid nature of the UNHRC and the involvement of NGOs, leads to a further process of hybridisation as they facilitate the involvement of more actors. First, the creation of NGO networks can facilitate the participation of NGOs that do not have consultative status. NGOs without consultative status would usually be excluded, but through networks they get some access to participation. Second, NGOs generate space for the participation of individuals.

The ECOSOC Resolution 1996/31 allows for the submission of written statements by NGOs.[58] In practice, at the UNHRC, joint statements are submitted by coalitions of NGOs. For example, at the 27th Council Session, a joint written statement was submitted on 'The Rights of the Child in Family Environments'.[59] This coalition included two global NGOs with general consultative status, Save The Children International and World Vision International, but it also involved smaller NGOs with special consultative status. In addition, a number of NGOs without consultative status could be heard. A footnote to the joint statement states that Child Rights International Network (CRIN), Defence for Children International – Costa Rica, Eurochild Global Initiative to End All Corporal Punishment of Children, and Truth and Reconciliation for the Adoption Community of Korea (TRACK), which are 'NGO(s) without consultative status, also share the views expressed in this statement'.[60] NGO networks and coalitions have facilitated the participation of NGOs that would otherwise have been excluded from the debates and discussions. NGOs that are 'outside' the formal participation mechanisms become part of the process. The UNHRC is thus not just a 'Third Space' for states with membership, but also allows for the participation of excluded actors.

NGOs create spaces for individual actors to take part in the dialogue within the UNHRC. In 2013 and 2014, the UNHRC heard oral statements from individuals who were invited by NGOs to speak. These individuals included: Rachel Fraenkel, a mother of a man kidnapped in Israel, invited by UN Watch to speak at the 26th Council Session,[61] representatives from the European Union of Jewish Students,[62] and the daughter of the Chinese political leader Wang Bingzhang.[63] Facilitating their access to the UNHRC does not mean that these individuals are truly participating in decision-making,[64] but it does challenge the view that states are the only actors in international decision-making.

In this section of the chapter, the empirical aspect of hybridity has been used to highlight the plurality of actors and the combination of informal practices that are used by NGOs to influence proceedings at the UNHRC. The evidence of hybrid IOs at the international level and the further hybridisation that takes place within the UNHRC challenges the dominant narrative that states are the sole subject in international decision-making.

This merely empirical use of hybridity exhibits limitations, however, as it risks overlooking the power dynamics between these different actors at the UNHRC.[65] Rosa Freedman documents the speech given by Mr Gibreil Hamid, a refugee from Darfur, to the UNHRC in 2008.[66] She critically noted that, as Mr Hamid talked of killings, bombs, fires and gang rape, the state delegates within the Council continued their conversations.[67] This instance of inattention at the UNHRC highlights the underlying power dynamics between states and non-state actors in international decision-making. It is these power dynamics and the reaction of states to the participation of NGOs that will be explored in the next part of this chapter, using the more critical element of hybridity.

Role of NGOs in international decision-making

The importance placed on NGO participation in the UNHRC mandate and the Institution-Building Package raises a question about the nature of the relationship between NGOs and states in practice. Hybridity, or the mixture of two entities to create a third entity, rarely, if ever, implies 'parity'.[68] Rather, the critical aspect of hybridity highlights the disguised power dynamics within hybrids.[69] It is this more critical aspect that can be used to uncover the place of power in international decision-making.

NGOs and states are not treated equally at the UNHRC. One such example is the politicisation of the state-led process for obtaining NGO consultative status. This specific criticism falls outside of this discussion on the relations between these entities at the UNHRC, but has been highlighted elsewhere.[70] The relationship between NGOs and states is often discussed in the literature using legal, doctrinal and linguistic analysis. Scholars use the terminology from Article 71 of the UN Charter and ECOSOC Resolution 1996/31 to consider the role of NGOs. This part of the chapter will consider this latter approach to NGO engagement at the UNHRC and subsequently show that using hybridity can help to develop a more nuanced approach to the power relations characterising interaction between states and NGOs. Then it will consider this complex relationship by exploring the types of NGO participation and how NGOs and states interact at the UNHRC.

The status of NGOs

Traditionally in international legal scholarship, states are the lawmakers and non-state actors have a subsidiary role. The language of the UN Charter is suggestive of a subsidiary role for NGOs. Although there is no definition of NGO in the Charter, Dianne Otto has emphasised that the Charter understands NGOs as '*not* governmental organizations'.[71] She has argued that this negative definition highlights the negative position of states towards NGOs and their attempt to place NGOs at the peripheries of international decision-making.[72] Paragraph 18 of ECOSOC Resolution 1996/31 confirms that the nature of participation of NGOs is more limited than the participation of states. The scope for NGO participation is further limited as Article 71 confines 'consultation to the areas covered by ECOSOC'.[73] These provisions seem to confirm a view within public international law that states are the primary actors in international decision-making and the role of NGOs is secondary.[74]

A more flexible approach to understanding the role of NGOs was developed in the linguistic analysis of these legal instruments. Scholars have explored the role of NGOs by using a range of descriptors for NGOs. There has been a shift in the way NGOs are described and some have suggested that this invokes a change in the relationship between states and NGOs.[75] Whereas initially NGOs had 'consultative status', there is a shift in favour of discussing 'partnerships' between states, IOs and NGOs.[76] Peter Willetts notes that 'the term *consultative status* was deliberately chosen to indicate a secondary role'.[77] 'Consultation' implies advice giving, rather than the NGOs being part of the decision-making process.[78] This consultative role can be seen to reinforce the state-centric nature of international decision-making. Placing NGOs in partnership with states could invoke equality;[79] it is suggestive of 'power sharing [and] cooperative arrangements'.[80] Yet, this does not go as far as a 'model of mutuality', where 'non-state actors benefit from the same power as subjects of international law in the formulation and implementation' of law.[81] Moreover, it is not clear whether this rhetorical device of 'partnership' is 'disguis[ing] entrenched power relations'.[82]

Hybridity, used as a critical analytical lens, can be applied to unpack this relationship. Whilst the formal status of NGOs suggests that non-state actors are not equal to states, the next section will show that the extent to which NGOs can influence the agenda or draft resolutions in the UNHRC suggests that there are significant spaces for the participation of non-state actors.

Participation at the UNHRC

NGOs can participate in formal mechanisms, as outlined in the UNHRC mandate and Institution-Building Package, but hybridity (as a lens that investigates how two entities interact) uncovers the informal channels of participation. The formal mechanisms of written and oral submissions are restricted in respect of word length or time, limiting the space for participation. In contrast, understanding the UNHRC as a 'Third Space' uncovers spaces in which NGOs can influence states. Hybridity 'reshapes the terms of the binary'[83] between subject and object to highlight not only the role of participation, but also the role of informal participation, in discussing the actors in international decision-making.

When it comes to the formal mechanisms, the ECOSOC procedures and the Institution-Building Package restrict the participation of NGOs at the UNHRC. ECOSOC Resolution 1996/31 even outlines the length of written submissions depending on the nature of the status granted to the NGO: general consultative status allows 2,000 word submissions and special consultative status allows only 500 words for submissions to the ECOSOC, and 1,500 words to other subsidiary bodies.[84] The UNHRC modalities of the different formats of debate outline how an NGO should participate, often restricting the types of comments that can be made.[85] In contrast, for the Universal Periodic Review, 'relevant stakeholders will have the opportunity to make general comments'.[86] There is limited time given for NGO oral submissions; two or three minutes depending on the type of proceeding and even this can be reduced if Member States overrun in their submissions. Furthermore, when they observe UNHRC proceedings in Room XX at the Palais des Nations or have to give oral submissions, NGOs have to take seats at the back of the room, behind the state delegates. This symbolic conceptualisation of NGOs as marginal, peripheral or secondary is further highlighted as state delegates talk at the back of the room or use their mobile phones during the time allocated to NGOs.[87]

Whilst the formal mechanisms for participation are thus restricted, there are mechanisms in place that enhance NGO participation, in particular the use of video. Recently, the UNHRC introduced using video messages for oral submissions so that NGOs can send in their comments without paying for a trip to Geneva.[88] This provides for an opportunity to enhance both the geographical representation and the plurality of the NGOs that take part in Council sessions. Although the time available will still be limited, this change to increase participation is suggestive of the importance of NGOs to the UNHRC.

Despite the restrictions to their submissions, NGOs are participating at the UNHRC using informal mechanisms. For example, NGOs are involved in the drafting process of resolutions,[89] often through informal lobbying.[90] At the 17th Council Session held in 2011, Resolution 17/19 on 'Human rights, sexual orientation and gender identity' was discussed. ARC International stated that they 'worked closely with activists in South Africa, Geneva and elsewhere to encourage the South African delegation to consider more positive language in the resolution'.[91] This coalition of NGOs and states shows a collaborative relationship: 'NGOs were consistently given the opportunity to make interventions, and to provide suggestions on the text, and South Africa carefully considered all suggestions, by States and NGOs alike'.[92] In this portrayal of the drafting of Resolution 17/19, NGOs are treated as equal partners. The Serpentine Bar, where state delegates, NGO representatives and political elites gather, mingle and discuss the UNHRC proceedings is a 'Third Space' that facilitates interactions and creates space for participation. It is in these informal spaces that NGOs are able to influence the agenda of human rights protection.

Whilst the more formal mechanisms for participation place NGOs at the peripheries, this cooperative relationship between states and NGOs in

Resolution 17/19 and the informal lobbying shows that there are spaces for NGOs to participate as equals at the UNHRC. Taken together, the formal and the informal practices show a nuanced power dynamic. Yet, it is states that have the final say at the UNHRC because only states vote on resolutions. Hybridity, in its critical sense, highlights the power dynamics between entities; it uncovers practices that challenge perceived views of the place of NGOs, even if states appear to dominate proceedings.

Conclusion

The role of NGOs in international decision-making has been reluctantly acknowledged in international legal scholarship.[93] Yet, questions remain as to how to measure their role.[94] This chapter has shown that hybridity can be used in an empirical sense to collect evidence of the plurality of actors in international decision-making. Using a two-part framework of membership and participation, this chapter conceptualised the UNHRC and NGOs as hybrid bodies. The hybrid nature of these bodies allowed for more informal participation by actors that would otherwise have been omitted from discussions on international decision-making, such as some smaller NGOs and individuals. This highlighted the plurality of different actors that are participating in international decision-making and thus challenged the state-centricity narrative in international law.

In addition to this empirical aspect of hybridity, hybridity has a more critical aspect that was used to unpack the power dynamics between different actors at the UNHRC. The legal instruments facilitate some role for NGOs, but they also outline that NGOs are not equal to states in the UNHRC. What this legal, doctrinal and linguistic analysis cannot conceptualise is the informal participation undertaken by NGOs. Using hybridity, this chapter uncovered and acknowledged the importance of the informal spaces of NGO participation. Despite the restrictions of the formal mechanisms of participation, there is potential for genuine NGO engagement and influence at the UNHRC.

Remaining questions for international legal scholars are the effect of NGO participation on the legitimacy of international decision-making, and how to hold NGOs accountable.[95] Hybridity as a lens goes some way to address this question by identifying the different actors and discussing their respective roles in international decision-making. In particular, hybridity exposes the complex 'hybrid' nature of the NGO networks, which facilitate the informal participation of NGOs that are omitted from the UNHRC proceedings. However, international legal scholarship has not established criteria for determining the 'constituency' that holds these actors to account.[96] Hybridity as a lens, with both empirical and critical aspects that focus on interactions between entities, does not provide a normative framework with which to demarcate a constituency for international decision-making. In this sense, hybridity is not helpful in deriving statements about the viability or desirability of NGOs' role in decision-making processes, for instance, whether it is reasonable that they lobby in the case of specific countries or groups affected by the respective proceedings. In discussing NGO participation at the UNHRC, the utility of hybridity is thus limited to identifying actors and practices and examining power dynamics between actors to give a more complex picture of the role of NGO participation.

Notes

Special thanks to Law and Global Justice at Durham Law School, for financially supporting a trip to the United Nations Human Rights Council in Geneva in June 2014.

1 The number of NGOs and States that were registered as attending in the Report for the 27th Council Session (8 to 26 September 2014). UNHRC, 'Report of the Human Rights Council on its twenty-seventh session' (22 December 2014), UN Doc A/HRC/27/2.
2 Alan Boyle and Christine Chinkin (2007) *The Making of International Law* (Oxford: Oxford University Press), 43.
3 Charter of the United Nations, 24 October 1945, 1 UNTS XVI, Article 71.
4 Over 3,900 NGOs have ECOSOC consultative status. See also Thomas Davies (2013) *NGOs: A New History of Transnational Civil Society* (London: Hurst).
5 Jean d'Aspremont (2011) 'Conclusion: Inclusive Law-Making and Law-Enforcement Processes for an Exclusive International Legal System', in Jean d'Aspremont (ed.), *Participants in the International Legal System; Multiple Perspectives on Non-State Actors in International Law* (London: Routledge), 425–39, 429.
6 Jörg Kammerhoder (2011) 'Non-State Actors from the Perspective of the Pure Theory of Law', in d'Aspremont, *Participants in the International Legal System,* 54–63.
7 d'Aspremont, 'Conclusion', 431.
8 Note that Jan Nederveen Pieterse (2001) divided hybridity into three claims, theoretical, empirical and normative, in 'Hybridity, So What? The Anti-Hybridity Backlash and the Riddles of Recognition', *Theory, Culture and Society* 18(2–3): 219–45, 238.
9 Jan Nederveen Pieterse (2009) *Globalization and Culture: Global Mélange* (Lanham, MD: Rowman & Littlefield), 120.
10 Kate Parlett (2011) *The Individual in the International Legal System: Continuity and Change in International Law* (Cambridge: Cambridge University Press), 41.
11 Pieterse, 'Hybridity, So What?', 238; Marwan M. Kraidy (2002) 'Hybridity in Cultural Globalization', *Communication Theory* 12(3): 316–39, 334.
12 Steve Charnovitz (2006) 'Nongovernmental Organizations and International Law', *American Journal of International Law* 100(2): 348–72, 362.
13 Dianne Otto (1996) 'NGOs in the UN System: The Emerging Role of International Civil Society', *Human Rights Quarterly* 18(1): 107–41, 110; Zoe Pearson (2004) 'Non-Governmental Organisations and International Law: Mapping New Mechanisms for Governance', *Australian Yearbook of International Law,* 23: 73–103, 73.
14 Boyle and Chinkin, *Making of International Law*; Otto, 'NGOs in the UN System'; Peter Willetts (2000) 'From "Consultative Arrangements" to "Partnership":

The Changing Status of NGOs in Diplomacy at the United Nations', *Global Governance* 6(2): 191–212, 191.

15 Martti Koskenniemi (1991) 'The Future of Statehood', *Harvard International Law Journal* 32(2): 397–410, 397.

16 Aoife O'Donoghue (2013) 'International Constitutionalism and the State', *International Journal of Constitutional Law* 11(4): 1021–45, 1024.

17 Charnovitz, 'Nongovernmental Organisations and International Law', 348.

18 Boyle and Chinkin, *Making of International Law.*

19 Jean d'Aspremont (2011) 'Introduction: Non-State Actors in International Law: Oscillating between Concepts and Dynamics', in d'Aspremont, *Participants in the International Legal System,* 1–21, 2; Lassa Oppenheim (1905) *International Law,* vol. 1 (London: Longmans), 341.

20 Robert McCorquodale (2014) 'The Individual and the International Legal System', in Malcolm Evans (ed.), *International Law* (Oxford: Oxford University Press), 280–308, 281.

21 Ibid. 282: Rosalyn Higgins (1995) *Problems and Process: International Law and How we Use it* (Oxford: Clarendon Press), 50.

22 Kammerhoder, 'Non-State Actors', 54–63.

23 Clive Archer defines an international organisation as 'a formal, continuous structure established by agreement between members, whether government representatives or not, from at least two sovereign states'. Clive Archer (2002) *International Organisations* (London: Routledge), 35.

24 Thomas Sommerer and Jonas Tallberg (2016) 'Transnational Access to International Organizations 1950–2010: A New Data Set', *International Studies Perspectives* 0: 1–20; Jonas Tallberg, Lisa M. Dellmuth, Hans Agné and Andreas Duit (2016) 'NGO Influence in International Organizations: Information, Access and Exchange', *British Journal of Political Science,* first view, 1–26.

25 Sommerer and Tallberg, 'Transnational Access', 2.

26 Ibid.

27 Ibid.

28 Ibid.

29 Ibid. 7.

30 Homi K. Bhabha (1994) *The Location of Culture* (London: Routledge).

31 Paul Routledge (1996) 'The Third Space as Critical Engagement', *Antipode* 28(4): 399–419, 406.

32 See Ian Clark (1998) 'Beyond the Great Divide: Globalization and the Theory of International Relations', *Review of International Studies* 24(4): 479–98, 479; Saskia Sassen (2013) *Deciphering the Global: Its Scales, Spaces and Subjects* (London: Routledge), 6.

33 See Richard Collins (2011) 'Non-State Actors in International Institutional Law: Non-State, Inter-State or Supra-State? The Peculiar Identity of the Intergovernmental Organization', in d'Aspremont, *Participants in the International Legal System,* 311–25, 311.

34 O'Donoghue, 'International Constitutionalism', 1021.

35 *Reparation for Injuries Suffered in the Service of the United Nations* (Advisory Opinion) [1949], ICJ Report, 174. See e.g. International Law Commission, 'Draft Articles on the Responsibility of International Organizations', in *Report of the International Law Commission on the Work of its 63rd Session* (2011), UN Doc A/66/10.

36 O'Donoghue, 'International Constitutionalism', 1024.

37 For example, the International Union for Conservation of Nature (ICUN) has been labelled hybrid because of its members that include government, NGOs, scientists and businesses. See Timo Koivurova (2010) 'Protecting the

Environment or Preventing Military Conflict: Policy Dynamics', *Environment Policy and Law* 40(4): 166–71, 166.

38 John Baylis, Steve Smith and Patricia Owens (2013) *The Globalization of World Politics: An Introduction to International Relations* (Oxford: Oxford University Press), 535.

39 Constitution of the International Labour Organisation, 1 April 1919, Article 1(2); Article 3(1).

40 Zoe Pearson (2008) 'Spaces of International Law', *Griffith Law Review* 17(2): 489–514, 493.

41 Charnovitz, 'Nongovernmental Organisations and International Law', 363.

42 See the role of NGOS in the United Nations Framework Convention on Climate Change at the Rio Earth Summit in 1992. Jessica Mathews (1997) 'Power Shift', *Foreign Affairs* 76(1), 55.

43 UN General Assembly (UNGA), 'Human Rights Council', 3 April 2006, UN Doc Res 60/251, para. 5.

44 Rosa Freedman (2013) *The United Nations Human Rights Council: A Critique and Early Assessment* (London: Routledge), 118.

45 UNGA Res 60/251, paras 7 and 8.

46 Ibid., paras 6 and 11.

47 UN Charter 1945, Article 71.

48 UNGA Res 60/251, para. 11.

49 ECOSOC, 'Consultative Relationship between the United Nations and Non-Governmental Organizations' (25 July 1996), UN Doc Res1996/31, paras 22 and 23.

50 Ibid., paras 29, 30, 32(a) and (b).

51 UNHRC, 'Institution-Building of the United Nations Human Rights Council' (18 June 2007), UN Doc A/HRC/RES/5/1, para. m.

52 UNGA Res 60/251, preamble.

53 Rosa Freedman (2013) 'Third Generation Rights: Is there Room for Hybrid Constructs within International Human Rights Law?', *Cambridge Journal of International and Comparative Law* 2(4): 935–59, 941.

54 E. A. B. Rudman (2011) 'Promoting Conversations in a State-Centric Reality: Queer and Feminist Perspectives on the Consultative Structure Set up by the United Nations under Article 71 of the UN Charter', *South African Yearbook of International Law* 36: 163–82, 167.

55 Karima Bennoune (2012) '"Productive tensions": Women's Rights NGOs, the "Mainstream" Human Rights Movement, and International Lawmaking', in Cecilia M. Bailiet (ed.), *Non-State Actors, Soft Law and Protective Regimes: From the Margins* (Cambridge: Cambridge University Press), 125–50.

56 Bruce K. Rutherford (2008) *Egypt After Mubarak: Liberalism, Islam, and Democracy in the Arab World* (Princeton, NJ: Princeton University Press), 16.

57 See Danielle Beswick in this volume.

58 ECOSOC Resolution 1996/31, para. 30.

59 UNGA, 'Joint written statement submitted by Save the Children International, World Vision International, non-governmental organizations in general consultative status, Groupe des ONG pour la Convention relative aux droits de l'enfant, Defence for Children International, Geneva Infant Feeding Association, International Federation of Social Workers, International Social Service, Plan International, Inc., SOS Kinderdorf International, Terre Des Hommes Federation Internationale, non-governmental organizations in special consultative status' (26 August 2014), UN Doc A/HRC/27/NGO/25.

60 Ibid., 4.

61 Tovah Lazaroff, 'Rachel Fraenkel Tells UNHRC that Kidnapping of her Son is "Every Mother's Nightmare"', *Jerusalem Post*, 24 June 2014, http://www.jpost.

com/Operation-Brothers-Keeper/WATCH-Rachel-Fraenkel-speaks-to-UN-Human-Rights-Council-360357 (accessed August 2014).

62 European Union of Jewish Students, 'Jewish Students Raise their Voice at the UN Human Rights Council', 25 March 2013, http://www.eujs.org/news/press-releases/jewish-students-raise-their-voice-un-human-rights-council (accessed May 2014).

63 'Clash at UN: China Tries to Stop Testimony by Daughter of Jailed Democracy Leader Wang Bingzhang; Democracies Rally to her Defense', *China Aid News*, 19 March 2014, http://www.chinaaid.org/204/03/clash-at-un-china-tries-to-stop.html (accessed May 2014).

64 See Mahdev Mohan (2009) 'The Paradox of Victim-Centrism: Victim Participation at the Khmer Rouge Tribunal', *International Criminal Law Review* 9(5): 733–75, 750.

65 Kraidy, 'Hybridity in Cultural Globalization', 318.

66 Rosa Freedman (2014) *Failing to Protect: The UN and the Politicisation of Human Rights* (London: Hurst), p. xiii.

67 Ibid.

68 Pieterse, 'Hybridity, So What?', 224.

69 Kraidy, 'Hybridity in Cultural Globalization'; Steven L. Arxer (2008) 'Addressing Postmodern Concerns on the Border: Globalization, the Nation-State, Hybridity, and Social Change', *Tamara Journal of Critical Organisation Inquiry* 7(1/2): 179–99, 196.

70 Kerstin Martens (2004) 'Bypassing Obstacles to Access: How NGOs are Taken Piggy-Back to the United Nations', *Human Rights Review* 5(3): 80–91, 84; Peter Willetts (2006) 'The Cardoso Report on the UN and Civil Society: Functionalism, Global Corporatism, or Global Democracy?', *Global Governance* 12(3): 305–24, 317.

71 Otto, 'NGOs in the UN System', 107.

72 Ibid. 110.

73 Ibid. 109.

74 Parlett, *The Individual in the International Legal System*, 41.

75 Willetts, 'From "Consultative Arrangements" to "Partnership"', 191.

76 Pearson, 'Non-Governmental Organisations and International Law', 89.

77 Willetts, 'From "Consultative Arrangements" to "Partnership"', 191.

78 Ibid.

79 Ibid. 192.

80 Kenneth Anderson (2000) 'The Ottawa Convention Banning Landmines, the Role of International Non-Governmental Organizations, and the Idea of International Civil Society', *European Journal of International Law* 11(1): 91–120, 109.

81 Makene Moïse Mbengue (2011) 'Non-State Actors in International Environmental Law: A Rousseauist Perspective', in d'Aspremont, *Participants in the International Legal System*, 372–89, 381.

82 Pearson, 'Non-Governmental Organisations and International Law', 90.

83 Amar Acheraiou (2011) *Questioning Hybridity, Postcolonialism and Globalization* (London: Palgrave Macmillan), 93.

84 ECOSOC Resolution 1996/31, para. 31(d) and (e) and 37(e).

85 See e.g. Office of the High Commissioner for Human Rights, 'A Practical Guide for NGO Participants: United Nations Human Rights Council', February 2013, http://www.ohchr.org/Documents/HRBodies/HRCouncil/PracticalGuideNGO_en.pdf (accessed March 2016). For Interactive Dialogues on Special Procedures, presentations should 'relate to reports under consideration or to the [Special Procedures] mandate'. Similarly, for Interactive Dialogues with High Commissioner for Human Rights, NGOs should relate their presentations to the reports, updates or High Commissioner's mandate.

For General Debates, the NGO should discuss the relevant Agenda Item that is under consideration.

86 Human Rights Council (HRC) Resolution 5/1, 'Institution-Building Package', para. 31.

87 Rosa Freedman, *UNHRC*, p. xiv.

88 Office of the High Commissioner for Human Rights (2015) 'NGO Participation in the Human Rights Council', http://www.ohchr.org/EN/HRBodies/HRC/Pages/NgoParticipation.aspx (accessed June 2015).

89 Charnovitz, 'Non-Governmental Organisations and International Law', 349.

90 See Jens Steffek (2013) 'Explaining Cooperation between IGOs and NGOs: Push Factors, Pull Factors, and the Policy Cycle', *Review of International Studies* 39(4): 993–1013, 993.

91 ARC International (2015) '17th session of the Human Rights Council', accessed 31 January 2015, http://arc-international.net/global-advocacy/human-rights-council/hrc17 (accessed January 2015).

92 Ibid.

93 d'Aspremont, 'Conclusion', 428.

94 Ibid. 429.

95 Holly Cullen and Karen Morrow (2001) 'International Civil Society in International Law: The Growth of NGO Participation', *Non-State Actors and International Law* 1(1): 7–39, 15, 29; d'Aspremont, 'Conclusion', 428.

96 Ronald Tinnevelt and Thomas Mertens (2009) 'The World State: A Forbidding Nightmare of Tyranny? Habermas on the Institutional Implications of Moral Cosmopolitanism', *German Law Journal* 10: 63–80, 77. See also Neil Walker (2008) 'Beyond Boundary Disputes and Basic Grids: Mapping the Global Disorder of Normative Orders', *International Journal of Constitutional Law* 6(3–4): 373–96, 391; Aoife O'Donoghue (2014) *Constitutionalism in Global Constitutionalisation* (Cambridge: Cambridge University Press), 54–86.

Part II

Hybridity in history and culture

Chapter 6

From Romanised subject to sophisticated code-switcher

The formation of thought on hybridity and the spread of Roman culture

Gareth Sears

Introduction

The study of the Roman world, and in particular the incorporation of subject peoples into the political and cultural ambit of Rome, has long been concerned with how native peoples reacted to the Roman habitus, how they used what can be called the Roman material culture and whether, in effect, hybrid cultures were produced. The last century and a half has seen considerable evolution of thought on the exact processes of acculturation by which native populations became more 'Roman' with, in general, a move away from a model where Rome imposed Roman culture onto the conquered to much more nuanced models that see, certainly, the evolution of hybrid cultures but also an appreciation of the ways that individuals and communities could adopt different cultural stances in different situations. Romanists have thought a lot about the process which was, and often still is, referred to as Romanisation (although some are more squeamish than others about the term for reasons that I will explain below) and lessons drawn from these debates should be useful for any field where hybridity has become a concern. Roman studies have also come to benefit from analyses in other fields regarding hybridity or identity studies, with 'hybridity' or 'hybridisation' often being used in place of Romanisation to better describe cultural interactions. This chapter will examine the evolution of ideas about Romanisation and the application of other models of cultural hybridity to the Roman world, problematise them and provide examine the way in which such models can be applied to epigraphic culture, language and acculturation and particularly through one case study – the cult of the god Ba'al Hammon/Saturn – and its construction by the urban populations of the region.[1]

The vexed problem of Romanisation

Romanisation has been the dominant paradigm since Mommsen coined the term 'Romanising', with regard to the civilising mission of Rome in his *Romische Geschichte*, and Haverfield renamed it 'Romanisation' in his work on Roman Britain.[2] For both, the Roman takeover of the Western Mediterranean was followed by the imposition of Roman culture. Colonies from Colchester in Britain to Timgad in modern Algeria should be microcosms of Rome: with their fora, temples, grid-plans, baths and amphitheatres they were supposed to be mini-Romes with plans for emulation by other communities. Those who acquiesced to being Romanised had made a conscious decision on the value of being Roman and adopting Roman ways of doing things, becoming more civilised in the process. Their usage of Roman material goods gave them the feeling, the spiritual sense, of being Roman. The touchstone text for this model was Tacitus' *Agricola*, written at the end of the first century CE and describing the activities of the writer's father-in-law as governor of Britain in 77–85 CE. Agricola 'civilised' the British chiefs so that expertise in Latin and the toga became coveted and then: 'Step by step they were led to things which dispose to vice, the lounge, the bath, the elegant banquet. All this in their ignorance, they called civilisation, when it was but a part of their servitude.'[3]

The model described above was the product of academics from European cultures that held their own empires, and their gift of civilisation to the conquered, as an obvious good. In addition, for those empires that held territory in the former Roman empire there were clear links to be made between the beneficence of Rome and French or Italian rule in North Africa. Exploration of Roman remains replete with Latin inscriptions and late antique churches helped to legitimise the present; the colonisers were reclaiming Christian-European lands.[4] The privileging of 'Roman' material, cities, villas and art in the provinces, rather than the 'native' settlements and material culture and the countryside, was a result of this thinking.[5]

Ideally there would be no hybridisation in the Romanisation model. A successful end result would be the production of Romans rather than Romano-Britons or Romano-Africans; Romanisation was simply the process of transforming the imperial subjects into Romans. However, as Hingley points out, even Haverfield recognised that Romanisation was not always uniform, resulting in cultural mixing, and was not always deep.[6] The product of this school of thought can be seen in the clear view of many academic works that the advanced results of the provincial civilisations were the product of 'Romans', not Hispano-Romans for instance, despite the fact that most scholars could recognise that immigration to the provinces from Italy was limited.

Romanisation was not the only model during the first half of the twentieth century. Collingwood, in the 1920s and 1930s,[7] for instance, saw a fusion, albeit imperfect and failed, that created a Romano-British culture. Yet it was not until the aftermath of the European colonial adventure that attacks on a state-driven Romanisation of grateful, passive, natives started in earnest.[8] In the 1960s and 1970s academics, particularly from the Maghreb, began to address the character of native–Roman interaction in Africa.[9] Bénabou, for instance, pointed to evidence of physical, cultural and religious resistance to Rome.[10] The postcolonial reaction returned agency to the indigenous population but also pointed to the works of the colonial era that played down the scale of revolts and any continuity with the pre-Roman period. Instead of a Roman-inspired cultural package that had led to the creation of a Romanised society which the native populations (apart from those on the barbarian fringes of the provinces) accepted, more or less passively, resistance and cultural permanence of the native population was emphasised.

Postcolonial studies provided a necessary corrective to the earlier reconstructions of Roman Africa. As was recognised early on though, such postcolonial approaches, just as those that emphasised the Roman at the expense of native, preserved a clear dichotomy of Roman and native, of Romanisation or resistance.[11] Two defined cultures are often still seen as acting in opposition to each other. In reality, different communities and individuals reacted to Roman rule and culture in much more nuanced ways depending on, for instance: social position, gender, pre-existing power structures, circumstance and what they felt was most beneficial to them at a particular moment.[12] Important here is the difficulty in reading literary material. For instance, even if Apuleius, writing a Greek-influenced Latin novel at the end of the second century CE, was being accurate in describing himself and the heritage of his home-town, Madauros, as half-Numidian and half-Gaetulian (so fully 'native') this should not mean that he did not also conceive of himself as Roman, a citizen of the Roman empire.[13] His mockery of other Africans who could not speak Latin properly goes some way to demonstrating the complexity of Romano-African identities in the second century.[14]

Apuleius demonstrates the problem of defining ethnicity in the ancient world. That question is now, essentially, at the heart of all examinations of the process of cultural change, of cultural hybridisation, in the conquered regions of the Roman empire. Romanists are no longer as secure in their sense of the 'Roman' as were Haverfield or Mommsen.[15] There was a clear legal definition of a Roman citizen and individuals and communities could become citizens. What made a person, an object, or belief 'Roman' is far less clear and was mutable and negotiable depending on context;[16] the Romans themselves changed over time and adopted non-Roman ideas and objects. So, for instance, although the Latin colonies in Italy of the fourth and third century BCE can be seen as quintessentially Roman in the respect that they were founded by the Republican state in order to control territory, there were clearly both 'Roman' and 'Greek' ideas at play in their planning and conception; Republican Rome was itself heavily influenced by the architecture and organisation of eastern cities such as Alexandria, Phillipi and Antioch.[17] So when Romans founded cities in Spain from the second century BCE, and local populations were influenced by them, they were not unproblematically 'Romanising' but were taking on wider central and east Mediterranean practices; communities in Africa and Spain had also been directly influenced by Phoenician colonisation from at least the eighth century BCE.[18] Indeed, in the immediate aftermath of the Roman conquest of Carthaginian territories in Africa and Sardinia, the existing populations continued to employ elements of Punic (the culture of the Carthaginians and other Phoenician colonies) material culture and religious ideas in their communities, or undertook new usages of Punic culture, rather than simply importing 'Roman' ideas.[19]

The way that Romanisation is conceived has changed, particularly since the 1990s. For most academics Romanisation is no longer an imposition by the state, nor a one-way process. Romanisation now provides a model where individuals took on elements of what could be perceived as 'Roman' culture, whilst maintaining or changing elements of 'native' culture in order to improve materially their lives and also, importantly, it is not seen as precluding the possibility that 'native' ideas could influence 'Roman' culture. Several academics in the early 1990s produced models that changed the paradigm from a 'top-down' process to one driven by local elites who wished to adopt Roman practices and acquire goods to project power and status to their own peoples and neighbouring groups; Roman or Roman-style products then diffused from the elites into wider society.[20] As part of this process 'Roman' culture was adapted by local populations, producing Romano-provincial/sub-provincial hybrid cultures; this is a very different Romanisation to that envisaged by Haverfield.[21]

The continued use of 'Romanisation' as a term has been criticised because of the way that it defines the debate over cultural change through the prism of Rome.[22] Despite such attacks 'Romanisation' remains dominant in much academic discourse. Partly because there is a long history of using it but also because it conveys a sense of a process by which some populations made use of elements of what could be termed 'Roman' culture in order to change their lives or to maintain and improve their status. Romanists in parts of continental Europe also tend to use the term 'Romanisation' more than British scholars, as Rome being the civilised progenitor of their Western European societies is relatively unproblematic.

Developments in thought about cultural interaction and individual/community agency have been influenced, in recent decades, by social scientists such as Giddens and Bourdieu.[23] The importance given to community agency and the multi-faceted nature of identity has contributed to a move beyond Romanisation or resistance to examinations of communities who were using elements such as Latin epigraphic practice, something far more sophisticated than simple emulation or rejection of Rome.[24] These approaches to identity often using the language of hybridity have moved away from the simple binary opposition of native/Roman seen in both traditional and postcolonial analyses of Roman occupied regions.[25] An example of the more nuanced approaches to cultural change and hybridisation can be seen in the study of linguistic 'code-switching'.[26] Such studies have shown that different languages employed on the same inscription could convey different information, appropriate to the linguistic culture. So, whilst the steady increase in the use of Latin in inscriptions, first alongside Punic in some cities, could show hybridisation, and even Romanisation, interpretations have developed over time. First it has been noted that Punic was used in private settings for much longer than in public ones, suggesting that sophisticated choices were being made about when to employ a particular language.[27] Then it is clear that some bilingual inscriptions, for instance at Lepcis Magna, have standard Roman titles, such as consul or holding tribunician power, in the Latin text, but in the Punic the sense of the terms is conveyed – so head of the army and having the power of the ten rulers respectively; in others imperial titles only appear in the Latin text; some inscriptions also reveal individuals appearing with different names in the Punic and Latin.[28] Such usage appears to be the product of intertwined ideologies – the desire among the local elite to appeal to the Roman state, and to show their cultural power as wielders of Latin, but also to assert their heritage to each other and the general populace of the city. Although such an individual might seek to display different versions of their identity in different situations these identities cannot be held totally separate; they inform each other. It is worth noting though that, whilst there is a clear desire to preserve Punic script and Punic names on bilingual building inscriptions, the very act of putting up a building inscription is clearly aping a Roman cultural practice. Carthaginian period texts had been, as far as we can tell, largely focused on religious dedications.[29] Thus, these decisions, although complex in generation and impact, can be seen as producing a hybrid epigraphic culture.[30] It is worth noting that these bilingual hybrid forms only existed for a relatively short time until being abandoned for Latin-only texts.

Case study: the cult of Saturn and Caelestis

In this section I want to show how hybridity and the other issues discussed above might be approached by examining the way that the cults of Ba'al Hammon/Saturn changed in Roman Africa.[31] Africa is, in many ways, the ideal place to test the arguments outlined in the previous section given its centrality to the postcolonial reaction against simple 'Romanisation' and the quality of the evidence in terms of archaeology, literature and epigraphy for the region. This is not withstanding the privileging of 'Roman' cultural artefacts such as literary texts and cities rather than rural sites. This section will argue that, whilst the cults were not static and did come to incorporate elements that might be considered 'Roman', there are more interesting ways of reading the material connected to the ambitions and needs of elite and non-elite urban actors alike than readings of 'Romanisation' or even hybridity.

Ba'al Hammon and his consort Tanit were the supreme deities of the Carthaginian pantheon.[32] It was to the two that Roman and Greek authors alleged the Carthaginians sacrificed humans, particularly children.[33] The deities had multiple open-air sanctuaries, often in places situated at high altitude, with votive inscriptions set up to them by their devotees. In addition there were the *tophets*, or child cemeteries, where deposition of burnt new-borns in urns sometimes also incorporating animal and bird bones (as offerings, as substitutions of some sort), was practised under the auspices of the gods.[34]

During the Roman period the deities were equated to Roman gods – Ba'al to Saturn and Tanit to Caelestis.[35] The adoption of Roman names for the gods happened through a gradual process. The earliest usage of Saturn appears in the first century BCE, but Ba'al continued to be used in some cities into the second century CE.[36] An early example of the use of Saturn for the god can be seen on a stela from the Tarhuna plateau in modern Libya. Here the neo-Punic script names the god Ba'al whilst the Latin names the god *Sapurnus* (sic).[37] Just as with human names the deities' names given in the neo-Punic and the Latin are not transliterations but reflect different naming strategies in the two languages; there is only one preserved attempt to render Ba'al into Latin characters.[38]

During the first three centuries CE some open-air sanctuaries dedicated to Ba'al and Tanit were replaced with 'Roman'-style temples with statues of the deity within the shrine and an altar placed before the temple. At Thugga (Dougga) and Thuburnica (Sidi-Ali-Bel-Kassem) temples were built during the second century CE alongside pre-existing sanctuaries, although the exact chronology of these changes, and whether the sites saw lapses in use, is often unclear.[39] Other purpose-built temples, for instance at Thamugadi (Timgad), do not appear to have been built over sanctuaries but incorporated, as did many Romano-African temples, large courtyards where stele were deposed. However, not all Roman period sanctuaries to the gods were temple structures. Perhaps the most famous open-air sanctuaries are those of Saturnus Balcaranensis on the Djebel Bou Kourneïn (the Mountain of the Two Horns), across the bay from Carthage, and the complex at Thinissut (Bir Bou Regba), which were built and developed as open-air sanctuaries with small shrines until their abandonment.[40]

The deposition of stele to the gods in the sanctuaries of the Roman period was not a static, unchanging rite. Some incorporated Latin text and over time increasing numbers incorporated the divine epithets of Roman gods; most stele, as with those of the Punic period, remained anepigraphic. Over time the depictions of Saturn, dedicants and offerings became more 'classical' in style, although Punic signs such as the 'Sign of Tanit' (a stylised female figure[41]) or other earlier symbols remained in use for some time. Many academics have read the dedicators as coming from the lower ranks of the Romano-African population, partly because of a lack of inscriptions, but also because where names of dedicants are included they often do not bear the *tria nomina* (the three elements of a Roman name, praenomen, nomen and cognomen – for instance, Caius Iulius Caesar) of Roman citizens; where elites were involved they were of African origin.[42] Imperial officials rarely dedicated stele or built temples to Saturn or Caelestis and the worship of Saturn does not appear to have been incorporated into the official pantheon of Roman colonies such as the refounded Carthage.[43]

Academics have emphasised different elements and come to different conclusions about the developments described above. Some emphasised Romanisation and argued that elites – whether of Roman, non-Roman or mixed descent – wanted to maintain the cults but adapted them to Roman understandings of religion.[44] Many academics have stressed considerable continuity despite Romanisation across the Punic and Roman periods, with Hurst, in his recent study of the Roman era structures in the *tophet* area of Carthage suggesting that Roman temples to deities connected to Saturn-Caelestis were built on the site by the late second century CE.[45]

Postcolonialists, for instance Bénabou, argued that much of what is described above shows tacit resistance to the Romans and their pantheon by African elites and non-elites, with elite 'Romans' ignoring the Saturn cult.[46] This does not mean that the postcolonialists entirely rejected the concept of borrowings from 'Roman' culture, nor that they claim easy continuities with the pre-Roman past, but that whilst Africans integrated different ways of expressing religious belief into their cults, the essence was consciously non-Roman.[47] Frend linked both arguments pointing to the Saturn cult as part of a long-term expression of religious belief in the region which also fed into the particular brands of Christianity and Islam expressed there; decline of the cult and its replacement by Christianity was tied to its Romanisation in the early third century.[48] This approach viewed elements of North African society as unchanging and permanent, in itself the problematic descendant of ideas that had African society as passive, waiting to be developed by Rome or France.[49]

As we saw above the dichotomy Romanisation–resistance has proved unfruitful in providing an explanation of change and continuity. Indeed 'continuity' in itself is of limited analytical use.[50] Just like the adoption of new methods of expression, 'continuity' is neither unchanging nor negative, it is a specific decision made by individuals and communities on how their lives, institutions and beliefs are organised, rather than the absence of a decision. Furthermore, as McCarty has pointed out with regard to the cult of Saturn at specific centres such as Thugga or Henchir el-Hami, these 'continuities' with the past are often far less apparent when the archaeological material is examined in detail – cults of the gods are reborn, adjusted or indeed started in the Roman period – some 'continuities' are created.[51]

If the cult of Saturn and Caelestis does not show straightforward continuity with the past and we may suspect narratives of 'Romanisation' or 'resistance', what do we take from Romano-Africans' experience and use of the cults? If we start with the dedicators of stele, temples and other gifts to the gods, whilst there is a clear separation between provincial officials, and the high elite of Roman colonies like Carthage, who did not dedicate to Saturn, and the elites of the cities of Roman Africa who did, the state of our evidence does not allow us to see whether imperial officials did or did not take part in festivals dedicated to Caelestis or Saturn instead of dedicating temples. Certainly the lack of an official space for the deities in the religious hierarchy of these cities did not prevent the construction of large temples in their honour complete, and indeed sometimes replete, with Latin inscriptions in Roman colonies; it is hard to believe that these structures were not important in the religious and psychological landscape of imperial elites, of self-conscious Romans, local Romano-African elites and the poor alike. At Carthage, for instance, by the fourth century CE a street containing many temples had come to be known as the *via Caelestis*, the goddess's temple apparently included a large, Latin, building inscription (according to a late literary source) and the festivals of the goddess appear to have drawn all manner of individuals including the future bishop, Augustine of Hippo, who came from the local elite of a provincial town.[52] Likewise, even if most urban dwellers were not dedicating stele to Saturn with Latin inscriptions they could not have escaped Latin inscriptions in honour of the gods in their towns, nor the festivals to the official gods of the city or in honour of the emperors. Of course individual reactions to all of these elements of 'Roman-ness' might have varied considerably.

Essentially we are seeing different registers of ambition among different groups leading to differential religious expression within a community. There was little to be gained for the high provincial elites or imperial officials in making a link to Saturn. Imperial officials such as provincial governors, who spent a short term of office in Africa before moving on to another posting elsewhere, are unlikely to have understood the centrality of the cult to Romano-African populations and the most powerful provincials were interested in impressing those governors. On the other hand, local elites were embedded in their communities and needed to take a stance both vis-à-vis the latter and vis-à-vis high elites. The non-elites who dedicated anepigraphic stele may not have been literate, so that any text – Punic or Latin - may not have been important compared to the image; prior to the fourth century BCE all stele at Carthage had been anepigraphic anyway.[53] What was important to them was the act of devotion, the place, the people involved, as well as the objects used. Whilst a lack of concern for the Latin text can be seen as resistance, there are reasons to doubt that the people involved in the deposition of the stele would have thought of, subconsciously or consciously, or experienced, the ritual in such binary terms. As was noted above people were increasingly incorporating elements into their devotions that could be described as 'Roman'. The symbols of the cult were increasingly classicising and many stele did include Latin inscriptions; some individuals were making decisions to purchase or commission such 'hybrid' objects – others would have been exposed to them as they deposited their own anepigraphic material.[54] Another important and unknown element is the commissioning process; presumably the dedicant was in some way reliant on the competences of the sculptor, which may not always have included Latin.

Non-elites would also have observed the activities of the local elite and their attempts to maintain their social standing with a complex use of symbols, some of which could be understood as 'traditional' and some 'Roman', if we wished to categorise them in this way. A concentration on Saturn and Caelestis could be seen as an attempt to stress their group's permanence to the general populace and those of other Punic and native cities through their devotion to the ancestral major deities. It could also, however, be seen as accommodating with Roman power either by the non-elites, by the elites themselves or by Roman immigrants or officials by increasingly using Roman names, or as a powerful display of knowledge of Roman-ness – an appeal to cultural cachet. In reality, the response to the 'Romanisation' of the cults would have been complex at both the community and regional level and, in some way, negotiated and agonised over in an attempt to serve the needs of religion, politics and fashion.

How we read Saturn cult and its relationship to hybridity is made more complex by the nature of the spread of the cult. Saturn and Caelestis had not been the ancestral deities for many Africans before the second century BCE, when the spread of *tophets* out of Carthage and a few other coastal cities began; the cult spread further under Roman rule than it had in the Carthaginian period.[55] As McCarthy has shown, some cities appear to have substantial breaks in practice and use of sites dedicated to Saturn in the first two centuries CE. Although McCarthy does not cite it, Carthage itself might show such a pattern as the *tophet* was abandoned following the city's destruction in 146 BCE and then as much as several centuries later, perhaps the second century CE, new temples, possibly to Caelestis and Saturn, were established in the area. What is most interesting about this is not 'continuity' of cult as Wilson has it but the persistence of knowledge at the site that this was sacred to Ba'al/Saturn and Tanit/Caelestis over, potentially, several centuries.[56] It suggests that either the site occupied a key place in the cultural memory of even the reformed Carthage or that, even though not used for a long time, the place had the quality of a 'lieu de mémoire' across time.[57] Even if there had not been continuity of memory at Carthage whereby generations passed knowledge of the meaning of the site down, even if there were substantial breaks, possibly there were exposed Carthaginian stele that could be compared to those of continuously occupied sites.[58] The reuse of a site, after a break, might still be seen by a community as evoking 'continuity' with the past and a return to ancestral values even if there were considerable differences between practices.[59] Over the long term, when there had been a break in practice, considerable external influences from other cults, 'Roman' or otherwise, might have been introduced without this being seen as anything other than traditional; practices were undertaken as seemed appropriate to the religious, political and cultural situation. However the deities were exactly conceived and represented, there was a concern to propitiate the chthonic gods of Africa throughout the Roman period – as Caelestis, Ba'al Hammon, the *Genius Terrae Africae* (the Spirit/Personification of the African soil/land), or a *Dea Patria* (goddess of the country/fatherland). The worship of these deities may have been conceived as harking back to the past, as long-term 'continuity', but was as much to do with present realities – fertility, the success of the city – and these, if we want to think in this way, were the hybrid realities of pre-Roman, eternal spirits of place, Latin inscriptions and built temple complexes.

This section has demonstrated that the archaeological and epigraphic material for the cult of Ba'al Hammon/Saturn does not support simplistic readings of cultural change. Instead, as might be expected given the argument above, the formation and reproduction of each cult at each individual city could be understood in different ways by different groups or individuals, depending on their own needs, experiences and cultural capital.

Conclusions: hybridity and beyond

The Roman interpretation of Ba'al Hammon/Saturn did lead to what we might describe as a hybrid cult drawing on a range of 'Roman', 'pre-Roman' and indeed other Mediterranean styles of art and architecture, nomenclature and so on. The relationship was, of course, complex and 'hybridity', whilst on one level an interesting way of escaping the binary division inherent in some postcolonial approaches to Roman Africa, as well as of looking at the use of a varied palette of rites, deities, spaces, material culture to call (presumably) on divine power, could be limiting if used incautiously as a way of thinking about the construction of cults of Saturn and Caelestis in the first few centuries CE. Catch-all terms such as 'hybridity', 'continuity', 'resistance', 'Romanisation', 'innovation', do not satisfactorily in and of themselves describe all the process of change and developments shown in these cults. A focus on these concepts tends to be reductive. Judging the exact 'Roman'-ness of a community or a response to a particular god does not take us very far.

More interesting is an examination of the motives of those creating, perpetuating and (sub)consciously hybridising the cults. As part of this, comparisons of the exact development of cults at different locations can help to identify differences in approaches to ostensibly the same god and, in doing so, allow the historian or archaeologist to suggest particular motivations for a community. At many African cities we can see the impact of a range of actors – local elites who paid for buildings and dedicants, presumably from across society, who set up stele to the gods. 'Romanisation' and 'hybridity' might provide a way of understanding how the actors created the spaces – both physical and conceptual – but it is not subtle enough in understanding the 'why'. Instead examinations of the range of responses to the gods across and within communities, the nature of individual city cults, and how these were informed by those of other cities (both elites and non-elites would have travelled between cities), need to look at the messages conveyed in the cults, the agency of those involved and the roles that such cults played in urban life.

Notes

1 Gareth M. Sears (2011) *The Cities of Roman Africa* (Stroud: History Press).
2 Theodor Mommsen (1854–85) *Römische Geschichte* [Roman history], vols 1–3 (Leipzig: Reimer & Hirsel), 5; Francis Haverfield (1923) *The Romanization of Roman Britain*, 4th edn (Oxford: Clarendon Press). For discussions of Romanisation and Haverfield see Philip W. M. Freeman (1997) 'Mommsen to Haverfield: The Origins of Studies of Romanization in Late 19th-C Britain', in David J. Mattingly (ed.), *Dialogues in Roman Imperialism: Power, Discourse, and Discrepant Experience in the Roman Empire*, Journal of Roman Archaeology Supplementary Series 23, 27–51; (2007) *The Best Training-Ground for Archaeologists: Francis Haverfield and the Invention of Romano-British Archaeology* (Oxford: Oxbow), esp. 1–42; Richard Hingley (1997) 'The "Legacy" of Rome: The Rise, Decline and Fall of the Theory of Romanization', in Jane Webster and Nick Cooper (eds), *Roman Imperialism: Post-Colonial Perspectives* (Leicester: Leicester Archaeology Monographs 3), 34–8; Hingley (2000) *Roman Officers* (London: Routledge), 111–55; Louise Revell (2009) *Roman Imperialism and Local Identities* (Cambridge: Cambridge University Press), 5–10; David J. Mattingly (2011) *Imperialism, Power, and Identity: Experiencing the Roman Empire* (Princeton, NJ: Princeton University Press), 203–9; Gareth M. Sears (2014) *Cities in the Roman World*, Oxford Bibliographies Project (Oxford: Oxford University Press).
3 Tacitus, *Agricola* 21; translated by A. J. Church and W. J. Brodribb, London 1874.
4 See the attitudes collected in Abdallah Laroui (1970) *L'histoire du Maghreb, un essai de synthèse* (Paris: Maspero), 53; and David J. Mattingly (1996) 'From one Colonialism to Another: Imperialism and the Maghreb', in Jane Webster and Nick Cooper (eds), *Roman Imperialism: Post-Colonial Perspectives* (Leicester: Leicester Archaeology Monographs 3), 49–69. On the use of the Roman past in Italian and German fascism see: Volker Losemann (1999) 'The Nazi Concept of Rome', in Catherine Edwards (ed.), *Roman Presences: Receptions of Rome in European Culture, 1789–1945* (Cambridge: Cambridge University Press), 221–35; Katie Fleming (2007) 'Fascism', in Craig W. Kallendorf (ed.), *A Companion to the Classical Tradition* (Malden, MA: Oxford University Press), 342–54; Massimiliano Munzi (2012) 'Italian Archaeologists in Colonial Tripolitania', *Libyan Studies* 43: 81–110. On Haverfield and the British empire see Hingley, *Roman Officers*, and Freeman, *Best Training-Ground*, 499–535.

5 See Hingley, *Roman Officers*, 150–1, on the privileging of military, villa and major urban sites of Roman Britain before the 1990s over rural sites and small towns. A major factor behind this preference was because dressed stone, inscriptions and mosaics were more impressive to modern eyes than the remains of a wooden round-house.
6 Hingley, *Roman Officers*, 117–19.
7 Robin G. Collingwood (1932) *Roman Britain* (Oxford: Clarendon Press).
8 Mattingly, 'From one Colonialism'; Sears, *Cities of Roman Africa*, 9–10.
9 Marcel Bénabou (1976) *La Résistance Africaine à la Romanisation* (Paris: Maspero); see also Laroui, *L'histoire du Maghreb*. Work on resistance in its myriad forms has also benefited from ideas coming out of 'Subaltern Studies'.
10 Bénabou, *La Résistance*.
11 For example, see C. R. Whittaker (1978) 'Review of "Marcel Bénabou 'La résistance africaine à la romanisation"', *Journal of Roman Studies* 68: 190–2; Yvon Thébert (1978) 'Romanisation et déromanisation en afrique: histoire décolonisée ou histoire inversée?', *Annales: Économies Sociétés Civilisations* 33: 64–82, 76–80.
12 David J. Mattingly (1997) 'Africa: A Landscape of Opportunity', in Mattingly, *Dialogues*, 117–39.
13 Apuleius, *Apology* 24.
14 Ibid. 98.
15 A. Bernhard Knapp and Peter van Dommelen (2010) 'Material Connections: Mobility, Materiality and Mediterranean Identities', in Peter van Dommelen and A. Bernard Knapp (eds), *Material Connections in the Ancient Mediterranean: Mobility, Materiality and Identity* (London: Routledge), 1–18. There has also been a shift away from a simplistic reading of a particular set of objects archaeologically marking off an ethnic group known from literature such as the Goths or Vandals.
16 John C. Barret (1997) 'Romanization: A Critical Comment', in Mattingly, *Dialogues*, 49–64.
17 Alicia Jiménez (2010) 'Reproducing Difference: Mimesis and Colonialism in Roman Hispania', in van Dommelen and Knapp, *Material Connections*, 38–63.
18 Thébert, 'Romanisation', 76; Sears, *Cities of Roman Africa*, 13–30.
19 Serge Lancel (1995) *Carthage: A History* (Oxford; Blackwell), 428–46; Peter van Dommelen (2001) 'Cultural Imaginings: Punic Tradition and Local Identity in Roman Republican Sardinia', in Simon J. Keay and Nicola Terrenato (eds), *Italy and the West: Comparative Issues in Romanization* (Oxford: Oxbow Books), 68–84.
20 One of the clearest expressions of this is Martin Millett (1990) *The Romanization of Britain* (Cambridge: Cambridge University Press), a model where Romanisation was driven by local elites self-Romanising as part of the game of social competition and, from them, elements of Roman culture trickled down to non-elites.
21 Simon J. Keay and Nicola Terrenato (2001) 'Preface', in *Italy and the West*, pp. ix–xii.
22 E.g. David J. Mattingly (1997), 'Introduction', in Mattingly, *Dialogues*, 7–24, 8–11; see also Hingley, *Roman Officers*, arguing that the term should continue to be used to make clear the underlying assumptions surrounding interpretations of cultural change. Webster suggests using 'creolization' to describe the cultural processes in conquered communities; Jane Webster (2001) 'Creolizing the Roman Provinces', *American Journal of Archaeology* 105(2): 209–25.
23 Anthony Giddens (1984) *The Constitution of Society: Outline of the Theory of Structuration* (Berkeley, CA: University of California Press); see Revell, *Roman Imperialism and Local Identities*, 10–15, for an example of the use of structuration theory.

24 Mattingly, *Dialogues*; Jiménez, 'Reproducing Difference'.
25 See Mattingly, *Imperialism, Power, and Identity*, 203–45 and 'discrepant identity' for a similar model; See for instance de Londras, Ch. 4 in this volume on the benefits of the move away from binary oppositions that 'hybridity' allows.
26 James N. Adams (2003) *Bilingualism and the Latin Language* (Cambridge: Cambridge University Press).
27 Sergio Fontana (2001) 'Leptis Magna: The Romanization of a Major African City through Burial Evidence', in Keay and Terrenato, *Italy and the West*, 161–72.
28 E.g. Joyce M. Reynolds and J. B. Ward-Perkins (2009 [1952]) *Inscriptions of Roman Tripolitania*, enhanced electronic reissue by Gabriel Bodard and Charlotte Roueché, http://inslib.kcl.ac.uk/irt2009 (accessed May 2016), 319, 321. See Josephine C. Quinn (2010) 'The Reinvention of Lepcis', in *Meetings between cultures in the ancient Mediterranean: Proceedings of the 17th International Congress of Classical Archaeology*, Rome 22–26 Sept. 2008, *Bolletino Di Archeologia Online*, 52–69; Adams, *Bilingualism*, 213–21.
29 There are very few surviving Punic inscriptions that are not connected to religious practice, but inscriptions such as *Corpus Inscriptionum Semiticarum* I 5510, which commemorates the seizure of Akragas by a Carthaginian army, suggests that there may have been others that were destroyed in antiquity.
30 Sears, *Cities of Roman Africa*, 69–73. This formation of this Romano-Punic epigraphic culture could be seen as a clear example of the construction of a hybrid culture.
31 Beyond the relationship between Latin and pre-Roman languages, which was mentioned above, another key example of hybridity would be the appearance of 'Roman' style buildings and cities in areas that had previously been unurbanised; see Sears, *Cities of Roman Africa*.
32 Ibid. 52–64.
33 Ibid. 18–19. The evidence for child-sacrifice is inconclusive at best.
34 The word *tophet* derives from the description of a place of child sacrifice near Jerusalem (Jeremiah 19: 6) and has been applied to child cemeteries in the Phoenician colonies – there is no evidence that this was what the Carthaginians called the sites, nor incontrovertible evidence that child sacrifice, rather than cremation, took place in them. Bonnet has challenged the distinction between sacred site and cemetery as unreal for Punic religion; Corinne Bonnet (2011) 'On Gods and Earth: The Tophet and the Construction of a New Identity in Punic Carthage', in Erich S. Gruen (ed.), *Cultural Identity in the Ancient Mediterranean* (Los Angeles, CA: Getty Research Institute), 373–87, 378.
35 Usually anyway; some cities chose other Roman deities. For instance the large coastal city of Hadrumetum seems to have linked Ba'al Hammon with Pluto rather than with Saturn – see Alain Cadotte (2007) *La Romanisation des dieux: L'interpretatio romana en Afrique du Nord sous le Haut-Empire* (Leiden: Brill), 333–41.
36 Cadotte, *La Romanisation*, 26–9.
37 *AE* 1980: 900.
38 See Fontana, 'Leptis Magna'; Adams, *Bilingualism*, 213–40. The one known attempt is a dedication by a soldier of the garrison at Carthage who dedicated a stele to the god at Thuburbo Maius, *AE* 1954: 53: 'Consecrated to Balamon Augustus. Marcius Mansuetus, soldier of the first urban cohort, of the century of Kapito, a stationarius, has acquitted his vow with a willing soul.'
39 Marcel Leglay (1961–6) *Saturne Africain: Histoire; Monuments I and II* (Paris: CNRS), 207–20, 276–86; Matthew M. McCarty (2012–13) 'Continuities and Contexts: The Tophets of Roman Imperial-Period Africa', *Studi Epigrafici e Linguistici* 29–30: 12–17; Cadotte, *La Romanisation*, 29, 31–5; Sears, *Cities of Roman Africa*, 57.

40 Leglay, *Saturne Africain*, 32–73, 97–100; Hédi Dridi and Meriem Sebaï (2008) 'De Tanesmat à Thinissut: Nouvelles observations sur l'aménagement d'un lieu culte africain', in *Lieux de cultes: Aires votives, temples, églises, mosquées: IXe Colloque international sur l'histoire et l'archéologie de l'Afrique du Nord*, Tripoli, 19–25 Feb. 2005 (Paris: CNRS), 101–18, 110–15.
41 See the National Bardo Museum, 'A votive stele under the form of the so-called "Tanit" sign', 28 Dec. 2011, http://www.bardomuseum.tn/index.php?option=com_content&view=article&id=113%3Astele-votive-en-forme-du-signe-dit-de-tanit&catid=42%3Apuniques-&Itemid=29&lang=en (accessed May 2016).
42 Leglay, *Saturne Africain*, 401–6; W. H. C. Frend (1952) *The Donatist Church: A Movement of Protest in Roman North Africa* (Oxford: Clarendon Press), 80–3; see also James B. Rives (1995) *Religion and Authority in Roman Carthage from Augustus to Constantine* (Oxford: Oxford University Press), 142 ff. for a more nuanced version of this position.
43 Leglay, *Saturne Africain*, 402; Rives, *Religion and Authority*, 146.
44 E.g. Paul-Albert Février (1976) 'Religion et domination dans l'Afrique romaine', *Dialogues d'histoire ancienne* 2(1): 305–36; Rives, *Religion and Authority*, 146–7; Cadotte, *La Romanisation*.
45 Henry R. Hurst (ed.) (1999) *The sanctuary of Tanit at Carthage in the Roman Period: A Re-interpretation*, Journal of Roman Archaeology Supplementary Series 30, esp. 9–14 and 91–101.
46 Bénabou, *La Résistance*, 334–40, 370.
47 Ibid. 261, 263.
48 Frend, *Donatist Church*, 76–86, 333–6.
49 Cf. *L'histoire du Maghreb*; Mattingly, 'From one Colonialism'.
50 McCarty, 'Continuities and Contexts', and Josephine C. Quinn (2011) 'The Cultures of the Tophet: Identification and Identity in the Phoenician Diaspora', in Gruen, *Cultural Identity in the Ancient Mediterranean*, 388–413, on the *tophets*.
51 McCarty, 'Continuities and Contexts'.
52 Quodvultdeus, *Book of the Promises and Predictions of God* 3.38.44; Augustine, *The City of God*, 2.4 and 26.
53 Hélène Bénichou-Safar (2004) *Le Tophet de Salammbô à Carthage: Essai de Reconstitution*, Collection de l'École Française de Rome, 342 (Rome: École française de Rome); Quinn, 'Cultures of the Tophet', 400.
54 See Sears, *Cities of Roman Africa*, 69–73.
55 Matthew M. McCarty (2010) 'Soldiers and Stelae: Votive Cult and the Roman Army in North Africa', in *Meetings between Cultures in the Ancient Mediterranean, Bolletino Di Archeologia Online*, 1–10.
56 Roger J. A. Wilson (2001) 'Review of J. T. Peña; J. J. Rossiter; A. I. Wilson; C. Wells; M. Carroll; J. Freed; D. Godden, Carthage Papers, and H. Hurst, The Sanctuary of Tanit at Carthage in the Roman Period', *Journal of Roman Studies*, 91: 198–200, 200.
57 Pierre Nora (1997) *Les lieux de mémoire 1* (Paris: Gallimard).
58 Most of Punic Carthage had been levelled when the new Roman colony was constructed in the last decades BCE.
59 McCarty, 'Continuities and Contexts'.

Chapter 7

Hybridity and the ancient western Mediterranean

Phillip Myers

Introduction

The Iberian Peninsula, since antiquity, has been a place of cultural exchange.[1] Within the context of liberal frontiers, ancient Iberian settlements highlight a significant degree of hybridisation, which suggests that interactions between Iberian and eastern Mediterranean peoples created a broader context for cultural homogeneity, rather than specific 'orientalising' or later 'Romanising' effects suggested by previous scholars. Both Greek and Phoenician traders settled port towns on the periphery of Iberia to access the wealth of silver, gold and metals, and introduced eastern images through trade. Greeks from Phocaea and elsewhere also travelled to Iberia to trade for silver, and settled along the coast of Catalonia at Ampurias, following the fall of Phocaea to the Persians in the mid-sixth century BCE. The Phocaeans interacted with a people named the Indecetani, whom they cohabited with, residing first on a small island off the coast, but later moved to the mainland and constructed a *diopolis*, or twin city. Phoenician settlements are seen across the southern Mediterranean coast of Spain, and further Phoenician settlements are found along the Atlantic coast as well, both along the western Spanish and North African coastline. The most prominent Phoenician city in the far western Mediterranean is Gadir (modern Cadiz), and was perhaps the largest of the Phoenician communities in Spain. Gadir was also a *diopolis*, but did not have a hybrid community – Gadir appears as a religious site and the main population was located on the mainland at Castillo de Dona Blanca, named Didyme, or twin city by Strabo.[2]

Within Iberia, the Phoenicians interacted with two primary groups, the Tartessians and the Turdetanians. The silver trade brought great wealth to the Tartessians, a people who lived near Huelva some 80 kilometres west of Seville and northwest from Cadiz were the Phoenicians primary trading partner until the sixth century. The Tartessians were succeeded by the Turdetanians, a large federated tribe that controlled much of the Guadalquivir valley, around Colina de los Quemados (Cordoba), from the sixth to third centuries BCE. In both instances, these economic relationships proved the basis for cultural exchange. With this great wealth came the importation of ideas: art, sculpture, language and technology. The influx of these extra-Iberian aspects began to influence Iberian culture in the art, coinage and fragmentary literary evidence showing a hybridised language. The core argument of this chapter is to address the questions of how contact between Iberian and eastern Mediterranean cultures created hybrid cultures, and how hybridity is viewed by modern scholars. These two questions can be addressed by examining three topics: by considering both the physical evidence of hybridity from Cadiz and Ampurias in tandem with acculturation and identity studies within the scholarly tradition. On the latter topic, the bibliography is vast, and will be addressing a few core concepts such as 'creolisation' and 'orientalisation', which are used in a similar manner to 'Romanisation', a theory which had dominated Roman studies since the late nineteenth century.

One of the major fallacies within acculturation studies is the concept that one culture completely abandons its identity for another. This stems from a theory called 'Romanisation', coined by Theodor Mommsen and was first published in 1885 in the fifth volume of the *Römische Geschichte*. Mommsen's theory attempted to explain Roman empire-building through the transformation of frontiers into provinces, as well as to account for the cultural evolution towards a homogeneous Roman culture.[3] Mommsen's theory imagined a binary relationship between 'civilised' and 'native' groups, with one being inherently superior, which causes the native to appropriate civilised traits, while abandoning native cultural aspects. 'Romanisation' relied heavily on the textual over archaeological evidence.[4] A similar term, 'orientalisation' appeared among Spanish discussions of Phoenician presence in Iberia in the mid-nineteenth century, and is a staple of Phoenician acculturation studies in Spain. 'Orientalisation' follows a similar acculturative process, but has not been extensively debated in contrast to 'Romanisation'.[5] Putting aside the ghost of Mommsen, who does not need to be resurrected for the purpose of public execution, '-isation' acculturation models are problematic because of the presumption of cultural conquest by one group over another.

In contrast to the existing host of acculturation studies formulated by scholars, I would assert that local hybridisation occurred in a local context among Iberian communities with dynamic variation. No single acculturative model has the scope to address all of the variations seen in how Iberian communities reacted to cultural input.[6] This is because *as a process* it is incorrect to assume a desired terminal outcome of cultural contact; Iberians in contact with Greeks and Phoenicians did not become *as them*, but adopted similar traits, and created a compound identity. Reece stated in regards to Roman Britain that the people there, following the Roman conquest 'became more Gaulish, more Rhinelandish, more Spanish, a little more

Italian, a very little more African, and a little more Danubian', recognising that identity is highly complex and evolutionary.[7]

The establishment of permanent Greek and Phoenician communities in southern Iberia has been reconsidered by scholars recently as concepts of colonisation and imperialism have been challenged, along with the form and function of early settlements.[8] The term 'colonisation' will not be applied because the settlements found in the early stages of Phoenician contact with the western Mediterranean do not represent the typical image of the colony; many early settlements were initially developed for trade, and not designed to control territory.[9] Alternatively, the terms 'presence' for Greek settlements, and 'pre-colonisation' have been applied by scholars in relation to Phoenician and Greek communities in an attempt to disengage from the problematic linear acculturation models previously explored in the nineteenth and early twentieth centuries.[10] The 'presence' model suggests that, in the Greek context, the spread of Greek culture in Iberia was spread by traders, rather than by direct colonial contacts. Trade was facilitated by a series of small ports called *emporiae*, while the Phocaeans only had two towns: Emporion and Massalia (Marseille). Evidence of Greek wares is commonly seen through the fourth century BCE in Iberian communities. In contrast, Phoenician 'pre-colonisation' is an extension of 'orientalisation', but creates a conceptual precursor to colonisation, where a cultural affinity emerges. 'Pre-colonisation' correctly identifies that trade contacts did spread culture, however the concept is linked to ideas of imperialism and colonialism, which does not appear to be the case in the pre-third century BCE Iberian experience.

In the case of the Greek and Phoenician period in Spain, the literary evidence is too sparse to create a cohesive image, but the physical evidence emphasises that from the eighth to fifth centuries, the relationships between Iberians, Greeks and Phoenicians were made concrete through the economic relationships. The ancient sources, specifically Herodotus, blended fact and fable in the construction of historical narratives.[11] In contrast, the archaeological evidence shows that indigenous culture did not simply cease to be Iberian, but rather a dynamic organic evolution of cultural traits emerged within the Iberian sphere of influence.

The Greeks in the West: Emporion and hybridity

The first appearance of permanent Greek settlements in the West is in the sixth century at Massalia (Marseille), founded by Phocaeans fleeing the Persian conquest of their home.[12] Emporion was founded shortly after Massalia on the island of San Martin de Ampurias in modern Catalonia. In the mid-sixth century BCE, the city was relocated to the mainland.[13] Emporion was created as a *diopolis* with the Indecetani, a local group of Iberians.[14] Emporion is an interesting case for the study of hybridity because of the inherent political equilibrium, economic cooperation and urban development seen at Emporion and also across the region. Emporion's residents cooperated for mutual security and had an a combined legal system (*politeuma*), but each community had an independent government, and minted their own coinage.[15] The Indecetani coins were issued in bronze asses, whilst the Greek drachma was issued in silver, which indicates that Indecetani coins were used for daily transactions, and the Greek drachma for larger transactions.[16] Many of the Iberian issues are heavily influenced by Greek imagery, and the minting of the high-value drachma may suggest an admiration of Greek identity. Both Iberian and Greek mints persist into the Roman era, which has led some scholars to the conclusion that Rome was responsible for the creation of the *Emporitani Hispani* because the Romans did not see a difference between Greek and Indecetani.[17]

Beyond the physical urban hybrid image is the wider geographical and economic hybridity seen at Emporion. Within the region around Emporion, known as the *chora* or hinterlands, several communities formed during the sixth and fifth centuries, primarily developed for agricultural purposes (Figure 7.1). The site of Mas Castellar de Pontos, a site 20 kilometres northwest of Emporion, was occupied from the fifth to third centuries BCE, and features large pits for agricultural products to be stored.[18]

Several Indecetanian settlements of this nature existed at sites bordering Emporion's presumed territory, suggested by the generally uniform nature of placement of these communities, but this may also have been because of suitable locations for *oppidum*-style settlements.[19] Another aspect of the region of Indecetani settlements is a locally produced and traded greyware pottery, which is seen in every settlement around Emporion, and some far to the north. The images on the pottery were influenced by Greek motifs, but it was produced at nearby Ullastret, a major Indecetani *oppidum* southwest of Emporion. The greyware pottery has been employed to define the Indecetan cultural and economic regions due to small quantities of the pottery found elsewhere beyond this region, which primarily focuses around Emporion and Ullastret. Furthermore, this pottery appears within the fifth to third centuries BCE, and begins to decline in quality around the mid-third century.[20]

The specific cause of this decline is unknown, but speculatively it may be due to the Second Punic War, and ultimately the capture of Emporion in 195 BCE by the Roman consul Cato. The Emporitani are seen by Roman writers as a hybrid community, the residents are referred to as the Spaniards of Emporion (*Emporitani Hispani*). Livy seems to be arguing that resistance to Cato stemmed from the Spaniards of Emporion, but it may be more likely this was a regional resistance, as he references 'aristocrats from other states' seeking shelter at Emporion. As Cato's legion was 'ravaging more widely' Emporion was the only settlement that had erected significant fortifications. The misinterpretation by Livy is that resistance

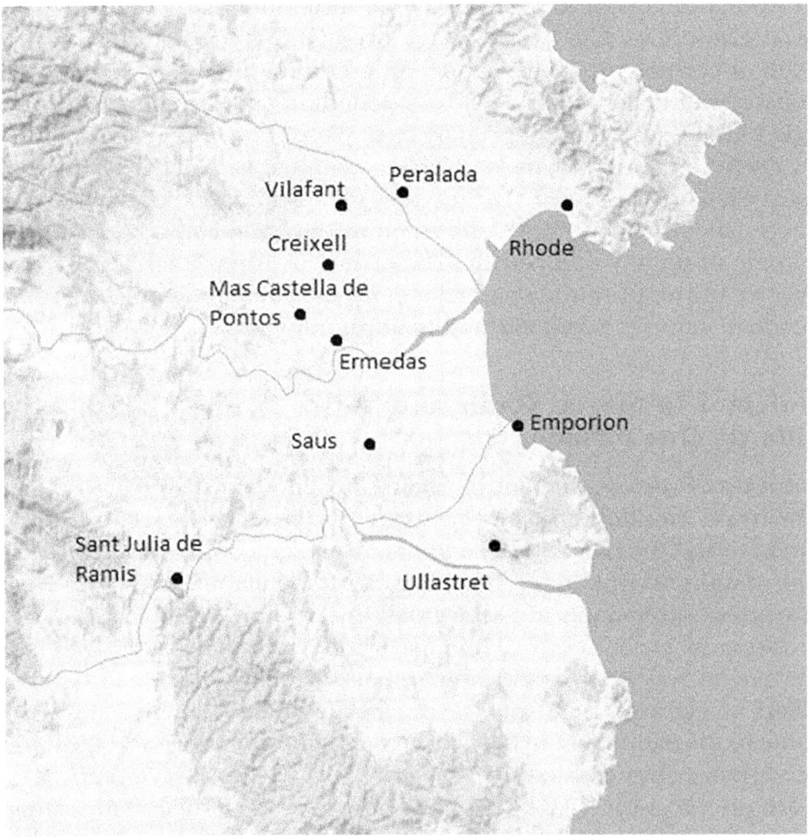

Figure 7.1 Map of the Emporitanian hinterland and Iberian settlements along the *chora*. Emporion and Rhode are Greek settlements, and the Iberian communities are easily identified along the western perimeter.

came only from the Emporitanians, but in reality the resistance included other settlements within the federation. What Livy's statement highlights is that not only was the Emporion-Indecetani relationship an economic and cultural federation, but also a political alliance, emphasising the depth of hybridity in the regional view. Following Cato's capture of Emporion, a building programme was undertaken to enhance the city: the walls were reconstructed, refurbishing existing temples and redeveloping the marketplace (*agora*), with a new addition of Greek-styled housing. Even within this context of increased construction, the rural hinterland still remained largely Iberian through the second century. The evidence indicates that in the Roman period, local identities persisted, as terms such as *Emporitani*

Hispani indicates a deep level of hybridisation of Greek and Iberian culture, so that Romans may not have been able to differentiate between the two groups at Emporion. The hybrid image presented at Emporion provides an excellent perspective on Greco-Iberian acculturation, as Greek identity is negotiated within an Iberian context, highlighting the dynamic nature of the Indecetani. Emporion is a primary example of how two groups cohabited to create a hybrid urban landscape, complete with legal systems to represent each group, while in the broader regional context they formed a cohesive economic network, which is seen in the archaeological evidence in the trade of pottery and cereals. The economic interdependency form an image of a strong cultural regional identity, a fusion between Greek and Indecetanian cultural, economic and political frameworks.

Phoenicians in Iberia: Gadir and Castillo de Dona Blanca

In contrast to Greek settlement in Spain, the Phoenicians created many settlements on the southern coast between the Pillars of Herakles (Straits of Gibraltar) and the Balearics. The Phoenicians settled near native *oppida*, near the mouths of rivers, or on small islands off the mainland (Figure 7.2). These types of settlements are seen in all of the early Phoenician towns. Gadir, the most prominent of Phoenician settlements in the far western Mediterranean, was settled according to tradition on a small island beyond the Pillars of Herakles near the Tartessian kingdom at Huelva. Founded sometime in the eighth century, Gadir served as the primary port-of-call for traders carrying silver east to Carthage and Tyre. The literary references to Gadir are prolific, with several legendary heroes of the Trojan War visiting the far west.[21] Most notable of these heroes was Hercules, who completed his tenth labour stealing the cattle of Geryon.[22] Gadir was located on an island off the coast named Erytheia, with two adjacent islands named Kotinoussa and Antipolis. A coastal Phoenician settlement at Castillo de Dona Blanca (Puerto de Santa Maria) was founded about the same time at the island site and located approximately 10 kilometres northeast of Gadir was the mainland port (Figure 7.3).[23] In this discussion, it is more valuable to examine the impact of Phoenician trade on Iberian communities rather than examining the Phoenician settlements themselves, due to the apparent lack of hybrid elements in Phoenician urbanism. However, evidence indicates that Iberians were receptive to a number of oriental cultural, technological and administrative elements.

All three types of impacts stem from trade. The impact of eastern Mediterranean trade on Iberian culture can be seen in the way that local elites sought out eastern Mediterranean goods for prestige purposes. The bulk of Phoenician trade goods imported were painted pottery in exchange for silver, which is reflected in the rapid development of the

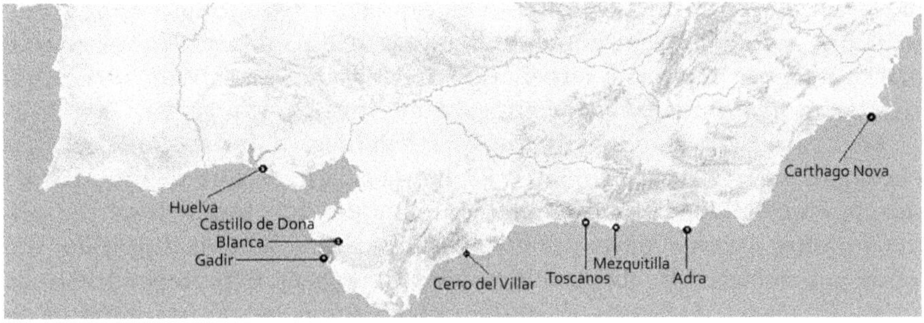

Figure 7.2 Major Phoenician settlements, around sixth century BCE.

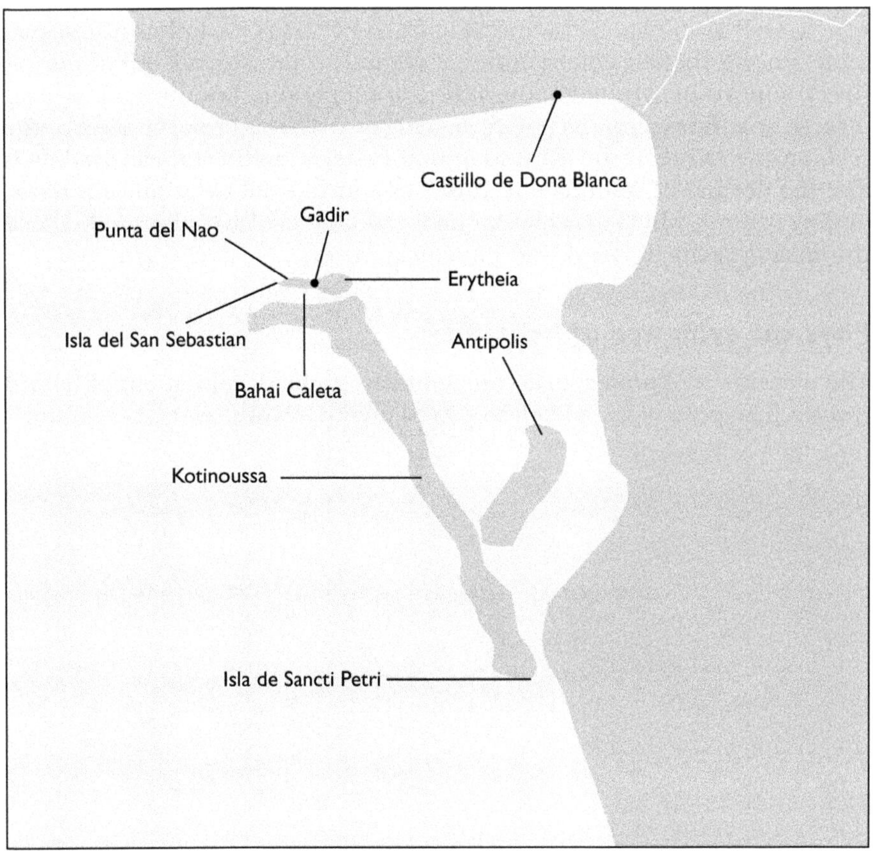

Figure 7.3 Regional map of Gadir and Castillo de Dona Blanca, around sixth century BCE.

mining industry in the seventh and eighth centuries, alongside the infrastructure to facilitate movement of goods from inland sites to coastal markets. These networks, largely operated by Iberian labour, indicate a significant investment in these endeavours.[24]

The Tartessian kingdom is the best example of interaction and the development of tertiary commercial markets, which spread oriental art throughout the Guadalquivir valley. Initially the Tartessians were the primary trading partner for eastern Mediterranean merchants, but when the silver was depleted in the Huelva region, Tartessos experienced its own 'crisis' in *c.*540.[25] Tartessos' dwindling silver supply began to inhibit trade and Greek traders sought other communities to trade with via land routes along the Vinalopo and Segura rivers. In response, Tartessos undertook the development of transportation of mineral resources from inland regions in exchange for Greek imports; Iberian elites were trading Greek wares to the Iberian interior as Attic wares began to appear within the peninsula, as well as Phoenician wares (Figure 7.4).[26] This evolution of internal trade among Iberian communities is central to the spread of culture, as Greek imports penetrated beyond the littoral regions, but does not appear in large quantities until the mid-fifth century.[27] What is important about the relationship between the Tartessian and eastern Mediterranean traders is that the decline of resources at Tartessos spurred the creation of interior mining centres, which may have in turn encouraged Tartessians to become secondary traders of Greek and Phoenician wares.

Physical evidence of hybridity

The movement of pottery also can be linked to the development of hybrid images. The pottery most likely depicted mythic scenes, as seen commonly

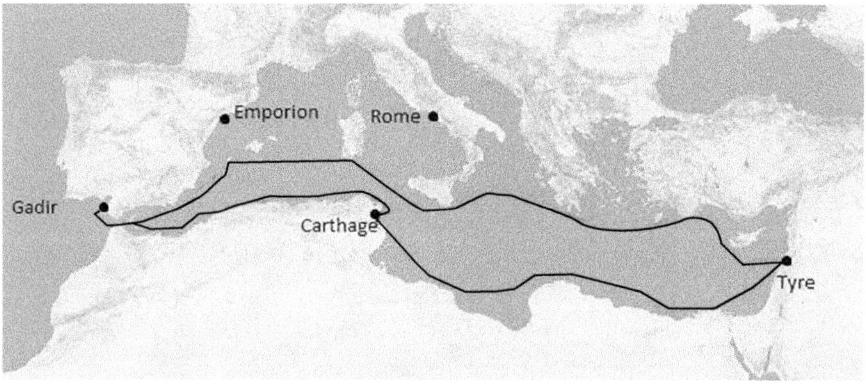

Figure 7.4 Route of Phoenician trade; the northern route is the western route – the southern route was for ships returning from Gadir to Tyre via Carthage.

among Greek pottery, but few fully intact examples from this period survive. However, hybridised images are seen in stone sculpture which does survive; the Museo Arqueologia of Madrid holds several sculpted anthropomorphised funerary pieces featuring images such as sirens, gryphons, sphinxes and a human-headed bull. This style of sculpture appeared in the Tartessian region of Huelva in the sixth century, and later spread to other communities in the Guadalquivir. These techniques were rapidly incorporated into local funerary burials and local statuary traditions which removed the dependency on foreign imports of this type to generate prestige.[28] Prior to the sixth century, Iberian sculpture was absent of these traits, which suggests two primary avenues of transmission: either these images emerge via interpretation or, as Phoenician settlements in Iberia expanded, craftsmen were imported. The latter may have been more likely, as the settlement at Castillo de Dona Blanca,[29] located across the Bay of Cadiz from Gadir, and at Toscanos,[30] situated at the mouth of the Velez river, showed elements of monumental construction. These techniques were rapidly incorporated into local funerary burials and local statuary traditions which removed the dependency on foreign imports of this type to generate prestige. In some instances, Greek imports are found in great quantity in burials.[31] The methods employed in these sculptures exhibit distinctive Hellenic traits: centaurs and satyrs are some of the most iconic images which appear to have been imported.[32] The importation of skilled labour into the region may have been due to the development of Phoenician and Greek communities; it may have been far less expensive to generate local sculpture than have sculptures imported from the East. In turn, if trained sculptors would be retained by local Greek and Phoenician elites, this in turn would suggest the development of regional supply of goods, including the employment of local labourers as stonecutters, builders and transportation of raw materials. Many regions in Iberia had a history of stonecutting for statuary, so Greek and Phoenician elites may have co-opted this industry alongside mining for the purposes of acquiring local materials for sculpture production. Presumably, this sculpture was traded with Iberian communities, and potentially local Iberian artists attempted to reproduce or synthesise local sculpture. Equally likely is that Iberian artisans were apprenticed, or that foreign artisans were hired by Iberian elites. Other avenues of acquisition may have occurred, but leave just as little evidence to how these situations evolved. Nonetheless, the outcome was that Iberian art was influenced heavily by oriental influences.

The best examples of oriental influence on artistic styles comes from a series of funerary monuments, which depict a variety of mythical beasts, not seen prior to Phoenicio-Iberian contact. The distribution of funerary stele featuring oriental images ranges widely: a sphinx was found at Agost in Alicante, an anthropomorphised bull at Balazote in Albacete, a siren at Corral de Saus in Valencia, and a griffin at Elche in Alicante.[33] Although the location of these monuments varies widely, the evidence would suggest that oriental influences were transmitted by imported pottery with these images. Notably, these sites were located well away from Greek and Phoenician settlements, highlighting the distribution of imported goods, either through secondary traders, or if located on rivers, may have been visited by eastern Mediterranean traders.

Writing appears alongside sculpture and trade as another indication of Greek influence on Iberian culture. The first appearance of an Ionian script in Spain first appears within the Tartessian sphere as early as the mid-fifth century, which notably was the same region that had adopted Greek sculptural techniques, and the development of writing coincided with the expansion of Greco-Iberian trading as evidenced by two fragmentary letters:[34] one found at Emporion and the other at Pecha Maho.[35] The first letter suggests economic activities and trade links between Emporion and the nearby settlement of Saigantha. The author recommends the services of the barge operator whose job was to guide ships to the harbour. Saigantha has been suggested to be Saguntum; the Greek name for the city was Zakantha. The author is assumed to be Phocaen due to the dialect. This letter highlights the commercial connections of Emporitanians with Iberians because the letter names the Iberians, but also that the letter is suggesting that other Greeks employ these services. The second letter, found in southern France near modern Narbonne, was written sometime in the mid-fifth century and references six people in total, several who are designated as witnesses to the exchange and that the business was conducted in Emporion. The letter discussed the sale of an *akation* and a shipment of what may have been oil.

These two letters, in conjunction with the development of indigenous sculpture, are indicative of how Iberians and Greeks interacted in the sixth and fifth centuries. The empowerment of local elites to begin engaging in trade missions to the interior caused the importation of Greek pottery in latter half of the fifth century to reach its pinnacle due to the increased demand of minerals, which further spurred the Iberian trade networks to expand to fulfil the needs of Greek enclaves.[36] These traits appear to have evolved more dramatically with wealthier communities such as at Emporion as discussed earlier. The circumstances for the development of an Iberian hybridised Greek script is unclear, but the adoption of writing is clearly linked with trade. These technical skills should be seen as generally developing synchronously; the incorporation of writing appears alongside the expansion of interior trading with the Meseta, but also the appearance of Greek and Phoenician wares and sculpture.

Interactions between Greeks, Phoenicians and Iberians before the sixth century show a dynamic economic framework of exchange. Before the sixth century, exposure to pan-Mediterranean culture was driven by the trade and exploitation of natural resources by foreign interests. As I have shown in this chapter, the Greek and Phoenician settlements were developed initially as *emporiae*, but within a few decades of establishment evolved into towns. The aim of these settlements was primarily trade-based, but they were also communities, and integrated into the cultural landscape by sharing art, language, funerary practices, food preferences and technology. In the sixth century, the Phoenician communities in southern Iberia were challenged not only by political instability in the eastern Mediterranean, but also the appearance of the Phocaeans in northeast Iberia. Although this was not a direct territorial confrontation, relations between Greeks and Phoenicians appeared largely neutral, as both types of goods were freely transported within Iberia. Relations between Greeks and Punic settlements appear to remain neutral until the third century when the Barcids, a powerful Carthaginian family, expanded their interest in southern and south-eastern Iberia. Throughout the majority of the first millennia, trade and acculturation appears to have been the norm among the foreign and indigenous communities of Iberia, which suggests that this was not a 'colonial' period in the modern sense, but a period of incorporation of Iberia into the wider pan-Mediterranean network.

Ultimately, the image of the ancient world perhaps is more connected on a variety of levels: spurred by economic interest, the genesis of a pan-Mediterranean culture begins to emerge in the first half of the first millennia, developing dynamically in a regional, organic manner. The ancient world of the Mediterranean was neither 'Romanised' nor 'orientalised', but began to follow along a general cultural trend towards a very broad cultural homogeneity, and rather than losing all traces of original culture, local culture became hybridised with traits from several influences to appear somewhat more like those the Iberians interacted with. Until the age of empires dawned, the ancient world, at least culturally, was developing towards a semi-homogeneous state with local variation through a replicative interpretation of cultural inputs via economic relations with the wider Mediterranean.

Notes

1 This chapter was written in tandem with my PhD dissertation on acculturation in Roman Spain, and therefore many of the elements present within this discussion relate primarily to pre-Roman contact, but evidence from within the Roman period will be present due to the fluid nature of cultural exchange.

2 Strabo, *Geographia* 3.5.3: 'However, notwithstanding their vast number, its inhabitants possess an island, in length not much above a hundred stadia, and in some places only one stadium in breadth. Originally the city in which they dwelt was extremely small, but Balbus the Gaditanian, who received the honors of a triumph, added another to it which they called the New Town. These two form the city of Didyme, which is not above twenty stadia in circumference. In it, however, they are not pressed for room, because few live at home, the majority passing their lives on the sea, some too dwelling on the opposite continent,

and particularly on a little island adjacent on the account of its excellence.' Mela 3.46; cf. M. Aubet (1994) *Tiro y las colonias fenicias de Occidente* (Barcelona: Bellaterra, DL): 229.

3 R. Hingley (2005) *Globalizing Roman Culture: Unity, Diversity, and Empire* (New York: Routledge), 91–2.

4 This was primary evidence used by Mommsen, Haverfield and Collingwood's arguments for the Roman mission to bring civilisation to the frontier; T. Mommsen (1885): *Römische Geschichte* [Roman history] (Leipzig: Reimer & Hirsel); F. Haverfield (1905) *The Romanization of Britain* (London: British Academy); R. G. Collingwood (1923) *Roman Britain and the English Settlements* (London: Biblo & Tannen Publishers). On classical texts employed, see J. Huskinson (2000) 'Essay One: Looking for Culture, Identity and Power', in J. Huskinson (ed.), *Experiencing Rome: Culture, Identity and Power in the Roman Empire* (London and New York: Routledge), 21; G. Woolf, (1997) 'Beyond Romans and Natives', *World Archaeology* 28(3): 339.

5 C. Riva and N. Vella (2006) 'Debating Orientalization: Multidisciplinary Approaches to Change in the Ancient Mediterranean', *Equinox* 10: 1–170.

6 The bibliography on acculturation studies is too extensive to list here; on the rejection of 'Romanization' see D. Mattingly (2008) *An Imperial Possession: Britain in the Roman Empire, 54 BC–AD 409* (London: Penguin); and (2011) *Imperialism, Power, and Identity: Experiencing the Roman Empire* (Princeton, NJ: PUP); J. Barrett (1997) 'Romanization: A Critical Comment', in D. Mattingly (ed.), *Dialogues in Roman Imperialism: Power, Discourse, and Discrepant Experience in the Roman Empire.* JRA Supplementary Series 23 (Leicester: JRA), 51–66; cf. Hingley, *Globalizing Roman Culture*; Woolf, 'Beyond Romans and Natives'; P. W. Freeman (1993) 'Mommsen through to Haverfield: The Origins of Romanization Studies in Late Nineteenth-C. Britain', in Mattingly, *Dialogues*, 27–50. On North Africa, see E. Fentress (2006) 'Romanizing the Berbers', *Past and Present* 190(1): 3–33; S. Fontana (2001) 'Leptis Magna: The Romanization of a Major African City through Burial Evidence', in S. Keay and N. Terrenato (eds), *Italy and the West: Comparative Issues in Romanization* (Oxford: Oxbow), 161–72; D. Cherry (1998) *Frontier and Society in Roman North Africa* (Oxford: OUP); D. Mattingly (1996) 'From one Colonialism to Another: Imperialism and the Maghreb', in J. Webster and N. Cooper (eds), *Roman Imperialism: Post-Colonial Perspectives* (Leicester: Leicester Archaeology Monographs), 49–69. On Roman Britain, see M. Millett (1990) *The Romanization of Britain* (Cambridge: CUP); M. Henig (1995) *The Art of Roman Britain* (Ann Arbor, MI: University of Michigan Press); M. Green (2011) *The Gods of the Celts* (Stroud: History Press); Green (2003) *Symbol and Image in Celtic Religious Art* (London: Routledge); Green (1997): 'Images in Opposition: Polarity, Ambivalence and Liminality in Cult Representation', *Antiquity* 71(274): 898–911; Green (1998) 'God in Man's Image: Thoughts on Genesis and Affiliations of Some Romano-British Cult Imagery', *Britannia* 29: 17–30. For a summary of the evolution of identity studies, see J. Webster (2002) 'Art as Resistance and Negotiation', in S. Scott and J. Webster (eds), *Roman Imperialism and Provincial Art* (Cambridge: CUP), 24–52; and L. Revell (2009) *Roman Imperialism and Local Identities* (Cambridge: CUP), 1–39.

7 R. Reece (1988) *My Roman Britain* (Cirencester and Oxford: Oxbow), 11.

8 M. Aubet (2001) *The Phoenicians and the West: Politics, Colonies and Trade* (Cambridge: CUP), 257–304, applies the term 'colony' loosely to Gadir, as well as other Phoenician settlements in Iberia, but clearly challenges these conceptions earlier, 200–1. Early interpretations employed colonial language: R. Carpenter (1925) *The Greeks in Spain* (New York: Bryn Mawr); A. Garcia y Bellido (1936)

Los hallazgos griegos de España (Madrid: Centro de Studio Historicos) and (1948) *Hispania graeca* (Madrid: Centro de Studio Historicos). For a brief history of acculturation studies, see Webster, 'Creolizing'.

9 On Phoenician settlements, see M. Aubet (1995) 'El comercio fenicio en Occidente: balance y perspectivas', in *I Fenici: Ieri Oggi Domani* (Rome: Accademia Nazionale dei Lincei, Consigli Nazionale delle Ricerche), 227–43. On Greek settlements, see P. Rouillard (2009) 'Greeks in the Iberian Peninsula: Forms of Exchange and Settlements', in M. Dietler and C. López-Ruiz (eds), *Colonial Encounters in Ancient Iberia: Phoenician, Greek, and Indigenous Relations* (Chicago: University of Chicago Press), 131–54.

10 This is a vast topic and I will not discuss it in detail: general works include A. J. Graham (1982) 'The Colonial Expansion of Greece', in *The Cambridge Ancient History* (Cambridge: CUP), vol. 3, 83–162, 163–95, and J. Boardman (1999) *The Greeks Overseas* (London: Thames & Hudson), 212–18. On the Greek 'presence' in the west, see W. Kimmig (1983) 'Die grieschische Kolonisation im westchen Mittelmeergebiet und ihre Wirkung auf die Landschaften des westlichen Mitteleuropa', *Jahrbuch des Romisch-Germanischen Zentralmuseums* 30: 5–78. Extensive bibliographies and more recent surveys are found in A. Dominguez (1991) *La polis y la expansión colonial griega in Siglos VIII-VI* (Madrid: Editorial Sintesis), 109–61; A. Dominguez (1993) 'La colonización y el comercio griego en la Península Ibérica', *Hispania Antigua* 17: 469–86; R. Olmos (1991) 'Le facteur grec a Malaga et dans le context des intrallations pheniciennes du littoral andalou', in J. Gran Aymerich (ed.), *Malaga phenicienne et punique* (Paris: Recherche sur les civilisations), 123–33; A. Dominguez and C. Sanchez (2001) *Greek Pottery from the Iberian Peninsula: Archaic and Classical Periods* (London: Brill); A. Dominguez (2006) 'Greeks in the Iberian Peninsula', in G. R. Tsetskhladze (ed.), *Greek Colonisation: An Account of Greek Colonies and Other Settlements Overseas,* vol. 1 (Leiden: Brill) 429–505; on Phoenician 'pre-colonization' see Aubet, *Phoenicians and the West,* 194, 200–1; S. Celestino Perez (2009) 'Precolonization and Colonization in the Interior of Tartessos', in Dietler and López-Ruiz, *Colonial Encounters,* 229–54.

11 The first account is related to the misadventures of a merchant named Colaeus who inadvertently arrived in Tartessos, thereupon acquiring a vast fortune, which later enables his dedication of a great bronze vessel adorned with mythic beasts to the temple of Hera in Samos. Herodotus 4.152 claims this event as the cause for the close friendships between Samos and Cyrene, which may place this event c.630 BCE; on the date of Cyrene's foundation, see S. Stucchi (1989) 'Problems Concerning the Coming of the Greeks to Cyrenaica and the Relations with their Neighbours', *Mediterranean Archaeology* 2: 73–84; A. Laronde (1990) 'Greeks and Libyans in Cyrenaica', in *Greek Colonists and Native Populations* (Oxford: Clarendon Press), 169–80. A Phocaean expedition made contact with Tartessos and established a relationship of *philia* with the 'silver king' Arganthonis, enabling trade to be conducted and bringing the mineral wealth, specifically silver, to Phocaea. This may have led to a permanent colony being established nearby with a donation of land. Herodotus 1.163–8 claims the Phocaeans discovered much of the western Mediterranean, including exploring the Adriatic and Tyrrhenian Seas and Iberia. On Greek relations with local communities, see Dominguez, 'Greeks in the Iberian Peninsula', 429; For a detailed analysis of this tale, see R. Olmos (1989) 'Los griegos en Tartessos: una nueva contrastación entre las fuentesarqueológicas y las literarias', in *Tartessos: Arqueología Protohistórica del Bajo Guadalquivir* (Barcelona: Editorial AUSA), 505.

12 Justin 43.3; for a list of Greek and Roman authors that discuss the foundations of Massalia, see K. Lomas (2010) 'Beyond Magna Graecia: Greeks and Non-Greeks in France, Spain, and Italy', in K. H. Kinzl (ed.), *A Companion to the Classical Greek World* (Oxford: Blackwell), 183.

13 X. Dupre (2005) 'Terrocotas arquitectonicas prerromanas en Emporion', *Empuries* 54: 103–23; Dominguez, 'Greeks in the Iberian Peninsula', 476; A. Dominguez (2012) 'The 1st century of Massalia: Foundation, Arrival of Migrants and Consolidation of a Civic Identity', in A. Hermary and G. R. Tseskhladze (eds), *From the Pillars of Hercules to the Footsteps of the Argonauts,* Colloquia Antiqua 6 (Leuven: Peeters), 61–82.

14 It seems unclear where this name comes from, either if this was place-naming in agreement with Stephanus of Byzantium; A. Dominguez (2013) 'Greeks and Non-Greeks in the City of Emporion and the Construction of their Different Identities', *Electrum* 20: 30–1, or if this were a Roman appellation based on coinage (*Untika-Indika*); M. Garcia-Bellido and C. Blazquez (2001) *Diccionario de cecas y pueblos hispánicos* (Madrid: Consejo Superior de Investigaciones Cientificas), 50.

15 Strabo 3.4.8: 'The Emporitans formerly lived on a little island off the shore, which is now called Old City, but they now live on the mainland. And their city is a double one, for it has been divided into two cities by a wall, because, in former times, the city had for neighbors some of the Indicetans, who, although they maintained a government of their own, wished, for the sake of security, to have a common wall of circumvallation with the Greeks, with the enclosure in two parts – for it has been divided by a wall through the center; but in the course of time the two peoples united under the same constitution, which was a mixture of both Barbarian and Greek law – a thing which has taken the place in the case of many other peoples.' Livy 34.9.1: Even at that time Emporiae consisted of two towns separated by a wall. One was inhabited by Greeks from Phocaea, whence came the Massilienses also, the other by the Spaniards; but the Greek town, being entirely open to the sea, had only a small extent of wall, of less than four hundred paces in length, while the Spaniards, who were farther back from the sea, had a wall three miles around. A third class of inhabitants, Roman colonists, was added by the deified Caesar after the final defeat of the sons of Pompey, and at present all are fused into one mass, the Spaniards first, and later the Greeks, having been received into Roman citizenship.

16 On Iberian coinage at Emporion, see M. Garcia-Bellido and C. Blazquez, *Diccionario de cecas y pueblos hispanicos,* vol. 2, 387–96; on Greek coinage, ibid. 138–141; P. Rippoles (2012) 'La numismatica', in X. Aquilué (ed.), *Empuries: Municipium Emporiae* (Rome: 'L'Erma' di Bretschneider), 131–8.

17 Livy 34.16.4–5: They ravaged more widely, since the enemy was scattered in flight. This had no less influence than the defeat of the previous day in causing the Spaniards of Emporiae and their neighbours to submit. Many citizens of other states as well, who had taken refuge in Emporiae, surrendered. All of these the consul treated kindly, and after refreshing them with wine and food sent them home.

18 E. Pons (2002) *Mas Castellar de Pontos (Alt Emporda) : Un complex arqueologic de'epoca iberica (Excavaciones 1990–1998)* (Girona: Museu d'Arqueologia de Catalunya-Girona), 587–94; D. Asensio and E. Pons (2004–5) 'La troballa d'un crater atic de figures roges en el jaciment iberic del Mas Castellar (Pontos, Alt Emporda)', *Quaderns de Prehistoria i Arqueologia de Castello* 24: 199–211.

19 *Oppida* are common in Iberian settlement patterns, typically seen as fortified hilltop settlements with agricultural satellite communities. Ruiz de Arbulo (1992) 'Emporion: Ciudad y Territorio (s. VI-I aC). Algunas reflexiones preliminares', *Revista d'arqueologia de Ponent,* 18: 59–74. E. Sanmarti (1989) 'Emporion,

port grec a vocation ibérique', *Atti Taranto* 29: 92–4, claims the *chora* was located towards the south where evidence of Greek anchorages have been located, X. Nieto and J. P. Nolla (1985) 'El yacimiento arqueológico submarino de Riells-La Clota y su relación con Ampurias', *Cypsela* 5: 143–62; cf. E. Sanmarti (2009) 'Colonial Relations and Social Change in Iberia (Seventh to Third Centuries BC)', in Dietler and López-Ruiz, *Colonial Encounters*, 49–90, again claims the western territory may have been part of the *chora* and employed for agricultural purposes.

20 On distribution, see A. Martin (1988) 'Algunes precisions mes sobre la ceramic iberica indiketa decorada amb pintura blanca', *Fonaments* 7: 47–56.

21 Strabo claims Odysseus travelled beyond the Pillars of Heracles, and shields adorned the Temple of Athena in Odysseia to recount the sojourns of Odysseus, 3.2.13, 3.4.3–4; Justin states Teucer landed at Carthago Nova and settled at Callecia, 44.2–3; Strabo 3.4.3. Other heroes visited Gadir: the Athenian Menestheus, who contributed fifty ships to the Trojan War: Apollodorus, *Library* 3.10.8; p Homer, *Iliad* 2.557; Strabo states Menestheus had a settlement named after him (possibly Castillo de Dona Blanca) with an oracle that offered sacrifices to him, while Themistocles allegedly was honoured by the Gaditanians with a statue; Strabo 3.1.9; Philostratus *Life of Apollinius of Tyna* 5.4; Teucer's girdle and the golden olives of Pygmalion were housed in the temple of Hercules at Gadir; Philostratus 5.5.

22 Hesiod, *Theogony* 287–8; Herodotus, *Histories* 4.8.1; Apollodorus, *Library* 2.5.10; Justin, *Epitome of Trogus* 44.4.15–16; Ibycus fr. 282A; Aeschylus, *Heracleidae* fr. 37; Avienus, *Ora Maritima* 264–5.

23 Pliny, *NH* 4.22 states there are three islands, but discusses only Kotinoussa and Erytheia, Pliny's discussion echoes Strabo in n. 2. Pliny claims Timaeus and Polybius as sources and notes the various names of Erythreia: *Insula Iuonis* by the natives, and Aphrodisias by the Gaditanians, and Erythreia stems from name for the Red Sea: Erythræn, which Pliny claims as the origins of the Phoenicians. Strabo 3.5.3 states Antipolis was the closest to the mainland, and contained temples to Heracles and Cronus. A. Neville (2007) *Mountains of Silver and Rivers of Gold: The Phoenicians in Iberia* (Oxford: Oxbow), 93, states that large quantities of *murex trunculus* shells have been found, indicating dye manufacturing, and the lack of Phoenician occupation may suggest the island's industrial nature warded away residents.

24 Neville, *Mountains of Silver*, 148–9; Aubet, *Phoenicians and the West*, 281–5.

25 On the penetration of Greek wares, see M. Almagro (1970) 'Hallazgos de época visigoda en Almodóvar del Pinar (Cuenca)', *Trabajos de Prehistoria* 27: 437–8; M. Almagro (1992) *Las necrópolis ibéricas en su contexto mediterráneo* (Seville: Congresso de Arqueologia Iberica), 159–73; Dominguez and Sanchez, *Greek Pottery*, 79.

26 On relationships between Tartessos and adjacent polities, see M. Aubet (1982) 'Zur problematik des orientalisierenden Horizontes auf der Iberischen Halbinsel', in H. G. Niemeyer (ed.), *Phönizier im Westen (Die Beiträge des Internationalen Symposiums über 'Die phönizische Expansion im westlichen Mittelmeerraum' in Köln vom 24. bis 27. April 1979* (Mainz: Madrider Beitrage), 309–35; M. Aubet (1990) 'El impacto fenicio en Tartessos: las esferas de interacción', *Cuadernos Emeritenses* 2: 29–44.

27 It is clear that imports began to be moved inland during the sixth and fifth centuries, see distribution maps in P. Rouillard (1991) *Les Grecs et la Peninsule Iberique du VIIIe au IVe siècle avant Jesus-Christ* (Paris), 114–15 and 118–1–9. Typical objects found in this period are Ionian B2 type cups, P. Rouillard (1982) 'Les colonies grecques du Sud-Est de la Péninsule Ibérique: Etat de la question',

I *Focei dall'Anatolia ll'Oceano*, *PP* 37: 417–31. Similar evidence has been found in the Greek wreck off Point Lequin, France, see L. Long, J. Miro and G. Volpe (1992) 'El pecio griego arcaico de la Pointe Lequin (Porquerolles, Francia)', *Revista de arqueología* 134: 199–234. Greek imports appear to be used as luxury wares, with emphasis on larger burials with high-quality Attic goods.

28 For a summary of burial typologies in Iberian burials pre-contact, see A. Gonzalo (1997) 'The Funerary World and the Dynamics of Change in Southeast Spain', in Margarita Diaz-Andreu Garcia and Simon Keay (eds), *The Archaeology of Iberia: The Dynamics of Change* (London: Routledge), 85–94; A. Bettencourt (2008) 'Life and Death in the Bronze Age of the NW of Iberian Peninsula', in F. Fahlander and T. Oestigaard (eds), *The Materiality of Death: Bodies, Burials Beliefs* (Oxford: Archeopress), 99–104; M. Subira *et al.* (2011) 'Fire and Bones: Bronze Age III in the North-Eastern Iberian Peninsula', *Coll. Antropol.* 35(2): 565–76. See also R. Fort *et al.* (2013) 'An Analytical Study of Iberian Iron Age Stone Sculptures and their Surface Marks', *Archaeometry* 55(3): 391–406.

29 D. Ruiz Mata (1994) 'El poblado fenicio del Castillo de Dona Blanca: Introduccion al yacimiento', in E. Rosello and A. Morales (eds), *Castille de Dona Blanca: Archaeo-Environmental Investigations in the Bay of Cadiz, Spain (750–500* BC*)* (Oxford: BAR), 7; Ruiz Mata (1993) 'Los fenicios de epoca arcaica – siglos VIII/VI a.C. – en la Bahai de Cadiz: Estado de la cuestion', in A. Tavares (ed.), *Os fenicios no territorio portugues* (Barcelona: Cuadernos de Estudios Mediterraneos), 48.

30 H. G. Niemeyer (1990) 'The Phoenicians in the Mediterranean: A Non-Greek Model for Expansion and Settlement in Antiquity', in J. P. Descoeudres (ed.), *Greek Colonists and Native Populations* (Oxford: Clarendon Press), 480.

31 The tomb at Los Villares features two set pieces of Greek imports: a series of dining or ritual banquet pieces; J. Blanquez (1990) *La formacion del mundo iberico en el Sureste de la Meseta: Estudio arqueologico de la necropolis ibericas de la Provincia de Albacete* (Albacete: Instituto de Estudios Albacetenses), 222–6; and the second set contained fifty-three pieces of black glaze and red-figure pottery, with the tomb itself topped with a statue of a horseman; Blanquez (1992) 'Nuevas consideraciones en torno a la escultura iberica', *Cuadernos de Prehistoria y Arqueologia Universidad Autónoma de Madrid* 19: 121–43; Blanquez (1993) 'El mundo funerario albacetense y el problema de la escultura ibérica: La necrópolis de los Villares', in *Arqueología en Albacete* (Toledo: Universidad Autónoma de Madrid), 11–28.

32 On mythological creatures in Iberian statuary, see the centaur of Royos in R. Olmos (1983) 'El centauro de Royos y el centauro en el mundo ibérico', in *Homenaje al Prof. M. Almagro Basch II* (Madrid: Ministero de Cultura), 377–88, esp. 379; T. Chapa (1986) *Infujos griegos en la esculturea zomorfa iberica* (Madrid: Consejo Superior de Investigaciones Cientificas): the sphinx, 251 and griffon head, 252 from Alicante, human-headed bull from Albacete, 259, and a siren's wing from Valencia, 249. The distribution of this style of statuary is indicative of the spread of Greek technical skills.

33 Chapa, *Infujos griegos*, 251–9.

34 On the relationship of trade and language, see J. De Hoz (1994) 'Griegos e íberos: testimonios epigráficos de una cooperación mercantil', in P. Cabrera, R. Olmos and E. Sanmartí (eds), *Iberos y Griegos: Lecturas desde la diversidad, Huelva Arqueológica* 13(2): 259–60; on the development of an Iberian-influenced Greek alphabet, see De Hoz (1985–6) 'La escritura greco-ibérica', in *Studia Palaeohispanica: Actas del IV Coloquio sobre lenguas y culturas paleohispánicas, Veleia 2–3,* (Leoia: Instituto de Ciencias de la Antiguedad, Universidad del Pais Vasco), 285–98; De Hoz (1989) 'La epigrafía focea vista desde el Extremo

Occidente', in *Actas del VII Congreso Español de Estudios Clásicos III* (Madrid), 179–87; De Hoz (1993) 'La lengua y la escritura ibéricas, y las lenguas de los íberos', in F. Villar and J. Untermann (eds), *Lengua y Cultura en la Hispania Prerromana, Actas V Coloquio sobre Lenguas y Culturas Prerromanas de la Península Ibérica* (Salamanca), 635–66.

35 The commentary on these letters is extensive, so I have listed only the most relevant discussions: on the first letter, see E. Sanmarti and R. A. Santiago (1987) 'Une lettre grecque sur plomb trouvée à Emporion (Fouilles 1985)', *ZPE* 68: 119–27; R. A. Santiago (1990) 'En torno a los nombres antiguos de Sagunto', *Saguntum* 23: 123–40; Santiago (1993) 'Epigrafía dialectal emporitana', in E. Crespo, J. L. García and A. Striano (eds), *Dialectologica Graeca: Actas del II Coloquio Internacional de Dialectología Griega* (Valladolid: Autoria), 281–94. For the second letter, see M. Lejeuneand J. Pouilloux (1988) 'Une transaction commerciale ionienne au Ve siècle àPech Maho', *CRAI* 526–35.

36 Dominguez and Sanchez, *Greek Pottery*, 1–170; Rouillard, *Les Grecs et la Peninsule Iberique*, 117–23.

Chapter 8

Legal hybridity in Shakespeare

Revisiting the post-colonial in *The Tempest* and *Cymbeline*

Eric Heinze

Our courtiers say all's savage but at court; Experience, O thou disprov'st report![1]

Introduction

The study of legal hybridity is by definition inter-disciplinary. The distinctness of any given socio-scientific discipline will already have faced age-old doubts, but makes no sense at all if we are to understand hybridity. Authors in the late nineteenth and early twentieth century sought to grasp law as a closed system, hence as a self-contained scholarly discipline. Today, by contrast, we are more inclined to view a legal regime as, so to speak, fluidly quasi-autonomous. Law's fundamental concepts, principles and practices draw their meanings within broader social contexts.[2] As cultures mingle, a pluri-disciplinary standpoint lends itself to exploring both the formal and the informal, both the institutional and the social processes that merge to create legal systems.

Since the mid-twentieth century, postcolonial studies have focused on the destruction or subjugation of cultures through imperial power. The notion of hybridity equally recognises imbalance and coercion within colonial dynamics; but it emphasises transformations at both ends of, or rather along the entire spectrum of those dynamics. It also covers experiences beyond conventional settler colonialism. Hybridity certainly arises through imposition and coercion, but proceeds also through strategic self-interest or indeed through ambient and diffuse assimilation. Today, for example, a state seeking to regulate the internet may adopt rules already implemented by the US, perhaps because of material benefits of so doing, or perhaps because US dominance leaves few other feasible options. Alternatively, such a state may devise its own rules, but already steeped in technological concepts generated within US internet practice, an influence which might well be seen as cultural imperialism. Distinctions between (a) the coercive imposition of a norm, (b) the free choice to embrace that norm and (c) the assimilation of it through diffused concepts or values, are not always manifest even within cultures, let alone across cultures (see Figure 8.1).

Even within full-fledged colonial contexts, it may not always be apparent which doctrines or practices the coloniser imposes coercively, which ones the colonised accepts willingly from the coloniser, which ones the coloniser accepts willingly from the colonised, which ones diffuse spontaneously from the coloniser to the colonised, and which ones diffuse spontaneously from the colonised to the coloniser. Those concepts of 'imposition', 'coercion', 'acceptance', 'willingness', 'diffusion' and 'spontaneity' turn out to be more matters of judgement than matters of fact, and can breed considerable controversy. Today, for example, the question as to whether human 'rights' are an alien imposition *by* the West, or are a welcome borrowing *from* the West, or were indeed already part of this or that culture before the West ever arrived, appears far from settled. Answers to that kind of question often end up linked to the position on human rights that a given protagonist wishes to achieve from the outset.

In this chapter, I shall probe William Shakespeare's *The Tempest* and *Cymbeline* for insights into legal hybridity first emerging in early modernity,

— On s'américanise de plus en plus...

Figure 8.1 Drawing by Sempé [Jean-Jacques Sempé], *Quelques philosophes* (Paris: Denoël, 1984), 8.

as European colonialism is newly under way. Both late plays present a 'Jacobean' Shakespeare, attentive to the emerging seventeenth-century politics of absolute sovereignty with which European colonialism will become closely linked. In the first section, I review a progression from classical humanist, to postcolonial, and then to hybridity readings of late Shakespearean political drama. In the second section, I revisit, from a hybridity standpoint, a Shakespearean challenge to the myth of savagery as lawlessness, used to justify European conquests of non-European lands. In the third section, I recall well-known theories of colonialism as symbolised through sexual conquest, again contrasting the hybridity perspective. In the fourth section, I examine broader themes of mutual cultural exchange. In the final section, I argue that *Cymbeline's* shift to a hybridity model represents broader historical challenges to pre-existing political and legal assumptions.

Humanism, postcolonialism, hybridity

Classical humanist interpretations of art seek to identify experiences – 'truths' – that transcend time and place, history and culture. Rarely has humanism staked that claim more confidently than in readings of classical drama, from Shakespeare through to Corneille, Racine or Schiller. One generation of pupils after another has snoozed through lessons in which Hamlet, Horace, Britannicus or Don Carlos strut as universal figures plunged into universal struggles against universal obstacles.

For ages a work like *The Tempest*, too, had been read as a universal fable, unfolding in a fairy-tale nowhere because its humanist themes of self-realisation and reconciliation could presumably be discovered everywhere. A deeply wronged yet instinctively paternal Prospero, so it was thought, seeks only to nurture his untainted daughter Miranda. He fruitlessly strives to civilise the ungrateful 'native' Caliban. And he aims only to redress injustices wrought upon his lost Milanese domain, preparing it for enlightened rule under a meticulously initiated Ferdinand, son of the Neapolitan King Alonso.[3]

That humanist-universalist perspective has, since the mid-twentieth century, faced dogged attacks. Feminism, new historicism, cultural materialism and postcolonial studies have dissected that 'universal', seeing in it not the self-actualising lives of humans on all four continents, but rather a rhetorical strategy for naturalising privilege within repressive hierarchies, strategically justifying existing power structures under the mantel of a self-evident moral code.[4] With the tide of 1960s de-colonisation movements, new understandings of Prospero's isle were afoot. The Martiniquais Aimé Césaire rewrote the play, calling it *Une Tempête* (1969), and bearing the hallmarks of anti-colonialist critique associated with Frantz Fanon's *Peau noire, masques blancs* (1952) or *Les Damnés de la Terre* (1961). Césaire gives voice to a Caliban politically and psychologically colonised, yet having gained critical consciousness of the mental processes of colonisation, as he rebels against European domination.

But are those altogether recent insights? Did Césaire's Caliban ever really differ from Shakespeare's? Or is Césaire quarrelling with a naïvely humanist *Tempest* that was never Shakespeare's to begin with? Following pathways traced by Michel Foucault, Jacques Derrida or Judith Butler (as reflected in the literary criticism of John Dollimore, Terence Eagleton, Stephen Greenblatt, Graham Holderness, Paula Pugliatti and many others), no one today can easily read *The Tempest* other than as the story of a politically absolutist patriarch practising pervasive surveillance and control upon a commodified daughter and a degraded, brutalised Caliban, all in preparation to transform his Milan – England, of course – from a factious medieval backwater into the engine of a modern, global empire.

By the late twentieth century, readings and performances of *The Tempest* were passing from classical humanism to more critically minded postcolonial approaches. Its regime of power was increasingly deemed violent and oppressive. That approach contrasts with humanist readings, which viewed Prospero's realm as generally benign, and saw actual or threatened violence, if at all, only in the supposed savagery of the colonised.[5] Domination within Prospero's brave new world runs in one direction only. It emanates from the privileged European male, exercised upon his underlings. Of course, Prospero's Milan has itself become subordinated within the Neapolitan king's imperial structure – but, should Prospero's plot succeed, no more than Elizabeth's England will become 'subsumed' within James's Britain, only to emerge as dominant after all.

The edgier a political barb, the more an early modern writer must encode it. The techniques of political hegemony that Prospero is perfecting – controlling bodies by engineering minds – become packaged as the play's famous 'magic'. Meanwhile, in a tell-tale sign of the late Shakespeare's newly Jacobean world, that sovereign absolutism which Prospero is confecting, he also dissimulates through an accusation against his usurping brother Sebastian: 'he needs will be/Absolute Milan'.[6] Sebastian's political subordination under Naples is, of course, from Milan's standpoint, patently non-absolutist.[7] Over his own little shipwrecked domain, it is rather our avocational island sage who manufactures his hermetically sealed absolutism.

Power descends from this seventeenth-century autocrat upon Miranda, who remains vigilantly preserved as endogenous to a culture of European supremacy,[8] anticipating the ethnically pure enclaves that white overlords would later form within their colonial outposts.[9] That same power descends upon Caliban, indigenous yet enslaved, and rendered culturally exogenous within his own land.[10] It descends upon Ariel, Prospero's culturally appropriated agent.[11] Most importantly – at least, for Prospero's designs – power descends upon that Milanese-Neapolitan socio-political microcosm, that 'ship of state', which he lures into his dominion, a vessel carrying Europe's highest and lowest social orders, where all burst out into a revealing conflict with each other.

The sudden arbitrariness of social relations upon that ship, as a lowly boatswain impudently commands a king and his noble retinue,[12] raises precarious questions about the integrity of the seemingly natural hierarchy topped by Prospero, and of the seeming superiority and inferiority of the rival cultures subsumed within it. Caliban rebels from the periphery of power, but resistance, he forever learns anew, is futile. Meanwhile Ariel,[13] and even Miranda[14] or Ferdinand,[15] may well rebel closer to power's source, but with no greater success.[16] Those colonial dynamics had already been well prepared in another of the later dramas, *Antony and Cleopatra*, in which an Egyptian culture and its customs all fall prey to a Roman – decoded: 'European' – imperial project.

Those postcolonial readings by no means lack universal elements of their own. The adjective 'Global' has ended up appended to 'Shakespeare' as if it were an honorific, like 'Professor' or 'Doctor', yet with greater awareness of its postcolonial context. Macbeth today walks and talks in Burundi, China or Uruguay with the same panache he had once flaunted in a 'Scotland' propped up inside an early Jacobean 'Globe'. Such approaches largely depart, however, from the naïve universalisms of traditional humanist readings. In an age when a 'universalism' looks like little more than a particularism with an army – and yet that insight had already emerged in Shakespeare[17] – we view history as a succession of particularisms, clashing yet also combining to generate human cultures in flux and often in crisis. In a bygone humanist era, foreign troupes used performances of Shakespeare to tell *our* 'universal' stories. In a postcolonial era, they use the playwright to tell *their own* 'universal' stories. That is where hybridity theory enters, ushering us into a subsequent era of Shakespearean readings, and of legal theory: from the classical humanist to the postcolonial, and then to the 'post-postcolonial'. The 'universal' neither survives in its traditional, unilaterally Western forms, nor altogether perishes under the postcolonial onslaught. Universalism instead becomes an arena of constantly interacting cross-culturalisms.

Throughout the years in which *The Tempest* had emerged as 'the' Shakespearean play for postcolonial critique,[18] *Cymbeline* went mostly ignored. That neglect results in part from its lesser stage popularity. More importantly, *Cymbeline* was readily overlooked because it could never so easily fit mid-twentieth-century assumptions about colonialism as an affair of sheer one-way domination. *Cymbeline* directly challenges such readings. It presents a more ambiguous, two-way or even multilateral panorama of imperial relationships. If *The Tempest* is 'the' postcolonial play, then *Cymbeline* is 'the' hybridity play.

In *Cymbeline*, neither law nor society proceed with the one-way dynamics of superiority and inferiority, at the levels of both formal dominance and informal attitudes, which we witness in the more conventionally colonial setting of *The Tempest*. *Cymbeline's* loci of power and culture are polycentric. They are geographically and politically unstable, mutually shaping each other. *The Tempest's* new world may seem prophetically fixed upon an early modern present, with Ireland as well as Mediterranean or Caribbean locations long cited as its 'real' site.[19] But *Cymbeline's* present is less mysterious. A conquered Wales is expressly included among the play's main sites. The plot moreover rehearses the same contemporary, imperial power dynamics against the background of a historical predecessor, a time when Britain is itself a vassal of Rome.

The most important touchstone for imperial politics among Renaissance intellectuals is Roman history. In all Shakespearean political drama, of course, past events mirror the dramatist's own time. Only in *Cymbeline*, however, is that juxtaposition rendered almost pedantically explicit, as if the dramatist is spelling out that we scour history for critical templates of current affairs. Through a dual temporality, allowing Shakespeare to fashion a simultaneously ancient and contemporary plotline, *Cymbeline* presents a hybrid Britain as simultaneously colonising and colonised. Its ancient story shows a colonised Britain rebelling against Roman imperial power. Its modern one shows Britain incorporating that same imperial ethos into its own conquest over Wales, a Wales standing in for Ireland as well as other prospective conquests near or far. Law and culture become both imposed by and imposed upon *Cymbeline's* Britain.[20] It is surely those ambiguous intercultural relationships (see Figure 8.2), different from the more conventional domination pattern of *The Tempest* or *Antony and Cleopatra*, which have left *Cymbeline* ignored within postcolonial readings of Shakespeare.

Figure 8.2 Drawing by Michael Ffolkes (1967), in *Punch*, 4 September 1967, 341.

Although schools of legal realism have long construed law within informal as well as formal norms and processes, legal hybridity depicts that 'real' as multicultural. Multiculturalism arises sometimes through benign, spontaneous interactions, as in *The Comedy of Errors* when, in tourist mode, Antipholus of Syracuse sets off to 'view the manners' of Ephesus, to '[p]eruse the traders, gaze upon the buildings'.[21] Just as often, however, cultural interface issues from violence. When, after *The Tempest's* end, Prospero abandons the island, he will leave behind a Caliban bruised by years of servitude, yet conscious of the perils of justice and injustice in the world beyond its shores. In *Cymbeline* – even leaving aside a happy end which seems deliberately implausible, culminating as it does in the suspiciously nonchalant reconciliation of colonial overlords with their underlings – the cultivation of critical social, political and legal consciousness proceeds through breaches of cultural insularity, experiences of cultural interface. Sometimes those experiences are peacefully constructive, sometimes they are fortuitously violent.

'Mulmutius who made our laws'

'This island's mine'[22], spews Caliban, first emerging on stage, at Prospero. Those words might sound like the rant of any of the disgruntled vassals who populate Shakespearean drama,[23] seemingly amplified by the underling's garden-variety 'laziness': 'There's wood enough within.'[24] Caliban continues, however, by reciting a lineal interest in the land, the very hallmark of rule-of-law legality as embodied above all by the European aristocracy: 'This island's mine by Sycorax my mother,/Which thou tak'st from me.'[25] Caliban's claim is entirely of the type that constitutes ownership and dominion in Shakespeare's Europe; and of the type rehearsed elsewhere in the corpus – often less plausibly, but with more institutional and military power behind it[26] – with the dual aim of establishing title and challenging any subsequent usurpation of it. Caliban includes both elements. *The Tempest*, then, by no means lacks hybridity of its own. Caliban appropriates and turns the language of European law, the European language of institutional power and public right, back at the European. Still, that is as far as Caliban will ever benefit from hybridity. He learns the European language with which to name injustices inflicted by the European. He names them in European terms, and in that he learns to understand justice as the European understands it, yet he cannot overcome them.[27]

John Locke would later define colonised peoples as primitive, precisely through their supposed incapacity to recognise proprietary rights in land.[28] But had Shakespeare already challenged that myth? Caliban may well find 'civilised' European languages good for nothing but 'to curse',[29] but deploys the most important language of all, the language of European law,[30] against the European who has simultaneously imposed and violated it.

Caliban lacks a European status of legal personhood both within his conventional relationship to Prospero of master and servant,[31] but also of coloniser and colonised. Prospero's dismissal of Caliban's claim 'is itself performative of the discourse of colonialism, since this particular reticulation of denial of dispossession with retrospective justification for it, is the characteristic trope by which European colonial regimes articulated their authority over land to which they could have no conceivable legitimate claim'.[32] *The Tempest* strongly links those two sets of socio-legal relationships, the former offering a template for the latter. Prospero's 'civilisation' elicits the rule of law as a regime reserved for an exclusive set of full-fledged legal subjects, normatively justifying an exploitative labour regime: 'We cannot miss him: he does make our fire,/Fetch in our wood and serves in offices/That profit us.'[33] Prospero's is a regime of coercion, both crude and subtle,[34] in which, as the dramatist suggests elsewhere, 'strong possession' prevails 'much more than . . . right'.[35] Shakespeare almost anticipatorily responds to Locke that even if 'primitives' *did* speak the language of European land law, exactly as Caliban has learned to do, they would still be posited as uncivilised, and deprived of their land, on other spurious grounds. Caliban's ability to protest in the language of European legal and political concepts allows us to locate in *The Tempest* a critique of emerging colonialism, as opposed to a blithe endorsement of or complicity in it, just as *The Merchant of Venice, Othello* and even *Titus Andronicus* admit critical stances towards the racism or anti-Semitism directed at the Prince of Morocco, Shylock, Othello or Aaron.

In *Cymbeline's* politically climactic scene, Caius Lucius, an emissary of Caesar Augustus, has arrived in Britain to demand a hefty annual tribute, still unpaid as part of Britain's geminating rebellion against Roman rule. In terms admittedly more elaborate than Caliban's, Cymbeline's core claim is nevertheless identical: 'We do say then to Caesar/Our ancestor was that Mulmutius which/Ordained our laws'.[36] Within an imperial framework, law emerges as a hallmark of the civilised. Yet like Caliban to Prospero, Cymbeline – otherwise scarcely linked to Caliban, as surface appearances so strongly differentiate them – turns that reasoning back upon the imperial power. Cymbeline insists to Rome that Britain had been civilised, it had possessed its own native law, before Rome had ever arrived. In hybrid mode, he speaks Roman legalism back to Rome, incorporating the language of the empire in order to challenge it. Britain had not been a lawless place to which law was brought, but instead, in hybrid mode, became a locus of imperial law layered upon Britain's pre-existing indigenous law.

Like Caliban, Cymbeline depicts the loss of Britain to Rome as an act of non-law, of law-defeating violence, albeit paraded as rationality and civilisation. It is those ancient, native British laws which 'the sword of Caesar/Hath too much mangled'.[37] The forthcoming rebellion becomes a defensive violence, a violence of redress, a violence against violence, a violence to undo imperial violence, in contrast to the violence with which Britain subdues Wales. Accordingly, the 'repair and franchise' of Rome's destruction of the Britons' laws 'Shall by the power we hold be our good deed,/Though Rome be therefore angry.'[38] Caliban aspires to such rebellion, but enjoys only a parody of it in the plot he contrives with the buffoon Stephano against Prospero. Yet another deception from within the empire comes to mock the colonial subject.

Caliban sometimes hints at a golden-age story of life before the European father and daughter arrived, back in the days when he could still call himself, at any rate applying European rules, 'mine own king'.[39] Locke will theorise the non-existence of that principle, indeed of law itself, among non-Europeans in order to justify the 'introduction of law', that is, the imposition of a European order, within the 'new' world. Cymbeline nonetheless impugns the illegitimacy of that manoeuvre on the Romans' part. Both Cymbeline and Caliban invoke the empire's own legal rules to show how it is the empire that turns those embodiments of political rationality into arbitrariness.[40] What links them is the drive to speak the language of the empire against the empire.

The politically foundationalist mythmaking[41] is vintage. Caliban's life had undoubtedly been better before Prospero's arrival (although it was then Ariel who had fallen victim to Sycorax[42]). Similarly, Cymbeline now recites his own national creation myth: 'Till the injurious Romans did extort/This tribute from us *we were free*'.[43] That story, too, has a golden-age quality, the said Mulmutius, invoked now in his law-giving capacity for the second time, being a legendary figure.[44] 'Mulmutius made our laws,/Who was the first of Britain which did put/His brows within a golden crown.'[45] To be sure, Cymbeline's inadvertent suggestion of a primordial autocracy – Mulmutius was not 'elected', nor 'proclaimed', nor 'anointed', but rather 'called Himself a king'[46] – slightly clouds the 'freedom' narrative.

What robs the Britons of that ancient freedom is, on Cymbeline's rendition, the imperial 'Caesar's ambition,/Which swelled so much that it did almost stretch/The sides o' th' world.'[47] Cymbeline omits, of course, his own domination over Wales – spoken of in terms identical to those directed by Prospero against Caliban[48] – not to mention the bondage he imposes in imprisoning his daughter Imogen for her debatable breach of obedience. Similarly, when Prospero fastidiously recites his brother's usurpation of Milan and opportunist delivery of it to an imperial Naples, he omits reference to his own mirror-image overthrow of Caliban's sovereignty.

Does British 'freedom' in *Cymbeline* flow merely from the domination of the local imperialist as opposed to the domination of the distant one? Does Prospero 'civilise' his island merely by replacing one autocrat, Sycorax, with another, himself, even while he will decry his overthrow in Milan by his brother (a series of overthrows[49] spoofed in Caliban's hope that Stephano will overthrow Prospero)? Be that all as it may, just as Caliban exclaims to

Prospero, so does Cymbeline to Rome, that law, the hallmark of 'civilisation', had indeed existed, in the form recognised by the colonising power itself, before the empire arrived. British law in *Cymbeline* emerges as a hybrid of Roman law built upon a previously existing British law.

Caliban's 'acquisition' of law remarkably mirrors his 'acquisition' of language. Both *lex* and *lingua* become markers of a civilisation he is presumed to lack, a presumption based not on their absence so much as on Prospero's discounting of them. He turns out to learn – European – language through a process of cross-cultural exchange, a *quid pro pro,* the hallmark, at least as among privileged European males, of formally equal contractual reciprocity. Caliban possesses what many an intellectual property lawyer would call 'local knowledge'. Like his lineal claim itself, that knowledge becomes devalued and then appropriated, since, in exchange for learning the 'culture' of Prospero's language, Caliban has surely provided the information about 'nature' more essential to survival:

> When thou cam'st first,
> Thou . . . /wouldst . . . /teach me how
> To name the bigger light and how the less,
> . . . and then I loved thee
> And showed thee all the qualities o'th' isle,
> The fresh springs, brine pits, barren place and fertile.[50]

Caliban concludes the idea with an ironic image of reciprocity, 'Cursed be I that did so!'[51] The curse is rendered in exchange for the deception he experiences once Prospero's conduct proves non-reciprocal: 'You taught me language, and my profit on't/Is I know how to curse.'[52] Hybridity proceeds, as in many colonial situations, through exchange. Yet the model of exchange remains by no means that of the classical contractual paradigm of two formally equal actors each disposing of full-fledged legal personality. Instead, what might between two Europeans have been Caliban's private-law property rights over the isle's resources faces the same fate as any public-law rights he ought to have in lineal succession over the land's sovereignty. The name 'Caliban' indeed recalls 'cannibal'[53], the kind of savagery attributed by the coloniser to the native, yet for which the play offers not a hint of evidence. Caliban's existence comes to be defined by the European perception of him. It is 'Prosper', by contrast, who consumes the native's time and resources to his own benefit and to the vassal's detriment.

'My youth I spent much under him'

Also in conversation with Lucius, Cymbeline's adopted son Cloten – given his socio-political rank, the arch-knucklehead in the Shakespearean corpus – offers resistance with words less erudite than his step-father's.

Cloten rattles off a simplistic nationalist myth of self-sufficiency, bolstered even by an ethnically stereotypical jab at Italians' noses, which Shakespeare might well have heard, particularly among anti-Catholic contemporaries: 'Britain is/A world by itself; and we will nothing pay/ For wearing our own noses.'[54] This is at best the 'resistance' of the Little Englander. Cloten will later assume the role of the British imperialist interfacing with the Welsh vassal. On a chance encounter, he immediately takes Guiderius for a – by definition – lawless Welsh peasant through a similarly unthinking stereotype: '[W]hat are you/That fly me thus? Some villain mountaineers?/I have heard of such. [. . .] Thou art a robber,/A law-breaker, a villain. Yield thee, thief.'[55] Impermeability to cross-cultural exchange equates, in Cloten, with overt stupidity.

Cloten's astute mother, Cymbeline's second wife and the play's conspicuously unnamed 'Queen', makes the same point in shrewder, sinister terms. Far from a Britain breathing the air of freedom away from Rome, she depicts an independent Britain through the nationalist, geographically claustrophobic imagery of being 'ribbed and paled in'.[56] That image anticipates the dawning era of absolute sovereignty, of Bodin and Hobbes, whereby the political and legal regime comes to be grasped as impenetrable, reiterating, albeit more astutely, her son's disdain of influences outside the British court. Appealing to a nostalgic Elizabeth cult under James I, and recalling the glory of triumph over the Spanish Armada, Shakespeare has the Queen portray an admittedly more probing vision, but still of Britain as 'a world by itself':

> Remember, sir, my liege,
> The kings your ancestors, together with
> The natural bravery of your isle, which stands
> As Neptune's park, ribbed and paled in
> With oaks unscalable and roaring waters,
> With sands that will not bear your enemies' boats,
> But suck them up to th' topmast. A kind of conquest
> Caesar made here, but made not here his brag
> Of 'Came and saw and overcame'. With shame –
> That first that ever touched him – he was carried
> From off our coast, twice beaten; and his shipping,
> Poor ignorant baubles, upon our terrible seas,
> Like eggshells moved upon their surges, cracked
> As easily 'gainst our rocks.[57]

Cymbeline, his Queen, and Cloten unite, then, in opposing Rome. If Cloten speaks irrational xenophobia, however, and his mother absolutist nationalism, Cymbeline's language is different. In cosmopolitan and hybrid mode, Cymbeline challenges Rome like a Roman. Cymbeline rejects the empire, but, he will soon openly avow, it is an empire from which Britain has had much to learn, and that has spurred within Britain a consciousness of equal sovereign authority – echoed, again, by Caliban only through parody.

Lucius leaves the court uttering the words of the oppressive, violent empire: 'War and confusion/In Caesar's name pronounce I 'gainst thee. Look/For fury not to be resisted.'[58] With imperial manners, however, Lucius meticulously distinguishes between that hostile political gesture and a code of personal honour. He maintains a diplomatic courtesy, which, Shakespeare goes out of his way to display, Cymbeline returns in kind.[59] Cymbeline recalls a time of political cooperation with Rome, and his personal pride taken in it: 'Thy Caesar knighted me'.[60] The admitted anachronism, orders of chivalry being medieval and not Roman, evokes a simultaneously personal and political rapport idealised through values of absolute, indeed ontological, and quasi-kindred loyalty. It suggests deep cultural intermingling, which is echoed in other elements of the play: for example, the names of the British characters randomly distributed between local and Greco-Roman types, sometimes blended in the same person, as the King's son Aviragus has been raised as 'Cadwal', while his brother Guiderius has gone by the name of 'Polydore', and Imogen will assume the Latinate name 'Fidele'.

'Knighting' is conventionally performed through a genuflection, an image which Cymbeline then follows up in bathetically sexual terms with the recollection (read also, 'nighting'), 'my youth I spent/Much under him'.[61] With or without the bawdy allusion, that image portrays an intimate past shared by the two men, a theme echoed in the eroticism among cultural-political adversaries, alternating between enmity and admiration, in some of the other political dramas, e.g. between Coriolanus and Aufidius, or, albeit in a vein of unilateral conquest, between Henry V and Kate. Although ages and dates are left somewhat vague and often anachronistic, Cymbeline suggests a 'youth . . . spent . . . under' an at least somewhat older Caesar, the traditional posture of the older male assuming the sexually active, and the younger, the passive position. Yet the symbolic power relation, recapitulating that of empire and vassal, is hinted by Cymbeline in terms of both political domination and genuine attraction, in arch-opposition both to the outright sexual exploitation to be practised by Giacomo upon Imogen, to the European fear of miscegenation directed at Caliban, or to the association of Cleopatra with prostitution (although her erotic liaison with the defeated Mark Antony displays greater parity, even intermittent dominance on the Egyptian's part). That ambiguity, standing in for the uneasy yet inevitable blending of cultures under imperial rule, will become one of the play's central themes, when Giacomo undertakes the symbolic sexual ravishing of Cymbeline's daughter.

That hybrid ambiguity of empire contrasts with the rigidly, one-way colonial dynamics of *The Tempest*, where inter-ethnic sexuality retains the taboo[62] already present in *Titus Andronicus, The Merchant of Venice* or *Othello.*

Cymbeline, by contrast, boasts, 'of him [Caesar] I gathered honour'.[63] That honour gained from a personal and indeed erotic bond with Caesar becomes not only a point of pride, but also the self-same, paramount Roman value which Cymbeline will then deploy in his rebellion against Rome. Cymbeline notes uprisings elsewhere in the empire: 'the Pannonians and Dalmatians for/Their liberties are now in arms, a precedent/Which not to read would show the Britons cold;/So Caesar shall not find them.'[64] He concludes, that very honour, 'Which he [Caesar] to seek of me again perforce/Behoves me keep at utterance [i.e. to the utmost]'.[65]

'Poor tributary rivers'

Giacomo's name, contemporary Italian and not ancient Roman, allows Shakespeare not only in Britain but also in Rome to paint a panorama of early modern Europe as not only spatially but also temporally hybridised. An imperial domain facilitates characters' vast geographical movements in the play, tirelessly leaping between Britain and Italy as if one were just down the road from the other. History, too, is in motion, hybridising culture on its way. With Europe's classical revival already long under way by Shakespeare's time, ancient sources of politics and culture blend willy-nilly with contemporary ones.[66] The poet's dawning seventeenth century dwells, so to speak, just down the road from Mediterranean antiquity, as displayed generally by the wealth of Greco-Roman and classical plots, themes, sources, images, and allusions in the Shakespearean corpus and throughout Renaissance, Baroque, and Neo-Classical art. Shakespearean hybridity is, in that sense, a hybridity of hybridity. It revisits an already deeply hybrid classical antiquity (as captured in the present volume in Gareth Sears's chapter), intertwined with the hybridity of early modern Europe.

Cymbeline may be launching a rebellion, but his daughter's bedchamber stands replete with Roman art: 'it was hanged/With tapesty of silk and silver; the story/Proud Cleopatra when she met her Roman.'[67] Such a 'story', as we are seeing, remains altogether well embedded in the play. It, too, is a story of Rome's sexual qua imperial conquest in the vassal state of Egypt, where 'Cydnus swelled above the banks'.[68] At the room's chimney we find a rendering of 'Chaste Dian bathing', recalling another classical scene of erotic intrusion.[69] Imogen falls off to sleep with yet another, and particularly terrifying Ovidian tale of sexual conquest. 'She hath been reading late,/The tale of Tereus. Here the leaf's turn'd down/Where Philomel gave up.'[70]

Mirroring her father's youthful days, Imogen, too, faces a Roman world imperially, sexually predatory, yet at the same time culturally abundant and alluring. Admittedly, she too is not beyond uttering an anti-Roman ethnic stereotype, albeit in a moment of outrageous provocation by Giacomo.[71] Like her father, however, her British world is nonetheless immersed in the Roman. That British court in revolt against Rome remains suffused by

Roman-Italian values and aesthetics, as if Shakespeare is paying a cultural tribute to that same Renaissance Italy which much of his Protestant, English nationalist audience rebukes.[72] No such open embrace of European culture is heard from Caliban, who only ever suffers at its hands. In Salman Rushdie's words, however, 'the empire writes back'. It is to this supposed savage that Shakespeare gives *The Tempest's* most eloquent verses in that European language which Caliban claims to despise:

> Sometimes a thousand twangling instruments
> Will hum about mine ears; and sometime voices,
> That, if I then had waked after long sleep,
> Will make me sleep again, and then, in dreaming,
> The clouds methought would open and show riches
> Ready to drop upon me, that when I waked
> I cried to dream again.[73]

Hybridity may remain stronger, or at any rate more benign, in *Cymbeline* than in *The Tempest*, but thus far it still seems to flow mostly from Rome to Britain – the British assimilating Roman culture, but not vice versa. It is in *Cymbeline's* parallel politics, Britain over Wales, that an empire is shown susceptible to learn from the political underling. A heretofore sheltered Imogen had grown up hearing only the myths of civilised courtly life as opposed to the savagely rural. Wandering dangerously through rural Wales disguised as a peasant boy, Imogen marvels at the welcome and the refuge with which she is greeted.[74] Imogen realises that an empire, including her own, 'breeds monsters', while the vassal nation – she hints that, under local law, Wales is bound to funnel that same kind of 'tribute' into the British court which Cymbeline now refuses to send to Rome – offers something 'sweet'. 'Th'imperious seas breeds monsters; for the dish/Poor tributary rivers as sweet fish.'[75]

Meanwhile, in a parallel journey, Imogen's husband Posthumous finds in the empire a refuge, a place of escape from persecution by the king in Britain. If Caius Lucius bears the oppressive face of empire, the patrician Philario bears its benign, cosmopolitan face. Philario receives Posthumous into his Roman *domus*, which stands as a mythologised *pax romana* in miniature, gathering under his roof Roman, Gallic and British subjects – even if Giacomo will exploit that situation, reasserting empire's more predatory side, when he plots to diminish Posthumous through the seduction of Imogen.

'New heaven, new earth'

That layering of imperial dynamics, with Britain presenting both a conquered nation and a conquering empire, brings the complexities, ambiguities and contradictions of hybridity into focus more clearly than in any other play in the corpus, in contrast not only to *The Tempest* but also to other imperial plotlines. Owen Glendower may boast of his English-language fluency, yet in the highly defensive posture of an ultimately defeated Welsh nationalism. Kate may marry Henry V, yet only thereby regaining a residual influence over her wholly defeated France. Cleopatra may have seduced Julius Caesar and may adore Mark Antony, yet always asserts her cultural difference, her orientalised 'Egyptian-ness' with relish.

Although Shakespeare, from his earliest works, displays a knowledge of natural sciences at a level generally typical of educated individuals of his time, a momentous departure surfaces in *Cymbeline*. In his convulsive dream, Posthumous's sees his four deceased family members attending the Roman god Jupiter.[76] That sequence has been taken to hint at Galileo's recent observations of the planet Jupiter orbited by four moons, news that rapidly spread through Europe. The metaphysical, i.e. simultaneously material and moral deterioration of the medieval Christian, Aristotelian-Ptolemaic worldview pervades the Renaissance and the Shakespearean corpus, but what now transpires is God's unified empire, which had once enveloped our static and eternal earth, giving way to a multi-imperial universe. Jupiter 'rules' its four 'vassal' moons, just as it, corresponding to our earth and its moon, travels as vassal under the rule of the sun. Gone is that pristine, universal macrocosm, that unified, Great Chain of Being already nostalgically recited by Ulysses in *Troilus and Cressida*.[77] Replacing it is a multiple layering of ever-shifting macro- and microscosms. Unsurprisingly, it is in these later, Jacobean plays that social, national and class differences are not merely in tension – which we already find in the poet's earliest writings – but in perilous contingency, mutation and interchange, and indeed in an active process of cultural as well as material hybridity.

Meanwhile, Cymbeline's Queen, a powerful woman replacing the sorceress type of earlier plays, has turned chemistry student – mixing, hybridising substances in order to discover their potential combinations and latent properties,[78] undermining any biblical view of fixed and eternal 'types' created by God's will. As with cultural hybridity, some such admixtures can become salutary, others combustible, indeed lethal. A new society recapitulates a new cosmos, just as the earlier one had reproduced its own.

The Tempest certainly sets up a similar imperial layering, since Milan under Prospero's brother has acquired a vassal status under the King of Naples, in parallel to Prospero's conquest of his Island. Still, no comparable tapestry of hybrid cultures appears to match that of *Cymbeline*. To the contrary, Prospero's fixed project is to shift Miranda, like Henry's Kate, into a marriage within that larger imperial structure. After Shakespeare, the French classical dramatists Corneille and Racine will carry the torch of imperially layered, culturally hybridising plotlines, also frequently echoing modern politics through ancient histories.[79] They will confirm that consciousness of political and cultural hybridity as a European one – all the more remarkably, since neither of them would have had any knowledge of the Shakespearean stage. Both will synthesise, as does Shakespeare in England, local versus imperial political struggles as processes germane to the formation of the post-Westphalian state.

Notes

Many thanks to Nicolas Lemay-Hébert for his comments on a previous draft of this chapter, as well as Rosa Freedman and Philipp Lottholz for their efforts which have helped to bring about the current chapter. Citations to Shakespeare in this chapter refer to *The Oxford Shakespeare* (individual plays (Oxf[4])).

1 *Cym.* 4.2.33–4.
2 See generally e.g. Roger Cotterrell (1992) *The Sociology of Law*, 2nd edn (London: Butterworths LexisNexis); Eugen Ehrlich (1989) *Grundlegung der Soziologie des Rechts* [Fundamental Principles of the sociology of law], 4th edn, ed. Manfred Rehbinder (Berlin: Duncker & Humblot); Simone Goyard-Fabre (2000) *Essai de critique phénoménologique du droit* [Essay on a phenomenological critique of law] (Paris: Klincksieck); Jacques Vanderlinden (1996) *Anthropologie juridique* [Legal anthropology] (Paris: Dalloz).
3 See critically e.g. Meredith A. Skura (2004) 'Discourse and the Individual: The Case of Colonialism in *The Tempest*', in Russ McDonald (ed.), *Shakespeare: An Anthology of Criticism and Theory 1945–2000* (Malden, MA: Blackwell), 817–44, 817.
4 Cf. e.g. Skura, 'Discourse and the Individual', 818–19.
5 See e.g. Paul Brown (1994) "This thing of darkness I acknowledge mine': *The Tempest* and the Discourse of Colonialism', in Jonathan Dollimore and Alan Sinfield (eds), *Political Shakespeare: Essays on Cultural Materialism* (Manchester: Manchester University Press), 72–87, 80–1; Francis Barker and Peter Hulme (2002) 'Nymphs and Reapers heavily vanish: The discursive Contexts of *The Tempest*', in John Drakakis (ed.), *Alternative Shakespeares* (London: Routledge), 195–209, 205. Like all such metholdological divisions, of course, we should not overdraw that between humanist and post-colonial critique. Skura, for example, reminds us that not all traditional humanist scholars overlook Prospero's oppressiveness or Caliban's suffering. See Skura, 'Discourse and the Individual', 817–18.
6 *Tmp.* 1.2.108–9.
7 That mode of ironic self-revelation is by no means unique. Recall the disguised and spying Henry V's jibe at a common foot soldier 'you speak this to feel other men's minds', *H5*, 4.1.120–1. Recall indeed Antonio's slur, 'The devil can cite Scripture for his purpose.' *Merchant of Venice*, 1.3.95.
8 Prospero reproaches Caliban, 'Thou dids't seek to violate/the honour of my child'. *Tmp.* 1.2.347–8. That accusation is traditionally taken to suggest attempted rape. Cf. e.g. Stephen Orgel (1987) 'Introduction', in William Shakespeare, *The Tempest*, ed. Orgel (Oxford: Oxford University Press), 1–87, 28–9; Alden T. Vaughan and Virginia M. Vaughan (2011) 'Introduction', in William Shakespeare, *The Tempest*, ed. Vaughan and Vaughan (London: Bloomsbury), 1–138, 60. Caliban by no means denies having wished sexual intercourse, at least to counter the colonial invasion by 'peopl[ing]' the island 'with Calibans'. *Tmp.* 1.2.349–50. Presumably, however, any form of miscegenation would, from Prospero's and Miranda's viewpoint, violate her 'honour', even if Caliban's

actual conduct had consisted of nothing more than non-intrusive courtship. On anxieties about hybridisation, similar to those about miscegenation, see works cited in this chapter; text accompanying n. 80.

9 See e.g. Louis Couperus (1900) *De stille kracht* [The hidden force] (Amsterdam: L. J. Veen).

10 *Tmp.* 1.2.332–44, 363–4.

11 *Tmp.* 1.2.270–1, 294–6.

12 *Tmp.* 1.1.20–48. Cf. e.g. Barker and Hulme, 'Nymphs and Reapers', 202. That theme largely distinguishes the later 'Jacobean' from the earlier 'Elizabethan' Shakespeare. In the early and middle plays, class divisions are constantly challenged, and mobility at times evident, yet the overall socio-legal order remains intact. The 17th century, by contrast, leads Western Europe towards the consolidation of nation states, in which monarchs, at least for a time, achieve greater absolutism. Class divisions beneath them become more random, as is perhaps best captured by *All's Well That Ends Well.*

13 *Tmp.* 1.2.42–4.

14 *Tmp.* 1.2.467–76.

15 *Tmp.* 1.2.465–7.

16 For a review of scholarship on *The Tempest* from post-colonial, feminist, Foucauldian and other critical perspectives, see e.g. Vaughan and Vaughan, 'Introduction'.

17 See e.g. *Antony and Cleopatra,* 4.6.5 (Octavius Caesar declaring, before his triumph over Marc Antony's faction, 'The time of universal peace is near.').

18 See e.g. Skura, 'Discourse and the Individual', 817.

19 See e.g. Vaughan and Vaughan, 'Introduction', 39–54 (reviewing theories about the location of Prospero's Island).

20 Cf. Eric Heinze (2009) 'Imperialism and Nationalism in Early Modernity: The "Cosmopolitan" and the "Provincial" in Shakespeare's Cymbeline', *Journal of Social and Legal Studies* 18(3): 139–68.

21 *Comedy of Errors,* 1.2.12–13.

22 *Tmp* 1.2.331.

23 Cf. e.g. Eric Heinze (2009) '"Were it not against our laws": Oppression and Resistance in Shakespeare's Comedy of Errors', *Legal Studies* 29: 230–63, 247–58.

24 *Tmp* 1.2.314.

25 *Tmp* 1.2.331–2. Cf. e.g. Barker and Hulme, 'Nymphs and Reapers', 204.

26 *Henry V* famously recites the corpus's most specious lineal and biblical land claim to justify England's invasion of France. *H5,* 1.2.35–100.

27 But see Barker and Hulme, 'Nymphs and Reapers', 206 (noting Caliban's success in complicating Propero's plans).

28 John Locke (1988) 'Second Treatise of Civil Government', in *Two Treatises of Government,* ed. Peter Laslett (Cambridge: Cambridge University Press), 265–428, ch. 5 and secs. 41–9.

29 *Tmp.* 1.2.363.

30 See Eric Heinze (2013) '"Where be his quiddities now?": Law and Language in Hamlet', in Michael Freeman and Fiona Smith (eds), *Law and Language: Current Legal Issues,* vol. 15 (Oxford: Oxford University Press), 201–20 (examining the role of manipulated language in law).

31 See Heinze, 'Were it not against our laws', 234–5 (applying Hegel's concepts of master and servant).

32 Barker and Hulme, 'Nymphs and Reapers', 204.

33 *Tmp.* 1.2.311–13. Cf. e.g. Barker and Hulme, 'Nymphs and Reapers', 204.

34 See Eric Heinze (forthcoming 2016) 'Selecting the Memory, Controlling the Myth: The Propaganda of Legal Foundations in Early Modern Drama', in *Injustice, Memory and Faith in Human Rights* (Aldershot: Ashgate).
35 *King John*, 1.1.40. Cf. e.g. Albert R. Braunmuller (1989) 'Introduction', in William Shakespeare, *King John*, ed. Braunmuller (Oxford: Oxford University Press), 1–93, 50–1; Eugene Giddens (2005) 'Introduction', in William Shakespeare, *King John*, ed. Giddens (London: Penguin), pp. xxi–lxvi, xlix–l. A parallel can also be drawn to Richard II's snipe, just before his deposition, at Bolingbroke: 'They well deserve to have,/That know the strong'st and surest way to get.' *R2*, 3.3.198–9. Construing strictly Caliban's lineal claim, Prospero does indeed 'depose' him. See this chapter, text accompanying n. 41.
36 *Cym* 3.1.52–4. Cf. Phyllis Rackin (1990) *Stages of History: Shakespeare's English Chronicles* (Ithaca, NY: Cornell University Press), 4 (noting that '[t]he ideology of the "Ancient Constitution"' had emerged in early modernity 'to assert the antiquity of English liberties in order to legitimate a new political consciousness').
37 *Cym.* 3.1.54–5.
38 *Cym.* 3.1.55–7.
39 *Tmp.* 1.2.342. On lineal succession, Caliban would indeed have been king between the times of Sycorax's death and Prospero's arrival (*Tmp.* 1.2.279–84). Cf. e.g. Barker and Hulme, 'Nymphs and Reapers', 203.
40 See Heinze, 'Where be his quiddities now?' (examining the relationships between rationality and arbitrariness in legal and political language).
41 Cf. Heinze, 'Selecting the Memory'.
42 *Tmp.* 1.2.257–91.
43 *Cym.* 3.1.46–7 (emphasis added). Cf. John Pitcher (2005) 'Introduction', in William Shakespeare, *Cymbeline*, ed. Pitcher (London: Penguin), pp. xxi–lxxviii, lxi (observing, 'In *Cymbeline* there are rewritten stories and untrue histories in every scene').
44 See editor's note at *Cym* 3.1.53, Oxf[4], p. 155.
45 *Cym* 3.1.57–9. Parallels can be drawn to the 'sceptered isle', 'band of brothers' and similar speeches and images in the English histories sketching myths of primordial unity. Cf. e.g. Heinze, 'Where be his quiddities now?', 211–12. Cf. also e.g. Heinze, 'Imperialism and Nationalism', 376.
46 *Cym.* 3.1.59.
47 *Cym.* 3.1.46–7.
48 See this chapter, text accompanying n. 1. Cf. Heinze, 'Imperialism and Nationalism', 387–8.
49 Cf. e.g. Barker and Hulme, 'Nymphs and Reapers', 204.
50 *Tmp.* 1.2.332–8. The eminent mid-20th-century Shakespeare scholar Frank Kermode displays the traditinal humanist interpretation: 'The colonists were frequently received with this kindness, though [the natives' – EH] treachery might follow.' Kermode treats 'treachery', as Barker and Hulme observe, 'as if this were simply a "fact" . . . without seeing that to speak of "treachery" is already to interpret, from the position of colonizing power, through a purported "description"'. Barker and Hulme, 'Nymphs and Reapers', 204–5.
51 *Tmp.* 1.2.339.
52 *Tmp.* 1.2.362–3.
53 See Orgel, 'Introduction', 25–6; Vaughan and Vaughan, 'Introduction', 30–6, 59–62.
54 *Cym.* 3.1.12–14.
55 *Cym.* 4.2.72–7.
56 *Cym.* 3.1.19.

57 *Cym.* 3.1.16–29.
58 *Cym.* 3.1.64–6.
59 *Cym.* 3.1.67, 83–4.
60 *Cym.* 3.1.68.
61 *Cym.* 3.1.68–9. On Caesar's 'swelling', see this essay, text accompanying n. 49 and 70.
62 *Tmp.* 1.2.347–50. As Brown observes, 'the proof of Propsero's power to order and supervise his little colony is manifested in his capacity to control . . . his *subjects'* sexuality, particularly that of his slave [Caliban – EH] and his daughter', attesting 'Prospero's triumphant ordering of potentially truant or subversive desires in his body politic.' Brown, 'This thing of darkness', 81 (author's emphasis). Skura adds that 'Caliban's attempted rape of Miranda can be seen as an expression not merely of sexual but also of territorial lust'. Skura, 'Discourse and the Individual', 818 (citing Orgel).
63 *Cym.* 3.1.69.
64 *Cym.* 3.1.72–5. Cf. Heinze, 'Were it not against our laws', 376–7.
65 *Cym.* 3.1.70–1.
66 See e.g. Rackin, *Stages of history*, 1–5.
67 *Cym.* 2.4.68–70.
68 *Cym.* 2.4.71.
69 *Cym.* 2.4.82.
70 *Cym.* 2.2.44–6. That Roman story would lay the ground for Lavinia's victimisation in the crudely decadent imperial drama *Titus Andronicus.* See e.g. Eugene M. Waith (1994) 'Introduction', in William Shakespeare, *Titus Andronicus,* ed. Eugene Waith (Oxford: Oxford University Press), 1–69, 27–8. The tale of Tereus and Philomel becomes all the more potent in an early modern Europe where women's legal or social safeguards against rape are unreliable at best, even if a royal princess could, of course, enjoy greater protection.
71 *Cym.* 1.6.152 (referring to a 'stew' of Roman sexual degeneracy). Cf. Heinze, 'Were it not against our laws', 386.
72 See e.g. Giddens, 'Introduction', p. xlix.
73 *Tmp.* 3.2.135–42.
74 See this chapter, text accompanying n. 1.
75 *Cym.* 4.2.35–6.
76 *Cym.* 5.3.124–216.
77 *Tro.* 1.3.84–133. Cf. Heinze, 'Were it not against our laws', 252.
78 *Cym.* 1.5.6–23. Cf. Stephen Orgel (1996) 'Introduction', in William Shakespeare, *The Winter's Tale,* ed. Stephen Orgel (Oxford: Oxford University Press), 1–83, 46; John Pitcher (2010) 'Introduction', in William Shakespeare, *The Winter's Tale,* ed. Pitcher (London: Methuen), 1–135, 55–6.
79 Cf. Eric Heinze (2010) '"He'd turn the world itself into a prison": Empire and Enlightenment in Jean Racine's Alexander the Great', *Law and Humanities* 4(1): 63–89.

Chapter 9

Hybridity and the Ottoman

What can we learn from the Ottoman statebuilding framework?

Mark Kirkham

> *There is nothing more difficult to take in hand, more perilous to conduct, or more uncertain in its success, than to take the lead in the introduction of a new order of things.*
>
> Nicolò Machiavelli[1]

Introduction

For over six hundred years the Ottomans managed to govern one of the largest empires that have ever existed. Governing in one of the most culturally diverse areas on the planet, Ottoman rule managed not only to adapt but also to thrive. In order to keep its authority and legitimacy, each of the empire's communities had to feel that the central authorities were acting in their interests, which required a high degree of dynamism and adaptability by the state. In this context, hybridity – as a concept which helps understand the combination of political systems – gives us insights into these instruments of imperial control. Balancing the role of the state against the needs of religious, cultural and social actors was a key characteristic of the flexible political system of the Ottoman empire. In recent years, hybridity as a concept has emerged and has been used to describe many aspects of human existence. Within this context a new framework has emerged, in the form of critical transculturalisation, understanding the role of the state as mediator. The Ottoman example is actually a good one, underscoring how the state can stabilise intercommunity relations through a mediating approach. This chapter explores how the Ottomans approached state formation and how their approach could adapt and inform current statebuilding models.

Hybridity – exploring the term

Hybridity has been explained in many ways from being just the natural result of immigration, or simply the mixing of two or more races – as was the case in racial and cultural studies – or even just describing the very nature of language. As Said argues in *Orientalism*, 'every domain is linked to every other one, and nothing that goes on in this world has ever been isolated and pure of any outside influence'.[2] The aspect of hybridity most debated is primarily cultural. Scholars such as Nakagama and Krizeks argue that hybridity is many things – it is 'universal and particular, to be the source of identity and difference'[3] – while others such as Young argue that it is simply the notion that something can be 'simultaneously the same but also different'.[4] Andrew Hammond, on the other hand, asserts that hybridity is the creation of a new identity where hybridity 'denotes the way that elements from diverse, seemingly contradictory cultures can, without losing their uniqueness, meet and combine to create a third space of identity'.[5] Some argue that hybridity is simply the new term for 'cross-cultural encounters' which have been a 'regular feature of world history since the earliest days of the human species existence'.[6] It is certainly true that to some degree cultures have mixed over time and exhibited features of what we would call a hybrid culture today. Thus, what do theorists seek to achieve by identifying hybridity within a specific culture? I argue that hybridity is a lens to understand how different actors react to the process of inter-cultural hybridisation. By recognising the hybrid nature of the process, actors such as the state can enhance their ability to predict and adapt to the emerging recognition of a hybrid culture. The adaptation and recognition to the pre-existing process of hybridisation, in practical terms, could inform policy practices of state and non-state actors. If there is any utility in practice to the recognition of hybrid culture, this could have the greatest positive impact in the sphere of statebuilding. Hybridity and hybridisation are arguably at play during the interaction between the 'local' and the 'international' during the creation of new state entities.[7] This makes a strong case for looking at hybridity in such circumstances in more detail, which I will do through the concept of critical transculturalism.

Critical transculturalism: how does it inform our understanding of the state?

Before attempting to demonstrate how hybridity could inform the practices of statebuilding, it appears important to discussion the specific contribution of hybridity discussions to cultural studies. The alternative to recognising that cultures are hybrid and can be reconciled within a 'transculture' is cultural divisions and imperialism. Professor Martinex-Echazbal argues that societies must push for 'a kind of brokerage, an exchange, a give-and-take, a process whereby both parts of cultural equation are modified and give way to a new socio-cultural conglomerate'.[8] Kraidy asserts that critical transculturalism is an alternative perspective from the traditional frameworks articulated around cultural imperialism and cultural pluralism.[9] Table 9.1 captures the main features of cultural imperialism, cultural pluralism and critical transculturalism, respectively.

Table 9.1 Cultural imperialism, pluralism and critical transculturalism

	Cultural Imperialism	*Cultural Pluralism*	*Critical Transculturalism*
Concept of culture	Holistic	Pluralistic	Synthetic
Conception of global culture	Monoculture	Multiculture	Transculture
Central trope	Dominance	Resistance and/ or adaption	Hybridity
Site of agency	Structure	Individuals and or/community	Social practice
Scope of agency	Global	Local and contextual	Translocal and intercontextual
Empirical focus	Material/ Institutional	Local and contextual	Material and discursive and textual
Relation between structure and agency (process)	Dialectical	Dialogical	Dialectical and dialogical
Relation between structure and agency (outcome)	Determination	Interaction and intertextuality	Articulation (lopsided)
Media focus	Production and distribution	Reception and text/message	Production, text and reception and reproduction
Relation of state to external	Too weak	Too strong	Mediator/referee

Source: Kraidy, *Hybridity or the Cultural Logic of Globalization*, 149.

Kraidy argues that transculture is a way of moving away from the 'models of domination and resistance' in the process of the merging of cultures.[10] The critical difference is clear: within transculture, there is no assumption of moral high ground of any particular cultural traits. However, creating this new relationship is far more difficult in practice than in theory. With regard to the means to achieve this new understanding of the world, Kraidy proposes that critical transculturalism is primarily to be achieved through 'social practice'.[11] Social practice according to Kraidy is the site of agency, the means to creating this transculture. However, under the existing political structures, pursuing the ideal of a transculture appears remote. Still, Kraidy acknowledges that 'it may be productive to contemplate a positive role for the state'.[12] It could become the focus of state forces to develop policy that enhances and speeds up the process towards transculture, but the methods may be very different from the policies currently being pursued.

Kraidy suggests a different role for the state, one that plays the role of independent arbitrator, while societal practices pursue change.[13] However, he does not distinguish between the respective scope of developed states and developing states, whose different ranges of capacities may vary to a great extent. In so-called 'developed' states, the state has greater capacity and can influence significantly the trajectory of social change, and can therefore be more ambitious in its goals for social change. Therefore, the scope of ambition should be adapted to the local realities, for example states can develop ambitious goals if the resources and societal legitimacy are firmly established. However, in societies where the state fundamentally lacks both of these core elements, Kraidy's 'mediator/referee' dichotomy could also have some real resonance.[14] *Prima facie*, a good example where a state took such a role is the Ottoman empire.

Reflecting on the Ottoman state and the impact on communities

The Ottomans' approach to governance is a good case of a state that played a 'mediator/referee' role in order to manage the diverse population that lived under its rule. The 'foundation of Ottoman power was the result of brokerage across boundaries, especially religious ones'; as a result, the Christians and Muslims in the Ottoman empire worked towards 'laying the foundations of a hybrid state'.[15] In order to find out how this was done, it is important first to understand how Ottoman society treated the 'other' (those with a significantly different cultural/religious background to the majority). The Ottoman empire lasted from 1299 to 1923 – considering the dramatic changes the world went through over those centuries, this demonstrates a considerable level of longevity. The Ottoman state started out from humble beginnings as just one tribe amongst many in the geographic area we call Turkey today. From the very start in 1299 when Osman founded the Ottoman dynasty, the foundations of the state were not based upon one clearly homogeneous people. This is because the state formed by Osman was not exclusively formed around the Ottoman Turks. Many immigrants from all over the Middle East and Europe established themselves within the Ottoman community. The result of this migration combined with military success set a precedent for the new state, built around compromise and the use of local power structures to rule effectively.

Ottoman policies from the beginning were a hybrid between the Byzantine laws, which used to dominate the area, and the nomadic traditions of the Oghuz Turks. Policies were therefore made with both the indigenous and migrant population in mind. As Yetisgin argues, the 'Ottoman ruling practices had its merits in dealing with mixed communities quite different from each other'.[16] In fact, this is one of the crucial reasons for the success of the Osman dynasty, and the Ottoman state's method of ruling attracted support from throughout the Middle East. As time went on there was an active surge of migrants moving into the Ottoman community. This growth of a diverse population could be argued to be one of the key factors in the Ottomans long-lasting success.

> The Ottomans' success was their official recognition that the diversity over the territories over which they ruled required the adoption of flexible administrative practices that could accommodate the needs of different religions and different cultures.[17]

So which specific policies did the Ottoman state model introduce that allowed for the maintaining of a diverse community while maintaining stability? The main instrument used by the Ottomans was the millet system which was 'a loose administrative set of central-local arrangements, it was a script for multi religious rule'.[18] The millet was organised by a boundary manager system that utilised local community institutions. The Patriarch of the Orthodox Church is one example of this. Their role was to maintain internal cohesion while collaborating with the Sultanate and Divan that made up the Ottoman imperial administration. Table 9.2 makes clear the framework that the Ottoman state utilised to administer the millets.

The millets were a system employed by the Ottoman state to arrange communities based upon religious or ethnic groups. This system and the spiritual-secular fusion that the Sultanate personified can give a glimpse of how critical transculturalism could be achieved on the state level. As Donald Quartart argues, '[t]he [sic] Ottoman Policies of pragmatism and flexibility attracted a host of support regardless of religion of social rank'.[19] Community leaders who maintained the peace and paid their dues, for example, 'would be rewarded with continued appointment and increased opportunity for wealth'. However, those community leaders who failed to maintain the peace across the different communities would have 'lost their livelihoods and more often, their heads'.[20] This mechanism for control although fairly crude meant that local community leaders were strongly encouraged to maintain peaceful relations and the status quo. The key emphasis here is that the state formally integrated religious leaders into

Table 9.2 Fundamental structure of the Ottoman state

Ottoman official classification	*Administrative and political framework of the Ottoman empire*
The Sultan	Head of government and state
The Divan	The executive arm of government
Boundary Manager	Executive leaders of different communities (the Patriarch led the Greek Orthodox community)
The Millet	The administrative format of different communities recognised by the Ottoman state (e.g. Jewish Millet, Greek Orthodox Millet and the Kurdish Millet)

the state structure and strongly encouraged them to maintain minimum standards of governance. Non-religious leaders played a similar role: 'local chiefs and notables at a rural level and neighbourhood chiefs (*mahalle başi*) and guild leaders (*kethüdâ*) also organised their communities' for the Ottoman state.[21]

As a result, the relationship between communities for the most part was relatively cordial. The marketplace exemplified this relationship, where Jews, Christians and Muslims would not only trade with each but would sometimes form 'business associations'.[22] Gilles Veinstein notes that in the local courts of Avlonya, Muslims and Jews testified for each other and often would act as guarantors for each other.[23] Bruce Masters argues that this paints a 'relatively harmless picture of intercommunal relations in Arab cities of the seventeenth century', although in the long run, as he points out, different religious groups did tend to 'cluster together' to form more homogeneous groups.[24] The difficulty with the assertions made by Masters and Veinstein is that, depending upon the location within the empire, especially in a multi-layered system, each city or area would have had different experiences of inter-communal relations. The sheer duration of the Ottoman period makes it incredibly difficult to make assertions about the nature of Ottoman society beyond the time periods and locations of the authors cited. Furthermore, the relatively cordial relationship portrayed by the authors above is not unanimously supported. The Ottomans did indeed institutionalise some brutal practices and they did reinforce existing divisions at different times in their history. Jaber argues that the Ottoman state 'literally legalized instruments of oppression'.[25] In addition, 'Non-Muslim millets suffered serious social, political and legal disabilities'.[26] However, on closer analysis, it is important to remember that Jaber reflects on the later days of the Ottoman empire. For instance, Jaber discusses the historical period when millets were demanding independence; however, this was not the case until the mid-nineteenth century. Hence, it is important to take into account the distinction in time periods. In addition, the other authors quoted here such as Imber have subjected Ottoman history to a considerable revisionist process, which demonstrates that it is not as clear cut as Jaber articulates.

What became the dominant discourse of the Ottoman state from a European perspective during the latter part of the Ottoman period was that it was an Islamic state imposing its will over parts of Europe, Africa and the Middle East through brutal force and repression. Particular elements within Europe went out of their way to portray the Ottoman empire as a danger. Protestant clergy in 1578 claimed that the Ottoman empire 'employed both slavery and strict hierarchical administrative cadres in which everyone feared for his life'.[27] Towards the end of the Ottoman empire was labelled the 'Sick Man of Europe' by Tsar Nicholas I, an empire which had failed to adapt to modernity. However, to conclude with Imber's words, '[d]espite all the stereotypes and preconceptions to the contrary, inter Ottoman group relations during most of the Ottoman history were good relative to the standards of the age'.[28]

How did the Ottomans treat migrant populations?

The complex arrangement of laws around minorities and the Sultan also tell a different story to the picture portrayed by the European elites. The Sultan at the centre of the Ottoman state had in fact a difficult role and balance to maintain within the empire. The Sultan was just one of many titles such as the Emperor or Caesar ('Kaysar'), Caliph and Basileus (King) that the rulers decided to take as an official title as the empire expanded. This was to emphasise to local populations that, even though the state had changed in its fundamental nature, the Sultan would ensure some form of continuity of old practices. The new regime was a hybrid between a secular autocracy and a theocracy. Legitimacy therefore was split between those who determined religious law and those who determined secular law. This was in stark contrast to the universalist rule in Byzantium, which was based on the idea that the Emperor was the living embodiment of God and therefore above the rules of man. Each identity was emphasised strongly to each separate community, but the Sultans were careful to be seen as defenders of minority rights. As Barkey argues, despite the overwhelming influx of Muslim populations into the Ottoman empire and the Ottoman state acquiring a stronger Islamic identity, the Sultan was more interested in the title of Caliph as the 'protector of Islam'.[29] Very few Sultans ever took the pilgrimage to Mecca, because conventions and tradition of multi-religious coexistence meant that the Sultanate came to refrain from overtly preferential treatment for individual groups. Sometimes, however, Sultans did go out of their way to strengthen people's trust in the institutions. When Ottoman expansion took itself into Europe through the conquest of Byzantium, Mehmed II started to claim descent from the 'Komnenian lineage, a noble Byzantine dynasty'.[30] By stating a link to this European dynasty, one of the most noble in origin, Mehmed II intended to garner Christian support for his rule.

Often Ottoman Sultans would invest their own personal funds in huge infrastructure projects within the provinces to demonstrate their commitment to the communities in those provinces. Ahmet III built a huge public foundation in Istanbul which exemplified the Sultans' long tradition of funding personally the maintenance of 'mosques, soup kitchens and fountains almost everywhere in the empire'.[31] Sultans also went to great lengths to honour the Shia branch of Islam by renovating the Karbala and Nejef shrines, which are deemed to be among holiest places for the Shia Muslims. The symbolic nature of these gestures demonstrates a willingness to recognise the importance of subjects who were not part of the Sunni majority.

A principle of local rule by the Ottomans became an important tool for the state. The rulers of Ottoman provinces enabled a porous 'evolution of Ottoman policy by placing importance on local connections'.[32] For example, the tradition of local rule in Moldavia and Wallachia persisted for over 200 years until as late as 1711 because of the perceived treachery by the princes during the campaign against Russia.[33] The relationship between the Sultanate and the Crimean Khans developed an interesting twist as the Sultans declared that the Khans would be heirs to the Ottoman throne if the bloodline ended. Damascus was ruled directly by the Sultan until in 1708 the province of Damascus was given a locally born governor and the ability to gather local taxes, maintaining security and preventing revolts as a means to quell resistance to the centre.[34] In contrast to the customary practice of modern states, which seek to centralise and to only use formal government institutions to enact policy, hybrid government was used to decentralise powers to allow local initiatives while preserving the central political vision. Community-based welfare initiatives became a key instrument for individual communities to contribute to the welfare of the people. To this end 'internal taxes' were collected to push forward projects, including new schools, hospitals and local infrastructure.[35] In the 1830s, the Bulgarians took a further step to create their own 'special school system' which was unique in building a 'secular' school where both girls and boys would be educated.[36] This demonstrates that the power over certain aspects of the state was being devolved by the Ottoman state and may have played an important role in maintaining the status quo.

The integration and embrace of minority religions into Ottoman culture was present from the very foundation of the state. The Jewish community underwent expulsions and persecutions all over Europe, such as the Spanish expulsion in 1492, and collectively fled to the Ottoman empire. The Jewish community enjoyed a 'more complete equality' in Turkey than anywhere else in Europe at the time.[37] Sultans also spent a considerable amount of time trying to understand and support the Jewish and Christian communities. Attending church services and performing religious rituals of the three main religions came to be seen as one of the Sultans' most important duties. In the passage below Mehmed II or the Conqueror (who ruled as Sultan from 1444 to 1481) is described as a ruler who dedicated time to listening and appreciating Christian traditions and listening to their concerns.

> My fellow residents in Pera told me that he [Mehmed II] entered their church [St Dominicus] and took a seat in the choir to observe the ceremony and the manner of the worship service. At his request they also celebrated a Mass in his presence . . . He discussed the laws and rites of the Christians with them as well, and, when he heard that the churches were headed by bishops, he even desired that a bishop be appointed for

> the care of the Christians and promised to do everything in his power to provide his unlimited assistance. But how could anyone who learned from afar of his wars and victories, of the great size of his army, and of his fame and majesty imagine him to possess such simple frankness, or, if he did hear of it, not admire it.[38]

This underlines the fact that minorities and different religious faiths were prioritised at different times during the life of the empire. However, Mehmed II was not the exception when it came to individual Sultans' attitudes towards minority religious groups. When Mahmud II (who ruled from 1808 to 1839) visited Rumelia, he made a speech where he proclaimed that:

> You Greeks, Armenians and Jews, you are all my servants of God, and you are all my subjects – just as good as the Muslims, your beliefs are different, but you all obey the laws and my imperial orders.[39]

As Karateke argues, there was early recognition that if 'people were allowed to practice their religion freely' then as long as the state produced stability and functioned at a basic level, the people were for the most part satisfied to live under Ottoman rule.[40] Particular community leaders expressed some positive evaluations of their experience during Ottoman rule. One example is Samuel De Medina, a sixteenth-century rabbi who in 1566 emphasised that the Jews were able to 'live happily and prosperously'.[41]

This is an indication that the non-Muslim minorities in the empire were at least considered important enough for the Sultan to put considerable effort into appeasing them. In one important way, there is a similarity between contemporary statebuilding projects and the Ottoman experience. The Sultan had to ensure that local structures would remain loyal to the central state and these local entities would continue to implement policy on the central state's behalf. This experience, which aimed at integration, cannot be said to represent Ottoman policy throughout the period of its predominance. Churches for the most part were not repaired and new ones were not commissioned.[42] In the long term, the Ottomans prioritised the Muslim population, as it made up the vast majority throughout most of the Ottoman empire's life span.

Yet, for the most part, sultans made an active effort to be seen to embrace minority religions in order to maintain their own power base. We must be careful in the assessment of why these sultans made the effort to embrace minorities. Certain sultans ruled at a time of dramatic change in the empire, where newly conquered territories were being integrated into the empire and where large-scale mass movements were taking place. Mehmed II presided over a significant expansion of the Ottoman territory, including Constantinople, Serbia, Morea, Bosnia, Albania and Moldavia. Mahmud II took the throne during the Greek war of independence, which eventually was lost by the Ottomans. It was in the interest of sultans to be at least seen as a benevolent leader who did not disregard large parts of a population, as it was the sultan's responsibility to maintain stability in the empire. During a time of conflict, populations which did not have a natural Muslim affinity would resist any far-reaching reforms by the Ottoman state. As Faroqhi argues, 'Ottoman rulers did not assume that religious unification was a precondition for the successful functioning of the state'.[43] This indicates that there was a longer term philosophical understanding of how the state should function, which was passed down through the generations and goes beyond the actions and words of individual sultans.

The role of secularism in the Ottoman empire

Another aspect of the Ottomans' strategy was to balance religious interests with secular principles in order to create stability within the central state. This contrasts with the European perspective at that time which deemed the Ottoman empire to be 'a kind of ecclesiastical state within a Muslim super state'.[44] Part of state administration, elites such as the Ottoman '*kul*-servants', went through a thorough process of education which focused on a wide-ranging syllabus that did not only involve Islamic aspects of statecraft.[45] Education for Ottoman officials took place primarily at the Enderun School which was linked directly to the Palace of the Sultan. Ottoman officials came to understand a tradition known as *adab* which instilled a sense of the world beyond just Islam and legitimacy of the Ottoman state. Barkey argues that the sultans were instrumental in promoting a balance between 'the forces of religion and the forces of the secular'.[46] The most famous example of the role of secular laws was when the 'Kanun of Suleman' allowed the charging of interest on loans by 10 per cent throughout the empire.[47] This shows that the Ottoman administration could contradict Islamic law in particular circumstances. However other cases – such as laws against money laundering – came about purely because Islamic law did not actually cover that particular area. Islamic law came to be seen by the Ottomans as a tolerant basis on which all other laws could be applied. Saray even goes so far to say that Ottoman law was best described to be based upon four basic principles: 'Justice, equality, tolerance and human needs'.[48] Interpretation of Islamic law, therefore, was key, but the Ottomans demonstrated the potential for a mix between spiritual law and secular law.

The role of the Ottoman millets

At the core of the Ottomans' imperial system was a mechanism called 'millets'. The millet system meant that different religious communities had a degree of autonomy about how laws were made and applied. The millets are a good example of how an external power (a system built on relative toleration, i.e. the Ottoman state) can ensure that local elites (such as the Greek Orthodox Church) adhere to standards set out by the central state while also allowing local elites to exercise authority. The millets themselves were primarily religious institutions with a dual role; they served as an official representation of the state but also enabled disputes to be resolved without involving the state-run Islamic courts run by the Divan. The Divan, otherwise known as the Imperial Council, was effectively the cabinet of the government. The millets were a key instrument for the Sultan and the Imperial Council to exercise control over the many different and diverse populations that lived within the boundaries of the Ottoman empire.

The millets represent a considerable devolution of government. As a result, religious minorities effectively had semi-sovereign capabilities, which could be used to keep the peace and to allow local custom to integrate within the general polity. The representatives of the individual millets were even given 'rights to collect tax, education [to run their own education system] and run judicial and religious affairs'.[49] The reason for this is described by Cahnman: 'If they attempted a forced integration [transformative agenda], they might not have been able to exploit the traditional skills and tax capacities of the subject peoples'.[50] The concern for the Ottoman administration was to promote business while also prompting reform. Stability and taxes were the primary concerns of the Ottoman state. The Ottomans 'were content to tolerate the existence of a wide variety of local practices', as they were more interested in 'efficiency than uniformity'.[51] The *Zimme* (people or communities to whom promises had been made), which the Christian and Jewish communities came to be part of, were protected because in Islamic law the *Zimme* or *Ehl-I Kitap* were 'people of the book' and therefore had a right to have their being and property protected.[52]

In some cases, members of different religious communities would become accustomed to living with each other and integrate to a certain extent. Scholars such as Jaber argue that non-Muslims suffered 'serious social, political and legal disabilities' within the millet system.[53] However although *prima facie* the millet system displays segregation, the Ottoman state allowed a considerable amount of religious and cultural integration. The city of Aleppo (in modern-day Syria) is a striking example, as particular quarters designed for particular religious sections became 'homogenous in social and economic status'.[54] A common practice, if not 'culture', was established throughout the Ottoman empire for families to cluster together based more upon social and economic lines rather than according to religion. In the Kurdish quarter, which in the mid-eighteenth century actually had no Kurds left from the 'original settlement', in the early twentieth century 93 per cent of the population were actually Christian.[55] In general, most families chose where they wanted to live and this was often not in the quarters designed initially to house them.

The way that the Ottoman state dealt with the management of the millets was through representation by well-regarded religious leaders who were respected in their communities. The Sultan and/or Divan would consult each religious leader to discuss how best to proceed with state policy in regard to each minority. If there was unrest in any particular area, religious leaders would be called upon along with provincial governors to suggest solutions to the unrest. In some instances, the religious leaders were given considerable power to create local laws, which would bind millets rather than the Sharia law. The Ottoman rulers treated the millet representatives as 'corporate bodies' and they were encouraged to perpetuate their own 'internal structures'.[56] As Jackh argues, the millets almost 'represented themselves to the Sultan as if they were foreign powers'.[57]

The main administrative mechanism that the Ottomans used to manage the Greek Orthodox millet was the position of the patriarch. Patriarchs are the key religious leaders in the Greek Orthodox Church, they wield substantial authority and are usually well respected within the community. During the fifteenth century this role extended even further than it does today, impacting almost every area of Christian life, they were part of the state and were part of its judicial and administrative core. This was emphasised by Sultan Mehmed II who remarked: 'Be the Patriarch in [happiness] and have our friendship on anything you wish and enjoy all your privileges, as all the patriarchs before you also had.'[58] These privileges were a key mechanism to draw the patriarchs into the Ottoman state system. The Ottomans saw the patriarch's position as an opportunity to prevent the possibility of a hostile population turning against them. This became part of an incorporation and integration policy which came to be known as *Istmalet*, which drew in local elites through incentives and concessions, with the end goal of assimilation.[59]

Yet the patriarch's administrative capabilities were limited, as the Ottomans first and foremost wanted the patriarch to pay taxes and to prevent him from becoming a threat to the central state. The patriarch was portrayed as an Ottoman representative, 'he was given the rank of vizier [third rank below the Sultan] and provided with Janissaries [the Sultan's personal bodyguard] to protect him'.[60] The *berat*, an official document giving the patriarch authority over the Christian Orthodox community, had to be bought from the Ottoman state with the approval of the Sultan. Without the approval of the Sultan no institutional endorsement of the patriarch's authority could be gained. Administratively, this document was essential for the patriarch to deal with 'community issues, administrative and educational activities', but it also allowed the church to form its own court system.[61] These courts were allowed to deal with civil matters such as marriage but had to leave 'penal issues' to the Muslim courts.[62] The *berat* also meant that the patriarch would become recognised by the Ottoman state as a fiscal unit. This is demonstrated by Patriarch Jeremie in 1544:

> I took on the engagement to give yearly to the Imperial Treasury as a *mukataa* the sum of four thousand pieces of gold on the condition of being the Patriarch of Istanbul-the-well-protected and of dependent domains and the regions and the countries of Moldavia and Wallachia. Accordingly, I was given the imperial berat.[63]

This is significant insofar as those who were part of a local community but also part of a religious group would maintain their own 'sense of community', but also embrace a collective narrative.[64] On the other hand, the long-term impact of persisting with the millet as a system of governance rather than just a temporary mechanism is that difference started to become an entrenched norm. Hourani argues that the millets 'perpetuated the idea of separateness' in the long term, between Muslims and non-Muslims.[65] This may be the reason why the Ottoman state system came to be seen as the sick man of Europe.

The long-term impact of Ottoman state policy

The partial cultural fusion and effective stabilising policy pursued by the Ottomans also rested upon the authority of the central state. The system had worked around an adherence to the Sultan's imperial orders and to ensure revenues generated from tax collection reached the centre. The main issue with this policy was that as soon as this imperial structure disintegrated and lost authority each community moved towards locally articulated national and religious doctrines. The defeat of the empire in the First World War had a major impact on the confidence the people had in the millet system.[66] By the nineteenth century the demands for 'independence not reform" were difficult to ignore.[67] After the defeat in the First World War, imperial authority started to erode and rebellions against the centre were increasingly dealt with by coercive force. In the case of the Kurds, this 'strengthened [Kurdish] nationalism'.[68] The Kurdish millets earlier on in Ottoman history were prepared to work within the empire, but they came to express nationalism and a desire for national sovereignty. The long-term assumption that the Ottomans relied upon was that the continuation of their particular brand of indirect rule would always be sustainable, but no imperial rule has been able to last indefinitely.

Conclusion: the relevance of the Ottoman empire for current statebuilding practices

Current statebuilding projects within the Middle East do not recognise the significance of these historical circumstances but continue to use the benchmarks of sovereignty and democracy. As Dixon argues, '[n]eo-conservatives and liberal interventions subscribe to the idealistic belief that external powers can successfully re-engineer states into Western capitalist democracies'.[69] Based upon a secular understanding of the state, these projects are frequently blind to the multi-faith dynamic, which continues to play a significant role. In Iraq this was reflected in how the constitution was formulated: the 'Sunni Arab minority which constituted 20% of the population were excluded from the negotiations in 2005 to form an Iraqi constitution'.[70] The premise of the liberal democratic statebuilding project is that legitimacy should come from the people; but the application of this premise has ignored that fact that within local communities religious figures still play a role. For example, the Mahdi army that came to oppose the newly formed Iraqi government was formed based upon religious elites and principles. As Dodge has shown, the Mahdi army was formed around Al Sadr's religious charity, run by a cleric appointed by Al Sadr's headquarters in Najaf.[71] The Mahdi army rose to prominence in 2004 and was the first coherent military force to actively confront Coalition forces in a sustained manner. Clearly the religious authorities had the ability to form alliances and to function actively to oppose the state if turned into enemies. The integration of existing structures therefore could benefit both the state and cultural/religious leaders in the pursuit of common goals.

Comparing this modus operandi with the Ottoman experience, it is the lack of recognition of traditional religious actors in the Middle East which appears to be a major issue. This fuels initial resentment, as democracy to demonstrate its appeal must be fully functional and in states such as Iraq this was not the case. Despite the shortcomings of their imperial rule, the Ottomans went to considerable lengths, especially during periods of instability, to ensure their rule would embrace both secular and religious values. This chapter has demonstrated that the state has been and could be an important agent in the pursuit of adaptable policy frameworks. The Ottoman model could be an inspiration to utilise the idea of the 'meditator/referee' to reflect the diversity of cultures that exist within countries currently going through the process of reconstruction such as Iraq and Afghanistan. However, the Ottoman style millet system has its limits, especially the long-term entrenching of local political actors, which opposed the overall political project. An adapted version of the millet system could thus also harm the pursuit of the ideal of transculturalism as described by Kraidy. The risks of engaging with these local religious entities could encourage nationalism on a local scale, which can increase division and weaken central rule in the long term. Neverthless, the functional model the Ottomans employed could help inform practitioners in their pursuit of alternative policy options that could stabilise the state in the short and medium term, allowing long-term reform to be gradually fed through at a grass-roots level.

Notes

1 Nicolò Machiavelli (2003) *The Prince* (London: Longman Revised Editions), 24.
2 Edward Said (1978) *Orientalism* (London: Routledge), 11.
3 Thomas K. Nakayama and Robert L. Krizek (1995) 'Whiteness: A Strategic Rhetoric', *Quarterly Journal of Speech* 81(3): 291–309, 302.
4 Robert J. C. Young (1995) *Colonial Desire: Hybridity in Theory, Culture and Race* (London: Routledge), 20.
5 Andrew Hammond (2007) 'The Hybrid State: Hanif Kureishi and Thatcher's Britain', in Joel Kuortti and Jopi Nyman (eds), *Reconstructing Hybridity: Post-Colonial Studies in Transition* (New York: Rodopi), 221–40, 222.
6 Jerry H. Bentley (1993) *Old World Encounters: Cross-Cultural Contacts and Exchanges in Pre-Modern Times* (Oxford: Oxford University Press), p. vii.
7 Roberto Belloni (2012) 'Hybrid Peace Governance: Its Emergence and Significance', *Global Governance* 18(1): 21–38.
8 Lourdes Martínez-Echazábal (1998) '*Mestizaje* and the Discourse of National/Cultural Identity in Latin America, 1845–1959', *Latin American Perspectives* 25(3): 21–42, 37; Marwan Kraidy (2005) *Hybridity or the Cultural Logic of Globalization* (Philadelphia, PA: Temple University Press), 148–61.
9 Kraidy, *Hybridity*, 148.
10 Ibid. 150.
11 Ibid.
12 Ibid. 157.
13 Ibid.
14 Ibid.
15 Karen Barkey (2008) *Empire of Difference: The Ottomans in Comparative Perspective* (Cambridge: Cambridge University Press), 55.
16 Memet Yetişgin (2014) 'The Ottoman Way of Governing Multi-Ethnic and Multi-Religious Communities', http://dergiler.ankara.edu.tr/dergiler/19/1157/13616.pdf (accessed July 2014), 1.
17 William L. Cleveland (1994) *A History of the Modern Middle East* (Boulder, CO: Westview Press), 43.
18 Lauren Benton and Richard Ross (2013) *Pluralism and Empires, 1500–1850* (New York: New York University Press), 92.
19 Donald Quartart (2000) *The Ottoman Empire 1700–1922* (New York: Cambridge University Press), 13.
20 Barkey, *Empire of Difference*, 147.
21 Ibid. 143.
22 Ibid.
23 Gilles Veinstein (1994) *Une communauté Ottomane: Les juifs d'Avlony à Valona dans la deuxième moitié du XVI siècle* (Aldershot: Variorium), 790.
24 Bruce Masters (2001) *Christians and Jews in the Ottoman Arab World: The Roots of Sectarianism* (Cambridge: Cambridge University Press), 33.
25 Abu Jaber (1967) *The Muslim world: A Quarterly Review of History, Culture, Religions and the Christian Mission in Islamdom* (Oxford: Hartford Seminary Foundation), 210.
26 Ibid. 220.
27 Yetişgin, *The Ottoman Way*, 138.
28 Colin Imber (2002) *The Ottoman Empire 1300–1650* (Basingstoke: Palgrave Macmillan), 175.
29 Karen Barkey (2014) *Political Legitimacy and Islam in the Ottoman Empire: Lessons Learned* (New York: Columbia University), 471.

30 Hakan Karateke, 'Legitimizing the Ottoman Sultanate'. http://lucian.uchicago.edu/blogs/karateke/files/2014/04/LEGITIMIZING-THE-OTTOMAN-SULTANATE.pdf (accessed July 2014), 24.
31 Quartart, *Ottoman Empire*, 94.
32 Ibid. 103.
33 Ibid. 27.
34 Karl Barbir (1980) *Ottoman Rule in Damascus 1708–1758* (Princeton, NJ: Princeton University Press), 19–20.
35 Howard Douglas (2001) *History of Turkey* (London: Greenwood Publishing).
36 Pierre Voillery (2000) *Le developpement des écoles parmi les populations de l'empire* (Paris : Turcica), 59–83.
37 Imber, *Ottoman Empire*, 221.
38 Georgius de Hungaria (1993 [1481]) *Tractatus de moribus, condictionibus et nequicia turcorum . . .*, ed. and tr. into German by Reinhard Klockow (Cologne: Böhlau; German title: *Traktat über die Sitten, die Lebensverhältnisse und die Arglist der Türken*), 225–7, quoted in Hakan T. Karateke (2005) 'Opium for the Subjects? Religiosity as a Legitimizing Factor for the Ottoman Sultan', in Hakan T. Karateke and Maurus Reinkowski (eds), *Legitimizing the Order: The Ottoman Rhetoric of State Power* (Leiden: Brill), 111–29, 125.
39 Helmuth v. Moltke (1835) *Briefe uber Zustande und Begebenheiten in der Turkei aus den Jahren* (Berlin), 131–42.
40 Hakan Karateke, *Legitimizing the Ottoman Sultanate* (Basingstoke, Palgrave), 125.
41 M. Goodblatt (1952) *Jewish Life in Turkey in the 16th Century as Reflected in Legal Writings of Samuel De Medina* (New York: Jewish Theological Seminary of America), 118.
42 Jaber, *The Muslim World.*
43 Suraiya Faroqhi (2010) 'The Ottoman Ruling Group and the Religions of its Subjects in the Early Modern Age: A Survey of Current Research', *Journal of Early Modern History* 14(3): 252.
44 Ernst Jackh (1944) *The Rising Crescent: Turkey Yesterday, Today and Tomorrow* (New York: Farrar & Rinehart), 525.
45 Barkey, *Political Legitimacy*, 475.
46 Ibid. 472.
47 Haim Gerber (1994) *State, Society and Law in Islam: Ottoman Law in Comparative Perspective* (New York: New York University Press),73–5.
48 Mehmet Saray (2003) *The Principles of Turkish Administration and their Impact on the Lives of Non-Muslim Peoples: The Armenians as a Case Study* (Ankara: Atatürk Araştırma Merkezi), 3–6.
49 Edwin Pears (1917) *Life of Abdul Hamid* (London: Constable & Co.), 26.
50 Werner Cahnman (1944) 'Religion and Nationality', *American Journal of Sociology* 49: 525.
51 William L. Cleveland (1994) *A History of the Modern Middle East* (Boulder, CO: Westview Press), 45.
52 Clote Cahen (1997) 'Zimme', *İslam Ansiklopedisi*, vol. 13 (Eskişehir: M.E.B.), 9.
53 Jaber, *The Muslim World*, 220.
54 Quartart, *Ottoman Empire*, 180.
55 Ibid.
56 Hugh Poulton (2000) *The Muslim Experience in the Balkan States, 1919–1991*, http://www.tandfonline.com/doi/pdf/10.1080/00905990050002452 (accessed June 2016), 47.
57 Jackh, *Rising Crescent*, 75.
58 Halil Inalcik (1991) *The Status of the Greek Orthodox Patriarch under the Ottomans* (Athens: Turcica), 407–37. Moltke, *Briefe*, 237.

59 Halil Inalcik (1954) *Foundations of Ottoman-Jewish Cooperation* (Jerusalem: Mossad ha-Rav Kook), 5.
60 Adam Gielgud (1866) 'European Turkey and its Subject Races', *Fortnightly Review* 6: 9.
61 Barkey, *Empire of Difference*, 135.
62 Inalcik, *Status of the Patriarch*, 407–37. Moltke, *Briefe*, 418–419.
63 Paraskevas Konortas (1989) *Considérations Ottomanes au sujet du statut du patriarcat orthodoxe de Constantinople* (Athens: Congrès International des Études du Sud-est Europeen), 221.
64 Albert Hourani (1946) *Syria and Lebanon* (London: Oxford University Press), 76.
65 Ibid. 63.
66 Nese Düzel (2001) 'Cumhüriyet'i Kuranlar Korktu' [The Founders of the Republic were frightened], http//www.radikal.com.tr/haber.php?haberno¼24546 (accessed Sept. 2015).
67 Roderic Davison (1954) 'Turkish Attitudes Concerning Christian Muslim Equality in the Nineteenth Century', *American Historical Review* 59: 853.
68 Hamit Bozarslan (2005) 'Türkiye'de Kürt Milliyetçiliği: Zımni Sözleşmeden Ayaklanmaya 1919–1925' [Kurdish nationalism in Turkey: from mutual contract to uprisings 1919–1925], in E. J. Zürcher (ed.), İmparatorluktan Cumhuriyetè Türkiye'de Etnik Çatışma [Ethnic clashes from empire to the republic] (Istanbul: İletişim Yayınlari), 89–123.
69 Paul Dixon (2009) *Hearts and Minds? British Counter-Insurgency from Malaya to Iraq* (London, Routledge), 209.
70 Ibid. 315.
71 Toby Dodge (2007) *The Causes of US Failure in Iraq* (London: Routledge).

Part III

New developments in hybridity and legal pluralism

Chapter 10

Legal and normative pluralism, hybridity and human rights

The Universal Periodic Review

Louisa Riches

Introduction

The international human rights project aspires towards the creation of a universal 'whole' in terms of the definition, recognition and protection of fundamental rights and freedoms, at the core of which is a liberal sensibility. However, the enduring stand-off between those accused of cultural violence in their attempt to universalise human rights and, on the other hand, cultural relativists who appear to use culture and traditions to justify human rights violations, is just one illustration of the difficulties besetting this claim to universality.

This chapter analyses the potential of one of the United Nations' (UN) monitoring mechanisms, the Universal Periodic Review (UPR), to mitigate these tensions via its creation of a unique space that accommodates a diversity of voices and opinions and fosters multi-directional interaction within a forum that is universal in terms of structure, scope and participation. As such, this chapter argues that normative pluralism is an apt theoretical framework to be applied to the UPR on the basis that it has the conceptual capacity to describe the UPR's protection and promotion of universal rights and freedoms without eroding cultural difference and sensibility.[1] Furthermore, a normative pluralist approach accommodates state-centrism, a key feature of contemporary international law, whilst also allowing for contributions from non-state actors.

The UPR's normative approach supports institutional development at both a state and international level whereby state sovereignty is acknowledged as being supreme yet open to scrutiny. A state's ratification of a human rights treaty, appearance at the UPR and acceptance or rejection of recommendations are all examples of the exercise of its sovereignty. The fact that there are no legal sanctions for those states that do not implement accepted recommendations contributes to the normative character of the UPR's process. Nonetheless, the focus on state law and international law at the UPR prompts discussion of the concept of legal pluralism although, it is argued, the concept in its various guises is neither a sufficient means of interpreting the UPR's function nor describing the dynamic at play. The coexistence, overlap or interplay of different legal systems, which are the key features of legal pluralism, will not of themselves secure the protection and promotion of human rights. This will be more successfully pursued via a normative process that lends itself to the sharing of norms and the development of institutions and institutional norms in a progressive way, more commonly attributed to normative pluralism.

The perspective adopted throughout this chapter is that, in the context of the UPR, legal pluralism is more helpfully understood as being a subset of normative pluralism. Furthermore, the pluralism at the heart of the UPR creates a broadly conceptualised hybrid space that accommodates similarity and difference, within which the hybrid and the non-hybrid can coexist. The first section of this chapter explains the UPR process and considers the UPR's genesis in the context of the creation of the Human Rights Council (the Council). The second section provides an overview of normative pluralism, with a brief summary of some key contributions to legal pluralism scholarship. It supports the proposition that legal pluralism is a species of normative pluralism and considers the connection between normative pluralism and hybridity in terms of human rights promotion and protection. This section closes by examining the means by which a normative pluralist space inevitably creates a space accommodating hybridity in a variety of forms.

The third section applies the preceding conceptual analysis to the processes occurring at the UPR. It presents the UPR's interactive dialogue as a space within which the approaches of state actors differ, some operating within a legal framework, while others put forward claims on a normative level. It also briefly illustrates the UPR's support of plurality in terms of the needs and challenges relative to individual states. The chapter concludes that the UPR creates a uniquely plural space that opens a realm of possibilities not driven solely by one or another international or regional institution, alliance or regime. Despite the inevitable pressures and political forces at play, ultimately the UPR succeeds in supporting a pluralistic approach to rights realisation, which allows a wide spectrum of concerns to be raised and recommendations to be made.

The UPR and universality

The UPR is distinct from other monitoring mechanisms in being cooperative in its approach, rather than adversarial or inquisitive, and by the fact it is structured around a state-led peer review with input from treaty bodies, civil society and human rights experts.

Resisting politicisation: the UPR's objective and distinctiveness

One of the objectives fuelling the creation of the UPR was to avoid the political interference and cultural violence that other UN bodies have been accused of. The need to resist politicisation and maintain the UPR's credibility was expressed by the President of the Council in his opening remarks at the UPR's 18th working group session. The President reiterated that recommendations made must focus only on human rights in order to 'maintain and "beef-up" the credibility of the UPR system' and that the state under review must respond to all recommendations.[2] Despite these assertions, politicisation and regionalism are inevitable when a body comprises representatives from a state's government as opposed to individuals that are independent and non-governmental.[3] Furthermore, regionalism is at the heart of the UN's structure, divided as it is into five regions,[4] with political allies often providing mutual support on the UPR stage.

Designed as 'a cooperative mechanism, based on an interactive dialogue, with the full involvement of the country concerned and with consideration given to its capacity-building needs', the UPR seeks to 'complement and not duplicate the work of treaty bodies'.[5] It is intended to provide:

> a universal periodic review, based on objective and reliable information, of the fulfilment by each State of its human rights obligations and commitments in a manner which ensures universality of coverage and equal treatment with respect to all States.[6]

Despite a focus on legal commitments, recommendations to the state under review are made by diplomats with a political mandate, and themes emerging during a state's UPR often betray a desire to maintain and/or pursue political harmony. During the working group session of China in 2013, for example, the strategic alliance between Syria and China was apparent: the representative of Syria applauded China's 'open' state report and recommended it continue to play an active role in the Council's work and continue to contribute to solving issues relating to human rights in a fair, objective and non-selective manner.[7] Whilst Russia welcomed China's human rights achievements, the UK expressed concern regarding restrictions on freedom of expression and association and urged greater transparency over the use of the death penalty.[8]

The UPR process

As Ruth Houghton notes in this collection (chapter 5), there 'is a plethora of actors participating at the international level' which itself contributes to a hybrid process. Civil society, comprising domestic non-governmental organisations (NGOs), international NGOs, and others affiliated to human rights matters, including the national human rights institution if there is one, and the media, is invited to make written submissions prior to the working group session. These submissions are then summarised and assembled by the Office of the High Commissioner for Human Rights (OHCHR) into a stakeholder report. A third source of information is a compilation prepared by the OHCHR based upon, for example, reports by special procedures, treaty committees and commissions of inquiry.

The key focus of the UPR is the working group session at the UN headquarters in Geneva, which lasts a mere three and a half hours.[9] Following the state's opening remarks there is an 'interactive dialogue' (considered below) in which reviewing states make comments and recommendations, to which the state under review must respond. The OHCHR then produces a summary report of comments and recommendations made and the state's response. The state should report upon its achievements against previously accepted recommendations in subsequent reviews.[10]

A 'universal' periodic review

A number of the UPR's features seek to counter criticisms levied at the Council's predecessor, the Commission on Human Rights, and to distance human rights discourse from allegations of white imperialistic supremacy. The choice of 'universal' in the UPR's naming carries various connotations. It is universal in the sense that: all states are subject to review; the review concerns all human rights commitments and obligations of a given state; and each state under review and each participating state is treated equally in terms of process and procedure.[11] Furthermore, prefacing the name of this mechanism with 'universal' supports the universalism that underpins international human rights principles, as encapsulated by the Universal Declaration of Human Rights (UDHR).

A key criticism levied at the Commission on Human Rights was its politicisation and selectivity in terms of those states subject to scrutiny.[12] The same cannot be said of the UPR.[13] The equal treatment of states is at the heart of the UPR's structure whereby *all* UN member states are subject to review. During its first cycle between 2008 and 2012, there was universal participation by all UN member states, one aspect heralded as evidence of the UPR's success, and this pattern looks set to continue. Secondly, whilst a treaty body focuses on the particular right it seeks to protect and is homogeneous in its approach, the UPR is not as restricted. Universality is achieved in terms of the UPR's mandate to address the situation in relation to *all* human rights commitments by a given state including legal commitments via human rights treaty ratification, voluntary commitments and those obligations pursuant to customary international human rights law. Further, a state will only report to a treaty body for those treaties ratified, whereas all states are scheduled for UPR regardless of their treaty commitments.[14]

UPR is thus not limited to a particular type or generation of rights; reviewing states raise various concerns and make recommendations across a broad range of civil and political as well as economic, social and cultural rights, from the abolition of the death penalty and commitments to eradicate the recruitment and use of child soldiers, to access to education for rural populations, employment opportunities and land rights.[15] Thirdly, a universal approach to the treatment of each state under review is embodied in the interactive dialogue which illustrates the UPR's equal treatment ideal and sets it apart as a cooperative mechanism (as opposed to adversarial or inquisitive).[16] Whilst the extent to which this element is truly interactive and truly a dialogue might be questioned, it importantly provides a space in which a plurality of voices and opinions are heard in equal measure. One criticism, however, arising from the peer element and equal treatment approach is that states with questionable human rights records are given the floor, albeit for a short amount of time, in which to comment and recommend on matters when the same or similar issues are far from resolved in their own 'back yard'.[17]

Contributing states are allocated the same floor time, although this is extremely limited – being as little as one minute and ten seconds, depending upon the number of states taking part. The dialogue is designed to be progressive and focus on capacity-building needs. It involves comment, reflection and feedback from the state under review which might include reports on progress, implementation and action taken to address nepotism and corruption within the state's government. In addition, there are examples of general requests for support from the international community to assist a state in meeting its obligations and addressing its challenges, as was the case during Afghanistan's second cycle UPR.[18]

The dialogue is not limited to the content of reports; during Cambodia's review in January 2014 protestors gathered outside the official entrance to the UN Palais des Nations in Geneva in response to the Cambodian government's violent crackdown on civil protests by garment factory workers earlier that month. The incident was referred to by a number of state representatives – twelve states expressed concern about the government's handling of the demonstrations, with the majority requesting a credible investigation into the incidents and a lifting of the ban on peaceful assembly. The response of the Cambodian delegation was simply that the ban on peaceful assembly was in line with the country's sovereign laws.[19] Therefore, notwithstanding the equal treatment characterising the UPR, a key consideration is whether its structure is sufficiently robust to support and contain the pluralism and hybridity of the communities, societies and cultures that convene and contribute to what is primarily a state-centric mechanism.

Legal and normative pluralism and hybrid human rights realisation

Legal pluralism

Contestations of the term 'legal pluralism' primarily revolve around what is meant by 'legal': what is 'law' and what is 'non-law'. Despite this, the general consensus is that legal pluralism allows for the coexistence of more than one legal order, and scholarship in the field has championed legal pluralism as a means to underscore the way state and non-state legal orders and norms coexist.[20] Institutional and human behaviour is influenced by a complex web and interplay of norms including legal, social, cultural and religious. It has been argued that legal pluralism can, therefore, be more properly understood as a 'species' of normative pluralism.[21]

A plurality of legal systems challenges a realist and monist state-based concept of law. In this sense legal pluralism shares with international law in general, and international human rights law in particular, a sensibility that challenges the sanctity of state sovereignty and the principle of non-interference[22] as a narrow approach that does not account for the plurality of norms influencing state and non-state behaviour. John Griffiths presented legal pluralism in his seminal 1986 piece as a challenge to legal centralism on the premise that legal pluralism accounts for the presence in a social field of more than one legal order, rather than the centralist approach whereby the state reigns over all legal/normative orderings.[23] Griffiths concluded that:

> a situation of legal pluralism – the omnipresent, normal situation in human society – is one in which law and legal institutions are not all subsumable within one 'system' but have their sources in the self-regulatory activities of all the multifarious social fields present, activities which may support, complement, ignore or frustrate one another . . .[24]

Here Griffiths describes an analytical framework underpinned by normative pluralism. Roderick Macdonald developed this, observing that legal pluralism 'denies the local hegemony of national legal orders and argues for multiple, overlapping, often non-geographically defined legal systems', adding that 'it opens inquiry into the impact of often conflicting implicit normative frameworks'.[25] He highlights the prevailing issue that legal pluralism 'presupposes the possibility of transnational coordination without establishing new formalized and explicit regimes to impose an international normative hierarchy'.[26]

This logic can be seen at play in the international human rights movement and the UPR. The individual and collective rights of the citizen previously considered to relate to the internal affairs of a state, and to be addressed without external interference, are now widely accepted as falling within the remit of international law and subject to the scrutiny of the international community. Brian Tamanaha argues that legal pluralists have 'jammed together' two divergent ways of seeing law as state law and non-state law and that the failure of legal pluralism is a symptom of this jamming together; non-state law is not law and should more properly be referred to as social norms.[27] This strikes a chord with William Twining's approach to legal pluralism as a species of social norms, with social norms being divided into legal and non-legal norms.[28] Gunther Teubner refers to the 'non-foundational foundation of law' and comments that it is constitutional theory that grounds legal authority.[29]

Similarly, Amitai Etzioni finds that attempts to couch human rights discourse in foundational precepts and justificatory language detracts from its success by implicitly supporting the view that human rights are particular to a certain society or culture, therefore undermining claims of universality.[30] Etzioni argues against relativism in its various forms and advocates cross-cultural moral judgement, noting that a failure to do so stops human rights discourse in its tracks. It becomes evident from these discussions that it is almost impossible to deal with 'legal' matters in an exclusive manner; a realisation that has manifest ramifications for the use of the concept of legal pluralism. Rather, the legal and non-legal inform one another and do so as part of a complex interplay of social, cultural and legal norms. It makes sense, therefore, to understand legal pluralism, as Twining does, as a 'species' of normative pluralism, and in particular as a subset comprising social norms sub-divided into 'legal' and 'non-legal', with both having a powerful influence over state, institutional and individual behaviour.

Normative pluralism

In part, normative change emanates from the development of legal principles and the process of standard setting in terms of the expressive function of law. Here, the law functions as a means to say something, to dictate action to conform to a social norm or aspire to an emerging norm and, therefore, operate in a symbolic manner.[31] The primary means by which international human rights are promoted is by encouraging states to commit to international human rights treaties and to introduce and implement domestic legislation accordingly. The UPR, however, promotes human rights principles and protection via other non-legal normative orders that may provide a more palatable basis for a state to base subsequent action upon. A state may prefer, for example, to accept a recommendation made by an ally with whom it already shares certain cultural and/or moral norms. Compliance can thus be justified in accordance with a non-legal normative order, rather than a legal one which the receiving state might perceive as a reinforcement of Western hegemony.[32]

It has been said that the current age of globalisation has seen a move away from the age of modernity characterised by a primacy of law and a return to the primacy of norms that prevailed in the pre-modern age.[33] Such primacy depends on the context; at the local level societal norms will be most prevalent, whereas legal norms may dominate the national level. Action that might be unlawful under international law, for example, might be justified as legitimate in accordance with a moral or cultural norm. Norms are distinct from values; a norm and its normative order relate to control and causation, prompting compliance or sanction when deviated from.[34] As noted above, a normative pluralist approach questions the (traditional) view that legal norms are separate from other norms. Due to a lack of law enforcement provisions for rights violations at the international level, human rights protection may be left relying upon normative ordering. It can thus be argued that it is not simply human rights law that influences state behaviour; it is the power and weight of different normative orders including cultural, religious and moral.

Conceptually, normative pluralism provides a means to comprehend the complex interplay of orders and processes at the UPR and may account for the engagement with international human rights discourse by certain autocratic countries that have previously viewed international human rights law and principles as an expression of a Western liberal agenda.[35] Furthermore, although there is no legal requirement *per se* that a state under review should accept any recommendations made to it, the weight of normative expectation on the part of the international community at the UPR is significant and assumes that states *will* accept a majority of recommendations received. Normative pluralism is thereby important when exploring the processes of international human rights promotion and diffusion by providing an effective means of understanding certain drivers of change and behaviour in this field. This process of overlap, interplay and norm sharing also creates an innately hybrid space with the capacity to accommodate and assimilate difference and plurality.

Hybridity

Hybridity is a 'conceptual lens' that can be used to analyse the international human rights movement in general and the UPR in particular. States are not homogeneous entities existing in separation from their political, geographical and cultural neighbours and arguably never have been. The territorial expansion of the Roman empire and colonialism are just two obvious examples illustrating the role of the hybridisation of tribes, clans, families and cultural traditions as well as legal norms and customs in the emergence of today's state system.[36] A plurality of cultural, social and legal norms exists both within the boundaries of a state and transcends borders as they spread in multiple directions. To perceive these cultures as 'internally coherent, seamless wholes' is a 'false assumption'; a recognition of the 'radical hybridity and polyvocality of all cultures' is necessary.[37]

The legal pluralist approach holds that legal systems are distinct and separate entities operating in parallel to one another, while a traditional reading of legal hybridity sees the creation of a 'new' legal system through the fusion (or conquest) of two or more systems that were previously distinct. Jennifer Hendry, on the other hand, observes that the process of norm dissemination can be understood in terms of transfer, transplantation and translation. Hendry prefers the concept of transfer as it 'provides a more nuanced option for the purposes of investigating an area as complex as intra-state normative plurality'.[38] Conceptually, hybridity encompasses processes of transfer and homogenisation, but its affiliation with colonialism means that as a concept and a way of making sense of the world we inhabit it has, unsurprisingly, been subject to as much criticism as support.[39] Hybridity's different guises and effects have prompted calls not for a single definition but for the development of an analytical framework that is intelligible and usable.[40]

Contemporary interest in hybridity is not unprecedented: S. P. Donlan in his work on legal and normative hybridity, in which he reviews the period between the twelfth and the nineteenth century, concludes that 'legal and normative hybridity is the rule; unified, national state law is the exception'.[41] It thus appears reasonable to understand the national legal orders of the states participating in the UPR as already hybrid products of centuries of hybridisation of different legal and normative frameworks. In this light, normative pluralism has the advantage of moving beyond the confines of the more restrictive concept of legal pluralism and accommodating the complexity emphasised by the hybrid perspective towards national legal orders. Such a conceptual framework has the potential to conceive of rights promotion and protection in a way that does not deny universal principles *per se*, but also allows for cultural specificity as to how that promotion and protection is accepted. As such, normative pluralism provides a means of describing the UPR's dynamic, whereas a broad concept of hybridity that supports the creation of non-homogeneous entities offers a means of interpreting the function of the UPR and its contribution to the processes of rights protection and promotion.

UPR encompassing normative pluralism and hybridity

This section explores the way the UPR encompasses normative pluralism and hybridity with reference to specific examples related to the interactive dialogue. The UPR's facilitation of a broadly conceived hybridisation process does not start with the interactive dialogue but it is there most visible. During that dialogue, multiple voices, identities and opinions gather to explore and encourage the adoption of human rights norms and agreed international standards of behaviour. Normative practice is disseminated amongst member states not only through the making, acceptance and implementation of recommendations, but also by making *ad hoc* requests and pleas. During Cambodia's review, for example, China asked for consideration and respect towards Cambodia's local customs and society (with reference to the Cambodian government's response to garment worker protests, noted above).[42]

State and non-state actor engagement

As with any such mechanism, the success of the UPR's output is largely determined by individual state input and not all states have access to the financial, diplomatic and structural resources of the likes of Western Europe and the US. Interviews with a selection of Commonwealth states reveal that a somewhat haphazard and uncoordinated approach characterised preparations for the UPR's first cycle and undermined the quality of state reports and civil society's capacity to engage.[43] Arguably, civil society has a more visible and active role in the reporting and monitoring of state progress in relation to treaty commitments than it does at the UPR. An NGO can submit a report directly to a treaty committee which is then provided in full to the state concerned. Furthermore, an NGO can apply to attend the treaty committee and make an official verbal submission. This is not so with the UPR.

Civil society representatives may attend the UPR working group sessions but only as observers. Whilst their physical presence is important (to be visible and present is to be acknowledged and there is scope for conversation outside of the formal setting), it has limited tangible impact. Most importantly, by the time of the working group session it is too late to influence state recommendations; representatives will generally have agreed their statement and recommendation(s) at a domestic level prior to arriving in Geneva. Those NGOs that convene and host side-events outside of the formal working group session, generally in the lunchtime slot or at the end of the day, acknowledge this. They nonetheless believe debate is worthwhile because it reinforces the particular challenges faced by the state and applies pressure for future action.[44] Nor does this mean that civil society plays little or no role in the recommendation-making process.

Prior to the working group session, (international) NGOs will lobby participating states to make certain recommendations, with the lobbying of smaller, less powerful states being more successful.[45] Furthermore, stakeholder submissions are available to the state under review to consider during its UPR preparation. The UPR thus provides a vehicle for stakeholders and civil society to influence recommendations and feed in opinions, research and recommendations on a broad spectrum of human rights concerns to be made available on the world stage. Whilst arguably relegated to the role of mute observer during the interactive dialogue, civil society can play an active role in the follow-up process by engaging in subsequent dialogue regarding a state's progress against recommendations, although this varies from one state to another subject to the resources at the disposal of both state and non-state actors.[46]

In terms of a state's engagement with the UPR process, in addition to the issue of available resources, the implementation of recommendations depends on the existence and effective functioning of national institutions and political processes. Without successful implementation the integrity and legitimacy of the UPR is undermined and normative change is stifled. Failure to follow up accepted recommendations is symptomatic of the limitations of a state-centric system. State (in)stability and the proliferation of weak, fragile and fragmented states[47] contributes to a view that the structure of the UN is outmoded for today's increasingly interconnected and interdependent globalised world, facing challenges that were not and could not be conceived by those orchestrating the UN's architecture. The state-centricity of the Council and the UPR, and their combined re-edification based on principles of state authority and sovereignty, reflects the limits of the Council's predecessor, the Commission on Human Rights. Paul Schiff Berman considers the hybrid reality of overlapping spheres of legal authority, noting that one response is for communities to either reimpose territorially based authority, by building both metaphorical and physical walls and boundaries, or seek universal harmonization via a 'world law'.[48] Reconfiguring the UN's state-centric composition faces the key stumbling block of the insistence of the tight grip of individual countries on their state sovereignty and the consequential need to amend, if not completely redraft, the UN Charter.

Conversely, the UPR's dependency on a state-centric structure serves to shine a light on a state's (considerable) human rights deficiencies, even though the direction and intensity of that light is determined by political affiliation and acrimony. The UPR's normative pluralist approach unmasks the cracks and fissures within a state's human rights machinery whilst serving to reinforce the strengthening and cooperative approach at the UPR's heart. This is apparent via themes emerging during the interactive dialogue and those concerns raised by civil society. Numerous recommendations were made, for example, to New Zealand during its second cycle review in January 2014 requiring it to better protect and enforce the rights of its indigenous populations, namely Maori and Pacific families, and to provide adequate redress for violations against the same.[49] The review of Afghanistan during the same period further demonstrates the UPR's capacity to highlight prevalent issues and concerns; recommendations clustered around the rights of women and children, the death penalty and the need to maintain protection of the right to freedom of expression, particularly with regard to human rights campaigners and journalists.[50]

The aspiration towards an interactive dialogue based upon objective concerns independent of regionalism and political affiliation and in favour of a universal approach to rights realisation is not without limitation. There is a risk that political allies will lavish praise that glosses over fundamental human rights issues within the state concerned, as already illustrated with reference to China's review in 2013. It is inevitable though that a state will be both praised and criticised for its achievements. The first cycle review of Tunisia in 2008 illustrates this point. Tunisia was praised for: 'the establishment of the Higher Committee on Human Rights and Fundamental Freedoms' (Kuwait); being 'among the first countries to adopt a Constitution that promotes values of equality, justice and freedom' (Palestine); and 'the strong democratic pluralist system in Tunisia' (Pakistan). In addition, the Philippines stated 'Tunisia's best practices in promoting and protecting human rights in the age of globalization could be set as an example'.[51] Such achievements rest on fragile foundations, given that three years after its first review it was events in Tunisia that sparked the Arab Spring.[52]

To suggest only positive comments were made would be misleading. Japan acknowledged that combating terrorism was important but emphasised the need to respect human rights whilst pursuing this objective; the UK expressed concern regarding the restriction of freedom of expression and the requirement for registration by political parties and NGOs; and Morocco requested 'concrete examples of judicial ruling relating to the promotion and protection of human rights'.[53] As a related but side-issue, whilst the UPR provides an arena for cooperative dialogue in a non-threatening manner, if rights monitoring machinery is functioning effectively we might question whether some warning of domestic and regional unrest should have been revealed during the UPR process. Explanations for the general Arab Spring blind spot amongst the human rights community have included overestimation by human rights activists of the stability of authoritarian regimes in the region and underestimation of the speed with which people were mobilised to take action. Another was that human rights groups were more focused on supply than demand, that is, the extent to which governments 'supplied' their subjects with basic human rights, as opposed to paying attention to the demands of the state's citizens.[54]

Normative pluralism and the accommodation of different paradigms

Both the comments and recommendations made and the response of the state under review may be influenced by the political relationship between the two states, as well as revealing something of the paradigmatic position of each. The accommodation by the UPR framework of such different positions is further evidence of the mechanism's capacity to accommodate plurality, both in terms of the plurality of states vis-à-vis one another and a state's internal plurality, as considered below.

The Syrian delegation's opening statement at its second UPR in 2011 was overtly political; it declared its commitment to universal human rights and the building of a democratic society but stated it was only willing to accept advice from certain African, Asian and Latin American countries.[55] The delegation's view was that Western countries had no right to provide human rights advice given their role in, for instance, conflicts in Libya and Iraq and, furthermore, their colonial legacy.[56] Syria's interactive dialogue occurred during the height of the Arab Spring; related to this, the US condemned the Syrian government for having committed gross violations of human rights against its own citizens in the form of 'mass arrests, arbitrary detentions, torture and targeted killing' that 'continued unabated', and called for President Assad to step down immediately.[57] Cuba made a point of order that the US's approach was entirely unacceptable because neither the Council nor any other UN forum was the appropriate environment for such a request. It fell to the President of the Council to restore order and remind all representatives to continue the process 'in the customary climate of respect',[58] although such a climate of respect leans heavily upon diplomacy and may do little to truly advance the protection of a society's weak and vulnerable population.

The approach of the Syrian government and its supporters might simply reflect a denial of violation, or may hark towards a justification for action during a state of emergency. Alternatively, decisions may be deemed legitimate in the broader context of the US's current and historical human rights abuses outside of its own territory as being indicative of acceptable norms of unilateral state behaviour (for example, Guantanamo Bay and the US's use of military unmanned aerial vehicles, particularly in parts of the Middle East). By comparison, rather than being based on a normative approach, the US's request for the resignation of the Syrian government might have been determined by legal principles, with the US perceiving the interpretation of Syrian national law by the Syrian government, and its actions towards its citizens, as fundamentally incompatible with international human rights law, regardless of the US's own previous and current actions. By situating legal pluralism as a subset of normative pluralism, and by the fact of the UPR's pluralist character, both possible paradigmatic approaches are plausible and neither trumps the other as possessing primary importance.

A primarily legalistic stance is evident again in the US's recommendation to Yemen during Yemen's first cycle review that the state 'step up enforcement of laws protecting women from rape and violence, criminalize spousal rape and treat honour killings no differently than murder'.[59] After postponing a response and examining the issue, during a subsequent Council session Yemen submitted that it accepted the recommendation with the qualifying statement that:

> What the recommendation calls 'spousal rape' does not exist. All marriages are concluded based on consent between the two partners, and a wife who wishes to separate from her husband on her own motion is entitled to file for divorce and for dissolution of the marriage in accordance with the Islamic sharia and the applicable Personal Status Act.[60]

This interpretation of national law and custom does not align with the US's position, or a Western approach, to the issue raised. Yemen's statement, however, suggests it considers its domestic law sufficient and fit for purpose. Remarkably, the Council appears not to have pursued the matter further. The exchange highlights the plurality of norms underpinning domestic law and custom and the extent to which religious practice informs the latter. It also exposes the Council's passive approach in this matter, the result being that a conflict of norms at the international level remains unresolved, one of the weaknesses of the pluralism that characterises the UPR.

The above are examples of plurality in terms of inter-nation interactions at the UPR. As a supplementary point, the operation of principles of legal and normative pluralism are also apparent at the UPR at an intra-state level. Currently ranked as the second most fragile state in the world,[61] Somalia provides an apt example of this. Somalia's second UPR review took place in January 2016 and the associated documentation highlights the deep-rooted challenges the country faces in terms of human rights protection, with all of its reports to relevant treaty bodies being overdue (bar one due in 2017), with one report overdue since 1984.[62] Given this, and societal infrastructure challenges highlighted by the launch in November 2014 of the first postal service in more than two decades,[63] the importance attributed by Somalia to engagement with the UPR should not be overlooked. Autonomous regions in Somalia, namely Somaliland, succeed in operating under a parallel legal and political system in coexistence with Somalia only on a normative level.[64] Furthermore, Somalia is characterised by plurality in terms of patriarchic and traditional orders alongside institutions of the modern state. Armed conflict has resulted 'in the total destruction of assets and infrastructure' in significant parts of the country, and the collapse of the rule of law in its southern and central parts.[65] In terms of the UPR, this situation illustrates both the positive and negative potential of normative and legal pluralism occurring in hybrid spaces of governance within states. Given the loss of a unified national entity combined with deep-seated, often patriarchal, societal practices, UPR recommendations involve longer term action dependent upon statebuilding and the development of the country's infrastructure and its capacity and will to address and regulate particular cultural practices.[66]

Whilst the examples of Yemen and Somalia demonstrate the UPR's inter-state and intra-state pluralism and its ability to accommodate fragile states, they also expose the UPR's key weakness; that whilst these states engage with the process, there is little evidence of any additional resulting support or potential for accepted recommendations to be subsequently implemented. Conversely, Argentina, ranked as a 'stable' state, provides a good example of the operation of normative pluralism within the UPR's hybrid space. Its interactive dialogue offered an opportunity to share on the world stage and in a cooperative environment the experience and difficulties Argentina faces and has faced as a state undergoing a process of 'memory, truth, justice and reparation', both as it emerges from a national crisis relating to the 'terrorist State that perpetrated crimes against humanity in the 1970s' and the more recent 'economic, social and political tragedy' at the start of the millennium due to 'a State that was absent for more than a decade'.[67]

Argentina's interactive dialogue provides evidence of the unique nature of each UPR and its potential for sensitivity towards the human rights situation of each particular state. Peer comments and recommendations were supportive of attempts at progress whilst being mindful of the further domestic action required. The state report presented an openness in terms of acknowledging past human rights abuses and current challenges, and advocated the importance of working in dialogue with civil society.[68] Although the stakeholder submission report raised concerns about the lack of consultation with civil society as part of Argentina's UPR preparation, civil society is evidently active with thirty-seven stakeholders having made submissions.[69] Finally, Argentina proactively engaged with the UPR process to the extent that it submitted an interim report following each of its first and second cycle reviews.

This section illustrates the different positions adopted by reviewing and reviewed states, the operation of the conceptual framework of normative pluralism and the UPR's capacity to accommodate legal plurality. It highlights that, although the UPR accommodates plurality, it does not resolve related tensions. The UPR is constructed, intentionally or otherwise, as a hybrid entity in the broadest sense; it allows for the sharing and dissemination of legal practice and social norms (legal and non-legal) as well as for the expression of legal and normative difference and offers a space in which heterogeneous and diverse actors sit alongside, and in opposition to, one another, and within which there is the potential to effect change, albeit in some cases more slowly than in others.

Conclusion

According to the preamble of the UDHR, 'it is essential to promote the development of friendly relations between nations'; the UPR is instrumental in this respect precisely because of its normative pluralist approach to human rights promotion and protection. This chapter has sought to present normative pluralism as a means of describing the UPR's dynamic and the hybrid lens as a means to assist with understanding its function, with reference to the development of multiple hybrid and normative (legal and non-legal) structures, as each country selects which recommendations to accept and (more importantly) implement. The UPR arena accommodates regional approaches to rights protection and promotion and hears multiple voices via multiple avenues in the development of rights discourse and hybrid cultural norms.

The concept of legal pluralism is not sufficient to describe the UPR's function because states are not legally held to account. Despite the parameters of the review including an assessment of progress against legal commitments, the approach is cooperative, not punitive. This creation of a safe space where multiple voices can be heard is a strength of the mechanism not a failing. A plurality of state and non-state actors participate in these sessions to make statements and recommendations that contribute to the dissemination of international human rights norms. The UPR therefore succeeds in promoting rights via an exchange of viewpoints and the sharing and transfer, though not necessarily convergence, of various political, cultural and of course normative (including legal) orders.

Although over two-thirds of recommendations made during the UPR's first cycle were accepted,[70] this indicator of the UPR's success should be treated with caution. The acceptance of recommendations is in part informed by the weight of the international community's expectations. Those states that are integrated into the international community, or aspire to be, seek to be seen as engaged with human rights discourse; those that are not and choose not to be, less so: 'countries are on the world stage during their review. No one wants to look bad.'[71] In a similar vein, a Bangladeshi government official commented that 'not wanting to be seen to be doing poorly creates a sort of competition to see who has done the most'.[72]

The UPR's capacity to give voice to all states provides the potential to move beyond the limits of a human rights discourse plagued by the conflict between universalism and relativism. It would be naïve, however, to disregard the risk inherent in championing a pluralistic and hybrid, cooperative approach to the promotion of, and compliance with, international human rights; namely that it provides scope for the very endorsement of practices that for a majority of states would qualify as fundamental violations of human rights norms. Embedded cultural norms forming the foundations of society that conflict with defined international human rights norms can be challenged but external actors cannot impose change without accusations of violating sovereignty. Obvious examples include the subjugation of women and child marriage according to traditional cultural practice or so-called religious principles. It is possible that the failure to conform to a norm is seen as an 'alternative conception of normativity' as opposed to a lack of human rights compliance,[73] and that when viewed through the hybridity lens, it is simply the reflection of a different cultural norm or way of being.

For all the faults and issues with the UPR mechanism, it does succeed in providing a stage that is structurally universal in terms of airtime, audience and participation, and on which numerous voices can be heard and opinions expressed and defended, without judgment or retribution and alongside a conscious determination to keep regionalism and political agendas at bay. Yet, despite the UPR's capacity to encapsulate the normative pluralism that characterises the international human rights field, it falls prey to ongoing challenges and dilemmas. The religious, cultural, moral and legal normative orders of communities, countries and regions vie for legitimacy within the UPR arena but, ultimately, it is left to each individual state under review to determine which recommendations made it will accept and what action, if any, will ensue. A state's response to the recommendations it receives will indicate (or betray) its politico-legal persuasions and the most influential normative order(s) for the government of the day. The success of the UPR mechanism will, ultimately, depend upon the extent to which action results from the recommendations accepted – a project for another day.

Notes

1 Michael Goodhart (2003) 'Origins and Universality in the Human Rights Debates: Cultural Essentialism and the Challenge of Globalization', *Human Rights Quarterly* 25(4): 935–64.
2 Author's own notes of comments made by Baudelaire Ndong Ella, Human Rights Council President during observation of the opening of the UPRworking group 18th session at the Palais de Nations, Geneva, 27 Jan. 2014.
3 Philip Alston (2006) 'Reconceiving the UN Human Rights Regime: Challenges Confronting the New UN Human Rights Council', *Melbourne Journal of International Law* 7(1): 185–224, 189.
4 The African Group, the Asian Group, the Eastern European Group, the Latin American and Caribbean Group (GRULAC), and the Western European and Other Group (WEOG). For a list of the members of each group, see 'Department for General Assembly and Conference Management – UN Regional Groups of Member States', http://www.un.org/depts/DGACM/RegionalGroups.shtml (accessed Nov. 2014).
5 Ibid.
6 UN General Assembly Resolution 60/251, 3 Apr. 2006, para. 5(e).
7 'Report of the Working Group on the Universal Periodic Review, China (including Hong Kong, China and Macao, China)', A/HRC/25/5, 4 Dec. 2013, para. 165, https://documents-dds-ny.un.org/doc/UNDOC/GEN /G13/188/55/PDF/G1318855.pdf?OpenElement (accessed Mar. 2016).
8 Ibid., paras 135 and 176.
9 The Council sought to address the time constraints prior to the start of the UPR's second cycle: 'Follow-up to the Human Rights Council resolution 16/21with regard to the universal periodic review', A/HRC/DEC/17/119, 19 July 2011.
10 Ibid., para. 2.

11 This ensures 'universality of coverage and equal treatment with respect to all States', as required, General Assembly Resolution 60/251, 3 Apr. 2006, para. 5(e).
12 In particular, the Commission on Human Rights came under fire from the 'like-minded group' of states comprising a number of developing states led by China that called for an end to all country-specific criticisms and urged a more general and cooperative set of procedures; see UN Information Service, 'Commission on Human Rights Opens Sixty-First Session', UN Doc HR/CN/1 107 (14 March 2005), and Alston, 'Reconceiving the UN Human Rights Regime', 204–6.
13 Although scepticism as to the UPR's potential to succeed where the Commission failed was raised at its inception, Nico Schrijver (2007) 'The UN Human Rights Council: A New "Society of the Committed" or Just Old Wine in New Bottles', *Leiden Journal of International Law* 20(4): 809–23.
14 There was some debate as to whether non-ratified treaty obligations should fall within the review, see Rosa Freedman (2011) 'New Mechanisms of the Human Rights Council', *Netherlands Quarterly of Human Rights* 29(3): 289–323, 299.
15 These are themes prevalent in many of the recommendations made to Afghanistan during its review on 27 Jan. 2014, 'Report of the Universal Periodic Review Afghanistan, Human Rights Council', 26th Session, A/HRC/26/4, 4 Apr. 2014.
16 General Assembly Resolution 60/251, 3 Apr. 2006, par. 5(e).
17 See comments made by the international NGO Human Rights Voices regarding recommendations made to Norway during the 19th session of the UPR by Iran, Russia, Saudi Arabia and Sudan, http://www.humanrightsvoices.org/site/developments/?d=12139 (accessed May 2014).
18 Author's own observation of the UPR working group 18th session, Jan. 2014.
19 'Report of the Working Group on the Universal Periodic Review: Cambodia', A/HRC/26/16, 27 Mar. 2014, paras 53, 91 and 93, https://documents-dds-ny.un.org/doc/UNDOC/GEN/G14/127/27/PDF/ G1412727.pdf?OpenElement (accessed Mar. 2016).
20 William Twining (2010) 'Normative and Legal Pluralism: A Global Perspective', *Duke Journal of Comparative and International Law* 20(3): 473–517, 474; see also Gad Barzilai (2008) 'Beyond Relativism: Where is Political Power in Legal Pluralism?', *Theoretical Inquiries in Law* 9(2): 395–416, 396.
21 Twining, 'Normative and Legal Pluralism', 473.
22 See Charter of the UN, Articles 2(1) declaring the sovereign equality of all members of the UN and 2(7) in support of the principle of non-interference.
23 John Griffiths (1986) 'What is Legal Pluralism?', *Journal of Legal Pluralism and Unofficial Law* 18(24): 1–55, 1, 3; described by Brian Tamanaha as '*the* seminal piece in the field, [which] set forth the concept of law that is adopted by most legal pluralists'; Brian Z. Tamanaha (2007) 'Understanding Legal Pluralism: Past to Present, Local to Global', *Sydney Law Review* 30(3): 375–411.
24 Griffiths, 'What is Legal Pluralism?', 39.
25 Roderick A. Macdonald (1998) 'Metaphors of Multiplicity, Civil Society, Regimes and Legal Pluralism', *Arizona Journal of International Comparative Law* 15(1): 69–92, 79.
26 Ibid.
27 Brian Z. Tamanaha (1993) 'The Folly of the 'Social Scientific' Concept of Legal Pluralism', *Journal of Law and Society* 20(2): 192–217, 208.
28 Twining, 'Normative and Legal Pluralism', 480–1.
29 Gunther Teubner (2004) 'Societal Constitutionalism: Alternatives to State Centered Constitutional Theory?', in Christian Joerges, Inger-Johanne Sand and Gunther Teubner (eds), *Transnational Governance and Constitutionalism* (Oxford: Hart Publishing), 3–28.

30 Amitai Etzioni (2010) 'The Normativity of Human Rights is Self-Evident', *Human Rights Quarterly* 32(1): 187–97, 195.
31 Scott N. Arnold (2000) 'Postmodern Liberalism and the Expressive Function of Law', *Social Philosophy and Policy* 17(1): 87–109; Cass R. Sunstein (1996) '*On the Expressive Function of Law*', *University of Pennsylvania Law Review* 144(5): 2021–53, 2021, discussed further in Louisa Riches and Simon Gardiner (forthcoming 2016) 'Racism and Homophobia in English Football', *International Journal of Discrimination Law.*
32 See the comments made by Syria during its review in the UPR's second cycle, as referred to in the following section.
33 Touko Piiparinen (2012) 'Exploring the Methodology of Normative Pluralism', in Jan Klabbers and Touko Piiparinen (eds), *Normative Pluralism and International Law* (Cambridge: Cambridge University Press), 35–63, 36.
34 Ibid., 39.
35 Etzioni, 'Normativity', 194, with reference to Singapore and China.
36 See e.g. Gareth Sears's and Philip Myers's contributions to this volume (Chs 6 and 7).
37 Seyla Benhabib (2002) *The Claims of Culture: Equality and Diversity in the Global Era* (Princeton, NJ: Princeton University Press), 25.
38 Jennifer Hendry (2013) 'Legal Pluralism and Normative Transfer', in Günter Frankenberg (ed.), *Order from Transfer: Comparative Constitutional Design and Legal Culture* (Cheltenham: Elgar Publishing), 153–70.
39 Bill Ashcroft, Gareth Griffith and Helen Tiffin (1998) *Key Concepts in Post-Colonial Studies* (London: Routledge); Homi K. Bhabha (1994) *The Location of Culture* (London: Routledge). For a comprehensive overview of the criticisms of hybridity, see Paul O'Connor (2014) 'Applying Hybridity: Rhythms of the Hajj, Tumblr, and Snowden', *Glocalism: Journal of Culture, Politics and Innovation* 2014(1), http://www.glocalismjournal.net/Issues/HYBRIDITY/Articles/Applying_Hybridity_Rhythms_Of_The_Hajj_Tumblr_And_Snowden.kl (accessed June 2014).
40 Marwan M. Kraidy (2005) *Hybridity, or the Cultural Logic of Globalization* (Philadelphia, PA: Temple University Press), p. iv.
41 Sean P. Donlan (2011) 'Remembering: Legal Hybridity and Legal History', *Comparative Law Review* (June): 1–23, 2.
42 Author's own notes observing the UPR working group 18th session for Cambodia, 28 Jan. 2014.
43 Purna Sen (2011) *Universal Periodic Review: Lessons, Hopes and Expectations* (London: Commonwealth Secretariat), 12 and 21.
44 Author's own notes attending a side event hosted by Alkarama, during Yemen's second cycle review, UPR 18th session, 29 Jan. 2014.
45 As this chapter's author was informed during informal discussions with an INGO representative; 18th UPR working group session, 28 Jan. 2014.
46 This may be due to resource implications and the level of commitment, as well as structural capacity.
47 Stefan Wolff (2011) 'The Regional Dimensions of State Failure', *Review of International Studies* 37(3): 951–72.
48 Paul S. Berman (2005) 'From International Law to Law and Globalization', *Columbia Journal of Transnational Law* 43: 485–556.
49 'Report of the Working Group on the Universal Periodic Review, New Zealand', A/HRC/26/3, 7 Apr. 2014, https://documents-dds-ny.un.org/doc/UNDOC/GEN/G14/131/43/PDF/G1413143.pdf?OpenElement (accessed May 2016).
50 'Report of the Working Group on the Universal Periodic Review, Afghanistan', A/HRC/26/4, 4 Apr. 2014, https://documents-dds-ny.un.org/doc/UNDOC/GEN/G14/129/52/PDF/G1412952.pdf?OpenElement (accessed May 2016).

51 'Report of the Working Group on the Universal Periodic Review, Tunisia', A/HRC/8/21, 22 May 2008, http://daccess-dds-ny.un.org/doc/UNDOC/GEN/G08/136/23/PDF/G0813623.pdf?OpenElement (accessed June 2014).
52 Eva Bellin (2012) 'Reconsidering the Robustness of Authoritarianism in the Middle East: Lessons from the Arab Spring', *Comparative Politics* 44(2): 127–49; Filipe R. Campante and Davin Chor (2012) 'Why was the Arab World Poised for Revolution? Schooling, Economic Opportunities, and the Arab Spring', *Journal of Economic Perspectives* 26(2): 167–87, 167.
53 'Report of the Working Group on the Universal Periodic Review, Tunisia', HRC 8th Session, Agenda item 6, GA, A/HRC/8/21, 22 May 2008, paras 27, 28 and 31.
54 Eric Goldstein (2013) 'Before the Arab Spring: The Unseen Thaw', Human Rights Watch, 13 Dec., https://www.hrw.org/world-report/2012/country-chapters/middle-east/north-africa-global.
55 A discussion of the ongoing civil war in Syria and the role of the international community in human rights terms, from a humanitarian perspective and in relation to international criminal law, is beyond the scope of the current chapter; it is acknowledged that this example is as a simple illustration.
56 'Report of the Working Group on the Universal Periodic Review, Syrian Arab Republic', A/HRC/19/11, 24 Jan. 2012, paras 7 and 10, https://documents-dds-ny.un.org/doc/UNDOC/GEN/G12/102/33/PDF/G1210233.pdf?OpenElement (accessed Apr. 2016).
57 Ibid., para. 31.
58 Ibid.
59 'Report of the Working Group on the Universal Periodic Review, Yemen' A/HRC/12/13, 5 June 2009, para. 93.13, https://documents-dds-ny.un.org/doc/UNDOC/GEN/G09/139/40/PDF/G0913940.pdf?OpenElement (accessed Apr. 2016).
60 'Report of the Working Group on the Universal Periodic Review, Yemen; Addendum, Views on conclusions and/or recommendations, voluntary commitments and replies presented by the State under review', A/HRC/12/13/Add.1, 23 Sept. 2009, recommendation 13.
61 Fund for Peace (2016) Fragile States Index, http://fsi.fundforpeace.org (accessed Apr. 2016)/.
62 'Compilation prepared by the Office of the United Nations High Commissioner for Human Rights in accordance with paragraph 15(b) of the annex to Human Rights Council resolution 5/1 and paragraph 5 of the annex to Council resolution 16/21: Somalia', A/HRC/WG.6/24/SOM/2, 23 Nov. 2015, https://documents-dds-ny.un.org/doc/UNDOC/GEN/G15/266/94/PDF/G1526694.pdf? OpenElement (accessed May 2016).
63 'Somalia profile', BBC News Online, 1 Mar. 2016, http://www.bbc.co.uk/news/world-africa-14094632 (accessed May 2016).
64 Brad Poore (2009) 'Somaliland: Shackled to a Failed State', *Stanford Journal of International Law* 45: 117–50.
65 'Report of the Working Group on the Universal Periodic Review, Somalia', A/HRC/18/6, Human Rights Council 18th session, 11 July 2011, http://daccess-dds-ny.un.org/doc/UNDOC/GEN/G11/145/90/PDF/ G1114590.pdf?OpenElement (accessed June 2014).
66 Ibid.; 'The Somali Penal Code covers "hurt", "grievous hurt" and "very grievous hurt" and Islam also prohibits female genital mutilation (FGM). However, FGM is widespread in Somalia and almost all Somali women and girls are subjected to this damaging practice', para. 19.

67 'Report of the Working Group on the Universal Periodic Review: Argentina', A/HRC/22/4, 12 Dec. 2012, https://documents-dds-ny.un.org/doc/UNDOC/GEN/G12/186/90/PDF/G1218690.pdf?OpenElement (accessed Apr. 2016), para. 7.
68 See e.g. reference in para. 21 of the Working Group report, the delegation's reference to the ongoing need to improve the situation in relation to detainees, and para. 22 regarding the pending adoption of domestic laws regarding the prevention of torture that it hoped to report to the Human Rights Council.
69 'Summary prepared by the Office of the High Commissioner for Human Rights in accordance with paragraph 5 of the annex to Human Rights Council resolution 16/21: Argentina', A/HRC/WG.6/14/ARG/3, 19 July 2012, https://documents-dds-ny.un.org/doc/UNDOC/GEN/G12/155/45/PDF /G1215545.pdf?OpenElement (accessed Apr. 2016).
70 Edward R. McMahon (2012) 'The Universal Periodic Review: A Work in Progress. An Evaluation of the First Cycle of the New UPR Mechanism of the United Nations Human Rights Council', *Dialogue on Globalisation Study* (Geneva: Friedrich Ebert Stiftung), 3.
71 Ibid. 13.
72 Ibid.
73 Macdonald, 'Metaphors of Multiplicity', 79.

Chapter 11

Deconstructing a sovereign right

The hybridisation of the anti-death penalty discourse in Europe

Jon Yorke

Introduction

The European Union (EU)[1] and the Council of Europe (CE)[2] have created a hegemonic position for the abolition of the death penalty and both regions are now initiating external projects to contribute to the global removal of the punishment. At the apex of a legislative alignment of the two regions' uncompromising human rights position is the EU's Charter of Fundamental Rights of the European Union, Article 2, which states, (1) '[e]veryone has the right to life; (2) No one shall be condemned to the death penalty, or executed',[3] and the CE Protocol No. 13 to the Convention for the Protection of Human Rights and Fundamental Freedoms, concerning the abolition of the death penalty in all circumstances, Article 1, which similarly states, '[t]he death penalty shall be abolished. No one shall be condemned to such penalty or executed.'[4] There can be no derogations from these absolute prohibitions, no re-creation of a capital judicial system, no training of executioners, no construction of a death row and no execution chamber or engineering of execution apparatus or formulation of lethal substances for such punishment.[5]

We need to understand how this legislation has solidified the abolitionist position and to do so necessitates placing the human rights perspectives alongside additional sources of influence and power. The overarching political science scrutiny of the death penalty is found most notably through what Michel Foucault termed the 'classical theory of sovereignty'.[6] The theory complicates the uncompromising human rights position by articulating a ruling conception – usually a Westphalian statist sovereign formation within a designated territory, based upon a varying theme of the theory of the social contract[7] – with the attaining of a Weberian 'monopoly over the legitimate use of physical force in the enforcement of its order'.[8] This monopoly over legitimate violence includes the political power and legal right of capital punishment and to sufficiently situate the reflexivity of such a position, we need to consider the paradigmatic figure of the 'public enemy' or the 'monster' who breaches the social contract. This protagonist is identified through the lens of the 'worst of the worst' criminal which had committed the 'most serious crimes'[9] and so is deserving of the ultimate punishment.

The 2001 'Dialogue' between two eminent French philosophers, Jacques Derrida and Elisabeth Roudinesco,[10] and the 2014 publication of Derrida's 'Seminar on the Death Penalty' (1999–2000),[11] reveals a useful discursive framework to assess the evolution of the political and legal processes administered within Europe towards people who commit the most serious crimes. Derrida and Roudinesco laid bare numerous agonistic exchanges which are cogent for the questioning of whether the classical theory of sovereignty can now stand in juxtaposition with the global movement for abolition.

This chapter uses this *agonism*[12] to analyse whether the European regions (both the European Union and the Council of Europe) can be viewed as promoting abolitionism within the social science approach to 'hybridity theory'. It seeks to reveal the interweaving filaments of discourse and praxis within the conflicts between abolitionism and retentionism. Borrowing from Freedman and Lottholz (this volume), hybridity occurs where there is resistance to domination. In this context, hybridity is applied for challenging head-on the *sovereign's domination* over individuals within a capital judicial system through to an execution. The analysis investigates whether the European regions can be identified as 'hybridiser(s)' of abolitionism. Or whether the praxis of abolition of the death penalty occurred organically – through mutually consensual weaving of discourses outside of any discernible trajectory of European institutions' abolitionism. Today, various contributory strands for promoting abolition are entwined, and a critical review of the different sources and fora of resistance against this punishment makes it clear that a strengthening of the abolitionist discourse has rendered global consequences for countries trying to prevent the cutting of the noose or blunting of the sword or bending of the needle.

This chapter first provides a working definition of the essential elements of hybridity discourse. The theory and practice of hybrid processes is found in various disciplines, such as plant biology, animal species and anthropology, and has now demonstrated a significant tributary within political science theory and in particular the investigations into the formulation and manifestation of sovereign power. Then the chapter engages with the Derrida/Roudinesco dialogue to frame the debate over the 'public enemy' and investigates whether, with the illumination of hybridity studies, the classical theory of sovereignty can now appropriately maintain the death penalty for such criminal protagonists, as they are labelled by states. The essential features of the European Union's and the Council of Europe's abolitionist discourse are then proposed to determine to what extent hybridity theory can further help understand the recent abolitionist phenomenon. A new understanding of abolitionism may be discerned through hybridity theory, and perhaps the theory's most significant contribution will be via a multi-faceted attack on this archaic vestige of statist sovereign privileging.

Approaching a political science discourse on hybridity

In its essentialist outcome, the process of hybridity – *hibrida* – produces a new phenomenon. Various entities (the contributors are not limited to two, and can be indeterminate) are brought together for a generative project. In effect, hybridity theory can set an action in motion or be used, *ex post facto*, to locate antecedent influences contributing to and producing different outcomes, creations and motions. The theory of hybridity is found in biology, for example, in plant hybridisation that produces a new plant variation which can occur synthetically and/or naturally,[13] and in 'gain-of-function' experiments to incorporate altered amino acids into pathogens to study effects to develop treatment plans in influenza pandemics.[14] Multi-faceted and multi-contributory factors also occur in animal hybridisation, in both same species and inter-species variants.[15] In anthropology, the effects of human procreation from inter-race intercourse is studied. Homi Bhabha adopted the theory of hybridization to demonstrate that imperial powers perpetuated postcolonial anxieties about mixed-race breeding and the essentialist claims of the purity of one race over another.[16] The disciplines of political science and sociology have utilised the anthropological perspectives and identified the discourse, processes and outcomes of systems which feed into theories of racism, fear of the 'other' and the tragic consequences which occur.[17] There is a reflexive nature to the theory of hybridity which attempts to correctly isolate various factors of influence and pressures for change and response. Haj Yazdih states that hybridity studies identify the 'blended, patch worked and layered influences' on a subject and/or outcome, and that '[c]onsiderations of hybridity run the gamut from existential to material, political to economic'.[18] Social science hybridity studies analyse political events through top-down and bottom-up, horizontal and shifting axes, and variable genealogy, to understand what was, what is and what might be. In effect, it is a study of the mutability of the boundaries of concepts, and Ien Ang notes that hybridity theory confronts and problematises these boundaries and so the theory is a heuristic device which can be used to analyse complicated entanglement.[19] Reflecting this entanglement, Piero Bassett states that, 'social customs, scientific discoveries, political experiences and technical innovations have always tended to merge together, giving rise to new realities'.[20]

The concept of 'new realities' for a very real future horizon of a 'death penalty free world',[21] has evolved from the global abolitionist movement.

The sovereign relationship with the death penalty has a vast history, and the political phenomenon which encapsulated the power and right to impose the punishment dates, at least, back to *c.*2000 BCE to the Hebrew Mosaic law in the Torah of the *lex talionic*, 'eye for an eye',[22] or in the adoption of the mandated punishments in the Code of Hammurabi in the Mesopotamian period *c.*1772 BCE.[23] In a qualitative observation, retributive forms of political sovereignty have sought to reserve for themselves the power and right to the death penalty for over 4,000 years. The weight of this historical burden significantly contributed to the observations of Günther Kaiser, Professor of Criminology and Head of the Max Planck Institute for Foreign and International Criminal Law, who stated in 1986 that 'there appears to be little hope that international bodies, whether private or official, will be able to achieve unanimity [among] the majority of countries concerning the restriction or abolition of capital punishment'.[24] Furthermore, Sir Leon Radzinowicz who was the first Wolfson Professor of Criminology, the founding Director of the Cambridge Institute of Criminology, and who had been a member of the Royal Commission on Capital Punishment (1949–53),[25] stated in 1999, in a dejected resignation, '[c]apital punishment has displayed throughout its chequered and frequently repellent history a truly exceptional degree of durability'.[26] This history and the lack of consensus against the death penalty at the international level meant that Kaiser and Radzinowicz could not envisage a 'reality' of the global abolition of the death penalty. The abolitionist movement was too fragmented at the time and had not yet begun to significantly 'weave' together to become a hegemonic force, and therefore the abolitionists' strength created by this enmeshing together of different performative strands had not yet been envisaged.

However, abolition is occurring. 'Little hope' has grown into a 'new reality' as the anti-death penalty hegemony is continually mobilising to bear down upon the decreasing retentionist states. The European regions, which are the focus of this chapter, have unified their abolitionist efforts successfully. The last execution on European soil occurred in Latvia in 1997.[27] Contrary to Kaiser's and Radzinowicz's unconfident reading of the potential of the abolitionist community, there is a regional mandate for abolition and a significant impetus for a global calling for retentionist states to reject the punishment and create a world without the death penalty. To help understand why Kaiser and Radzinowicz could not envisage the solidification of the abolitionist community, and in effect, imagine the different abolitionist strands coming together, we now engage with the philosophical debate on the classical theory of sovereignty. In effect, this debate represents the difficulty of emerging from the binary 'sovereign-and-citizen' analysis, and the neutralising of socially disruptive circumstances through recourse to capital punishment.

The Derrida-Roudinesco dialogue: the limits of Westphalian sovereignty

In the 2001 dialogue between Jacques Derrida and Elisabeth Roudinesco,[28] the two French philosophers discussed pre-selected 'great questions that mark our age'.[29] Amongst these was the issue of the 'death penalty and its necessary abolition'.[30] What followed was a discussion on the hegemonic apparatus which creates and seeks to maintain the punishment. Derrida stated:

> [a] 'deconstruction' of what is most hegemonic in philosophy should include a deconstruction of the death penalty, and everything with which it is in solidarity – beginning with a certain concept of sovereignty.[31]

For Derrida, there is a 'solidarity' or a necessary symbiotic relationship between sovereignty and the application of the death penalty and this ubiquitous matrimony is the disconcerting paradigmatic lens from which he provides his reading of European philosophy. He stated the '[f]act about the history of Western philosophy: never, *to my knowledge*, has any philosopher *as such, in his or her own, strictly and systematically philosophical discourse,* never has any philosophy *as such* contested the legitimacy of the death penalty' (emphasis in original).[32] In further vitiation, '[f]rom Plato to Hegel, from Rousseau to Kant (who was undoubtedly the most rigorous of them all), they expressly, each in his own way, and sometimes without much hand-wringing (Rousseau), took a stand *for* the death penalty' (emphasis in original).[33] Such philosophical dystopia was affirmed in Derrida's First Seminar on the Death Penalty at the University of California, Irvine, on 8 December 1999, when he stated:

> [n]ever is the state or the people or the community or the nation in its statist figure, never is the sovereignty of the state more *visible* in the gathering that founds it than when it makes itself into the seer and *voyeur* [voyante et voyeuse] of the execution of an irrevocable and unpardonable verdict, of an *execution* [emphasis in original].[34]

Derrida's interpretation of this philosophical tradition could not emerge from its alignment with Westphalian sovereignty. It included the Enlightenment theory of the social contract, Immanuel Kant's categorical imperatives,[35] the phenomenology of Emmanuel Levinas[36] and the literature of Maurice Blanchot,[37] as not having adequately solved the problem of how to deal with threats to the life of the sovereign and the life of his citizens. Hence, Derrida was of the opinion that there will always be circumstances where the death penalty would be viewed as necessary for the survival of the sovereign and his subjects. Jean-Jacques Rousseau, a favourite of Derrida's, had legitimised the punishment in his *Social Contract* through the execution of the 'public enemy'.[38] When a murderer breaks the 'right to life' clause, which is the foundational provision of the compact,[39] because survival is at stake, a binary position is proposed; either the sovereign or the individual ('public enemy', 'monster') will perish.[40] This binary position became a methodological platform to allow the privileging of the sovereign-versus-citizen binary. It has created the circumstance for the potential stifling of theoretical enquiry and prevented an analytical gaze to search for further contributory factors and influences.

In continuation of this, Derrida claimed that the Italian Enlightenment humanist, Cesare Beccaria, allowed for the death penalty in exceptional cases.[41] Beccaria is recognised as one of the main figures promoting the abolitionist discourse in modernity, and within his tract, *An Essay on Crimes and Punishment*, first published in 1764, he argued for the general abolition of the death penalty, but conceded that, '[t]here are only two grounds on which the death of a citizen might be held to be necessary'.[42] The first is when an individual 'retains such connections and such power as to endanger the security of the nation, when, that is, his existence may threaten a dangerous revolution in the established form of government'.[43] The second was when the death penalty is demonstrated to be a deterrent, but Beccaria argued that 'centuries of experience' had revealed that 'the ultimate penalty has never dissuaded men from offending against society'.[44]

This threat to sovereignty and security was also taken up by Jean Graven, Judge of the Court of Appeal in Geneva, following a death penalty symposium organised by the post-war abolitionists Albert Camus and Arthur Koestler in Paris in 1957.[45] Graven stated that the punishment should be reserved for 'those antisocial elements which can be stopped only by being eliminated, in the "last resort" . . . [w]hat then should be done with those individuals who have always been considered proper subjects for elimination?' Graven then answered his own question rhetorically, '[s]ociety has not the right to kill even these "monsters"!'[46] In 1961, James Avery Joyce critiqued Graven's propositions and stated that he had failed to empirically reveal how the death penalty was an adequate penological tool against present and future 'monsters'. Joyce argued that he had not understood the wider sociological issues associated with the commission of crime, as he asked, '[h]ow did we get these "monsters" anyway – national and international ones?'[47] Graven's thesis did not provide an answer because his reasoning was shackled to the absolute binary position. So Joyce can be viewed as engaging a nuanced understanding as he reveals that there is something more, something alternative, that can be offered to the death penalty debate than a lethargic resignation in accepting the binary position. Through this reading we can sow the seeds of hybridity discourse, and necessitate a recall of the foundational role of the sovereign in promoting and fostering the life of the populace (instead of killing its members): from reducing infant mortality to increasing life expectancy.[48] We can approach an understanding of this political process as we present concepts of human dignity in punishment which seek to ensure the preservation of life over death. In 1967, Marc Ancel argued that the capital judicial process possessed inherent irredeemable vicissitudes rendering it incapable of dealing with such complex penological issues. He stated:

> assuming [such human 'monsters'] did exist, who would decide it? The jury on the basis of an impression? The special judges on the basis of the particular conception they would have of their duties? Experts? Whether or not one wants to admit it, does not the taking of this road mean the admission that some human beings do not have the right to live or may have the right withdrawn from them? Here one approaches the worst ideas of totalitarian eugenicism . . . In a world pretending to be humane and to believe in universal human rights, the first right of a person is the right to life that society should guarantee him. Therefore, the first duty of the state is to abstain from killing.[49]

In *To his Fellow Citizens of France, on Death Punishments*, published in 1837, Jeremy Bentham provided a utilitarian thesis against the death penalty.[50] He argued that the punishment, rather than being used to maintain order and quell an impending threat, was a product of a 'sinister interest' of the sovereign and this repugnant sentiment could also be found percolating into 'public opinion'.[51] To propose an answer to Joyce's question above, and engage with Ancel's observations on the inherent vicissitudes of the capital judicial system, we can point to Bentham's 'sinister interest' as a significant basis for the adverse social environment which creates the public enemy/monster in the first place. It is because the death penalty cannot be dissociated from the effect of 'brutalizing society'[52] following executions. A harrowing feature of this punishment is that it keeps the *thanatos*, the death-drive, close to the surface of susceptible consciences.

The work of the nineteenth-century French historian and statesmen, François Guizot, is on the whole absent from abolitionist literature, but he did understand how to present a criminological position which implicitly considers Bentham's 'sinister interest', and effectively demonstrates how to neutralise this malevolence. Guizot stated, '[c]apital punishment, in spite of appearances, has not, even in a physical sense, the advantage of an immutable efficacy; for in suppressing a known enemy, it does not always suppress danger',[53] and he further explained, '[w]hat power seeks in the employment of capital punishment is security'.[54] Here Guizot argued:

> [p]unishments may destroy men, but they can neither change the interests nor sentiments of the people . . . [the government] may kill one or several individuals, and severely chastise one or several

> conspiracies, but if it can do no more than this, it will find the same perils and the same enemies always before it. If it is able to do more, let it dispense with killing, for it has no more need of it; less terrible remedies will suffice.[55]

These theories created the seeds for a new reality of abolitionism. They set in place a process of hybridisation as the beginnings of the interweaving of the different arguments against the death penalty and the dismantling of the citizen-versus-state, life/death, binary. Unless we are able to propose a more nuanced reading, we are left to be told by the retentionists that the death penalty is an appropriate penological tool in exceptional cases, and we will not be able to see and acknowledge that 'less terrible remedies will suffice' (i.e. a prison sentence for murders). Guizot provided a nuanced criminological analysis for the determination of the inefficacy of the death penalty. He laid bare the phenomena of danger, sentiment, conspiracy, effective punishment and humanitarian principles. What we can learn from Guizot, Bentham, Joyce and Ancel is that the death penalty is insufficient to deal with the technical political and criminological mechanisms required to reduce crime and thus maintain a state's societal equilibrium. This is against the binary position of the classical theory of sovereignty, which maintains that when the 'security' of the state is threatened the only possible outcome is either the death of the sovereign state or the attacker(s). Each of these positions is contingent upon whether the death penalty is employed; non-execution leads to the death of the sovereign and his subjects, and an execution leads to the life of the sovereign and his subjects. The abolitionist literature reviewed above demonstrates that this is an overly simplified and dangerous determination.

Identifying the 'new reality' of abolitionism: Roudinesco's disagreement with Derrida

In the 'Dialogue', Derrida then considered the manifestation of 'exceptional cases' through the Weimar constitutional public law theory of Carl Schmitt.[56] Derrida proposed the cogency of Schmitt for the theory on the 'limitations of sovereignty', and in articulating the eternal possibility of the death penalty he engaged with Schmitt's theory on 'the right to suspend the law, or the rule of law, the constitutional state'.[57] Article 48 of the Weimar Constitution (1919, with amendments through to 1933) enabled the president of the Reich to suspend the provisions of the constitution to formulate a 'state of exception' (for the quelling of disorder) and Schmitt explained that what 'characterizes an exception is principally unlimited authority, which means the suspension of the existing legal order'.[58] In Derrida's reading, there was no situating of post-war European law to curtail this 'unlimited authority', because in the use of emergency law the 'state suspends the law in the exception on the basis of its right of self-preservation', and the sovereign 'has the monopoly over this last decision'.[59]

It is well known that Article 48 provided the constitutional foundation for Hitler to create the sophisticated political, legal and military apparatus for the Final Solution, which included the extermination of many Jews, gypsies, disabled people and homosexuals. This was initiated for the mere fact of *who* they were; their crime was their *existence*.[60] This repugnant eugenicism was denounced in 1949–50 by the drafters of the European Convention on Human Rights. To prevent such illegitimate *thanatos* in the future the Council of Europe created the framework for a supranational region to protect human rights which elevated these rights over absolutist political considerations of the individual states. During the drafting debates, Henri-Pierre Teitgen, the *rapporteur* to the Committee for Legal and Administrative Affairs, stated, '[i]t is necessary . . . to create in advance a conscience in Europe which will sound the alarm',[61] and this is because 'the reason of state' is a 'permanent temptation', and 'Fascism and Hitlerism have unfortunately tainted European public opinion. These doctrines of death have infiltrated into our countries.'[62]

The drafters understood that the formulation of the European Convention on Human Rights would limit 'state sovereignty on behalf of the law, and for that purpose all restrictions are permitted'.[63] Hence the provisions for repudiating Article 48 and Schmitt's theory on sovereignty were set in motion, and the key mechanism was a 'conscience in Europe which will sound the alarm' to protect human rights. However, the possibility of the death penalty was reserved. In the European Convention on Human Rights, Article 2(1),[64] the punishment was allowed under the discretion of the Member States, and so it is clear that in 1949–50 the 'regional' rule of law was not yet fully articulated to provide for the severing of the death penalty from sovereignty. Therefore the abolitionist project has been ongoing.

Roudinesco recognised this evolution of European human rights against the death penalty and firmly disagreed with Derrida's position. It appears that Roudinesco had considered the policies of the Council of Europe, and the European Union, for the internal removal of the death penalty and the prerequisite requirement that all new Member States provide for abolition. In the 'Dialogue', she stated, 'it seems impossible to me that the death penalty could be reinstated in Europe',[65] but Derrida, in recalling Rousseau, Beccaria and Schmitt, replied, 'Oh, of course it could!',[66] and he further argued that:

> [a]s long as an abolitionist discourse has not been elaborated and effectively accredited (and this has not yet been done) at the level of unconditional principles, beyond the problems of purpose, exemplarity, and even the 'right to life,' we will not be shielded from a return of the death penalty.[67]

However, European abolitionist discourse *is* now 'elaborated' and 'effectively accredited', and this is why Roudinesco replied:

> I am among those who think that this is not possible. The abolition is inscribed into European law. It has become, in a way, *outside the law*, out of the reach of law, since it falls under a higher order, that of international treaties [emphasis in original].[68]

Roudinesco articulated the supranational nature of sovereignty within the European Union and the Council of Europe, and the role of legislation providing for abolition. Although she does not describe the political and legal events which led to abolition 'being inscribed into European law', she had identified the hegemonic moment, the 'new reality'. This is a product of the European Union and the Council of Europe being (symbiotic) hybridiser(s). Abolition *is* now elaborated and effectively accredited and it occurred most clearly through the 2002 Protocol No. 13 to the ECHR and the EU Charter of Fundamental Rights 2000 incorporated by the Lisbon Treaty in 2007. The Charter now has equal legal status to the Treaty[69] and in Article 6(2),[70] the Lisbon Treaty set in motion the weaving together of the two European regions into a homogeneous European project for the promotion of human rights.[71] There is now a solidified European legal mandate that is unconditionally against the death penalty.

For a clearer picture of how we arrived at this symbiosis of European perspective, we should briefly reflect on the origins of the current role of the European regions as abolitionist actors. The first initiatives against the death penalty did not find germination centrally within these regions but were set in motion through Member States' denunciation of the punishment, independent of any centralised, regional, discourse. So abolition was not a *top-down* phenomenon, but a *bottom-up* promotion of a rejection of the claimed special deterrent effect of the death penalty, and an elevation of the humanist and human rights perspectives. In the Council of Europe, all Western Member States had made the required legal provisions to renounce the death penalty for peacetime offences by 1981, with France being the last country to join.[72] This homogeneous rejection of the punishment for peacetime offences in Western Europe then provided an abolitionist impetus for the political organs of the Council of Europe and the European Union, initially through the 'parliaments', the Parliamentary Assembly of the Council of Europe,[73] and the European Parliament of the European Union[74] (then under the European Community). Thus, a common European abolitionist position began to emerge from the 1980s onwards and has evolved into the two European regions now promoting in a symbiotic way the abolition of the death penalty in all circumstances and without exceptions. This is certainly a new reality, which was not envisaged by most European policy-makers and civil society in the mid-1980s, through the 1990s. The privileging of the classical theory of sovereignty mistakenly over-simplified the issue and consequently mystified the road to abolition. Such theoretical privileging did not allow for a full engagement with the hybridisation process that has set in motion the 'possible' (of abolition) and did not identify the role of the European regions as 'hybridisers'.

Derrida could not pull his gaze from the possibility of the return of disorder in Europe, and he did not adequately consider the cogency of the hegemonic provisions created by the Council of Europe and the European Union. Roudinesco, however, understood that, through regional law, the Beccarian exception and Schmitt's public law theory are now denounced and neutralised. The 'worst of the worst' criminals in Europe will not be treated with the brutality they administered, and an application of retribution through death is abolished as archaic and a violation of human rights. At the regional level, this is most clearly evidenced through the litigation following the death sentence of Abdullah Öcalan, the leader of the Kurdistan Worker's Party, for uprisings aimed at destroying the integrity of the Turkish state.[75] In 2003, the Turkish government signed and ratified Protocol No. 13 and overturned his death sentence for terrorist offences against Turkey.[76] At the state level, the horrific events of the ETA attacks in Spain,[77] the London Tube and bus bombings,[78] the Beslan school attacks in South Ossetia,[79] the attacks in France (on the magazine headquarters of *Charlie Hebdo* and in other locations in Paris),[80] and the mass killings in Norway on the Island of Utoeya and during the bombings in Oslo,[81] were all dealt with by the Member States without a legislative reaction to reintroduce capital punishment. They demonstrated that, in order to neutralise the possibility of future attacks, states must teach that when terrorist violence is imposed which leads to loss of life, a humanitarian response is required which prioritises human dignity over retribution. The state should not be seen as the aggressor and instead transparently reveal why the terrorist's actions are wrong through punishment grounded in human rights principles.[82]

The European regions as hybridiser of the abolitionist discourse

The European Union has initiated a sophisticated alignment of policies, explored new strategies to meet future challenges, and in effect has woven together 'ideas' to stop the 'actual violence' of the state's death penalty system. The 2010 12th Annual EU-NGO Forum of Human Rights can be viewed as a clear expression of the EU as hybridiser of the abolitionist discourse, both internally and externally.[83] The Forum identified that '[t]he European Union is committed to enhancing and deepening its communication and exchanges with civil society organisations (CSOs) in the field of human rights and democratisation', and it received input from Member State governments, representatives of the European Commission, Council and Parliament, Member State judges, lawyers, academics and civil society.[84] During the Forum, the 'Working Group 1 on EU Instruments in the Fight Against the Death Penalty' affirmed that the 'global abolition of the death penalty ranks among the main objectives of EU human rights policy'.[85] The Working Group discussed how in applying the Lisbon Treaty it is necessary that the (then) newly created European External Action Service[86] adopt policies to support the Commission in maintaining internal abolition and also utilise the Common Foreign and Security Policy (CFSP), to promote abolition externally.[87]

Through the weaving together of the different aspects of the European abolitionist strategy and receiving multi-faceted and multi-disciplinary contributions, the Working Group established four 'key elements' which can be viewed as woven together within a hybridisation process: they are (a) coherence and consistency; (b) cooperation; (c) education and awareness raising; and (d) efficiency and effectiveness.[88] While it sought to infuse debates in other countries with abolitionist ideas and thus to hybridise them, and finally convince their partners to abolish the death penalty, the EU's strategy was thus hybrid in itself and foresaw action on multiple levels, through multiple channels and utilising multiple tools.

The Workshop linked up the different actors in the abolitionist community to ensure that the EU would provide technical support to regional bodies such as the United Nations, the African Union and the Arab League. The EU will share regional and country best practices and lessons learned. Within the facility of the four key elements, the Working Group also encouraged a multi-layered approach towards abolitionism, as it encouraged 'granting financial assistance and enhancing relations with third countries, in particular with neighbouring countries'.[89] It also encouraged a 'continuous, systematic and strategic consultation with NGOs to reassess local needs and situations on the ground regularly',[90] and 'support the World Coalition Against the Death Penalty initiative to set up an international database that could function as a forum through which the EU and NGOs can publish updates on their respective work and actions'.[91]

The Working Group recalled the 2005 Council Regulation No. 1236/2005, on the prohibition of trading in equipment that may be used in the administration of the death penalty.[92] It was the first regional instrument of its kind which provides a new deconstruction of the execution apparatus. The Regulation Article 3(1) prohibits EU Member States from the export of 'goods' which have 'no practical use other than for the purpose of capital punishment', and Article 4(1) prohibits the import of such 'goods' into Europe. The Working Group emphasised the need for the strengthening of the text, to specifically include the prohibition of the manufacture and trade of lethal substances for use in executions.[93] This advice significantly contributed to the 2011 Commission Implementing Regulation 1352/2011, which was adopted to specifically prohibit trade in lethal substances which are used in the execution protocol.[94]

An example of the Working Group's call for bilateral actions was witnessed during the debates on the EU-Libya Framework Agreement. Member of Parliament, Ana Gomes, stated, '[t]he Union cannot abstain from persuading Libya to commit itself to a moratorium on the death penalty and it demands that the Libyan authorities publish the identity of national and foreign citizens who are executed'.[95] Here Gomes was promoting the regional affirmation for abolitionist discourse on different levels. First, it is a specific topic for bilateral dialogue; second, the initiation of a moratorium would engender political, legal and social dialogue on the punishment in the country, and; thirdly, the transparency of the capital judicial process enables the global abolitionist community to provide critique through the use of UN Safeguards,[96] the ICCPR[97] and the Universal Periodic Review undertaken within the UN Human Rights Council.[98]

In individual cases, the EU engages defence attorneys and provides advice for *amicus curiae* briefs (submitted by a 'friend-of-the-court' who is not party to the proceedings) which presents to courts addition expert information on human rights issues. In the case of *Atkins v. Virginia*,[99] the US Supreme Court held that executing a mentally ill inmate was a violation of the Eighth Amendment's cruel and unusual punishments clause, and in *Roper v. Simmons*,[100] the court held that executing a juvenile offender was also a violation of the Eighth Amendment. In both cases the majority opinion cited the EU *amicus curiae* briefs, along with other briefs filed by third-country bar councils and NGOs. These decisions demonstrate how international opinion concerning mental health issues and children's rights is woven into the fabric of the US Supreme Court's reasoning.[101]

The European Union also contributes to political diplomacy and attracts global media attention in death penalty cases. The case of Meriam Ibrahim in Sudan, who was sentenced to one hundred lashes and then execution for sexual immorality and apostasy serves as a good example.[102] The Presidents of the European Union, Commission and Parliament called upon Sudan to revoke the sentences.[103] A general statement was also made by the EU spokesperson on the case,[104] and a presentation was made in the United Nations Human Rights Council.[105] A multi-pronged approach to the legal and political issues in the case was taken by the EU, including a general political statement, the initiation of bilateral diplomacy through the EU Delegation in Khartoum and support for the defence team which informed the domestic litigation and the petition in the African Commission on Human and People's Rights.[106] This weaving together of different strands of the abolitionist strategy was further strengthened by significant civil society utilisation of social media. Meriam and her family received support from Amnesty International[107] and a law student from the University of Manchester, Emily Clarke,[108] as they initiated petitions which both gained over one million signatures. All over the world the hashtags #SaveMeriam and #FreeMeriam trended on Facebook and Twitter to make her plight one of the most discussed human rights cases in 2014.[109]

At the multilateral level, perhaps the most striking example of the EU's role as discursive hybridiser is in the bi-annual UN General Assembly vote on the resolution on the moratorium of the death penalty. Since 1994, when the Italian government introduced a resolution for a worldwide moratorium, the EU has been at the forefront of generating a cross-regional alliance to produce a successful vote. In 2007 a European Parliament resolution stated that the EU will 'seek the co-sponsorship of countries in other continents'.[110] This it achieved with the cross-regional alliance consisting of Albania, Angola, Brazil, Croatia, Gabon, Mexico, New Zealand, the Philippines, Portugal on behalf of the EU, and Timor Leste.[111] It took six attempts over a period of thirteen years for the General Assembly to vote in favour of the moratorium, and the global network of 104 Member States voting in favour of the resolution, with 29 abstaining and 54 voting in opposition.[112] Since 2007, the General Assembly has witnessed a gradual but steady increase in member states voting for the resolution. In 2008, the vote was 106 in favour, 34 abstentions and 46 against;[113] the figures in 2010 were 109 in favour, 35 abstentions and 41 against;[114] in 2012 they were 110 in favour, 36 abstentions and 39 against;[115] and most recently in 2014, 117 in favour, 34 abstentions,and 37 against.[116]

Conclusion

At the dawn of the abolition of the death penalty in France, Michel Foucault wrote in the September 1981 edition of *Libération*:

> The way in which the death penalty is done away with is at least as important as the doing away. The roots are deep. And many things will depend on how they are cleared out . . . Do we want the debate on the death penalty to be anything other than a discussion on the best punitive technologies? Do we want it to be the occasion for the beginning of a new political reflection? Then it must take up the problem of the right to kill at its root.[117]

This chapter has argued that the classical theory of sovereignty does not 'take up the problem' of the death penalty at its root, but unhelpfully privileges political power within an ultimate recourse to a monopoly of death over criminals through maintaining an illogical binary. The very recent European history of sovereigns laying down the sword, and turning their backs on the death penalty, and the emerging European regional position against the punishment, through to the contributions of civil society, all demonstrate that the classical theory is now insufficient to provide an adequate reading of this criminological and human rights issue. It is clear that the abolition of the death penalty is achieved and maintained through a multi-faceted approach taken by the many actors contributing to a 'new reality' of abolition. Hence the death penalty should no longer be confined to a statist conception but should now be read as having 'glocalised' implications.[118] The local is no longer privileged and the local–global interaction impacts upon death sentences and executions. The punitive *thanatos* through putting people to death does not just reverberate within the borders of a country, but its consequences spill over, causing regional and worldwide ripples.

In this light, we must consider what impact the theory of 'hybridity' has had upon the evolution of the European abolitionist project. It is an empirical and legal fact that the Western Member States of the European regions removed the death penalty before a centralised discourse had been formed and consolidated. As expansion occurred, abolition became a prerequisite for membership for the joining states from Central and Eastern Europe. There may not have been any grand narrative initiating a hybridity function, but to understand contemporary European abolition we must view the interweaving of praxis and discourse. Even though the abolition of the death penalty in Europe moulded itself through an organic process, led by the solidification of the project domestically in Member States, the result has been the creation of the European regions as 'hybridisers' engaging the regional and global community at multi-faceted and inter-disciplinary levels. This means that to understand abolition in Europe we should not singularly focus on 'human rights' but identify all of the discursive forces which are joining together to maintain abolition. Of course, human rights have a major role to play, if not *the* major role. There will always be a need to strengthen the different strands of the abolitionist discourse.[119] So a deeper appreciation of a theory of hybridity for the continued denunciation of this punishment may significantly contribute to the preservation of Europe as a, 'death penalty-free zone'[120] and help work towards a 'death penalty free world'.

Notes

I would like to thank the participants at the workshop, 'Hybridity: Exploring Power, Social Structures, and Institutions Beyond the Liberal West', at the Institute of Advanced Studies, University of Birmingham, 13 Mar. 2014, for the discussions, and especially to Dr Rosa Freedman and Dr Nicolas Lemay-Hebert, for organising the workshop, and to Mr Philipp Lottholz, for helping put together this generative collection. I also thank Dr Mark Eccleston-Turner for the wider discussion of the theory of hybridity.

1 For a full discussion of the European Union's policies for the abolition of the death penalty see Christian Behrmann and Jon Yorke (2013) 'The European Union and Abolition of the Death Penalty', *Pace International Law Review Online Companion* 4(1): 1–79, http://digitalcommons.pace.edu/pilronline/39 (accessed June 2016).

2 For further discussion of the Council of Europe's policies on the death penalty see Jon Yorke (2010) 'Inhuman Punishment and Abolition of the Death Penalty in the Council of Europe', *European Public Law* 16(1): 77–104; Jon Yorke (2009) 'The Right to Life and the Abolition of the Death Penalty in the Council of Europe', *European Law Review* 34(2): 205–29; Agata Fijalkowski (2011) 'European Policy on the Death Penalty', in Austin Sarat and Jürgen Martschukat (eds), *Is the Death Penalty Dying? European and American Perspectives* (New York: Cambridge University Press), 268–91; Evi Girling (2006) 'European Identity, Penal Sensibilities and Communities of Sentiment', in Sarah Armstrong (ed.), *Perspectives on Punishment: The Contours of Control* (Oxford: Oxford University Press), 69–82.

3 The Charter of Fundamental Rights of the European Union, 18 Dec. 2000, OJ C 364/1, http://www.europarl.europa.eu/charter/pdf/text_en.pdf (accessed June 2016).

4 Protocol No. 13 to the Convention for the Protection of Human Rights and Fundamental Freedoms, concerning the abolition of the death penalty in all circumstances, *CETS* 187, 3 May 2002, http://conventions.coe.int/Treaty/Commun/QueVoulezVous.asp?NT=187&CM=8&DF=22/06/2014&CL=ENG (accessed June 2016).

5 See e.g. Commission Implementing Regulation (EU) No. of 20 December 2011 amending Council Regulation (EC) No 1236/2005 concerning trade in certain goods which could be used for capital punishment, torture or other cruel, inhuman or degrading treatment or punishment, *OJ* L 338/31, 21 Dec. 2011, http://eur-lex.europa.eu/LexUriServ/LexUriServ.do?uri=OJ:L:2011:338:0031:0034:EN:PDF (accessed June 2016).

6 Michel Foucault (2003) *Society Must Be Defended*, tr. David Macey (London: Penguin), 240.

7 See Thomas Hobbes (1996) *Leviathan* (Oxford: Oxford University Press); John Locke (1980) *Second Treatise of Government* (Cambridge: Hackett Publishing); Jean-Jacques Rousseau (1993) 'The Social Contract', in *The Social Contract and Discourses* (London: Everyman), 180–310.

8 Max Weber (1978) *Economy and Society*, vol. 1, ed. Guenther Roth and Claus Wittich (Berkeley, CA: University of California Press, 1978), 54.

9 The International Covenant on Civil and Political Rights, UN Doc. A/6316 (1996), Article 6, states that the death penalty should only be reserved for the 'most serious crimes'.

10 See Jacques Derrida and Elisabeth Roudinesco (2004) *For What Tomorrow . . . A Dialogue*, tr. Jeff Fort (Stanford, CA: Stanford University Press).

11 See Jacques Derrida (2004) *The Death Penalty*, vol. 1, tr. Peggy Kamuf (Chicago, IL: University of Chicago Press).

12 Beatrice Hannsen (2000) *Critique of Violence: Between Poststructuralism and Critical Theory* (London: Routledge), 7.

13 For a useful introduction to hybridity of plant variations, see Robert W. Allard (1999) *Principles of Plant Breeding*, 2nd edn (New York: Wiley & Sons).

14 Arturo Casadevall and Michael Imperiale (2014) 'Risks and Benefits of Gain-of-Function Experiments with Pathogens of Pandemic Potential, such as Influenza Virus: A Call for Science-Based Discussion', *mBio* 5(4), 1 Aug.

15 See Lisa A. Cutts (2008) 'Walking on the Wild Side: Classification and Liability for Owners of Wild-Domestic Animal Hybrids', *San Joaquin Agricultural Law Review* 18: 71.

16 Bhabha critiqued the colonial teachings on the danger of the 'other' and the preservation of the purity of a race ('self') to affirm power structures. See Homi Bhabha (1994) *The Location of Culture* (London: Routledge).

17 E.g. Michel Foucault observed that in understanding sovereign power the manifestation of racism was 'a way of introducing a break into the domain of life that is under power's control: the break between what must live and what must die', in *Society Must Be Defended*, 254.

18 Haj Yashida (2010) 'Conceptualizing Hybridity: Deconstructing Boundaries through the Hybrid', *Formations* 1(1): 31.

19 Ien Ang (2013) 'Together-in-Difference beyond Diaspora, into Hybridity', *Asian Studies Review* 27(2): 149–50.

20 Piero Bassetti (2013) 'Introduction', *Hybridity, Glocalism: Journal of Culture, Politics and Innovation*, http://www.glocalismjournal.net/Issues/Hybridity.kl.

21 For a comprehensive review of the processes for achieving a 'death penalty-free world', see Roger Hood and Carolyn Hoyle (2015) *The Death Penalty: A Worldwide Perspective*, 5th edn (Oxford: Oxford University Press).

22 See Irene Merker Rosenberg and Yale L. Rosenberg (2004) 'Of God's Mercy and the Four Biblical Methods of Capital Punishment: Stoning, Burning, Beheading, and Strangulation', *Tulane Law Review* 79: 1169; Samuel J. Levine (1998) 'Capital Punishment in Jewish Law and its Application to the American Legal System: A Conceptual Overview', *St Mary's Law Journal* 29(4): 1037; Beth A. Berkowitz (2006) *Execution and Invention: Death Penalty Discourse in Early Rabbinic and Christian Cultures* (Oxford: Oxford University Press).

23 See Erwin J. Urch (1929) 'The Law Code of Hammurabi', *American Bar Association Journal* 15: 7; William A. Schabas (2002) *The Abolition of the Death Penalty in International Law*, 3rd edn (Cambridge: Cambridge University Press), 3.

24 Günther Kaiser (1986) 'Capital Punishment in a Criminological Perspective', *United Nations Crime Prevention and Criminal Justice Newsletter* 12–13: 16, cited in Roger Hood and Carolyn Hoyle (2008) *The Death Penalty: A Worldwide Perspective*, 4th edn (Oxford: Oxford University Press), 13.

25 *Royal Commission on Capital Punishment*, Cmd. 8932 (1953), and see Roger Hood (2001) 'Leon Radzinowicz 1906–1999', *Proceedings of the British Academy* 111: 637–55, 651.

26 Leon Radzinowicz (1999) *Adventures in Criminology* (London: Routledge), 291.

27 The only country within mainland Europe that imposes the death penalty is Belarus, which is not a member state of either the Council of Europe or the European Union, see Council of Europe, *Abolition of the Death Penalty*, http://www.coe.int/t/dghl/standardsetting/hrpolicy/others_issues/death_penalty/default_EN.asp (accessed June 2016).

28 Derrida and Roudinesco, *For What Tomorrow*. The 'dialogue' was published by Stanford University Press in 2004, but it was originally published in France under the title, *De Quoi Demain* . . . by Librairie Arthème Fayard and Éditions Galilée, 2001.

29 Ibid., p. x.

30 Ibid.

31 Ibid., p. 88.

32 Ibid., p. 146.

33 Jacques Derrida (2004) 'Capital Punishment: Another "Temptation of Theodicy"', in Seyla Benhabib and Nancy Fraser (eds), *Pragmatism, Critique, Judgment: Essays for Richard J. Bernstein* (Cambridge, MA: MIT Press), 203.

34 Derrida, *Death Penalty*, 3.
35 Immanuel Kant (2004) stated, '[t]he penal law is a categorical imperative', and so, '[a]ll murderers, whether they have themselves done the deed, ordered it to be done, or acted as accomplices, must suffer the death penalty', in 'The Metaphysics of Morals', in *Kant: Political Writings*, ed. H. S. Reiss (Cambridge: Cambridge University Press), 157.
36 Derrida stated, '[t]o my knowledge, Levinas devoted only a single sentence to it in 1987, after its abolition in France: ""I don't know if you accept this rather complex system which consists in judging *according to the truth* and in treating the one who has been judged *with love*. The abolition of the death penalty seems to me an essential thing for the coexistence of charity and justice"'. Derrida and Roudinesco, *For What Tomorrow*, 146. Derrrida was citing Emmanuel Levinas (2001) 'Interview with François Poirié', in *Is it Righteous to Be? Interviews with Emmanuel Levinas*, ed. Jill Robbins (Stanford, CA: Stanford University Press), 51. However, Levinas had provided an interview in 1982 about the executioner, and was asked if he has a 'face' and thus initiated an ethical responsibility to the 'other' him/her (the subject to be condemned). Levinas's answer had a certain level of ambivalence in that he stated, '[y]ou are posing the whole problem of evil', and that, '[t]here is an element of violence in the state, but the violence can involve justice'.'Philosophy, Justice and Love', in Emmanuel Levinas (2006) *Entre Nous: Thinking-of-the-Other*, tr. Michael B. Smith and Barbara Harshav (London: Continuum), 90.
37 In the Death Penalty Seminars, Derrida focused upon Maurice Blanchot's critique of the 'reign of terror' in the French Revolution, see *Death Penalty*, 111–15, and he engages with Blanchot's identification of the relationship of law and death in 'Literature and the Right to Death', in Lydia Davis (1999) *The Station Hill Blanchot Reader: Fiction and Literary Essays* (New York: Station Hill Press), 359–400. Considering the capturing and legitimising of the use of capital punishment through the rule of law, Derrida's deconstruction is reflective of Blanchot's ubiquitous assertion, 'The law kills. Death is always the horizon of the law: if you do this, you will die', in Maurice Blanchot (1992) *The Step Not Beyond* (Albany, NY: State University of New York Press), 25.
38 Derrida and Roudinesco, *For What Tomorrow*, 143.
39 Michel Foucault stated, '[t]he jurists ask: When we enter into a contract, what are individuals doing at the level of the social contract, when they come together to constitute a sovereign? They do so because they are forced to by some threat or by need. They themselves do so to protect their lives. It is in order to live that they constitute a sovereign,' Foucault, *Society Must Be Defended*, 241.
40 Derrida and Roudinesco, *For What Tomorrow*, 17.
41 Richard Bellamy (1995) *Beccaria: On Crimes and Punishment and Other Writings* (Cambridge: Cambridge University Press).
42 Ibid. 66.
43 Ibid.
44 Ibid. 67.
45 Albert Camus and Arthur Koestler both authored prominent post-war publications against the death penalty. See Albert Camus (1988) 'Reflections on the Guillotine', in *Resistance, Rebellion and Death* (New York: Vintage Press), 173–234; Arthur Koestler (1956) *Reflections on Hanging* (London: Victor Gollancz).
46 Jean Graven (1961) *New Reflections on the Death Penalty*, published by the Institute of Comparative Law of the University of Paris, and reviewed in James Avery Joyce (1962) *The Right to Life: A Worldview of Capital Punishment* (London: Victor Gollancz), in his 'Appendix B, Postscript in Reply', 268.
47 Graven, *New Reflections*, 77, cited in Joyce, *Right to Life*, 268.

48 See Jon Yorke (2010) *The Right to Life and the Value of Life: Orientations in Law, Politics and Ethics* (Farnham: Ashgate Publishing).

49 Marc Ancel (1967) 'The Problem of the Death Penalty', in Thorsten Sellin (ed.), *Capital Punishment* (New York: Harper & Row), 20–1.

50 Jeremy Bentham (1831) *To his Fellow Citizens of France, on Death Punishments* (London: Robert Howard), 10–11. Bentham further argued: '[w]hatever may have been the case *antecedently* to this experience, – subsequently to the demonstration thus afforded of the needlessness and uselessness of this so highly objectionable mode of punishment, the leaving it unabolished, was everywhere without excuse. Nor could the practice have anywhere remained unabolished, but for the original influence of the abovementioned causes of error, and in particular, sinister interest, the progenitor of all the others. And therefore it is – that, to account for men's thus shutting their eyes against the light, – the force, by which they appear to have been closed, has thus been presented to your view.' Ibid. 12.

51 Ibid. 10–11.

52 E.g. see Hugo Adam Bedau, when he argued, '[b]rutalization studies test the long-held hypothesis that capital punishment actually encourages rather than discourages murder by setting a "savage example" for society to follow', in Bedau (1997) *The Death Penalty in America: Current Controversies* (New York: Oxford University Press), 136.

53 François Guizot (1848) 'A Treatise on Death Punishments', in *General History of Civilisation in Europe: From the Fall of the Roman Empire till the French Revolution* (Edinburgh: William and Robert Chambers Press, 1848), 258. Guizot affirmed, '[c]apital punishment . . . has lost its efficacy . . . whatever individual it may fix upon, in destroying him, it by no means neutralises the impending danger' (p. 259).

54 Ibid.

55 Ibid. 327.

56 See Carl Schmitt (1985) *Political Theology: Four Chapters on the Concept of Sovereignty*, tr. George Schwab (Cambridge, MA: MIT Press).

57 Derrida and Roudinesco, *For What Tomorrow*, 91.

58 Ibid. 12.

59 Ibid. 12–13.

60 See David Cesarani (2016) *Final Solution: The Fate of the Jews 1933–1949* (London: Macmillan); Hans Bolt (1971) 'Article 48 of the Weimar Constitution: Its Historical and Political Implications', in Anthony Nicholls and Erich Matthias (eds), *German Democracy and the Triumph of Hitler* (London: George Allen & Unwin), 79–97.

61 Council of Europe (1975), *Collected Edition of the 'Travaux Prêparatoires,' of the European Convention on Human Rights* (The Hague: Martinus Nijhoff), vol 2, 174.

62 Ibid., vol. 1, 40.

63 Ibid., vol. 2, 294.

64 *The Convention for the Protection of Human Rights and Fundamental Freedoms*, CETS 5, 1953, Article 2(1) states, 'Everyone's right to life shall be protected by law. No one shall be deprived of his life intentionally save in the execution of a sentence of a court following his conviction of a crime for which this penalty is provided by law.' The death penalty is now abolished in the Council of Europe, and when member states join they sign and ratify Protocol No. 6, and most have signed and ratified Protocol No. 13.

65 Derrida and Roudinesco, *For What Tomorrow*, 91.

66 Ibid.

67 Ibid. 137. Nils Christie similarly stated in negative dystopian propositions, 'the European ban on death by killing is far from safely established . . . [w]ith a political split, particularly if states were no longer interested in membership of the Council of Europe, forces in favour of reintroducing death as punishment might gain increased strength'. (2014) 'Death as Punishment', in Lill Scherdin (ed.), *Capital Punishment: A Hazard to a Sustainable Criminal Justice System?* (Farnham: Ashgate Publishing), 73.

68 Ibid.

69 The Treaty of Lisbon Amending the Treaty on European Union and the Treaty Establishing the European Community, 2007 *OJ* C 306/1; 13 Dec. 2007. Article 6(1) states, 'the Charter of Fundamental Rights of the European Union . . . which shall have the same legal value as the Treaties'. See The Charter of Fundamental Rights of the European Union, 18 Dec. 2000, 2000 *OJ* C 364/1.

70 The Treaty of Lisbon, Article 6(2) states, 'The Union shall accede to the European Convention for the Protection of Human Rights and Fundamental Freedoms. Such accession shall not affect the Union's competences as defined in the Treaties.'

71 The weaving together of the two European regions' abolitionist discourses is also reflected in the joint statements on the 'World and European Day Against the Death Penalty', which occurs every 10 October, see Joint Declaration by the European Union High Representative for Foreign Affairs and Security Policy, Federica Mogherini, and the Secretary General of the Council of Europe, Thorbjørn Jagland, on the European and World Day against the Death Penalty, 10 Oct. 2015, https://rm.coe.int/CoERMPublicCommonSearchServices/DisplayDCTMContent?documentId=090000168047ac48 (accessed Oct. 2015).

72 See Behrmann and Yorke, 'The European Union and Abolition'. France abolished the death penalty in 1981, and Western states became a *de facto* abolitionist region. The punishment was retained in Belgium but all death sentences were quashed, and it was abolished in 1996. In Ireland the punishment remained on the statute books but the last execution was in 1954, and the punishment was abolished in 1990.

73 E.g. Resolution 1044 on the abolition of capital punishment, text adopted by the Parliamentary Assembly of the Council of Europe, 25th sitting, 4 Oct. 1994.

74 E.g. Resolution on the Abolition of the Death Penalty in the European Community, 1980 *OJ* (C 327) 95.

75 See *Öcalan v. Turkey*, (2005) 41 EHRR 45, para. 157. This case was the first case the European Court of Human Rights considered which involved a member state's death sentence, and it was imposed upon a criminal designated as a public enemy of the Turkish state.

76 The European Court of Human Rights ruled that the original death sentence of Abdullah Öcalan, along with the unfair trial that he received, was a violation of ECHR Articles 3 (prohibition again inhuman punishment) and 5 (the right to liberty and security of the person).

77 For a timeline of the ETA attacks in Spain see BBC News (2011) 'Timeline: ETA Campaign', 28 Oct., http://www.bbc.co.uk/news/world-europe-11181982 (accessed June 2016).

78 See *Guardian* (2015) '7/7 Bombings: Capital to Mark 10th Anniversary of Terror Attacks', 28 June, http://www.theguardian.com/uk-news/2015/jun/28/77-london-bombings-10th-anniversary-terror-attacks (accessed June 2016).

79 See *Guardian* (2014) 'Ten Years After Beslan School Siege, Survivors Struggle to Make a New Life', 1 Sept., http://www.theguardian.com/world/2014/sep/01/beslan-school-massacre-ten-years (accessed June 2016).

80 See the EU's response to the various terrorist attacks in France, and in other European countries, 'Response to Foreign Terrorist Fighters and Recent Terrorist Attacks in Europe', by the European Council and the Council of the European Union, 12 February 2016, http://www.consilium.europa.eu/en/policies/fight-against-terrorism/foreign-fighters (accessed June 2016)
81 For a timeline of the terrorist attacks in Norway see BBC News (2012) 'Timeline: How Norway's Terror Attacks Unfolded', 17 Apr., http://www.bbc.co.uk/news/world-europe-14260297 (accessed June 2016).
82 This penal policy reflects the reasoning of Justice Langa, in *State v. Makwanyane and Mchunu*, Case No. CCT/3/94, 6 June 1995, '[a] culture of respect for human life and dignity, based on the values reflected in the [South African] Constitution, has to be engendered, and the State must take the lead. In acting this out, the State not only preaches respect for the law and that the killing must stop, but it demonstrates in the best way possible, by example, society's own regard for human life and dignity by refusing to destroy that of the criminal', para. 222.
83 See Final Report, *EU Human Rights Instruments and the Lisbon Treaty: State of Play and Way Forward*, 12th Annual EU-NGO Forum for Human Rights, Brussels, 12–13 July 2010, available at, http://www.eidhr.eu/files/dmfile/2010EU-NGOHRForumFinalReport.pdf (accessed June 2016).
84 Ibid. 8, '[c]ivil society is afforded an enhanced opportunity to contribute to EU policy development and at the same time the EU can better draw upon civil society experience and reflect upon lessons learned'.
85 Ibid. 7.
86 See the European External Action Service, http://www.eeas.europa.eu/index_en.htm (accessed June 2016).
87 See The Treaty of Lisbon, Title V, General Provisions of the Union's External Action and Specific Provisions on the Common, Foreign and Security Policy, Articles 21–46.
88 *EU Human Rights Instruments and the Lisbon Treaty*, 7–11.
89 Ibid. 8.
90 Ibid. 9.
91 Ibid.
92 Council regulation concerning trade in certain goods which could be used for capital punishment, torture or other cruel, inhuman or degrading treatment or punishment, (EC) No. 1236/2005, 27 June 2005; *OJ*, L 200/1, 30 July 2005.
93 This was necessary as the Appendix to Regulation No. 1236/2005 included the syringes used in lethal injection, but not the chemicals to be injected into the inmate. This provided a loop-hole, which could be exploited. See *R (on the application of Zagorski and Baze) v. Secretary of State for Business, Innovation and Skills*, [2010] EWHC 3110 (Admin).
94 Commission Implementing Regulation (EU) No. 1352/2011 of 20 December 2011 amending Council Regulation (EC) No. 1236/2005 concerning trade in certain goods which could be used for capital punishment, torture or other cruel, inhuman or degrading treatment or punishment, 21 Dec. 2011, *OJ*, L 338/31.
95 Remarks by Anna Gomes, *Debate: EU-Lybia Framework Agreement*, CRE 19 Jan. 2011, European Parlaiment Debate.
96 *Safeguards Guaranteeing Protection of the Rights of Those Facing the Death Penalty*, ECOSOC Resolution, 1984/50; *Additions to the Safeguards Guaranteeing Protection of the Rights of Those Facing the Death Penalty*, ECOSOC Resolution 1989/64; *Strengthening of the Safeguards Guaranteeing Protection of the Rights of Those Facing the Death Penalty*, ECOSOC Resolution 1996/15.

97 The International Covenant on Civil and Political Rights, UN Doc. A/6316 (1966), entered into force, 23 Mar. 1976.

98 See Office of the High Commissioner for Human Rights, the Universal Period Review, http://www.ohchr.org/EN/HRBodies/UPR/Pages/UPRMain.aspx.

99 *Atkins v. Virginia*, 536 US 304 (2002), Justice Stevens cites at 316, *Brief of Richard J. Wilson for the European Union as Amici Curiae Supporting Petitioner, McCarver v. North Carolina*, 533 US 975 (2001) (no. 00–8727).

100 *Roper v. Simmons*, 543 US 551 (2005), Justice Kennedy referred to the EU *amicus curiae* brief, at 576–8, and he stated, 'It is proper that we acknowledge the overwhelming weight of international opinion against the juvenile death penalty', p. 578.

101 Member state briefs include, the British Government's amicus curiae brief in *In Re Linda Carty* in the Texas Court of Criminal Appeals and *Shonda Walter v. Tennessee* in the United States Supreme Court, *Brief of the Bar of Ireland, the Bar Human Rights Committee of England and Wales, the International Bar Association's Human Rights Institute, the Paris Bar Association, as Amici in Support of Petitioner, Shonda Walter*, No. 15–650 (2016).

102 See Jon Yorke (2014) 'Meriam Ibrahim Saved from 100 Lashes and the Death Penalty' (OxHRH Blog, 28 June), http://ohrh.law.ox.ac.uk/meriam-ibrahim-saved-from-100-lashes-and-the-death-penalty (accessed June 2016).

103 Press release, 'Presidents of the European Union, Commission and Parliament Call on Sudan to Revoke Inhumane Apostasy Verdict', European Union Delegation to the Republic of Sudan, 10 June 2014, http://eeas.europa.eu/delegations/sudan/documents/press_corner/2014/20140610_en.pdf.

104 'Statement by the Spokesperson on the Death Sentence for Apostasy in Sudan', Brussels, 15 May 2014, http://eeas.europa.eu/statements/docs/2014/140515_01_en.pdf.

105 'Statement by H.E. Mr. Alexandros Alexandris, Ambassador, Permanent Representative of Greece on behalf of the European Union', United Nations Human Rights Council, Geneva, 19 June 2014. http://eeas.europa.eu/delegations/un_geneva/documents/eu_statments/human_right/20140619_hrc26_item4.pdf.

106 *Redress and Others, Urgent Appeal in Respect of Ms Meriam Yahia Ibrahim*, to Commissioner Soyata Maiga, Special Rapporteur on Women's Rights, African Commission on Human and People's Rights, Filed 10 June 2014.

107 Amnesty International (2014) 'Sudan: Woman Condemned to Death Released After International Pressure', 23 June, https://www.amnesty.org/en/latest/news/2014/06/sudan-releases-woman-condemned-death-after-international-pressure (accessed June 2016)./

108 Emily Clarke (2014) 'Government of Sudan Don't Execute Meriam Yehya Ibrahim', Change.org, 24 July, https://www.change.org/p/government-of-sudan-don-t-execute-meriam-yehya-ibrahim-for-being-christian-savemeriam (accessed June 2016).

109 E.g. see Meriam Ibrahim on her escape from death row, 'the world gave me hope': *Guardian*, 2 Feb. 2015, http://www.theguardian.com/world/2015/feb/02/meriam-ibrahim-pregnant-death-row-sudan-your-questions (accessed June 2016).

110 Resolution on the Initiative for a Universal Moratorium on the Death Penalty, European Parliament, Doc. (C74 E/775) 26 Apr. 2007.

111 See press release, Council of the European Union, General Affairs and External Relations, Luxembourg, 18 June 2007.

112 Moratorium on the Use of the Death Penalty, GA Res. 62/149, UN Doc. A/RES/62/149 (18 Dec. 2007).

113 Moratorium on the Use of the Death Penalty, GA Res. 63/168, UN Doc. A/RES/63/168 (18 Dec. 2008).
114 Moratorium on the Use of the Death Penalty, GA Res. 65/206, UN Doc. A/RES/65/206 (21 Dec. 2010).
115 Moratorium on the Use of the Death Penalty, GA Res. 67/176, UN Doc. A/RES/67/176 (20 Dec. 2012).
116 Moratorium on the Use of the Death Penalty, GA Res. 69/186, UN Doc. A/RES/69/186 (18 Dec. 2014).
117 Michel Foucault (2000) 'Against Replacement Penalties', in *Michel Foucault: Power: Essential Works of Foucault 1954–1984,* ed. James D. Faubion (London: Penguin), 459.
118 See Editorial (2013) *Glocalism, a Journal of Culture, Politics and Innovation* 1 (Nov.), http://www.glocalismjournal.net/Issues/Hybridity.kl (accessed June 2016).
119 Elsewhere I have argued that maintaining abolition of the death penalty is akin to a 'never-ending story', due to the fact that abolitionists need to keep monitoring the application of sovereign power in criminal justice issues, see Jon Yorke (2008) 'The Evolving Human Rights Discourse of the Council of Europe: Renouncing the Sovereign Right of the Death Penalty', in Yorke, *Against the Death Penalty: International Initiatives and Implications* (Farnham: Ashgate Publishing), 67.
120 See 'The Council of Europe a Death Penalty Free Area', http://hub.coe.int/web/coe-portal/what-we-do/human-rights/death-penalty?dynLink=true&layoutId=18&dlgroupId=10226&fromArticleId (accessed June 2016).

Chapter 12

Describing a rights realisation hybrid

The example of socio-economic rights

Ben T. C. Warwick

Introduction

Descriptions of the progression or regression of human rights situations often hide a complex reality. Rarely, if ever, will a policy or a *de facto* picture of rights enjoyment be entirely positive or negative. Instead, a situation of rights protection will usually be a hybrid of positives, negatives and stagnation for different groups and for specific rights. Yet often the description of human rights realisation suggests a blanket improvement or reduction in enjoyment.

This chapter provides an argument for greater nuance in descriptions of socio-economic rights realisation and suggests that hybridity can help to overcome the more simplistic descriptive approaches that are seen. In doing so, the chapter expands some of the contrasting and counterposed *rights, subjects, and directions of realisation.* The hybridities within socio-economic rights realisation are uncovered, and the detail and nuance portrayed in linear or 'flat' descriptions of socio-economic rights realisation are unpacked. To achieve these complications and uncoverings, the argument draws upon the anti-essentialist capacity of hybridity and upon its power to disrupt static categorisations.[1]

Essentialism, or the idea that 'particular characteristics can be identified with [a group] over time',[2] stands accused of 'obscuring the particularities and incommensurabilities' of identity diversities.[3] Hybridity has previously been seen as a corrective to essentialist groupings of or within identity, race and gender.[4] In these contexts it has been argued that there is a need to combat the 'lumping together' of diverse individuals into a single category. This, in turn, helps to prevent crude identity-based prejudice and discrimination and helps to overcome 'them' and 'us' perceptions.[5] In relation to these problems, thinking through hybridity[6] is valuable in complicating such routes to identity-based discrimination, by rejecting homogeneity, while still maintaining a coherence for the system or idea.[7] Rather than addressing this already well-developed literature on essentialism and identity and hybridity's role in this setting, this chapter faces in a different direction. It identifies descriptions of human rights progress as the essentialised category. In a similar, albeit far less dehumanising manner, such simplistic descriptions of rights progress also hide the 'particularities' of the picture and suggest a homogeneity that is absent. In turn, remedying such simplicity promises to improve the quality of the CESCR's monitoring and the effectiveness of advocacy surrounding the ICESCR rights.

The chapter makes its argument in two parts. The following section sets out the context of socio-economic rights and seeks to establish the problem that exists in describing the situation of these rights. The second section identifies hybridities in the rights themselves, in the subjects of the rights, and in the different 'directions' which rights realisation can move in. The conclusion of this examination (made in a final section) is that, in the absence of significant additional resources or reform, hybridity can add (or acknowledge) depth and nuance in descriptions of socio-economic rights realisation.

The context of socio-economic rights realisation

The United Nations human rights framework and its various mechanisms are highly important in the promotion and description of socio-economic rights realisation. Socio-economic rights at the international level are primarily[8] grounded in a portion of the International Bill of Rights; the International Covenant on Economic, Social and Cultural Rights (ICESCR).[9] This treaty is well respected and has been signed and ratified by 161 States. A dedicated Committee (CESCR), tasked with monitoring, development and promotion functions, supports the realisation of the socio-economic rights detailed in the ICESCR. Various UN Special Rapporteurs and Independent Experts (for example, in the areas of adequate housing, food, extreme poverty and health) also contribute on a more indirect basis to the promotion and protection of socio-economic rights.[10]

Much of the reporting, monitoring and commentary relating to socio-economic rights at the international level is shaped by a primary general provision of the treaty; Article 2(1). This criticised provision[11] requires that '[e]ach State . . . take steps . . . to the maximum of its available resources, with a view to achieving progressively the full realization of the rights recognized'.[12] The provision – known as the requirement of 'progressive realisation' – has been described as a sword and a shield for human rights.[13] The rights to health, to an adequate standard of living and to housing, for instance, require states to take steps towards securing such rights and can be used as a sword in this sense. The provision that the 'realities of the real world'[14] cause full rights realisation to take some time to be achieved and that states may face limited availability of resources[15] can be utilised as a shield, on the other hand.[16]

A range of institutional and procedural difficulties have compounded the textual vagaries of this important general provision[17] and have affected the effective monitoring of socio-economic rights realisation. The Committee on Economic, Social and Cultural Rights (CESCR) and the other UN human rights treaty bodies face 'chronic' resource shortages,[18] a mere six hours with which to examine and question states on five years' worth of human rights issues,[19] and a 2,500 word limit on their concluding reports so as to minimise the cost of translation to all of the UN's working languages.[20] This can result in overly simple depictions of the actualities of socio-economic rights achievement. Official observations by the CESCR can leave aside more complex renderings of the rights involved. For example, the Committee noted that in Germany 'the earnings gap remains considerable'[21] and separately that not enough has been done to 'improve the situation of older persons in nursing homes'.[22] Statements such as these give little consideration to finer questions such as the following. In which regions of Germany is the earnings gap at its widest? In which occupations or income groups do women fare the worst? Has the gap has been consistently large or were initial improvements offset by a later crisis or regressive policy? Apart from direct action to close the pay gap, do other policy measures offer indirect compensation for the pay disparity? In generalising its consideration, the Committee fails to provide a clear direction of where, when and why the pay gap is considerable. It also fails to adequately describe the impacts of income disparity upon the individual. These problems with taking a generalised approach might equally be applied to the issue of older persons' care or any number of other issues raised by the Committee.

Giving an appropriately nuanced description of rights realisation is central to encouraging and facilitating the 'targeted' approach that the Committee itself requires.[23] The CESCR notes the importance of clearly targeting and prioritising in taking steps towards the aim of realising all of the ICESCR rights.[24] If the Committee wishes to retain support and maintain a function in guiding policy, it must better facilitate such a targeting. For example, women's rights activists have criticised the capacity of the human rights movement to 'accommodate a complex, nuanced understanding of human rights violations'.[25] The use of broad strokes to highlight 'problems' and 'successes' in socio-economic rights realisation, however, gives states and civil society actors insufficient direction on what exactly needs to be prioritised. Assisting states in their targeted approach to rights realisation is, furthermore, of importance when it comes to optimally allocating expenditure in the context of severe resource constraints. According to the CESCR, targeting resources has a significant role to play in protecting the most vulnerable in society from the effects of a resource crisis.[26] Yet if such targeting is to be effective, a greater emphasis on complexity in the CESCR's descriptions and analyses is required.

This pressure for more intricate and directed descriptions of rights realisation is only likely to increase for the CESCR. As socio-economic rights scholarship and advocacy increasingly engages with macro-economic arguments and budget analyses, the CESCR will have to adapt its reporting method.[27] Elson pinpointed significant value in adopting a human rights approach to budgeting when she noted that, 'the worst that an economist can say of a government's budget is that it is "imprudent", 'unsound', "unsustainable", "inefficient", while the human rights advocate can say that it violates human rights'.[28] Yet, she also makes clear that this value is not self-fulfilling and that detailed scrutiny is necessary in order to fulfil this potential. Decisions on fiscal policy are not easily made on the basis of generalised assessments, but require meticulous analysis of the indicators, efficiency of spending, and competing demands upon the budget allocation process.[29] This is one of the gaps[30] that human rights practitioners must bridge.

Economic decision-making is predicated on mathematical variables and comparisons of the sort that are currently far removed from human rights reporting.[31] There is a degree of resistance,[32] with some good reason,[33] to reducing socio-economic rights violations to simple quantitative metrics or a version of a simple line graph. However, the predominance of mathematics in the world of economics means that resource decisions are currently dominated by such (purportedly) empirical judgements and inputs. Some current approaches to describing rights realisation effectively claim to synthesise complex variables into a simple positive or negative assessments of progress.[34] While such an approach is arguably well tuned for political efficacy, the economic decision-making sphere demands a finer analysis of the problem to be addressed. If there is to be further influence over economic policy, then temporal, sectoral and demographic variables must be even less collapsible in realisation descriptions.[35]

Of course, beyond the various advantages for the operationalisation of socio-economic rights that are detailed above, more detailed descriptions of realisation can also contribute to normative development of socio-economic rights. By identifying with greater specificity the aspect of a state's performance that constitutes progress, other states and civil society can better benchmark against these standards. And as socio-economic rights become the subject of complaints to the CESCR by individuals under the new Optional Protocol,[36] more clarity as to the normative content of the rights and their corresponding duties can only be a good thing.

In summary, there are pressures on the CESCR in two directions that make ensuring the best description of rights realisation difficult. On the one hand, the Committee is institutionally restrained in terms of time, finance and other resources. On the other, ever-increasing demands are placed upon the CESCR to keep pace with the requirements of the new, ambitious directions of advocacy and scholarship. These pressures are unlikely to be addressed with a single 'golden bullet' as they require continuous attention to reform of the CESCR, new strategies from civil society and continued (or increased) cooperation from states. Each of these measures requires a committed process of change. As the following section argues, hybridity can provide a more immediate – if partial – answer to the increasing pressures.

Hybridity analysis as a complicating descriptor?

To only speak of a broadly positive or negative process of rights realisation[37] is to leave much unexamined. This section addresses three areas of complexity that are inadequately addressed by this 'realisation process' moniker. In particular, it is argued that a hybridity analysis can take this simplified/aggregated whole of a socio-economic rights realisation process and usefully demonstrate its multi-stranded and complex nature. Statements on an 'improving human rights situation'[38] can serve to obscure the complex network of rights contained within such a broad heading. Yet, full recognition of the multiplicity of rights is essential if all rights are to be fully realised. Although the statement may be true as an overall account of the direction of rights protection, describing an 'improving human rights situation' does not account for the variations within such a situation. That is to say, any position of overall rights improvement or realisation, is a *hybrid* of multiple rights realisations. Recognising that the hybrid overall situation is made up of component 'base units', or individual rights stories, helps promote greater recognition of the complexities of rights realisation. This argument will be made through three examples. First the multiplicity of rights will be detailed, before demonstrating the duality of directions that rights realisation can take. The final element of this section will show how the differing locations of realisation can add further depth to the realisation hybrid.

Rights

It is suggested above that rights realisation might properly be thought of as a hybrid or a complex tangle that is made up of smaller elements. These elements are partly constituted of different rights and elements of rights. As such, descriptions of 'rights' realisation can be broken down to expose the realisation picture for each individual right. Rather than discussing in general terms the realisation of the whole gambit of rights, hybridity can prompt a more useful discussion of individual rights. This combines human rights concerns with a hybridity perspective that facilitates reflection on the contents and means of the hybrid's formation.[39] Hybridity theories also serve to prompt an interrogation of the of power dynamics within and surrounding such hybrid entities.[40]

With the help of hybridity, rights realisation can be conceived of as consisting of the realisation of multiple different rights. This is crucial to reflecting the differences that might exist, for example, between the progress made on the right to food and the right to health. Put differently, it is possible that the right to health will have seen vast improvements while improvements in the right to food have been more incremental, and descriptions of the overall picture of rights realisation should reflect this. If it is described as a hybrid situation, some indication of the variable levels of progress is given. 'Hybridity' can act as a necessary caveat to the description of a state's progress on implementing socio-economic rights.

Similarly, a picture of a single right can be further deconstructed to express the multiple duties that constitute the right. The right to food, for example, requires the economic and physical accessibility of food, the cultural acceptability of the food, and the availability of food of an adequate quantity and quality. As such, references (positive or negative) to the 'realisation of the right to food' inadequately pinpoint the elements of the right that are being successfully realised. Rather, it should be acknowledged that the right to food and other rights are complex hybrids of multiple obligations. Such an acknowledgement might adequately allow us to move beyond generalised descriptions and to capture greater nuance in our descriptions.

For a concrete example of how elements of a single right might conflict, one might turn to phenomenon of foodbanks in the UK. Various descriptions see foodbanks as a positive development, capturing community spirit and ensuring the provision of sufficient food for individuals.[41] However, the cultural unacceptability of food, for example, is not captured in such descriptions. Those in desperation or who are pushed towards a source of food aid may be unable to maintain their Kosher, Halal, vegetarian or vegan convictions[42] and it is also clear that there is a cultural reticence to receiving charitable 'hand-outs'. Individuals with experience of foodbanks describe the encounter as 'degrading', bleak,[43] humiliating[44] or shameful.[45] Any general description of this situation will be limited in its ability to capture both the positive and problematic features.

Subjects

In addition to deconstructing a right or a set of rights, hybridity might also allow a better identification of the subjects of such rights. The situations of human rights subjects or rights holders are seen more clearly when a smaller slice of a group is examined. Disaggregated data have been defined as 'data broken down by key characteristics, such as ethnicity, gender and so on'.[46] Conceiving of indicators and statements as inherently hybrid can help to utilise this practice which is already well-established and endorsed in the human rights field,[47] in order to further unravel the subject group. Unravelling the groups of rights holders through disaggregation helps to go beyond simply demonstrating and describing which right or which part of a right is being realised. It can add attention to *who* the rights are being realised for.

Hybridity can encourage acknowledgement of the 'fuzziness'[48] of group boundaries and the unravelling of closely delimited categories in order to establish the subgroups and 'elements' that make up the whole. The disposal of neat categories and a move towards fuzziness provokes more specific or individualised attention to the circumstances of human rights holders. Such attention is central to ensuring that policy, economic and administrative measures that are intended to improve rights protection and are adequately tailored and targeted towards the individuals in need.[49]

Various groupings are both formed by the actions of the individuals they contain, or are constructed by external observers. According to a sociological understanding, the basis for the groupings are attributes such as shared 'perceptions, attitudes, feelings and behaviours'.[50] Human rights terminology echoes this, as individuals are grouped, for example, according to religion or belief, sex, race, colour, political or other opinion. While this approach has undoubtedly afforded space for group-particular interpretations of rights to develop, it has occasionally come at the cost of recognising the linkages between group rights.[51] Thus, there have sometimes been descriptions of rights realisation that refer to progress for a specific 'group', such as 'the elderly',[52] with limited appreciation of the porous membership criteria for the group or the other characteristics of group members.

Yet, these aggregated groups can be interrogated to show that the category of 'rural dwellers',[53] for instance, consists of both male rural dwellers and female rural dwellers. A hybridity lens can thus be used in order to see 'rural dwellers' as the hybrid category and the different constitutive groups as the elements that are hybridised. Highlighting the hybridity of the category of 'rural dwellers' avoids overlooking the particular rights of some of these dwellers (for example, rural women[54]).

Beyond this, the group of female rural dwellers can be further unpacked to show that the group is made up of female rural dwellers who are mothers and those who are not. Hybridity theories reflect this division and subdivision, acknowledge the absence of a 'pure' base unit, noting instead the 'ongoing condition' and 'prior hybrisation' of groupings, cultures and institutions.[55] This kind of unravelling, although tedious, eventually leads to the dissolution of various categories and encourages a focus on the diverse individuals within them. Such an emphasis on the individual has traditionally been the underlying principle of human rights,[56] but is practically challenging in the context of national policy-making and country-level reporting.

The re-division or disaggregation of social groups with the help of a hybridity perspective gives an acknowledgement of the heterogeneities contained within all groups.[57] It highlights that, although members of groups can have related attributes, blind categorisation means 'idiosyncratic individual[s]' are 'perceptually depersonalised'.[58] Put differently, the constructed group can strip individuals of their particular and distinguishing features.

In repersonalising socio-economic rights accounts, hybridity can allow human rights reporting to more clearly respond to theoretical critiques. Reports might more consistently engage with intersectionality critiques and recognise that individuals can be constituents of more than one group.[59] It could do so by noting the hybrid nature of any 'categories' that are invoked and, in so doing, acknowledge that each category is itself formed of other sub-categories.

Incidentally, hybridity can also stimulate a focus on the interactions that take place within groups, and how these interactions are reflected in the 'public' or overall presentation of the group. In the cases of 'family'[60] and 'indigenous'[61] groupings, feminists have critiqued the tendency to leave intra-group dynamics and power relations unexamined. This often results in some members of a group benefiting from the classification more than others. Through its redrawing of the group boundaries, hybridity analyses can disrupt the discrete power of the groupings themselves. It can complement the feminist critique of unequal intra-group structures by assessing how the group (the hybrid) is constructed, and which components of the group have greatest power over its functioning and presentation.

Directions

The Committee on Economic and Social Rights in their supervision of the implementation of the ICESCR have claimed that the progressive realisation provision can be viewed as reflecting the 'realities of the real world'.[62] The Committee dwells, in particular, on the 'realities' of resource constraints in this context, acknowledging the possibility of 'backsliding'[63] or the adoption by a state of a 'retrogressive' measure that reverses rights realisation.[64] This is a highly important acknowledgement that the overall process of socio-economic rights realisation is not a one-way process. It acknowledges that rights realisation does not persistently move forwards but can also go backwards. However, the retrogression concept sets up a forwards/backwards dichotomy[65] and neglects the simultaneity of directions that can characterise rights realisation. The realisation of rights might better be described neither as forwards nor backwards, but as a hybrid realisation process.

It is possible for rights protection to be both improving and deteriorating at the same time. In a similar vein to what is argued above, this could take the form of the realisation of two separate rights moving in different directions. So although there might be serious and concerning backwards steps in the realisation of the right to food in a country due to damaging government policies, this might coincide with a celebrated expansion of free secondary education and a consequently improved realisation of the right to education. Indeed, although there are likely to be patterns of violation and achievement (backwards steps in the realisation of the right to food will often coincide with backwards steps in the protection of health rights, for example) it would be an unusual – and drastic – situation where the protection of *all* socio-economic rights was reduced at the same time. This very simple example shows the difficulty of references to 'rights realisation' and 'rights retrogression'. At the very least, a claim that there has been an improvement of socio-economic rights realisation should prompt the response 'which right(s)?'

This multidirectional realisation process can be further interrogated. As different rights can move in opposing directions in terms of protection, so too can different aspects of the same right. The right to food contains several obligations including the obligation to ensure the availability of nutritious food free from adverse substance and the obligation to ensure that such food is culturally acceptable.[66] A situation could arise where there have been great improvements in the availability of nutrient-rich food which coincide with the introduction of tough legislation to remove a type of culturally appropriate (for example, Halal) foods from the country. This situation is more nuanced than can be adequately (and concisely) captured in the overall realisation/retrogression binary.

Conclusions

Hybridity offers a novel method for describing socio-economic rights realisation by opening up categories and offering a more detailed and complex picture. This allows an added depth to be brought to analyses of the extent to which the rights have been realised, while also operating within the practical constraints of the available information, finance and time. In doing so, it begins a move away from broad statements of progress or regression, and avoids the impossibilities of describing every individual's rights situation.

The range of rights, and the obligations contained within them, deserves full and nuanced description to enable properly directed censure and a well-targeted response. A full appreciation of the different groups, subgroups and diverse characteristics within the 'group' should be reflected in descriptions of socio-economic rights realisation. Importantly, the combined directions of rights realisation also requires acknowledgement, as well as the multitude of different paces at different times. The 'interdependence and indivisibility' of human rights is an axiom of the system.[67] Yet, the importance of the overlapping rights and elements of those rights can be lost in broad descriptions of progress. Put differently, without unpacking and addressing the component elements of the rights realisation matrix, it is clear that some elements that make up that hybrid will be overlooked.

Acknowledging such complexities can assist in combating challenges faced in socio-economic rights monitoring and reporting. Such detail is vital in maintaining a strong connection between macro-economic and geopolitical debates and individual rights situations. This is important in effectively shaping economic policies, but also in remaining faithful to the socio-economic rights imperative of targeting resources towards realising the rights of the most vulnerable. Socio-economic rights realisation is already a complex hybrid; it should be acknowledged as such.

Notes

1 Jan Nederveen Pieterse (1994) 'Globalisation as Hybridisation', *International Sociology* 9: 171, 167.
2 Tracy E. Higgins (1996) 'Anti-Essentialism, Relativism, and Human Rights', *Harvard Women's Law Journal* 19: 90.
3 Lisa Lowe (1991) 'Heterogeneity, Hybridity, Multiplicity: Marking Asian American Differences', *Diaspora: A Journal of Transnational Studies* 1(1): 26.
4 Ibid.
5 Ibid. 30.
6 Anjali Prabhu (2012) *Hybridity: Limits, Transformations, Prospects* (New York: SUNY Press), 41.
7 Jan Nederveen Pieterse (2001) 'Hybridity, So What? The Anti-Hybridity Backlash and the Riddles of Recognition', *Theory, Culture and Society* 18(2–3): 229.
8 For other examples of socio-economic rights in international treaties, see *Convention on the Rights of the Child* (1577 UNTS 3, 1989); *Convention on the Rights of Persons with Disabilities* (GA Res. 61/106, 61 UN GAOR, Supp. (No. 49), UN Doc.A/RES/61/106/Annex II 65, 2006); *Convention on the Elimination of All Forms of Discrimination Against Women* (1249 UNTS 13, 1979).
9 *International Covenant on Economic, Social and Cultural Rights* (adopted 16 Dec. 1966, entered into force 3 Jan. 1976, 993 UNTS 3, n.d.).
10 United Nations Human Rights Office of the High Commissioner, *Directory of Special Procedures Mandate Holders*, 2013.
11 Overseas Development Institute (1999) *What can we Do with a Rights-Based Approach to Development?* (https://www.odi.org/sites/odi.org.uk/files/odi-assets/pubications-opinion-files/2614.pdf), 3.
12 The provision and the treaty as a whole also contain obligations which are to be fulfilled immediately (i.e. which are not subject to the progressive condition); *ICESCR*, article 2(1).
13 Sandra Liebenberg (2001) 'The Right to Social Assistance: The Implications of Grootboom for Policy Reform in South Africa', *South African Journal on Human Rights* 17: 252.
14 CESCR, *General Comment 3: The Nature of States Parties Obligations (Art. 2, Para. 1 of the Covenant)* (UN Doc E/1991/23, 1990), para 9.
15 Ibid., para 10; Resources are broadly construed to include non-financial assets; ibid., para. 13.
16 Or even an 'escape hatch' for states; Scott Leckie (1998) 'Another Step towards Indivisibility: Identifying the Key Features of Violations of Economic, Social and Cultural Rights', *Human Rights Quarterly* 20(1): 94.
17 For details of the disagreements during the drafting process, see Philip Alston and Gerard Quinn (1987) 'The Nature and Scope of States Parties' Obligations under the International Covenant on Economic, Social and Cultural Rights', *Human Rights Quarterly* 9(2): 172–3.
18 Michael O'Flaherty and Claire O'Brien (2007) 'Reform of UN Human Rights Treaty Monitoring Bodies: A Critique of the Concept Paper on the High

Commissioner's Proposal for a Unified Standing Treaty Body', *Human Rights Law Review* 7: 142.

19 Navanethem Pillay (2012) *Strengthening the United Nations Human Rights Treaty Body System* (Geneva: United Nations Human Rights Office of the High Commissioner), 31.

20 Ibid. 55.

21 UN Committee on Economic, Social and Cultural Rights, 'Concluding Observations of the CESCR: Germany' (UN Doc. E/C.12/DEU/CO/5, 2011), para. 15; CESCR, *Concluding Observations: Portugal* (UN Doc E/C.12/1/Add.53, 2000), para. 12.

22 UN Committee on Economic, Social and Cultural Rights, 'Concluding Observations of the CESCR: Germany', para. 27.

23 E.g. UN Committee on Economic, Social and Cultural Rights, 'General Comment 20: Non-Discrimination in Economic, Social and Cultural Rights' (UN Doc. E/C.12/GC/20, 2009), para. 36.

24 CESCR, *General Comment 3*, para. 2.

25 Johanna E. Bond (2003) 'International Intersectionality: A Theoretical and Pragmatic Exploration of Women's International Human Rights Violations', *Emory Law Journal* 52: 73.

26 CESCR, *General Comment 3*, para. 12.

27 Diane Elson (2006) *Budgeting for Women's Rights: Monitoring Government Budgets for Compliance with CEDAW* (New York: UNIFEM); Radhika Balakrishnan and Diane Elson (2011) *Economic Policy and Human Rights: Holding Governments to Account* (London: Zed Books); Aoife Nolan, Rory O'Connell and Colin Harvey (eds) (2013) *Human Rights and Public Finance: Budgets and the Promotion of Economic and Social Rights* (Oxford: Hart); Rory O'Connell et al. (2014) *Applying an International Human Rights Framework to State Budget Allocations: Rights and Resources* (London: Routledge).

28 Elson, *Budgeting*, 12.

29 Diane Elson, Radhika Balakrishnan and James Heintz (2013) 'Public Finance, Maximum Available Resources and Human Rights', in Nolan et al., *Human Rights and Public Finance*, 22–5.

30 For other hurdles see AnnJanette Rosga and Margaret L. Satterthwaie (2009) 'The Trust in Indicators: Measuring Human Rights', *Berkeley Journal of International Law* 27(2): 253.

31 For a contrast to the human rights-based approach to macro-economic policy, see Anita Ghatak (1994) *Macroeconomics: A Mathematical Approach* (New Delhi: Concept).

32 John M. Conley (2011) 'Measuring the World: Indicators, Human Rights, and Global Governance: With CA Comment', *Current Anthropology* 52(S3): 87; Maria Green (2001) 'What we Talk about When we Talk about Indicators: Current Approaches to Human Rights Measurement', *Human Rights Quarterly* 23(4): 1085.

33 Philip Alston (2005) 'Richard Lillich Memorial Lecture: Promoting the Accountability of Members of the New UN Human Rights Council', *Journal of Transnational Law and Policy* 15: 74–9.

34 Brian Root (2016) 'Numbers are Only Human: Lessons for Human Rights Practitioners from the Quantitative Literacy Movement', in Philip Alston and Sarah Knuckey (eds), *The Transformation of Human Rights Fact-Finding* (New York: OUP), 356–7.

35 Nolan has addressed the ways in which subdivisions have already been made in human rights budget work; Aoife Nolan (2013) 'Putting ESR-Based Budget

Analysis into Practice: Addressing the Conceptual Challenges', in Nolan *et al.*, *Human Rights*, 43.

36 'Optional Protocol to the International Covenant on Economic, Social and Cultural Rights', *United Nations Treaty Collection*, https://treaties.un.org/Pages/ViewDetails.aspx?src=TREATY&mtdsg_no=IV-3-a&chapter=4&lang=en (accessed Feb. 2016).

37 Or the 'action of making [rights] real'; *Oxford English Dictionary*, 'Realization', 2014.

38 Bruce Bueno De Mesquita, George W. Downs and Alastair Smith (2005) 'Thinking inside the Box: A Closer Look at Democracy and Human Rights', *International Studies Quarterly* 49: 450; Kyaw Yin Hlaing (2003) 'Myanmar in 2003: Frustration and Despair?', *Asian Survey* 44(1): 88; Jernej Letnar Černič (2008) 'Corporate Human Rights Obligations at the International Level', *Willamette Journal of International Law and Dispute Resolution* 16: 132.

39 Roberto Belloni (2012) 'Hybrid Peace Governance: Its Emergence and Significance', *Global Governance* 18: 22–4.

40 Pieterse, 'Globalisation as Hybridisation', 173; Belloni, 'Hybrid Peace Governance', 23, 24.

41 Jason Beattie (2012) 'PMQs "Food Banks Just Part of my Big Society": David Cameron Tries to Make Virtue of Rise in Hungry Surviving Only on Charity', *Mirror*, 19 Dec., http://www.mirror.co.uk/news/uk-news/pmqs-david-cameron-tries-to-make-1497959.

42 Although the Trussell Trust does try to accommodate vegetarian clients; Hannah Lambie (2011) 'The Trussell Trust Foodbank Network: Exploring the Growth of Foodbanks across the UK', *Report to the Trussell Trust* (Coventry SURGE), 4 n. 4.

43 Niall Cooper and Sarah Dumpleton (2013) *Walking the Breadline: The Scandal of Food Poverty in 21st Century Britain* (London: Church Action on Poverty and Oxfam, May), 6, http://www.church-poverty.org.uk/news/pressroom/resources/publications/walkingthebreadlinefile/at_download/file.

44 Lambie, 'Trussell Trust Foodbank Network', 30.

45 de Schutter in Rosaline Eccles and Larissa Kersten (2013), *Freedom from Hunger: Realising the Right to Food in the UK* (London: Just Fair), 16.

46 Ann Blyberg (2009) 'The Case of the Mislaid Allocation: Economic and Social Rights and Budget Work', *International Journal on Human Rights* 6(11): 125.

47 CESCR, *General Comment 13: The Right to Education (Article 13 of the Covenant)* (UN Doc. E/C.12/1999/10, 1999), para. 37.

48 Pieterse, 'Globalisation as Hybridisation', 171.

49 Chairperson of the CESCR, 'Letter Dated 16 May 2012 Addressed by the Chairperson of the Committee on Economic, Social and Cultural Rights to States Parties to the International Covenant on Economic, Social and Cultural Rights', 2012.

50 Michael A. Hogg (2006) 'Social Identity Theory', in Peter James Burke (ed.), *Contemporary Social Psychological Theories* (Stanford, CA: Stanford UP), 118.

51 Rachel Johnstone (2006) 'Feminist Influences on the United Nations Human Rights Treaty Bodies', *Human Rights Quarterly* 28(1): 151; Sandra Fredman (2011) 'Engendering Social and Economic Rights', in Beth Goldblatt and Kirsty McLean (eds), *Women's Social and Economic Rights* (Cape Town: Juta Law), 4–5.

52 CESCR, *Concluding Observations: Dominican Republic* (UN Doc. E/C.12/2010/3, 2010), para. 280.

53 CESCR, *Concluding Observations: Slovakia* (UN Doc. E/C.12/SVK/CO/2, 2012), para. 21.

54 Allison Smith-Estelle and Sofia Gruskin (2003) 'Vulnerability to HIV/STIs among Rural Women from Migrant Communities in Nepal: A Health and Human Rights Framework', *Reproductive Health Matters* 11(22): 142–51.
55 Belloni, 'Hybrid Peace Governance', 23.
56 Although there is increasing attention given to 'group' and 'collective' rights; Rosa Freedman (2013) '"Third Generation" Rights: Is there Room for Hybrid Constructs within International Human Rights Law?', *Cambridge Journal of International and Comparative Law* 2: 935; Philip Alston (1998) 'Making Space for New Human Rights: The Case of the Right to Development', *Harvard Human Rights Yearbook* 1: 4.
57 Hogg, 'Social Identity Theory', 117.
58 Ibid. 118.
59 This level of analysis, at least as far as women's rights are concerned, has been lacking; Johanna E. Bond (2003) 'International Intersectionality: A Theoretical and Pragmatic Exploration of Women's International Human Rights Violations', *Emory Law Journal* 52: 72–3.
60 'The' (as if there was a single version) family is 'treated as if it were a single actor with a single class position, standard of living, and set of interests'; Myra Marx Ferree (1990) 'Beyond Separate Spheres: Feminism and Family Research', *Journal of Marriage and the Family* 52: 867.
61 See e.g. Siobhán Mullaly (2007) 'The UN, Minority Rights and Gender Equality: Setting Limits to Collective Claims', *International Journal on Minority and Group Rights* 14: 263; Indeed, there is the inclusion of a statement reaffirming the equal rights of men and women in the landmark *Declaration on the Rights of Indigenous Persons (General Assembly, 'Declaration on the Rights of Persons Belonging to National or Ethnic, Religious and Linguistic Minorities')* (UN Res. A/RES/47/135, 1992), preamble. However, caution should be had here to avoid replacing one sort of blindness to power dynamics with another; Mohanty claims in a different context that feminist discourse can 'discursively colonize the material and historical heterogeneities' of groups and 'produc[e]/re-present . . . a composite, singular' group: Chandra Talpade Mohanty (1984) 'Under Western Eyes: Feminist Scholarship and Colonial Discourses', *Boundary 2* 12(3): 334.
62 CESCR, *General Comment 3*, para. 9.
63 A term used in Center for Economic and Social Rights (CESR) (2012) *Mauled by the Celtic Tiger: Human Rights in Ireland's Economic Meltdown*, 6, http://www.cesr.org/downloads/cesr.ireland.briefing.12.02.2012.pdf; Aoife Nolan, Nicholas J. Lusiani and Christian Courtis (2014) 'Two Steps Forward, No Steps Back? Evolving Criteria on the Prohibition of Retrogression in Economic, Social and Cultural Rights', in Aoife Nolan (ed.), *Economic and Social Rights after the Global Financial Crisis* (Cambridge: CUP), 125. For discussion, see also Joe J. Wills and Ben T. C. Warwick (2016) 'Contesting Austerity: The Potential and Pitfalls of Socioeconomic Rights Discourse', *Indiana Journal of Global Legal Studies* 23(2): 629–64.
64 CESCR, *General Comment 3*, para. 9.
65 Illustratively, despite the numerous mentions of progression/retrogression, the word 'stagnation' has been recorded once in the CESCR's comments and observations; CESCR, *Concluding Observations: Columbia* (UN Doc. E/C.12/1/Add.74, 2011), para. 13.
66 CESCR, *General Comment 12: The Right to Adequate Food (art. 11)* (UN Doc. E/C.12/1999/5, 1999), paras 8, 11.
67 Craig Scott (2014) 'Interdependence and Permeability of Human Rights Norms: Towards a Partial Fusion of the International Covenants on Human Rights', *Osgoode Hall Law Journal* 27(3): 769.

Chapter 13

From hybrid to cybrid?

The formation and regulation of online 'hybrid' identities

Kim Barker and Christina Baghdady

Introduction: a hybrid space?

The role and spread of law in an increasingly globalised society is constantly being challenged. One significant, and timely, example of this arises in the context of online social communities. These 'communities' have recently been credited with influencing political uprising,[1] and the ensuing political instability across the Middle East as a consequence of online uprising spread through an offline context. The legal – and political – mechanisms that have been deployed to act upon such activity are mechanisms that have not been suited to a particular form of community uprising. These online uprisings are potentially the result of new online, or 'virtual' communities – and identities – being established. If new identities and communities are growing to influence social movements, it is perhaps time that the mechanisms of control are suited to the challenges they face.

Offline mechanisms[2] are no longer suited to online social movements, and this became apparent during the Arab Awakening[3] – the spread of online uprising transferred from the virtual, online identities of those seeking change to the offline communities acting upon the strength of feeling. It is necessary to consider the scope of these 'new' identities and communities, and then, by extension, consider the mechanisms in place to address such challenges to established offline social norms and controls – legal or political. This chapter will consider the role of online communities in political change and consider the suitability of existing methods of control, or whether a hybrid approach to regulation and control would be preferable. The consideration here given to 'hybrid' approaches is taken to mean a combination of traditional, offline regulatory controls, along with dedicated online controls to create a blended system targeted at meeting the regulatory needs of the internet, but also of the users of the internet.

This chapter explores the current regulatory system of social media platforms through the events of the Arab Awakening, and through the lens of hybridity. The current regulatory mechanisms place the emphasis very much on the platform provider of social media and online spaces to regulate and control their environments, with legal regulation entering only where something cannot be tackled by a platform provider. Important social media and communicatory online platforms are therefore left open to abuse from a regulation perspective, but also open to abuse where these websites are used to orchestrate change. These online spaces – particularly those such as Twitter and Facebook – have played an increasingly important role in political change in recent years. However, where they have been instrumental in such change, there have been repercussions involving either punishment for those most active on social media or the suspension of all social media platforms. Physically and geographically disparate users of these platforms are converging and creating new communities online, to create a new social movement – this is a new form of activism. Whilst these acts can be seen as forces for good, this chapter considers the failures of governments to deploy traditional regulatory mechanisms to prevent and combat such movements. This chapter will therefore theorise the potential for a more successful approach to counteract cybrid activism. Arguably, there is the potential to view hybridity – and by extension within this chapter, cybridity – as a term broadly reflecting creolisation, particularly in an online context.[4]

This chapter will draw upon wide-ranging fields of inquiry and literature from law, cybernetics, politics and communications to support the overall argument that there needs to be a more cohesive system of regulation of the internet. In particular, to explore this argument, the discussions here will consider the current understandings we have of identity and community, and will assess through the Arab Awakening, how those identities are challenging existing internet regulatory methods because a failure to apply hybridity, or a disregarding of the cybrid nature of social movements online and offline, could lead to further revolutions. The discussions within this chapter will explore our understandings of online activism, and will attempt to theorise methods of online governance that could allow for more effective counteractions. It will consider how these have been supplemented by the rise of activist identities, and how these have been transformed through the rise of social media, before commenting on the need for a hybridised (cybrid) approach to quelling identity-led, community-based uprising, especially with the dawn of Web 3.0.[5]

Transformative communities – 'always on'

Within any consideration of online activism, consideration ought to be given to the community in which an uprising occurred. The discussions below will therefore explore the challenges in defining 'community' within the current phase of the internet – that is, within Web 2.0 and the rise of social media. Working definitions of community offer different interpretive approaches to these groups, but considered together, there are a number of commonalities which appear. It is these commonalities which provide the basis for the later discussions relating to the control of these communities, and the regulatory quelling of online activism. This discussion here will consider the definitional approaches to community, including the constructions of multiple identities that are used across several communities in the digital world.

Primarily, our understandings of community stem from traditional interpretations. Community can be defined either with reference to a place or locality: 'The people of a district or country considered collectively, especially in the context of social values and responsibilities; society.'[6] The definition is far from one-dimensional, and, as Bell indicates, the term 'community' is itself full of complexities.[7] Niven reiterates this, implying that the term is used widely but without any significant thought given to its context or meaning,[8] whilst Ladds advances the supposition that community will have a different meaning to each community.[9] This implies that those who recognise communities, and those who participate in them, will largely define such entities. It is however possible that those communities are also recognisable by their identity, and even the shared identity of the community members, through joint or collaborative interests and shared, 'common perspectives'.[10] This approach is premised on the notion that there is a community in existence because the members believe in it, as Anderson[11] indicates. As a result, the community believes in its existence, reflects it in their cultural practices.[12] Anderson's point here is one which is significant within the discussions of community more broadly – it is very much the definition which forms the foundation for the considerations of social media and hashtag communities which are discussed below.

Despite this, shifting cultural practices, together with globalisation[13] challenge traditional perceptions of 'communities'. We now speak not of citizens, but rather of 'netizens'[14] – such a transformation is attributable to different developments such as the removal of geographical, social and even political restraints. Nevertheless, the influence of culture and technology is now something shaping our social relations, and identities, in large part due to the 'intricate connection[s] between culture and technology',[15] with Borer arguing it is 'imperative to attempt to comprehend the impact of electronic media on human social relations and self-identity'.[16] Atkinson goes further, indicating that a definition of community is actually 'a shared understanding'[17] and is broadly based on a number of characteristics, which could include 'a communal mind',[18] whilst Weinreich advocates that there is a distinction between an offline community and virtual gatherings, because fundamental to his definition of communities is the need for face-to-face interaction.[19] This approach to defining a community faces challenges and difficulties when online communities are considered, because it appears possible that face-to-face interactions have been replaced by the connections developed through the use of the internet.

This is particularly true for the communities that arise in online games, and virtual worlds, which are in their genre diverse and unique environments.[20] Bell approaches these spaces and communities by identifying their characteristics rather than communities,[21] which in itself indicates that there are a number of challenges in defining communities online. It is this difficulty that has been partially addressed by authors such as Alemi[22] and Barker,[23] who attempt to define communities online through reference to those who participate within them. It is possible – in a gaming context – to see that there are different layers of community; the space itself as a community, but also particular user groups within these communities. One such example would arise in the form of griefers[24] – gaming characters that seek to cause disruption to the experience of other game users.

This too is broadly reflective of other communities online – especially in social media contexts. It is perhaps more applicable to online social media sites than to other online platforms on the basis that online social media sites are primarily designed to allow the creation of networks specific to an individual – each person who has a Facebook account will benefit from the common features of Facebook – for example, the ability to comment on posts, and also the ability to block certain users – but will see a different, personalised feed dependent upon their connections. In this way, it is perhaps possible to view Facebook on one level – and your unique collection of friends on another level – as an online community consisting of smaller, interconnected communities. This is however, not Facebook-specific, and can broadly be said to be applicable and resonant of *any* online platform that encourages participation rather than pure consumption. For example, this can be said to occur through other social platforms, and is perhaps most apparent through Twitter – the microblogging site, with over 900 million accounts.[25] The scale and size of the communities which can be created, and accessed online, and especially through Twitter, is worthy of note. Schroeder *et al.* indicate that Twitter was significant to the Arab Spring, seeing over one million tweets sent on just two days in 2011 in Egypt.[26] Over three million Arab Spring tweets have been analysed to reveal that over 196,000 users had over 500,000 connections between them.[27] As such, it is evident that the reach of social media, and online identities is significant, and offers potential for not only democratisation, but also for the rapid building of social capital and protest mobilisation,[28] thereby forming communities online.

Twitter, whilst allowing a network of the 'self' to be created through followers, and those that users follow, is a much broader global community. Twitter perhaps offers something more in the sense of 'community' or identity than other online platforms, especially through the making of connections through hashtags. Hashtags allow users to connect with other users whom they do not follow, to share experiences, opinions, grievances or resources. This also allows users to connect with others sharing a similar identity or perspective. One such example of this is through the so-called 'Black Twitter' hashtag, which has developed to form a community of tweeters, connecting with others in different communities, but with whom there is a resonance.[29] This hashtag is not one based on skin colour, but is one which instead is concerned with ethnicity and group affiliation – yet another form of community identity.[30] Whilst in one dimension, Black Twitter is nothing other than a hashtag, on another level it is representative of much more, including community, and cultural force, with almost a quarter of all black internet users having a Twitter account.[31] The significance of a hashtag, represents (in the words of users) the culture and the wider community of those with a shared common interest, and a shared identity.[32] Another example of the ways in which Twitter encourages its user base to form communities is visible through the use of hash-tagging to gain support for a particular movement – and one example of such uses was visible in the use of social media to spark the Arab Spring and chain of social (and political) uprising in the Middle East. Social media in this context can be viewed as a strand of activism, and even a strand of cyber-activism.

Defining a community can, therefore, have several potential strands – community itself is not capable of a 'catch-all' definition, and is in part, dependent upon characteristics and a sense of self. This sense of self allows us to connect with a community, be it virtual or otherwise. The use of, and reliance upon, technology is also something shaping our communities.[33] Technology is therefore a means through which identities can be created, communities developed and reconstructed. This is especially significant in that it is possible for identities online to be distinguished from offline identities. This is not the same thing as anonymity, nor is it the same as privacy – about which, much has been written elsewhere.[34] The distinction between identity online and identity offline is such that, as Jordan indicates, it is not that users are creating anonymity in cyberspace – instead users are constructing identities that can be used there, making a distinction and a division from their offline identities possible.[35] And this, in the context of social uprising, is significant in that it allows different identities to be used across communities.

It is partially through this connection of self with community that cyber-activism, and cyber-communities have emerged as leading movements in an increasingly connected world. These cyber communities are rarely defined, and are diverse and distinct, but share some common characteristics, which aids in their identification. In this respect, the term 'hybridity' is directly relevant to online community spaces and arguably reflects the term creolisation, which relates to the formation of new identities and inherited culture.[36] For online communities, creolisation is equally applicable and is largely unchanged as a term of understanding, but can in part be tweaked, to indicate that a hybridised online community inherits identity but forms new culture, thereby blending the two.[37] This is particularly evident where there is a cross-fertilisation of existing identity and culture, blended with new forms of telecommunications. This therefore develops through social interactions, and leads to situations where online communities and platforms act to protect their interests, and challenge the applicability of the offline regulatory models. Social media sites – but online platforms more broadly – have in recent years have sought – and continue – to challenge this paradigm, and foster new forms of activism.

Cyber activism: building communities?

Given the ease with which cross-fertilisation of communities and identities occurs online, it is little surprise that connections and large groups form irrespective of their geographical locations. These connections create online communities, and with it comes the potential for activism. The reliance on online connections to coordinate and to connect for shared causes creates systems of cyber-activism. The community aspects are the foundations for such activism, and develop their own set of norms premised on similar ideas to those advanced by Anderson that there is a belief and therefore there is respect. The discussions here will consider the role of community in activism, concluding that the difficulties of defining communities are not reduced by online interactions, but that these communities share some commonalities of more traditional offline communities.

The rise of so-called activism is not *per se* a 'new' element to the role the internet has in shaping our interactions and, perhaps even our society, whilst remaining connected to the sense of self. From the early campaigns to allow the vote for women, suffragettes and suffragists have been using media outlets to gain support for their particular cause.[38] Tactics such as leaflets, small letters and secret places for leaving notes and material all play a role in historic activism, and these tactics have not changed – the medium has. Ultimately, the actions are the same, but the method of communication and orchestration is different. However, as media have changed, so too has the reach of the medium, and this in the age of the internet has led to even greater opportunities to advance agendas. This potential now includes the ability to introduce and energise social and political change. It is through the blending of these two that social uprising has occurred, and perhaps it is because of the hybridisation of social media with political desire that events such as those dominating the Middle East since 2008 have occurred. Howard and Hussein indicate that the significance of social and mobile media cannot be underestimated, not least because these are mechanisms of spreading democratisation through means that the state simply cannot control.[39]

Given the difficulties in defining 'community' it is possible to envisage that there are also difficulties in determining the forms of control and regulation which are used in governing these communities. The practical challenges attached to discussions surrounding community embody themselves in the battles between those finding new techniques to communication against those who attempt to dismantle them. Cyberspace has become the latest platform on which those battles are played out, but is not by any means restricted in terms of the effects that new methods of communication have, as is discussed below.

In many respects, these difficulties are compounded online, not only through the dominance of End User Licensing Agreements to control the rights and interests of users in online platforms, but also through the jurisdictional difficulties the internet as a single space poses.[40] Controlling elements of this space is therefore also likely to prove difficult, not least because offline rules are increasingly being applied to online environments and spaces, where they are perhaps not suitable nor effective. This is not a new debate, but remains as relevant now as it was at the dawn of the internet era, with advocates such as John Perry Barlow advocating vociferously that governments have no right to claim jurisdictional competence over cyberspace,[41] whereas others, such as Goldsmith and Wu have suggested that it is unrealistic to not expect there to be some form of claim by offline authorities that their competence extends beyond territorial borders to the internet.[42] That is not however to say that there is a 'law of the internet' and in this, Easterbrook's 'Law of the Horse' is as resonant today as it was in 1996.[43] We have an increasingly diverse set of online platforms and an increasingly diverse set of online interactions. Similarly, we have an increasing number of offline laws and regulations that extend their reach into virtual platforms. However, there has been no design or concept of an 'internet law' or a specifically configured system of legal rules that applies exclusively to the internet. The futility of such an attempt is perhaps clear when social and video media and mobile interaction are considered – such a system may be a theoretical ideal but a practical enforcement challenge.

It is therefore seemingly apparent that communities can take different forms and can arise in different guises. Such communities may even arise purely for a particular campaign, but the definition of such communities is hard to pinpoint. Nevertheless, where a group of interested citizens connect – either in an offline campaign, or an online chatroom, through a Twitter hashtag, or even a Facebook group – it is clear that these can be representative of a wider identity, and therefore potentially also of a community, and will seemingly develop their own sets of norms, and are equally able to generate potential for concrete actions. Online communities are about more than just people 'expressing' interest online, but can also spur very concrete actions on the ground, which might even render any effective regulation of the online activities insignificant.

The Arab Awakening: a hybrid form of 'on' and 'off' line socio-political uprising?

25 January arose from a series of social injustices including unemployment, corruption, poverty and the cumulative effects of a security state. More significantly, however, the events of 25 January were little other than the domino effects of the uprising in Tunisia and stem directly from Bouazizi's political statement[44] of self-immolation on 17 December 2010.

All of these political statements, including coverage of the events in mainstream media, overlooked – initially – the rise of social media, and the connections between events in different territories and across different community groups. Once mainstream coverage of such events spread to include the Egyptian media, the events gained a higher level of momentum and greater attention across both mainstream and social media. This was a significant, but overlooked element to the uprisings, and became widespread because of the difference in language – once media coverage arose in Egypt, understanding and appreciation of the events spread widely across the entire region. This is something that Schroeder *et al.* have recognised, indicating that grievances individually across communities were insufficient to lead to action – the cumulative effect was of much greater significance.[45] This created links across social platforms, and political spectra, communicating shared injustices whilst enabling those aggrieved to awaken their insurgent consciousness.[46]

The sharing and cross-platform grievances were voiced through non-traditional media platforms. Whilst not unique, this was the first, widespread, mass formation of Twitter communities and use of platforms such as Facebook, Twitter, the blogosphere and direct communication applications such as Whatsapp and Viber.[47] Facebook groups such as that called 'Kolena Khaled Saeed'[48] – named in memory of the young man beaten to death by police in a cybercafé in Alexandria in 2010 – proved to be pivotal. Not only is this example one that highlights the strength of feeling concerning shared grievances, but it is also a key indicator of the bonds across communities in support of a shared cause, and this strength of feeling was facilitated for the first time by social platforms. This group became a core logistical tool in exposing government corruption and providing a voice for democracy advocates as: 'a portal for collective commiseration'.[49]

As a further example – Wael Ghonim (founder of the group) – is a significant figure, not only in terms of his role in establishing the group for shared grievances, but in his professional role as an employee of Google. Ghonim understood the need to communicate multilingually, and he played a pivotal role in facilitating the spread of the movement, not only on a region-specific basis, but also to allow Western observers to follow the events. The effect of this cannot be overestimated, especially given the predictions of Western leaders, such as Hillary Clinton, who stated on the eve of 25 January that 'the Egyptian government is stable',[50] with the Israeli military chief echoing this message later the same day.[51] This prevailing underestimation of the situation was prevalent, not only in Western governments, but also in Western academia, with Walt advocating that cascade revolutions are rare occurrences.[52] Despite the rarity of such cascade revolutions, forces were at play which toppled different regimes. The subsequent arrest of Ghonim on 28 January by state security, and the subsequent high-profile interview[53] following his release twelve days later, was symptomatic of the spread of the uprising; the sharing across platforms of links to the interview occurred on a large scale.

Online activism was at the root of the social movement behind the Arab Spring. Irrespective of whether or not Clinton and Walt were wrong, it is clear that Clinton's statement might have been of a much more strategic nature than an actual and honest assessment. And even if both Clinton and Walt underestimated the force of the movement, it does not mean that they also underestimated the role of social media. It is therefore evident that no matter what statements were made, and predictions offered, social media use was pivotal in the Arab Awakening as a movement of activism.

This phenomenon was not Facebook-specific, and was also evident through Twitter on a similar, if not larger scale. Before the resignation of ex-Tunisian President, Ben Ali,[54] tweeting and social media activism was a growing force. This force in the form of tweeting saw in excess of 1,000 tweets each day advocating for political change in Tunisia.[55] By 17 December 2010, when Bouazizi self-immolated, almost a quarter of Tunisian blog entries focused on elements of political change,[56] reflecting the strength of feeling, and a growing outward vocalisation of dissatisfaction with the situation within the country. The rise in blog entries was also significant because the blog entries were not only in French, but also in English,[57] once again reflecting the use of non-traditional platforms to reach a wider and more diverse base, connecting with others of similar opinions, and establishing a socio-political online activist community.

This is a significant difference to the situation and media use in Egypt, where the tweeting was spread much more widely, including the middle classes alongside liberals and the upper classes. This is in part due to the spread of internet access, and was a significant feature in Egypt, because this facilitated connections with the working poor – the 'zabbaleen' – and grievances were identified as similar across political and social class.[58] During the revolution in Egypt, 34 per cent of tweets relating to freedom in Egypt came from people geographically located outside of the country, but this had dwindled to 12 per cent by the time of Mubarak's resignation.[59] Internally however, the number of Egypt-related tweets increased significantly at the time of resignation and thereafter.[60] It is therefore apparent that the prolonged use of Twitter changed post-resignation from an activist platform to one providing instant news from a range of outlets, yet again evidence of non-traditional community contact. It is also significant that the bonds formed during the revolution were maintained with a different focus post-revolution. This platform was significant for a number of reasons, including real-time information – both nationally and internationally – and for the maintenance of links established during the mirrored online and offline activism.

The importance of Twitter in this context was crucial, even when the authorities attempted to shut down social media sites. This is a lesson that governments have repeatedly failed to learn. Three years later, Erdogan's Turkish government also blocked – for example – access to Twitter,[61] only to suffer a similar backlash as that experienced in Egypt in 2011. This seems to indicate a failure of authorities to recognise that such online activist communities associate with one another, but also form an identity amongst themselves. This identity translates into a culture of norms, akin to the 'associative relation between objects, communities, or spaces.'[62] This identity and establishment of norms – i.e. the use of Twitter to organise meetings and campaigns – is also akin to a system of non-state lawmaking.[63] The norms established identify the community, and the purpose of the community – the Twitter activism is effectively what guides the rules of the self-identified community members. The norms and virtual associations developed through social media communities and interactions can – and do – actually transform into – and symbolise – physical movements that can counteract the state in the form of street demonstrations. It is therefore not only the existence of communities and their norms as such, but their triggering of actual social and political protest, that concerns governments and seems to necessitate their reaction through the cybrid approaches to communities.

(On)line + (off)line = cybrid?

Online communities are not purely online – they currently reflect a blend of online and offline, and as such, regulatory mechanisms seek to apply offline controls to online spaces. Neither can exist without the other – they are co-dependent and coexistent, and this is clearly apparent from the use of social media and digital platforms to coordinate combined movements advocating change. A key feature is the blend between different disciplines on a global scale, and the ability to transcend boundaries. This is increasingly apparent where there is the combination of artificial intelligence, and online communicatory methods – such as those used during the Arab Awakening, and in the aftermath.

The aftermath of such politico-social uprisings saw alternative approaches to regulating the use of social media platforms. These alternative approaches by governments have included attempts to turn off internet access across countries such as Egypt, and even post-revolutionary Twitter policing.

It has also extended to YouTube and television broadcasts, with the effect that presenters have been suspended for political satire.[64] Cybrid approaches follow in this context, blending the artificial intelligence and monitoring of social media by state authorities with real-time interactions. Such intelligence first appeared in fictional works[65] – and is considered here as a potential future scenario – but now transcends the division between technology and the uses of it, blurring the two so that it is increasingly difficult to distinguish one from the other. It is therefore a cross between the offline and online; offline mobilisation of online activities, in a similar way to the blend between humans and artificial intelligence.

As cybrid entities and cybrid communities are now increasingly apparent, it is perhaps time to introduce a blended hybrid approach to regulating online social and political movements. Hybrid approaches ought therefore, to develop from merely being used as a lens to consider theoretical perspectives, to being deployed as mechanisms to instigate practical change, in a online context, 'cybrid' approaches. In our offline environments, reliance is placed upon law and social order to ensure that society operates smoothly and runs accordingly. Law and order are key elements to any form of society, or community, yet it is perhaps evident from the events surrounding the Arab Awakening that the reliance on offline methods of control was far from effective.[66] Cybernetic theory[67] suggests that regulation by governments of things which are ill-defined and messy will in turn be ill-defined and messy. Such a theory – when considered in light of undefined, and previously unconnected individuals coming together to champion a common, revolutionary cause such as the Arab Awakening – offers an insight into the difficulty of controlling a diverse spread of networked individuals. This also reflects accurately the state of regulability and control of online sites and online communities. Cybernetic theories have at various points been defined in various different ways, but include suggestions that cybernetics is about interaction across dynamic networks.[68] This has perhaps never been more widely applicable than in the context of online communities, and the Arab Awakening: – communications across complex networks were the key to this particular uprising, especially the cumulative effect. The use of social media to support and facilitate political change involved not merely the use of social platforms but the interaction with them. The change in the use of the internet, and its platforms suggests that internet users no longer merely 'surf the web' but are immersed in it, and contribute to it. This is particularly clear when there is some form of community and identity, and therefore whilst networked horizontalism is spoken of in connection to online movements, it is perhaps more appropriate to consider activism in a community context, which also includes community-developed norms.

In reality, it is presently difficult to conceive of what a cybrid method of regulation could look like, because of the dilemmas states face when confronted with online interactions and offline political gatherings. It is possible that a cybrid approach would be community-based – but to consider such a basis requires precise considerations of what our communities will look like in the future. It is equally possible to perceive that the current dilemmas facing states in terms of online and offline regulation is a hybrid blend of specific legislation addressing offline uprisings, and technological interventions shutting down communication systems. A workable model of cybrid regulation would see key features of the largest online communities used to consider a system of regulation which interacts with the offline political spaces. States have readily adopted norms relating to their international relations – adopting norms for combined online interactions and offline gatherings is a potential likely extension of statehood. Merely 'switching off' Twitter, Facebook and other communicatory platforms offers little in the way of quelling social uprising because technology and communications systems are now incredibly sophisticated. It is increasingly apparent that, as technologies develop, states and government bodies will inevitably advocate other approaches, including online spying, data collection and even perhaps digital counter-insurgency. Once again, this is further evidence of the mix between traditional and non-traditional methods of addressing activism which span different forms of media.

Networked communitarianism: tailoring community identities

Given the discussions above of the features of community, and social media interactions representing offline political consciousness, there are a number of other potential considerations of the foundations for social uprisings that have been orchestrated through previously unconnected communities. Castells,[69] and Hill[70] talk respectively about the differences between the social consciousness and, on the other hand, the *networked* consciousness of those directly involved in the uprisings between 2008 and 2011, both in Southern Europe, and the Arab states. Networked horizontalism and networked individualism have both been used as terms to describe the effects of these uprisings, which gained momentum through media use and coverage – be it traditional media, or social media. However, whilst networked horizontalism reflects the use of social media movements to spread messages and organise meetings in person, and networked individualism reflects the individuals as part of a network, neither of these terms truly reflects the community impact and community role in the uprisings and movements. As such, networked communitarianism is a more appropriate descriptor. Networked communitarianism, it is suggested, is much more reflective of the role both of those involved in the uprising – in person and online – and is also much more reflective of the role of the network – again, be it online or offline. Communities were pivotal in the social and political activism witnessed during these uprisings. In the same way that hacking activism is hacktivism, networked uprisings are effectively networked communitarianism.

The communitarianist aspects of the Arab Awakening reflect not only the cumulative, community effects and impact of the social media campaigns, but also the role of the networks in facilitating the changes in political regimes. It is also apparent from the role media coverage played that a ready ability to communicate to mass groups of people, across different languages and cultures, was a significant factor.[71] This does not however detract from the communitarian aspects of the Arab Awakening – the rise and deployment of Twitter communities, and of cyber-activists is something that has shaped social revolution in the past decade. No longer can the political and social elements of revolution and uprising be considered to be totally distinct from one another. Similarly, in any establishment of community, and of horizontal communities where leadership is not hierarchical, social norms must play a significant role. These aspects and elements of community identities therefore suggest that these communities are blended, and hybridised political spaces.

Conclusion: online communities – hybridised political spaces?

Digital interactions now encroach upon every aspect of modern life – the use of smartphones and tablets mean that online communities members are widespread, mobilised and increasingly connected. The cumulative effect means that interactions are possible not only through initiatives such as eVoting,[72] but also reflect mass mobilisation of social activists across boundaries both physical and virtual. This is also evident when it comes to political movements, and social grievances – mass use of Twitter enables people to connect with others in different communities that have shared complaints. This intersection of digital and analogue reflects the increased ability of modern society to shift paradigms and to cross barriers that would previously have prevented widespread outcries. The connections formed online spread across platforms, reaching people who would have previously not been contactable – this use of media is therefore not restricted to traditional news outlets, but is hybridised, and politically charged.

As our use of the internet has altered, it was perhaps expected that the regulation of it would also change. This change is still pending, and as Mubarak and Erdogan have discovered, simply attempting to 'switch off' the internet is an insufficiently reliable response to vocalised campaigns spanning the online and offline realms. Appropriate approaches to these cybrid online communities and subcultures is something which ought to benefit from attention, especially given the instability surrounding economies and political regimes such as those in Syria.

It is also concerning that online identities, represented as communities such as Black Twitter, fail to benefit from recognition offline by those in power. This is increasingly problematic in light of the 2010 Declaration by the United Nations that internet access is a fundamental right – preventing legitimate vocalisation of political and social grievances by turning off the means for online communities to communicate would therefore appear to fall foul of such a declaration.[73] Not only this, but in practical terms, it seemingly would lead to greater outcry from the online communities affected. It is apparent from the Arab Awakening that communities and identities are fluid concepts, blending the online and offline. This is especially the situation where community members associate with identities – both individual and collective – and form subcultures, as these tend to be politically charged. It is impossible and undesirable for a 'one size fits all' approach to be adopted. This is especially apparent in relation to the collation of contacts across various platforms, because, as reiterated by Bell, there are 'those that use cyberspace to advance their project, in the same way they might use other forms of communication'.[74]

This chapter has considered the forms of online community and identity that were prevalent during the significant social media uprisings in the Middle East. It is clear that defining identities and communities is far from straightforward, and these challenges are compounded when considering digital activism. Nevertheless, it is possible to perceive digital connections as forms of communities, and indeed, groups with shared connections, values and norms. Hybrid approaches to controlling the online environments are necessary – it is appropriate that hybrid controls govern hybrid subcultures and communities, and where these appear online, cybrid approaches are the key to politically charged identities. A failure to apply hybridity and a disregarding of the cybrid nature of social movements online and offline could lead to further cascade revolutions. The medium may have changed, yet the message remains the same, but as McLuhan indicated, sometimes the medium is also the message.[75]

Notes

1 Eike M. Rinke and Maria Röder (2011) 'Media Ecologies, Communication Culture, and Temporal-Spatial Unfolding: Three Components in a Communication Model of the Egyptian Regime Change', *International Journal of Communication* 5, feature: 1273–85, 1274.

2 Taken, for the purposes of this work, to relate to traditional legal regulatory mechanisms, i.e. legislation targeted at physical activity and predominantly non-internet-based provisions.

3 Referred to by Ramadan as something akin to an uprising on demand: Tariq Ramadan (2012) *The Arab Awakening: Islam and the New Middle East* (London: Allen Lane). Also more commonly referred to as the Arab Spring; see e.g. Philip N. Howard and Muzammil M. Hussain (2013) *Democracy's Fourth Wave? Digital Media and the Arab Spring* (Oxford: Oxford University Press), 3.

4 This will be discussed further in considerations of community below.
5 Cade Metz (2007) 'Web 3.0.', *PC Mag*, 14 Mar., http://www.pcmag.com/article2/0,2817,2102852,00.asp (accessed May 2014). Web 3.0 can be considered to show the development of internet usage from the current social networking phase to the expected developments of convergence technologies.
6 Oxford Dictionaries, 'Community', http://www.oxforddictionaries.com/definition/english/community (accessed May 2014).
7 David Bell (2001) *An Introduction to Cybercultures* (London: Routledge), 93.
8 Rosie Niven (2013) 'The Complexity of Defining Community', *Guardian*, 3 May, http://www.theguardian.com/voluntary-sector-network/2013/may/03/community-spurs-fans (accessed May 2014).
9 Debbie Ladds, quoted in Niven, 'Complexity'.
10 Kathleen M. MacQueen, Eleanor McLellan, David S. Metzger, Susan Kegeles, Ronald P. Strauss, Roseanne Scotti, Lynn Blanchard and Robert T. Trotter II (2001) 'What is Community? An Evidence-Based Definition for Participatory Public Health Programmes', *American Journal of Public Health* 91(12): 1929–38, 1929.
11 Benedict Anderson (1983) *Imagined Communities: Reflections on the Origin and Spread of Nationalism*, 1st edn (London: Verso).
12 Tim Edensor (2001) *National Identities and Popular Culture* (Oxford: Oxford University Press).
13 Bell, *Introduction to Cybercultures*, 95.
14 Jay Hauben (2010) 'Further Thoughts about Netizens', 1 June, http://http://www.columbia.edu/~hauben/CMC/netizen_thoughts.html (accessed May 2014).
15 Michael I. Borer (n.d.) 'The Cyborgian Self: Toward a Critical Social Theory of Cyberspace' http://reconstruction.eserver.org/Issues/ 023/borer.htm (accessed Feb. 2014).
16 Ibid.
17 Philip Atkinson (2011) 'A Study of our Decline', 7 Feb., http://www.ourcivilisation.com/define.htm (accessed May 2014).
18 Ibid.
19 Frank Weinreich (1997) 'Establishing a Point of View towards Virtual Communities', *Computer-Mediated Communication* 4(2), http://www. december.com/cmc/mag/1997/feb/wein.html (accessed May 2014).
20 F. Gregory Lastowka (2010) *Virtual Justice: The New Laws of Online Worlds* (New Haven, CT: Yale University Press).
21 Mark W. Bell (2008) 'Toward a Definition of Virtual Worlds', *Journal for Virtual Worlds Research* 1(1): 2–5.
22 Farnaz Alemi (2007) 'An Avatar's Day in Court: A Proposal for Obtaining Relief and Resolving Disputes in Virtual World Games', *UCLA Journal of Law and Technology*, 6: 2–52.
23 Kim Barker (2013) 'MMORPGing, Law and Lingo', in Michael Freeman and Fiona Smith (eds), *Law and Language: Current Legal Issues*, vol. 15 (Oxford: Oxford University Press), 417–33.
24 Ibid. 433.
25 J. Edwards (2014) 'Most People on Twitter Don't Actually Tweet', *Business Insider*, 11 Apr. 2014, www.businesinsider.com/twitter-user-statistics-2014-4 (accessed June 2014).
26 Rob Schroeder, Sean Everton and Russell Shepherd (2012) 'Mining Twitter Data from the Arab Spring', *Combating Terrorism Exchange* 2(4): 54–64.
27 Philip N. Howard, Aiden Duffy, Deen Freelon, Muzammil M. Hussain, Will Mari and Marwa Maziad (2011) 'Opening Closed Regimes: What was the Role of

Social Media during the Arab Spring?', http://papers.ssrn.com/sol3/papers.cfm?abstract_id=2595096 (accessed June 2016).

28 Ibid.

29 Soraya N. McDonald (2014) 'Black Twitter: A Virtual Community Ready to Hashtag out a Response to Cultural Issues', *Washington Post*, 20 Jan., www.washingtonpost.com/lifestyle/style/black-twitter-a-virtual-community-ready-to-hashtag-out-a-response-to-cultural-issues/2014/01/20/41ddacf6-7ec5-11e-9556-4a4bf7bcb (accessed May 2014).

30 See Axel Bruns and Jean E. Burgess (2011) 'The Use of Twitter Hashtags in the Formation of Ad Hoc Publics', *Proceedings of the 6th European Consortium for Political Research (ECPR) General Conference 2011, University of Iceland, Reykjavik*, http://eprints.qut.edu.au/46515 (accesed May 2016).

31 Ibid.

32 Michael Arcenaux (2013) 'Black Twitter's 2013 All-Stars', *Complex Tech*, 23 Dec. 2013, www.complex.com/tech/2013/12/black-twitter-all-stars (accessed May 2014); McDonald, 'Black Twitter'.

33 Borer, 'Cyborgian Self'.

34 See e.g. Paul Bernal (2014) *Internet Privacy Rights: Rights to Protect Autonomy* (Cambridge: Cambridge University Press).

35 Tim Jordan (1999) *Cyberpower: The Culture and Politics of Cyberspace and the Internet* (London: Routledge), 75.

36 Robin Cohen (2007) 'Creolization and Cultural Globalization: The Soft Sounds of Fugitive Power', *Globalizations* 4(3): 369–84, 373.

37 See the section of this chapter: 'The Arab Awakening: a hybrid form of 'on' and 'off' line socio-political uprising?'

38 Maria Braden (1996) *Women Politicians and the Media* (Lexington, KY: University Press of Kentucky), 1.

39 Howard *et al.*, 'Opening Closed Regimes'.

40 Jurisdictional concerns are outside of the discussion here.

41 John P. Barlow (1996) 'Declaration of the Independence of Cyberspace', Electronic Frontier Foundation, 8 Feb., https://projects.eff.org/~barlow/Declaration-Final.html (accessed May 2014).

42 Jack Goldsmith and Tim Wu (2006) *Who Controls the Internet? Illusions of a Borderless World* (Oxford: Oxford University Press).

43 Frank H. Easterbrook (1996) 'Cyberspace and the Law of the Horse', *University of Chicago Legal Forum* 1996: 207–16.

44 Peter Beaumont (2011) 'Mohamed Bouazizi: The Dutiful Son Whose Death Changed Tunisia's Fate', *Guardian*, 20 Jan., http://www.theguardian.com/world/2011/jan/20/tunisian-fruit-seller-mohammed-bouazizi (accessed May 2014).

45 Schroeder *et al.*, 'Mining Twitter Data'.

46 Paul Mason (2013) *Why it's Still Kicking Off Everywhere: The New Global Revolutions* 2nd edn (London: Verso), 85.

47 Samuel Gibbs (2014) 'Six Alternatives to Whatsapp Now that Facebook Owns it', *Guardian*, 20 Feb., http://www.theguardian.com/ technology/2014/feb/20/six-alternatives-whatsapp-facebook (accessed May 2014).

48 Translated as 'We are All Khaled Saeed'.

49 Howard *et al.*, 'Opening Closed Regimes', 15.

50 Haroon Siddique, Paul Owen and Adam Gabbatt, (2011) 'Protests in Egypt and Unrest in the Middle East: As it Happened', *Guardian*, 25 Jan., http://www.theguardian.com/global/blog/2011/jan/25/middleeast-tunisia (accessed May 2014); Mason, *New Global Revolutions*, 26.

51 Mason, *New Global Revolutions*, 26.

52 Stephen M. Walt (2011) 'Why the Tunisian Revolution Won't Spread', *Foreign Policy,* 16 Jan., http://www.foreignpolicy.com/posts/ 2011/01/15/why_the_tunisian_revolution_wont_spread (accessed May 2014).
53 Mona el-Shazly (2011) 'Interview with Wael Ghonim', *10 Masa'an* [10:00 pm], 8 Feb. 2011.
54 The second president of Tunisia from 1987 to 2011. Ben Ali resigned during a wave of street protests in 2011, partially attributed to the suppression of press freedoms. See BBC News (2011) 'Profile: Zine al-Abidine Ben Ali', 20 June, http://www.bbc.co.uk/news/world-africa-12196679 (accessed May 2014).
55 Howard *et al.*, 'Opening Closed Regimes', 11.
56 Ibid.
57 Ibid. 12.
58 Mason, *New Global Revolutions,* 6.
59 Howard *et al.,* 'Opening Closed Regimes', 17.
60 Ibid.
61 Kevin Rawlinson (2014) 'Turkey Blocks Use of Twitter After Prime Minister Attacks Social Media Site', *Guardian,* 21 Mar., http://www.theguardian.com/world/2014/mar/21/turkey-blocks-twitter-prime-minister (accessed May 2014).
62 Andreas Koch (2004) 'Nowhere and Now Here: Hybrid Nature of Communities and Spaces', *Networks and Communication Studies (NETCOM)* 18(3–4): 171–9, 171, 173.
63 Paul S. Berman (2011) 'Towards a Jurisprudence of Hybridity', *Utah Law Review* 11(1): 11–29.
64 Shahira Amin (2013) 'In Post-Morsi Egypt Journalists Toe the Military Line or Self-Censor', IndexCensorship.org, 3 Dec., www.indexoncensorhip.org/2013/12/post-morsi-egypt-journalists-toe-the-military-line (accessed May 2014)/.
65 E.g. Dan Simmons (1996) *Hyperion Cantos* (New York: Spectra); Dynamix (1994) 'Metaltech: Earthsiege' (video game) (Dynamix & FASA Corporation).
66 Kim Barker (2013) 'Online Games and IP: Battle of the Forms to Social Norms: Reconceptualising and Re-layering?', *SCRIPTed* 10(3): 320.
67 Defined as: 'the scientific study of control and communication in the animal and the machine'; Norbert Weiner (1948) *Cybernetics, or Control and Communication in the Animal and the Machine* (Cambridge, MA: MIT Press).
68 Elena Crippa (2011) 'Roy Ascott: Teaching Change', *The Tate,* 25 June, http://www.tate.org.uk/context-comment/blogs/roy-ascott-teaching-change (accessed May 2014).
69 Manuel Castells (2012) *Networks of Outrage and Hope: Social Movements in the Internet Age* (Cambridge: Polity Press), 18.
70 Symon Hill (2013) *Digital Revolutions: Activism in the Internet Age* (Oxford: New Internationalist Publications), 42.
71 Castells, *Networks of Outrage and Hope,* 60.
72 BBC News (2014) 'E-Voting Experiments End in Norway amid Security Fears', 27 June, http://www.bbc.co.uk/news/technology-28055678 (accessed June 2014).
73 David Kravets (2011) 'UN Report Declares Internet Access a Human Right', *Wired News,* 6 Mar., http://www.wired.com/2011/06/internet-a-human-right (accessed May 2014)/.
74 Bell, *Introduction to Cybercultures,* 163.
75 Marshall McLuhan (1967) 'The Medium is the Message', in *Understanding Media: The Extensions of Man* (New York: Signet), 23–5, 63–7.

Part IV

Hybrid approaches to peace, development and justice

Chapter 14

Hybrid approaches to peace and justice

The case of post-genocide Rwanda

Danielle Beswick

Since experiencing a devastating genocide in 1994, Rwanda has become a byword for the consequences of international inaction in the face of mass atrocities. The mantra of 'no more Rwandas' is regularly invoked, particularly by those seeking to generate an international response to campaigns of forced displacement and violence committed by states against their citizens. The country recently commemorated the twentieth anniversary of the genocide and many observers describe its achievements in those two decades as remarkable, even miraculous. Rwanda has enjoyed a prolonged period of relative domestic stability, avoiding the fate of many other states which slip into repeated cycles of civil war after experiencing conflict. The national economy has grown consistently and the government has attracted significant amounts of aid to finance its recovery, along with private investors impressed at the country's efficiency and its efforts to make doing business easier. It has held regular parliamentary and presidential elections since 2003, with reports of violence or overt intimidation relatively limited compared with many post-war states. In many regards, though with important caveats which will be discussed, Rwanda can be considered a stable state which has to a large degree moved on from its violent recent history.

This success is often attributed to the combination of external support and resources with 'home-grown' Rwandan strategies for reconstruction. Rwanda's post-genocide leaders have drawn upon the country's pre-colonial past to find ways to rebuild identity, justice and social relations. This reconstruction has however been reliant on aid and other forms of support from international actors. Accordingly, Rwanda has pursued a peacebuilding strategy which is strongly characterised by hybridity.

Hybridity is a somewhat slippery and often ill-defined concept. For the purposes of this chapter its value lies in allowing us to identify the ways in which individuals, institutions and processes involved in post-conflict peacebuilding may combine elements considered international or 'liberal' with those identified as 'local', including objectives or the methods through which these are pursued.[1] This emphasis on combination fits with Mac Ginty's conception of hybridity. He argues that:

> Notions of hybridity move us away from the binary combinations that can seem attractive in helping to explain the social and political world: modern versus traditional, Western versus non-Western; legal-rational versus ritualistic-irrational.[2]

Mac Ginty also links this to a discussion of the agency of local actors; not passive, voiceless, recipients but active in for instance engaging with, promoting, shaping, ignoring or subverting the liberal peace in any given context.[3] These two elements of Mac Ginty's view are particularly relevant for our discussion of Rwanda. It is a state dependent on international aid yet its leaders are fiercely independent and willing to risk its international relationships to maximise their agency in particular spheres, including foreign policy, security, identity policy, justice and reconciliation.

Reflecting the strong articulation of a 'Rwandan approach' to peacebuilding, the country is often cited by analysts and international actors as a positive example of local ownership of peacebuilding and reconstruction. The high level of national ownership by the Rwandan regime does however raise questions related to the dynamics of power and resistance, including between elites and non-elites and between national and local (subnational) levels. It is often noted that there is little space for political dissent, alternative voices and approaches in the 'new Rwanda'.[4] This chapter will explore the dynamics of hybrid peace through the Rwandan case in order to make two contributions to a discussion of hybridity. First, it will show that Rwanda's path to peace provides rich evidence of hybrid peacebuilding, particularly through the transitional justice system – gacaca (pronounced *ga-cha-cha*) – developed to deal with crimes of genocide. Second, it will draw on studies of Rwanda's 'local approaches' to argue that, in considering the nature of the peace being built, and the potential for hybrid solutions to enhance local agency, we must remain mindful of which 'local' actors are privileged and how hybrid efforts fit into wider political dynamics.

The chapter begins with a brief overview of the 1994 genocide and the challenges for peace, justice and social reconstruction which flowed from this. It moves on to discuss the genesis and pursuit of 'Rwandan solutions to Rwandan problems', in a context of dependence on external support. In doing so it draws on Mac Ginty's 'variable geometry of peace', showing that there is no simple Rwandan/international dichotomy, instead we must explore how 'local' Rwandan factors and 'liberal' international factors combine to create a hybrid or 'fusion' peace in this particular case via specific actors, institutions and processes.[5] The chapter then goes on to briefly discuss identity policy and social reconstruction efforts, demonstrating the Rwandan government's recourse to pre-colonial ideals of 'Rwandan-ness' in its search for ways to deal with the legacy of genocide. The subsequent section will look in more detail at a specific institution established to pursue justice for crimes of genocide – gacaca. Gacaca embodies hybridity. It was modified from a pre-colonial Rwandan dispute resolution system, updated and codified to address some, but not all, of the concerns of Rwandan and international actors over the quality and fairness of the trials, along with the human rights of the accused and of witnesses. The chapter will conclude that Rwanda's post-conflict peace may have some of the advantages of hybridity, carrying greater legitimacy and potential for sustainability than externally imposed peacebuilding approaches. Nevertheless, this case also shows that hybrid approaches which may seem to lend themselves to bottom-up, flexible and participatory peacebuilding can simultaneously reinforce patterns of authoritarianism and top-down control. It will therefore be important to continue to investigate manifestations of hybridity in depth, and to uncover the sources and directions of power and agency, if we are to understand their likely implications for peace.

The genocide and its legacy

The 1994 Rwandan genocide has fundamentally shaped the country's politics in the past two decades. It lasted for around three months and was ended not by the UN force based in the country but instead by a rebel group, the Rwandan Patriotic Front (RPF). The RPF was made up largely of former refugees who had returned to the country in 1990, sparking a civil war. Led by Paul Kagame, the RPF were primarily Rwandan Tutsi refugees, a minority ethnicity population exiled after the move to majority Hutu rule following the departure of Belgian colonial administrators in 1962. The RPF invasion force proved tenacious, militarily capable and resilient. In 1993 the Hutu-led Rwandan Government signed a peace deal, the Arusha Accords, to allow the RPF to operate as a political party in Rwanda. However before this agreement could be implemented the Hutu President, Juvenal Habyarimana, was killed when his plane was shot down over Rwanda.[6] Following his death, Hutu hardliners in his administration launched a programme of mass extermination to kill all Tutsi in Rwanda. The genocide led to the deaths of over 800,000 Tutsi and many thousands of moderate Hutu who supported power-sharing or tried to save Tutsi. It ended in July 1994 when the RPF took control of the capital, Kigali.[7]

The genocide and the way in which it ended have generated particular challenges for Rwanda. These are perhaps most pronounced in the arenas of identity, social reconstruction and justice.

Ethnic identity was the primary basis on which individuals were targeted for elimination. During colonial rule the ethnic Tutsi minority had been favoured by the Belgian administrators, who used physical and social markers, including wealth and physiognomy, to categorise individuals into ethnic groups and issue identity cards. These would later be utilised by those hunting Tutsi during the genocide. During the colonial period identities lost their prior fluidity, becoming fixed and linked directly to social status, access to government positions, higher education and other opportunities. Following independence in 1962 the majority Hutu, comprising around 85 per cent of the population, took power and Tutsi were removed from politics and marginalised from public life.[8] Over the course of the genocide the Hutu–Tutsi divide sharpened still further. After the genocide this division created the strong potential for victim–perpetrator associations to join oppressor–oppressed, and Rwandan–foreigner associations which had become attached to these ethnic identities in the preceding decades.[9] For the new government, ethnic identity posed a series of challenges including: how to separate, or try to differently combine, ethnic identity and political power; how to ensure blame for genocide crimes was allotted to individuals rather than a whole ethnic group; and whether the terms Hutu and Tutsi had any place in the post-genocide state. These challenges relate closely to both social reconstruction and justice.

Social reconstruction refers to the rebuilding of bonds between individuals and communities. After conflict it means, at its most basic, finding a way to live together and to imagine and work towards a shared future. It is closely related to the concept of reconciliation and often linked to forgiveness. The genocide created significant barriers to achieving this or building the minimal trust and sense of safety in which such efforts could begin to develop. The killings during the genocide were often highly personal and intimate encounters, between perpetrators and victims who knew each other as neighbours, friends or even relations.[10] Hutu who were in positions of trust and societal standing, including members of the security forces, as well as many teachers, local politicians and religious leaders, aided in the identification and commission of direct violence against Tutsi. Government and media exhortations that Hutu citizens should identify and kill Tutsi, in order to prove themselves as loyal Hutu, underpinned mass participation in the genocide programme and a sense of fear, duty and impunity for such actions.[11] In the months and years following, many Tutsi returned from extended periods of exile, but the safety of this minority in the midst of a Hutu majority and with a hard core of genocidaires threatening to finish the job from neighbouring Zaire made rebuilding trust and social bonds an extremely difficult undertaking.

Perhaps the most daunting task facing Rwanda's new regime was that of justice. The genocide was led by the state and security forces and carried out with a high degree of citizen participation. Whether out of belief in the cause of 'Hutu Power' promoted by the genocidal regime, a desire to use the genocide programme as cover for personal score-settling against particular Tutsi or for enrichment at their expense, genuine fear of the RPF and reprisals if the genocide were not completed, fear of the social and other consequences of not participating, or a combination of these factors, many Hutu followed the order to kill.[12] During their advance to end the genocide and in the aftermath the RPF detained hundreds of thousands of Hutu. With no national legal framework to try crimes of genocide it was not clear how Rwanda's own systems could prosecute the planners and 'footsoldiers' of genocide. The new regime was faced with a situation where many of Rwanda's trained legal professionals had either been killed or fled the country,[13] leaving national justice systems in disarray. Jails were often in a poor condition and extremely overcrowded, housing a prison population that the government now had legal obligations to adequately provide for. The options were few, constrained by resources and overwhelmed by the scale of the problem, and the needs in the justice arena were many. These included challenging the sense of impunity that had underpinned popular participation in the genocide, identifying and prosecuting perpetrators and protecting witnesses. These practical challenges stood alongside dilemmas which could affect the quality of the post-genocide peace, such as how to establish what had actually happened in different parts of the country during the genocide, what role citizens should play in the justice process, and whether amnesty should be offered for any particular crimes or groups of perpetrators. Any proposed solution to these challenges would also have to engage with a central dilemma in post-conflict justice: how to ensure perpetrators are held accountable for their actions and punished, providing 'retributive' justice, whilst also maximising opportunities for justice processes to contribute to healing relationships between victims and perpetrators and between communities more widely, through 'restorative' measures.[14] Retributive justice elements would go some way to challenging the sense of impunity which had driven wide-scale participation in the genocide, but in a small and densely populated state, where victims and perpetrators would be required to live together again, restorative justice was recognised by the new government as vital to rebuild trust and promote social healing and reconstruction.[15]

Building a hybrid peace after genocide

In responding to these challenges Rwanda, led by a Broad Based Government of National Unity (1994–2003) and subsequently by RPF-led coalitions, has enjoyed significant international support. This support reflected the failure of the international community and individual states to respond to the unfolding crisis in Rwanda, preventing or stopping the genocide. The involvement of Western external actors in peacebuilding and reconstruction has invariably seen the promotion of liberal peace in post-conflict societies.[16] This includes an emphasis on human rights, multi-party democracy and economic reform to promote private-sector investment and limit state control over markets. Rwanda's reliance on aid from Western states and institutions associated with the liberal peace meant that these elements were also expected to feature strongly in its reconstruction.

However, as Mac Ginty notes, not all states experience the heavy hand of liberal peacebuilders; some experience a 'lite' version and local actors do have agency in the process of continual negotiation over the form that the hybrid (liberal-local) peace takes.[17] It is possible for local actors to resist or coopt the preferences and efforts of liberal peacebuilders. He argues that the extent to which this is feasible depends on factors including the 'extent to which local actors retain power during a liberal peace transition'.[18] In Rwanda's case, the RPF achieved the comprehensive military defeat of the government which carried out the genocide. The discrediting of other political parties in the aftermath of the genocide left the RPF in a strong position to claim to speak legitimately for the country, even before their dominance as a party was cemented through elections in 2003 and subsequently.[19] This combination of Western guilt stemming from international inaction during the genocide, and the commanding position of the RPF, allowed the party to control the narrative and adopt a strong moral position vis-à-vis would-be liberal peacebuilders. The RPF control of information reaching the media and international actors, a deliberate and calculated strategy they pursued immediately after the genocide, is explored elsewhere in detail.[20]

The potential for local actors to influence the hybrid nature of the peace is also dependent on, amongst other factors, 'the ability of local actors to resist, ignore or subvert the liberal peace; and the ability of local actors to formulate and maintain alternatives to the liberal peace'.[21] As we have already suggested, the first of these criteria is influenced by guilt connected to Western inaction during the genocide and the political dominance of the RPF. The second, ability to formulate and maintain alternatives, is also of particular interest in the case of post-genocide Rwanda. As we will see below, in relation to identity policy, social reconstruction, and justice for crimes of genocide, Rwanda's leaders have promoted 'home-grown' approaches to reconstruction. These are presented as linking Rwanda's present and its future with a pre-colonial past characterised by social unity. The depictions of these home-grown solutions reflect Mac Ginty's description of local alternatives, in that they 'may not conform to perceptions of legitimate peacemaking or peacebuilding according to the liberal peace perspective, but they may have cultural purchase in the host society'.[22] Such claims of cultural purchase make it difficult for external actors to critique such initiatives and may make them more inclined to support, whilst seeking to subtly shape, such efforts as part of their drive for 'local ownership' and sustainability.[23]

The rest of the chapter will explore the content and implications of these efforts to present and maintain alternatives to the liberal peace, and to generate a hybrid peace shaped by local agency. It is however important at this stage to remind ourselves that though 'liberal' and 'local' may provide useful shorthand, in this case for international and Rwandan actors, we are dealing here with actors who are already in some senses hybrid. The returning refugees who have dominated Rwandan politics since the genocide were in many cases largely raised and educated outside of the country.[24] Their ideas on how peace should be rebuilt are not purely 'local', Rwandan, perspectives, if indeed such a thing exists, but instead are infused by experience and exposure to wider ideas via their encounters with others, within and outside Rwanda. This hybridity is what allows Rwanda's leaders to walk a somewhat unstable path between keeping donors and international supporters relatively happy on the one hand, and maintaining policy independence and fulfilling domestic goals related to regime legitimacy and peacebuilding on the other.

Rwandan solutions to Rwandan problems

Most analysis of Rwanda's post-genocide experience falls loosely into one of two broad camps. The achievements of domestic peace, economic growth and stability are often praised, but critics note the dominance of the RPF in politics, involvement of Rwanda in destabilising neighbouring Congo, and describe Rwandan society as one infused by fear under a regime of surveillance and characterised by self-censorship. Regardless of their normative evaluation of Rwanda under RPF rule, most analysts can however agree on the assessment that Rwanda displays a high degree of local ownership over its post-genocide peace-building.[25]

The creation of space for national ownership in order to shape the hybrid peace has been achieved through a range of methods. First is the control of information, including the careful production of images and narratives on the genocide and Rwanda's recovery from it, for consumption and reflection within Rwanda as well as by external actors.[26] Second is the government narrative which highlights international failure to prevent or halt the genocide, in order to deflect criticism of the approaches taken by the RPF in rebuilding politics, society and security.[27] Third, and perhaps most relevant for this discussion, is the consistent mantra that Rwandan solutions were needed to face the post-genocide challenges and that these had greater societal resonance and legitimacy than alternatives posed by outsiders. These Rwandan solutions were imbued with further legitimacy by tracing their origins to the pre-colonial era, with proponents arguing that the fact they predated external interventions in Rwandan society meant that they constituted an authentically Rwandan initiative. The strong thread of self-reliance which runs through the policies and narratives of Rwanda's leaders underpins both its claim to and its search for local ownership of the post-genocide peace.

The role of the past in the present

Since the genocide the RPF has drawn on pre-colonial models and practices in areas including the three we discuss here: identity, social reconstruction and justice. The choice to reference Rwanda's pre-colonial past whilst largely discounting and demonising its experiences under colonial rule is deliberate and has significant implications for domestic politics as well as Rwanda's external relations. The pre-colonial past in Rwanda has become highly idealised under the RPF, represented as a time of peace and unity between the Hutu, Tutsi and the Twa.[28] The period of colonial rule by Belgium is seen very differently, as a time during which differences between the three groups were given political significance. Ethnicity is portrayed in official government accounts of this period as becoming hardened, in the sense that mobility became impossible, and oppositional, defining (lack of) access to opportunities such as higher education and government positions. The linking of ethnicity to political power is argued by RPF representatives to have divided Rwandans during colonial rule and to have continued post-independence, underpinning Hutu political power and directly leading to the civil war and 1994 genocide.[29] The contrasting of pre-colonial unity with colonial and post-colonial division is used to support a strong government narrative of self-reliance. The divisions which underpinned the genocide are argued to be the product of external involvement in Rwanda, with the inference being that Rwandans cannot trust external actors and their agendas and must be self-reliant, looking to their own history and culture for solutions to the challenges facing post-genocide society.[30] Such sentiments have allowed Rwandan representatives to reject or seek to modify efforts by 'outsiders' to influence peacebuilding strategies.

In searching for 'Rwandan solutions' the strategy of the RPF has therefore been to emphasise pre-colonial mechanisms and practises which brought communities together. It does not however seek to import these wholesale from the past; modification is necessary to make them relevant for the needs and challenges of the contemporary state and society. The influence of external actors, seeking to promote the inclusion of liberal values in local solutions is what makes these efforts hybrid in nature. Cutting across this liberal-local dynamic there are two main narratives that have guided the process of transformation, infusing the RPF vision for post-genocide Rwanda: 'Never Again', and Rwandan-ness. 'Never Again' refers to the determination of Rwanda's ruling elite that the country will not experience another genocide. In domestic politics, it has informed the ways in which civic education and justice have been pursued, as well as underpinning a preference for a democracy which is consensus-based rather than confrontational, as we will see below.[31] It has also been discussed in other research in terms of its influence on Rwandan foreign and security policy, including peacekeeping and intervention in situations where there is the prospect of genocide.[32] 'Rwandan-ness', sometimes referred to as 'Rwandanicity',[33] has been consistently articulated as a goal by successive post-genocide governments, the aim being to transcend ethnicity and pursue national unity through a new national identity. This reaches back to a pre-colonial past as discussed above, but it is more than an ideal. A post-ethnic, or non-ethnic, identity has been firmly anchored in legislation and reinforced by disciplining practices.

Managing identity

Since the genocide there has been a concerted effort by Rwanda's leaders to remove ethnicity from public discourse. The legal framework through which the government seeks to formally regulate political behaviour includes: the 2003 Constitution, which outlaws discrimination on ethnic grounds amongst others; Law 47/2001 of 18 December 2001 instituting punishment for offences of discrimination and sectarianism, and Law 33/2003 of 6 September 2003 repressing the crime of genocide, crimes against humanity and war crimes. The labels of 'Hutu' and 'Tutsi' are regarded by the government as dangerous and too damaged to have any place in public discourse in the new Rwanda. Instead a shared Rwandan national identity is promoted, with symbolic changes such as a new flag and national anthem reinforcing the impression that post-1994 Rwanda is a new nation in which ethnicity has no place. The strong rejection of ethnic discrimination may support broad-based peacebuilding and also protect minorities, in line with liberal approaches to human rights. However, critics argue that by criminalising discussion of ethnicity the RPF is able to disguise the fact that Tutsi are disproportionately represented in positions of power.[34] Political dominance has also been reinforced by the use of the labels of 'divisionist' or holder of 'genocide ideology' to discredit political opponents.[35]

In designing its political system Rwanda faced pressure from donors who promoted a version of multiparty democracy in line with that agreed at peace talks in Arusha, Tanzania, before the genocide. Having political power allocated based on a principle of balancing ethnic identities to protect all groups, as pursued in neighbouring Burundi, was rejected by the victorious RPF on the grounds that this would perpetuate division and enable future internecine conflict.[36] The experience of the genocide, donor respect for the RPF role in ending this and the lack of other credible parties with which to negotiate a new form of politics led to a compromise, to the benefit of consensus-based politics promoted by the RPF and at the expense of more adversarial democracy favoured by the donors. The approach can be explained, as noted by Vandeginste, by 'the historical context and the politico-military balance of power at a critical juncture'.[37] This chimes with Mac Ginty's argument that hybridity and the degree of local agency exercised in defining hybrid solutions can be influenced by such factors. In spite of its aid dependence, the dominant position of the RPF has allowed it to exercise considerable agency in design of post-genocide politics and identity and the disciplining of opponents.

Social reconstruction

Social reconstruction is a second arena in which the RPF has reached into Rwanda's past to craft solutions to challenges in the present. One initiative which displays clear elements of hybridity is *ingando*. Ingando is part of what Straus and Waldorf refer to as a project of social reengineering in post-genocide Rwanda; a set of efforts to build a new nation and new national identity which includes government-mandated community participation in social projects.[38] Ingando are residential camps for Rwandans which incorporate activities focused on topics such as the historical unity of Rwandans, the need to tackle persistent genocide ideology, sensitisation on gacaca and HIV/AIDS, alongside physical exercise and military style training. They are run for groups of citizens including former combatants going through reintegration programmes, prospective university students, street children and released prisoners. They are tools for promoting social unity which draw loosely upon historical practices of military encampment, encouraging Rwandans to focus on national goals and put aside individual concerns.[39] The contemporary manifestations are very different to ingando of the past in their large-scale involvement of civilians, but their proponents insist they are a Rwandan solution rooted in the country's traditions. According to Purdekova, in line with the wider arguments of Mac Ginty and Richmond on 'local' peacebuilding,[40] this insistence on the indigenous nature of ingando provides it with greater legitimacy and serves to obscure the political nature and unstated consequences of the programme. Ingando is 'historically-embedded and yet a profoundly post-genocide government tool of social engineering whose effects range far beyond what we are led to believe by the camps' official descriptions'.[41] Mgbako describes the camps as a form of 'political indoctrination'.[42] Susan Thomson, who experienced ingando first-hand during her field research in Rwanda, describes it as one of the few state-sanctioned spaces where identity can be discussed.[43] This is particularly notable given the careful wider policing of public speech discussed previously. Thomson's interviews with her fellow participants however showed a lack of buy-in from Hutu, who instead saw it as an attempt to control their thoughts and actions. There are mixed views, but it is clear from these three studies, particularly that of Thomson, that the emphasis on national unity and on 're-education' to achieve this echoes wider attempts by the ruling elite to control political space in ways which reinforce its own dominance.

These brief accounts demonstrate that identity policy and social reconstruction provide some initial insights into the hybrid nature of Rwanda's post-genocide peacebuilding. In both cases the past is used to justify and shape approaches pursued in the present, but the result of this is to reinforce rather than challenge state power in general and the dominance of the ruling RPF in particular. Perhaps the clearest illustration of Rwanda's hybrid peacebuilding – particularly the straddling and blurring of categories such as traditional/modern and formal/informal – can be found in the justice system adopted to try crimes of genocide: gacaca. As we will see, this similarly draws on past practices and 'local' solutions, including large-scale citizen participation, but in its hybrid post-genocide form retribution has displaced restoration as the guiding principle.

Transitional justice: Gacaca courts

Wielenga and Harris succinctly describe the challenges of the justice sector in Rwanda by 2000: over 800,000 prisoners, a quarter of the adult population, awaiting trial and only twelve courts available to process them.[44] Reports by organisations such as Human Rights Watch documented prison overcrowding and everyday challenges of maintaining prisoner nutrition and health in squalid conditions. The lack of trained lawyers and judges, along with limited capacity of national court systems, meant that processing this backlog of prisoners would take decades and by some estimates over a century.

The solution adopted by the post-genocide government, gacaca courts, built upon and adapted a pre-colonial justice system. Traditional gacaca was used to adjudicate disputes between members of a community, with respected elders acting as mediators and judges in reaching a solution. It derived its legitimacy from popular participation. However, as has been noted in relation to other 'traditional' or 'indigenous' justice systems, including in Jackson's contribution to this collection, the system was narrow in its dispute focus and in its composition: patriarchal structures meant that women were marginalised and judges were male.[45]

Clark's research shows that Rwanda's leaders did not adopt gacaca lightly.[46] They recognised the limits of a community dispute resolution mechanism adapted to tackle more complex and serious crimes, including murder and sexual violence, on a large scale. He quotes an interview with a Rwandan Minister, who observed: 'we were highly conscious of the concerns of the international community. What would the rest of the world think of gacaca?'[47] Clark highlights the importance of Tutsi diaspora, particularly those returning from Europe and the USA, in influencing the post-genocide leadership to consider donor opinions when designing new policies.[48] This meant that gacaca would need to be changed in order to make it more compatible with approaches to human rights and justice in line with liberal peacebuilding. Even after agreement to proceed with gacaca was reached at elite level, many in the wider population remained unconvinced of its suitability, raising concerns as to whether it would provide a fair, or sufficiently punitive, forum for trying crimes of genocide. Wielenga and Harris,[49] similarly to Breed,[50] note that many Hutu who faced gacaca regarded their acts as being committed during a time of war, a time they characterised as a state of legal exception, and that as they were following orders of the state and its representatives they should not personally be punished. The then Minister of Justice recalled receiving heavy criticism from survivors and the media during the 1990s when he promoted gacaca, with critics accusing him of 'simplifying the genocide, seeking cheap popularity and promoting impunity'.[51] Nevertheless, the existing system had proved incapable of responding to the challenge and pressure from aid donors, crucial to Rwanda's recovery and reconstruction, meant a radical solution was required. An eighteen-month pilot of the gacaca programme proved its ability to expedite trials and sentencing compared to the slow national courts process.

Traditional gacaca was transformed into the system of 'gacaca courts' through a series of changes, as summarised in Table 14.1.

An Organic Law passed in 1996 began the process of establishing a legal framework to prosecute crimes of genocide.[52] Along with subsequent legislation it established categories of crime and a range of punishments which could be applied. Category One covered those who planned the genocide and their accomplices, leaders (military, political or religious), those who displayed zeal for their activities, and those who committed rape or sexual torture. Category Two criminals included those who killed during the genocide or whose aim was to kill, whether or not they succeeded, and their accomplices. Category Three covered those involved in crimes who did not have the intention of killing, and Category Four covered offences against property. Sentences for Category One ranged from twenty-five

Table 14.1 The transformation from traditional gacaca to gacaca courts

'Traditional Gacaca'	*Gacaca Courts*
Adjudicate local crimes and property disputes, mainly between family or community members	Adjudicated crimes under four categories under new laws
Legitimacy derived from popular participation	Legitimacy derived from the legal framework and mandatory popular participation
No powers of imprisonment, judgements focus on exchange and compensation	Powers include imprisonment for life and compensation, leniency offered for full confession
Emphasis on truth and reconciliation, restoring relationships	Emphasis on truth, reconciliation and punishment
Cases judged by male community elders	Cases judged by panels of *inyangamugayo*, elected, unpaid men and women over 21
Challenges of access for vulnerable groups, crimes such as sexual violence excluded	Prosecutions for range of crimes, personal, violent, property-related and sexual violence

years' imprisonment to the death penalty, though the latter was abolished in 2007. Categories Two and Three attracted sentences of imprisonment ranging from one year to life imprisonment and involvement in public works, whilst Category Four crimes required sentences of fiscal or material reparation.[53]

The establishment of this legal framework helped Rwanda's leaders to show adherence to the liberal preference for equality before the law. Along with provisions for appeals to superior courts, codification also provided some protection against the possibility of manipulation of the process at local level to suit personal aims of judges, community members or political agents. The election of judges, including women, lent legitimacy to the process and reduced fears that discrimination which had infused pre-colonial gacaca would affect its successor.[54] In these regards, Clark's characterisations of gacaca are apt. It is described as dynamic, a hybrid of 'traditional and modern elements',[55] but also rather than labelling it 'indigenous' he describes it as 'endogenous: initiated and synthesised within Rwandan society but – because of the complex nature of that synthesis, and how markedly current gacaca differs from the original practice that partly inspired it – viewed by much of the population as a new, and perhaps confusing or disagreeable, entity'.[56]

Despite the safeguards built into the gacaca courts, which help this 'local' solution to comply to a greater extent with liberal principles, one of the main critiques of gacaca is its inadequate protections for the accused and witness participants. Suspects appearing before gacaca do not have lawyers; testimony which could exonerate or incriminate them is expected to be supplied by the community. Community participation is mandatory and potential defence witnesses have reported that when others speak out in favour of defendants they have often then found themselves accused of crimes. Breed's observations[57] also describe the vilification of Hutu bystanders to the genocide, charged as accomplices for offering support or sustenance to killers, or for perceived ill-treatment of Tutsi they had sheltered from the killers. Such experiences deter others from speaking out, a result which replicates the wider pattern in contemporary Rwandan politics of citizens choosing silence to avoid punishment for departure from state-approved narratives on the genocide and for political dissent. This climate of fear, described by Thomson and Reyntjens[58] among others, is supported by another main critique of gacaca – its failure to consider crimes committed against Hutu, which were not technically part of the genocide against the Tutsi. Failure to consider crimes committed by the advancing RPF forces is detrimental to building a culture of human rights in Rwanda. It can be viewed as a 'victor's justice', promoting impunity for RPF crimes whilst attaching a collective sense of guilt to all Hutu.[59]

The balance of evidence presented by researchers suggests that the cumulative effect of the changes made to gacaca in its reinvention as gacaca courts has been to compromise the restorative elements of this transitional justice mechanism and strengthen punitive, retributive features.[60] In other words, though justice mechanisms might aim to rebuild relationships between victims and perpetrators as well as punishing offenders, the balance here appears to favour the latter. In line with Mac Ginty's argument, a strong local actor facing little domestic challenge, with a clear vision for reconstruction, has been able to shape the hybrid peacebuilding process. The results of hybridisation in this case have been conditioned by the heavy state involvement in managing the process and the social context in which it is situated. This is not to say that gacaca has played out identically across all jurisdictions; Clark argues that 'instances of local judges standing their ground [in the face of pressure from state representatives] represent important moments of local agency that remain under-recognised in most non-Rwandan critiques of gacaca'.[61] Nevertheless, such instances appear to be few and far between. Breed, Thomson and Ingelaere[62] are among the many critics of gacaca whose extensive field interviews and observations highlight the extent to which pressure is exerted on participants and judges, by state representatives and their own communities, to ensure gacaca does not overstep its carefully policed boundaries.

Conclusion

The Rwandan case illustrates that the approaches of both international 'liberal' and 'local' actors to peacebuilding are conditioned by their own histories and their interactions with each other, resulting in hybrid peacebuilding processes and outcomes. The liberal peacebuilders who have provided diplomatic and financial support for Rwanda since the genocide have been reluctant to apply pressure over the illiberal elements of its path to peace, largely due to guilt over international failings during the genocide. The dominant position of the RPF and its clear vision for peace and reconstruction allowed its leaders to carve out space for local agency in relation to liberal peacebuilders. The approaches followed, seen most clearly in the case of gacaca, are however also influenced by the sensitivities of Rwanda's leaders to the preferences of their international supporters, as well as the experiences of some Rwandans in exile. This combination of influences, which problematises the idea of neatly delineated 'liberal' and 'local' actors, results in complex hybridity.

The Rwandan case also shows that the adoption of historical practices, especially pre-colonial practices, can be a powerful way to imbue contemporary policies with legitimacy and authenticity. In doing so they can help to maximise space for the exercise of 'local' agency. Narratives emphasising self-reliance and local ownership may be aimed at external audiences, whose interference and criticisms can be muted by the claim to be doing what is culturally appropriate and relevant for Rwandans, regardless of liberal peacebuilder preferences. They may also be aimed at domestic audiences sceptical of a new regime which has been dominated by former refugees, many of whom grew up in exile. Working at these two levels, hybrid peacebuilding may well allow space for greater local agency, authenticity and a sense of national ownership in the aftermath of conflict. Notwithstanding this potential, the analysis in Rwanda's case suggests there is sound basis for concerns that 'local solutions' serve to reinforce and obscure a pattern of authoritarian behaviour by the government, one which seeks to control citizens in ways which may not serve durable peace. Samset's analysis of Rwanda's trajectory since 1994 argues that 'a repressive peace is surely better than no peace. But repression is a high price to pay.'[63] While a focus on hybridity may not allow us to make a judgement on whether the price is too high, or what its implications might be, it does at the least offer a way to begin to uncover sources of local agency, and to question which 'locals' gain from such hybrid solutions.

Notes

1 Within International Relations as a discipline there is a dynamic debate on the drivers of peace between states at an international level. There is also, particularly since the end of the Cold War, much dispute over how peace might be built within states following periods of violent conflict. One of the key threads running through these debates on prevention of both interstate and civil wars can be loosely referred to as the notion of 'liberal peace'. The terms 'liberal peace' and 'liberal peacebuilders' are used in this chapter to refer primarily to international actors pursuing a set of aims which are characterised as liberal, including promotion of multiparty democracy, free markets and the rights of the individual. However, the liberal peace is a 'broad church', containing contradictions and significant disagreements between its proponents as to the ways to construct a liberal peace, i.e. what counts as 'liberal peacebuilding'. Nevertheless, these terms remain useful in the context of this chapter because they allow us to capture a broad trend in international engagement with conflict affected states. They also provide a point of contrast with 'local' approaches to peacebuilding, which tend to emphasise the context-specific nature of conflict within states and the need for context-specific peacebuilding appropriately tailored to that situation. As the chapter will show, neither 'liberal' nor 'local' approaches can be considered in complete isolation from each other, particularly as local actors may seek – with some success – to influence peacebuilding by international actors and they may also choose to reflect the preferences of international actors in their 'local' or home-grown solutions. The chapter therefore seeks to engage with these wider debates on liberal and local approaches to peacebuilding by highlighting the extent to which they are mutually co-constituted. It does however acknowledge that the debate on liberal peacebuilding is vast and that it is dealing with only a small part of these wider currents. For background on liberal peace and peacebuilding, see Michael W. Doyle (2011) *Liberal Peace: Selected Essays* (London: Routledge) and Roland Paris (2004) *At War's End: Building Peace After Civil Conflict* (Cambridge: Cambridge University Press); for a critical perspective on the liberal peace see Susanna Campbell, David Chandler and Meera Sabaratnam (eds) (2011) *A Liberal Peace? The Problems and Practices of Peacebuilding* (London: Zed Books).

2 Roger Mac Ginty (2010) 'Hybrid Peace: The Interaction between Top-Down and Bottom-Up Peace', *Security Dialogue* 41(4): 391–412, 397.
3 Ibid. 402–4.
4 Filip Reyntjens (2004) 'Rwanda, Ten Years On: From Genocide to Dictatorship', *African Affairs* 103(4): 177–210; Filip Reyntjens (2011) 'Constructing the Truth, Dealing with Dissent, Domesticating the World: Governance in Post-Genocide Rwanda', *African Affairs* 110(438): 1–34; Danielle Beswick (2010) 'Managing Dissent in a Post-Genocide Environment: The Challenge of Political Space in Rwanda', *Development and Change* 41(2): 225–51.
5 Mac Ginty, 'Hybrid Peace'.
6 *The Economist* (2004) 'Who Shot Down the President's Plane? Special Report: Rwanda since the Genocide', 27 Mar., 26.
7 Gerard Prunier (2002) *The Rwanda Crisis: History of a genocide* (London: Hurst).
8 Ibid.
9 Nigel Eltringham and Saskia van Hoyweghen (2000) 'Power and Identity in Post-Genocide Rwanda', in Ruddy Doom and Jan Gorus (eds), *Politics of Identity and Economics of Conflict in the Great Lakes Region* (Brussels: VUB University Press), 215–42.
10 Lee Ann Fujii (2010) *Killing Neighbors: Webs of Violence in Rwanda* (Ithaca, NY: Cornell University Press); Jean Hatzfeld (2010) *A Time for Machetes: The Rwandan Genocide – the Killers Speak* (London: Serpents Tail).
11 Scott Straus (2008) *The Order of Genocide: Race, Power, and War in Rwanda* (Ithaca, NY: Cornell University Press).
12 Fujii, *Killing Neighbors*; Straus, *Order of Genocide.*
13 Phil Clark (2010) *Justice without Lawyers: Peace, Justice and Reconciliation in Rwanda* (Cambridge: Cambridge University Press).
14 Danielle Beswick and Paul Jackson (2014) *Conflict, Security and Development: An Introduction*, 2nd edn (London: Routledge), 188.
15 For a comparative analysis of the transitional justice mechanisms pursued in South Africa, Rwanda and Mozambique, which reflects on the ways retributive and restorative elements were pursued through these different approaches and their implications for post-conflict peace, see Lyn Graybill (2007) 'Pardon, Punishment, and Amnesia: Three African Post-Conflict Methods', *Third World Quarterly* 25(6): 1117–30.
16 Roland Paris (2002) 'International Peacebuilding and the *mission civilisatrice*', *Review of International Studies* 28(4): 637–56; Roger Mac Ginty (2008) 'Indigenous Peace-Making versus the Liberal Peace', *Cooperation and Conflict* 43(2): 139–63; Mac Ginty, 'Hybrid Peace'.
17 Mac Ginty, 'Hybrid Peace', 399.
18 Ibid. 402.
19 Reyntjens, 'Rwanda, Ten Years On'.
20 Johan Pottier (2002) *Reimagining Rwanda: Conflict, Survival and Disinformation in the Late Twentieth Century* (Cambridge: Cambridge University Press).
21 Mac Ginty, 'Hybrid Peace', 398.
22 Ibid. 403.
23 Ibid. 399; Oliver P. Richmond (2011) *A Post Liberal Peace* (London: Routledge).
24 Reyntjens, 'Rwanda, Ten Years On'.
25 Scott Straus and Lars Waldorf (2011) 'Introduction: Seeing like a Post-Conflict State', in Scott Straus and Lars Waldorf (eds), *Remaking Rwanda: State Building and Human Rights After Mass Violence* (Madison, WI: University of Wisconsin Press), 3–21; Nina Wilén (2012) 'A Hybrid Peace through Locally Owned and Externally Financed SSR–DDR in Rwanda?', *Third World Quarterly* 33(7): 1323–36.

26 Pottier, *Reimagining Rwanda*; Reyntjens, 'Constructing the Truth'.
27 Beswick, 'Managing Dissent'.
28 Republic of Rwanda, Office of the President (1999) *The Unity of Rwandans: Before the Colonial Period, Under Colonial Rule, Under the First Republic*, Aug. 1999, Kigali: Office of the President.
29 Ibid.
30 Clark, *Justice without Lawyers*, 135.
31 Mahmoud Mamdani (2001) *When Victims Become Killers: Colonialism, Nativism and the Genocide in Rwanda* (Princeton, NJ: Princeton University Press); Ingrid Samset (2011) 'Building a Repressive Peace: The Case of Post Genocide Rwanda', *Journal of Intervention and Statebuilding* 5(3): 265–83.
32 Danielle Beswick (2014) 'The Risks of African Military Capacity Building: Lessons from Rwanda', *African Affairs* 113(451): 212–31.
33 Stef Vandeginste (2014) 'Governing Ethnicity After Genocide: Ethnic Amnesia in Rwanda versus Ethnic Power Sharing in Burundi', *Journal of Eastern African Studies* 8(2): 263–77.
34 Reyntjens, 'Constructing the Truth'.
35 Beswick, 'Managing Dissent'; Samset, 'Building a Repressive Peace'.
36 Vandeginste, 'Governing Ethnicity'.
37 Ibid. 274.
38 Straus and Waldorf, 'Introduction', 4; see also Samset, 'Building a Repressive Peace', 272.
39 Anna Purdekova (2011) *Rwanda's Ingando Camps: Liminality and the Reproduction of Power*, Refugee Studies Centre Working Paper 80, Oxford: Department for International Development, University of Oxford, http://www.rsc.ox.ac.uk/files/publications/working-paper-series/wp80-rwandas-ingando-camps-2011.pdf (accessed Dec. 2014).
40 Mac Ginty, 'Indigenous Peace-Making'; Richmond, *A Post-Liberal Peace*.
41 Purdekova, 'Rwanda's Ingando Camps', 7.
42 Chi Mgbako (2005) 'Ingando Solidarity Camps: Reconciliation and Political Indoctrination in Post-Genocide Rwanda', *Harvard Human Rights Journal* 18: 201–24.
43 Susan Thomson (2011) 'Reeducation for Reconciliation: Participant Observations on Ingando', in Straus and Waldorf, *Remaking Rwanda*, 331–9.
44 Cori Wielenga and Geoff Harris (2011) 'Building Peace and Security After Genocide: The Contribution of the Gacaca Courts of Rwanda', *African Security Review* 20(1): 15–25, 16.
45 Tim Allen and Anna Macdonald (2013) *Post Conflict Traditional Justice: A Critical Overview*, JSRP Paper 3, Justice and Security Research Programme, London: International Development Department, London School of Economics and Political Science; Clark, *Justice without Lawyers*.
46 Clark, *Justice without Lawyers*.
47 Ibid. 58.
48 Ibid. 61.
49 Wielenga and Harris, 'Building Peace'.
50 Amanda Breed (2012) 'Discordant Narratives in Rwanda's Gacaca Courts', in Maddalena Campioni and Patrick Noack (eds), *Rwanda Fast Forward: Social, Economic, Military and Reconciliation Prospects* (London: Palgrave Macmillan), 29–44.
51 Clark, *Justice without Lawyers*, 59.
52 Organic law no. 8/96 of 30 August 1996 on the Organization of Prosecutions for Offences Constituting the Crime of Genocide or Crimes against Humanity Committed since 1 October 1990.

53 Breed, 'Discordant Narratives'.
54 Clark, *Justice without Lawyers*, 71.
55 Ibid. 70–1.
56 Ibid. 50.
57 Breed, 'Discordant Narratives', 35–7.
58 Susan Thomson (2011) 'The Darker Side of Transitional Justice: The Power Dynamics behind Rwanda's Gacaca Courts', *Africa: The Journal of the International African Institute* 81(3): 373–90; Reyntjens, 'Constructing the Truth'.
59 Wielenga and Harris, 'Building Peace', 22.
60 Ibid. 18.
61 Clark, *Justice without Lawyers*, 157.
62 Breed, 'Discordant Narratives'; Thomson, 'The Darker Side'; Bert Ingelaere (2012) 'From Model to Practice: Researching and Representing Rwanda's "Modernized" *Gacaca* Courts', *Critique of Anthropology* 32(4): 388–414.
63 Samset, 'Building a Repressive Peace', 277.

Chapter 15

Hybridity or coexistence?

The politics of legal pluralism in the West African countryside

Paul Jackson

Introduction

This chapter focuses on the political dynamics of legal pluralism, and, specifically, the concept of 'hybridity' as a lens through which power relations in local justice may be viewed. The relationship between local power, decentralised authority and justice at the local level is not frequently articulated, particularly in the context of donor-supported post-conflict reforms and what impact these have on justice processes at the local level. Reforms in the area of decentralisation, and justice/security sector reform, are often not seen as having a close link, probably because justice/security is seen as separate from political power issues, i.e. these interventions tend to have a more 'technical' focus.[1] It is the contention of this chapter that these interventions alter power structures and it is the politics arising from these structures that play an important – if not the most important – role in the outcomes of such reforms. Furthermore, the coexistence of formal and informal systems at a local level reinforces the power structures that support elites in the African countryside and prevent access to justice for those who are excluded from that elite. Legal pluralism may be seen as a problem (elites manipulating the system) or as a potential solution (providing a choice between remedies) for those seeking justice. In either case, the way in which these dynamics work in practice might mitigate against a hybrid approach, but might imply that a system of coexistence might be more practical.

If access to justice is so influenced by power arrangements, as proposed here, donor programmes in support of justice must become better at understanding and working with local politics, including abandoning dichotomies that are of little use in understanding reality (formal/informal, modern/traditional). Whereas many postcolonial African governments saw the chiefs as something of an impediment to modernising strategies, many have also enhanced their role, particularly since the 1990s, and have formalised their governance role.[2] However, the picture is frequently far more complex than traditional authority being either formal or informal and it is the negotiation of those relationships and links that remains important.

The reality on the ground is a form of fluid hybrid that is neither fully formal nor informal or, indeed, traditional or modern.[3] However, local systems do not necessarily represent simple 'bottom-up' approaches to security and justice development, rather they often represent the structures and machinery that is used by local elites as a means of control and social conformity. Opening access to justice to all members of communities requires empowerment of the marginalised within local power structures. Dismantling or reducing the power of local elites may be impractical in the short term, even if this form of liberalism is desirable. However, those engaged in security and justice programmes need to be aware of the implications of local political systems and of working with hybrid systems. If not, then the power of local elites may be enhanced and those who navigate the fluid hybrid systems (i.e. the end users of security and justice) will be disadvantaged.

This chapter argues that local power arrangements are important in determining people's access to justice and they also have a strong impact on the outcome of justice processes. Furthermore, these links are usually overlooked within internationally supported local government and justice reforms, where traditional authorities, like chiefs, are able to negotiate these institutions to maintain biases towards lineages and social categories, particularly youth and gender. Many international programmes that examine justice emphasise the development of formal justice systems, whereas traditional or customary law still provides the majority of justice decisions for the population, particularly in rural districts.[4] As Baker and Scheye[5] observe, there are a number of core assumptions underlying current international approaches to justice sector reform, including: (1) a lack of a formal justice system is tantamount to a lack of justice *per se*; (2) the formal state justice system is what people want; and (3) a formal state system of justice is sustainable. To these three, I would add that there is also an assumption that the traditional and formal systems are somehow unaffected by local power structures.

In the justice field, work by Beswick (this volume) and particularly Fowles (this volume) highlight the structural causes of human rights abuses, and Fowles proposes that this highlights a methodological failing in that abuses are frequently overlooked because the perspective of the investigators conditions them to focus on a case by case basis. Hybridity could be useful in shedding light on those areas within the justice sector by providing a lens through which to understand the structures that create human rights abuses (Fowles, this volume). I will argue that these structures have their own politics and that the politics of the traditional authorities themselves, their relationship with decentralised power structures and how they exercise power in decentralised roles, are important to justice outcomes.

What are we talking about when we talk about 'hybridity'?

The concept of hybridity has a long history in many different fields. Emanating originally from postcolonial approaches to culture and the work of Bhabha in particular, hybridity is something that occurs within a 'Third Space' that exists between the dominant and the dominated, the coloniser and the colonised, and the global and the local.[6] Essentially the Third Space is a contact zone where these alternative worldviews exist and where the unbalanced relationship between them constructs new forms of identity – a hybrid.

Within international relations, this has largely been taken up by a group of theorists looking specifically at the liberal peace and its limits, particularly Roger Mac Ginty, Oliver Richmond and Volker Boege.[7] Mac Ginty and Richmond have also developed this further in a posited 'local turn'.[8] Alongside these academic efforts to develop theory there has also been a long-run dialogue within the policy community on the state-centric approaches of many international agencies, reflected mainly within evaluations and case-study approaches that perhaps do not use the label of hybridity but make use of similar concepts of how state institutions and other actors interact.[9] At the same time, there is also a tradition within development studies that recognises hybridity as an alternative to the linear predictions of early development theory and the assumed linear trajectory of socio-cultural development from traditional to modern envisaged by Talcott Parsons, and perhaps more controversially within some interpretations of Weber.[10] Francis Fukuyama, for example, recognised this in a lecture in 2006 when he asked the question: 'Can informal institutions embedded within social norms [or *hybrid institutions*] be made to work more effectively for development outcomes in absence of a functioning Weberian state system?'[11] Clements *et al.* go on to outline a slightly different approach in changing the question to whether new forms of hybrid systems can evolve that will combine the best of both the Weberian and non-Weberian systems.

Given the longevity of dialogue relating to hybridity, one could represent this as being a new label for something that already exists rather than something that is actually new. However, the real value in using hybridity as a lens is that one can move away from divisions of the world into simple binary systems (state/non-state, traditional/modern, formal/informal) and recognise the fluidity of social systems and their politics. In particular, as Mac Ginty points out, it is also useful for moving away from ideas of 'pristine systems' espoused by some nationalist or ethnically based groups since it recognises that all human society is fluid to some degree. This also means that all social systems can be recognised as already being hybrid, i.e. there is no need to 'hybridise' them specifically, rather the analysis is of the effect of external and internal processes on changing the dynamics of hybrid systems, whatever they are labelled. As Mac Ginty characterises it, humanity is 'already tainted with the "original sin" of hybridity'.[12]

Mac Ginty characterises hybridity as being the result of the interaction between four core factors:

- the compliance powers of the liberal peace, or how far can liberal interventionists make people conform and punish detractors;
- the incentive powers of the liberal peace, or how far people will vote with their feet for security, Western justice, etc.;
- the ability of local actors to resist, ignore or adapt liberal interventions; and
- the ability of local actors to develop a viable alternative.

These are all greatly contested at local level, and there are clear links with other branches of literature within security sector reform, for example, and the contested nature of local ownership of security and justice programmes. This approach asks key questions, not least who are the owners, and whether they actually are the locals that require security and justice; or conversely, are they part of a political elite that maintains local systems for their own benefit?

In addition, the discussion of hybridity is also partly a discussion between balances of power between alternative sources of legitimacy and, as Foucault may have put it, between different forms of 'productive' power.[13] To some degree the extent of hybridity is partly a political choice and partly the result of institutional pressures arising from institutional constraints, including those who operate within those systems. This raises a number of issues around legitimacy and political power at the local level and part of any analysis of a hybrid system and what it means has to include a view of where the power lies within such systems and who exercises power and how?

Local power and chiefs in West Africa

Most of the power relationships in the countryside are not formalised, and remain relatively under-researched, and for justice, the lack of formalised legal frameworks leaves room for considerable leeway within decision-making. As an UN ECA Report states in 2007:

> Chieftaincy has continued to operate with large numbers of adherents, especially in rural areas . . . as custodians of customary law and communal assets, especially land. They dispense justice, resolve conflicts and enforce contracts. They also serve as guardians and symbols of cultural values and practices. Unfortunately, chiefs operate largely in an informal setting without clear definitions of their authority.[14]

In other words, the role of the chief is flexible and not always clearly specified, even if there are strong local traditions within which chiefs operate. Chiefs are largely under-studied and also misunderstood and yet the literature on hybridity and statebuilding recognises that capable democratic states must be based on some system of shared social values and that this might be achieved by incorporating indigenous institutions and norms, whilst adapting those systems to international expectations. This is not a new problem and is common in much British imperial literature as well as many more recent studies of the resilience and legitimacy of African institutions.[15] However, it has proved to be a consistent issue since the provision of justice in the countryside is predominantly tied up with local political systems as well as with the social, economic and political lives of many Africans, and the nature of the local political systems mean that incorporation, or even harmonisation, into a formal state institutional system as espoused by statebuilding, remains extremely difficult, even if it is generally desirable.[16]

Most current debates on the nature of the chieftaincy and consequent hybridity are located in a bigger debate about the nature of the postcolonial state and its failure.[17] The basic dilemma that hybridity, amongst other approaches attempts to address, is that the post-colonial state essentially emulates Western institutional governance, which is often at odds with traditional African cultural values and socio-economic conditions. The failure of the postcolonial state, the collapse of state infrastructure and the various forms of violence and structural oppression that have come from Western-style institutions that have been used as instruments of totalitarian, corrupt and frequently violent rule, have also meant that many people, particularly in rural areas, look to alternative, local and traditional institutions for security and justice.

In reality, most of these local systems are partly local/traditional and partly international/modern. This hybridity is part of the everyday reality facing most people, but the realities of power mean that only some people can make the most of existing in both worlds. Charles Piot, for example, is one analyst who looks in detail at these dilemmas in Northern Togo and he argues that, whilst the remote villages of the Kabre people of northern Togo appear to have all the trappings of a classic ‘out of the way’ African culture – subsistence farming, straw-roofed houses, and rituals to the spirits and ancestors – village life is in fact an effect of the modern and the global.[18] He goes on to argue that a simple dichotomy between local and international is misleading and does not represent the fluidity of everyday relations in Northern Togo, a situation that is also recognisable across West Africa.[19]

The question here is where is the power and who exercises it? Mac Ginty’s analysis above makes an assumption that the power relationship is really between international and local – as implied by the balance between incentives and resistance. This is undoubtedly true, but the hybrid approach requires a more detailed analysis of the nature of that resistance, including exploring who is offering resistance and why?

I have analysed the politics of chieftaincy systems elsewhere,[20] so within this chapter I wish to concentrate on the nature of power exercised by chiefs and traditional authorities usually in the face of a dysfunctional formal state justice system. Essentially chiefs themselves equate their control of local justice mechanisms to a source of power rather than a means of dispensing justice.[21] In addition, local justice systems do enjoy significant local support. As Lubkemann *et al.* point out in Liberia:

> People complain that that the formal court system is overly narrow in how it defines the case at hand, thereby failing to get at the underlying dispute, in contrast with the customary mechanisms' focus on resolving precisely those root issues. The focus on root issues rests on a culturally grounded assumption that incorrect or injurious behaviour usually stems from damaged and acrimonious social relations. Justice must work to repair those relations rather than merely treat the behavioural expressions that are only its symptoms.[22]

There are clear links with Beswick's (this volume) work here in looking at the political outcomes of transitional justice in Rwanda, but perhaps even more clearly with the approach taken by Fowles (this volume) in addressing the case-by-case approach rather than identifying the underlying problems. This approach is also particularly interesting in essentially developing a conservative way of maintaining social cohesion. Justice is as much about the maintenance of social control as of providing 'justice' in a Western sense, and this has powerful influences in terms of Stephen Lukes's idea of the 'third face' of power in arguing that the absence of conflicting interests does not necessarily mean that there is no underlying power relationship.[23] He goes on to say: 'the most effective and insidious use of power is to prevent such conflicts arising in the first place'.[24] Lukes's approach derives from Gramsci's analysis of the power of agents and their development of hegemony in shaping the interests of others, which leads to the conclusion that power operates by creating silences and so can operate through consensus as well as conflict. In the context of the African countryside this is particularly important given the complex and fluid mixture of formal state institutions (if they are there at all), traditional or customary systems like chiefdom courts and unseen systems of power that regulate social structures.

In the case of a West African chief, it is untrue to say that most chiefs are able to act as independent agents in isolation. Chiefs are regulated by the law in so far as they want to interact with national or international actors, but also traditional law in their day-to-day operation as a chief. In many parts of West Africa this social regulation and limitation on power is provided by a number of traditions, including powerful secret societies like Poro and Sande.[25] The local power of such societies was recognised in a series of seminal works on Liberia written by G. W. Harley in the 1940s, in particular his paper on 'masks as agents of Social control in Northeast Liberia'.[26] Importantly the local regulations within which the chief operates are a system designed to maintain social cohesion and so the exercise of traditional law is about maintaining social control.

This has a number of effects, including the maintenance of social structures in which an elite has a vested interest and where dissent amongst groups that do not benefit from such social conformity (youth, women or the excluded, typically) takes the form of Lukes's 'third face' of power in constituting a silence where conformity is taken as consent or absence of power conflict. This is backed up by work in Sierra Leone[27] but also significantly in Ghana by Crook, Asante and Brobbey,[28] who ran a detailed survey comparing different forms of dispute mechanisms at the local level that provides some interesting findings. In particular the Ghanaian research shows that the most traditional form of dispute mechanism concerning land was regarded as the least in tune with popular perceptions of justice since it represented a very narrow elite group who were able to manipulate local traditional justice mechanisms.

In other words, local justice systems reinforced the social systems they were derived from, including providing a mechanism for a local elite to reinforce and maintain their own power. This highlights a paradox: customary justice systems are popular yet retain a high degree of patriarchal/traditional order that itself forms a political system. Furthermore, those who are in favour of increased use of the customary sector in particular tend to make an assumption that, because more people use the system, it follows that they prefer it. In reality this might not be the case. Some may prefer that route, but others may be faced with little choice, or with significant social pressure to conform to the social regulation of secret societies. It is also illustrative of how traditional justice and the form of social reconciliation are perhaps not entirely benevolent or desirable for some of the local population. Impartiality and the rule of law is regarded as less important than the maintenance of community power relations. The research of Crook *et al.*[29] implies that either there has been a reduction in respect for local institutions or that chiefs are less respected as upholders of balanced justice (or both).

Powerlessness and exclusion from justice

The idea that justice is a major lever of political control exercised by a political elite over the general population becomes more clear when we examine the lack of access to justice of specific groups within society. In urban areas, there may be an option of a formal justice mechanism, usually a magistrates' court or an appeal court, but between 70 and 80 per cent of the population do not access these justice institutions. Instead they rely on access to local courts, presided over by a group of members appointed by the chief. Local courts may be dominated by local elites which makes them extremely risky in terms of getting a result. The local courts mainly investigate and make judgments based on customary law, and chiefs also have the power to set bye-laws in conjunction with predominantly male elders. This means that citizens do not necessarily know the bye-laws that apply to them; these may contravene human rights, be applied in an arbitrary manner or involve degrading treatment like the beating of children.[30] At the same time, there appears to be little chance that a poor person could bring a successful case against a chief or a member of a chief's family.

One additional factor is the continuing importance of kin groupings to rural society. Chiefs are themselves limited by ruling family and kin linkages and traditions within the rural hierarchy.[31] For example, family history is frequently taken into account in selecting people for formal positions, so if your ancestor was a chief then you are far more likely to gain a position of influence than a relative newcomer. Kinship also has the effect of restricting power to a particular ethnic group – the *indigenes* – or the original founders of that place. Because chiefdom and kinship is so tied to the land, legitimacy is usually tied to the length of time that a particular family has occupied a piece of land.

Clearly this places certain groups of people in an increasingly powerless position. Non-indigene (*stranger*) women and youth are in particularly vulnerable positions with almost no representation and no power to influence decisions in local courts. Paramount chiefs are frequently cited as hearing cases when they have no mandate to do this, and individuals who oppose the chief are likely to be ostracised from the community.[32] Rural West African society further isolates people from access to justice in that power is usually wielded by the elders, who are usually male. Young men are expected to obey their elders whilst (male) elders wield power in families, social groupings and justice forums like the courts. When discussing 'youth' it should be noted that this essentially means socially acceptable or fully participating in local society, having more to do with social status, belonging and kinship relations than with age.[33] The concept of youth is also linked to land, wealth and marriage and those who lack those things remain classed as 'youth'. The social exclusion of these 'youths' was identified as a key driver of conflict in Sierra Leone and also Liberia.[34]

Women in particular have been marginalised by the customary system of justice, although this may vary between different regions.[35] The customary system tends to govern domestic issues that concern many women whilst women also face higher barriers to entry to the formal sector in terms of financial and social issues.[36] The local system of managing domestic affairs, which is largely dominated by men, has produced a system that is institutionally biased against women and frequently violates women's constitutional and human rights. For example, if a woman brings a case against a husband, brother or farmer, then they are likely to be labelled as a 'bad woman' and socially ostracised, which represents a significant social cost.[37] At the same time, there is a strong traditional legacy within the customary system and during a large-scale participatory exercise within the chiefdoms in 2002, there were comments from women that expressed pleasure at being asked their opinion because they 'are not considered worthy of taking any challenging responsibility other than cooking and nursing children'.[38] The same report goes on to report polygyny (one man with several conjugal relationships), leviratic marriage (inheriting a brother's wife), collecting 'marriage tax' whilst girls were still at school, hearing serious rape cases in local courts rather than district courts (and therefore treating it as a minor case) and patrilineal inheritance were all 'rigorously supported by local courts'.[39] It is clear that many of these practices have continued within the customary system despite the introduction of human rights legislation, including the continuation of women having the status of 'minors' in many local courts.[40]

So where does that leave us? People seeking justice in the countryside of much of Sierra Leone and Liberia face something of a dilemma. Formal justice may not be present or functional, whereas customary justice systems are there but institutionally biased against some groups. Reflecting the hegemony of the society that created them, customary justice systems exist within complex systems of social hierarchies comprising secular power in the form of chiefs, but a heavily regulated social habitus controlled by secret societies. Whereas hybridity appears to be an attractive idea, as does the idea of resistance to externally driven justice reforms, power, hegemony and patriarchy can be hidden in hybrid approaches to local justice. That is not to imply that the formal system cannot also contain such bias, but a legal system that conforms with UN definition human rights, for example, is fundamentally incompatible with a system that reinforces social structures that are institutionally biased. This actually raises the question of whether 'hybridity' as a single, fluid system is possible at all, or whether what we are actually analysing is a form of institutional competition at the local level.

Conclusion: who are we going to be 'hybrid' with?

This chapter has explored the relationship between justice provision, hybridity and power at the local level in West Africa. Local power dynamics have a strong bearing on the extent to which rural citizens can gain access to justice despite efforts to decentralise power, and legally empower marginalised groups. Reform efforts have overlooked the inherent political dimensions of justice provision, which in rural Africa are deeply embedded in informal social structures, including kinship relations and secret societies, but which have also been shaped by the continuing influence of the chiefs and local social power structures. Whilst there remain several justice actors available to people, although the formal system may lack hegemony in many areas, local political elites, incorporating the chiefs, maintain control through their ability to enforce social conformity and to create silences where the access to particular avenues is rendered unavailable.

At the same time, the lens of hybridity is useful in this case because it emphasises the linkages between formal and informal, legal and customary sources of justice and therefore power. One can also say that hybridity represents the actually lived experience of most people on the ground and that is likely to remain so for the foreseeable future since the resilience of the local has been very strong in the face of violent centralisation, war and international intervention for more than thirty years.

For most people, justice is not dispensed from formal, modern systems but from a dense network of institutions at local level which may or may not be codified or even visible. These institutions constantly change and are subject to a variety of controlling bodies which regulate the meaning and enforcement of common law. Indeed, even the formal institutions of local and magistrates courts draw on common law rather than formal law in many of their cases, and this is open to interpretation and influence according to changing local customs. Different social structures exercise influence over justice processes and outcomes. These biases exist despite the public, national agreements, for example to enforce human rights legislation. Local power is at least partly exercised through the appointment to courts and through the role of elders within villages. As documented, this leads to institutional bias within the customary system, particularly against women and youth as defined in the Sierra Leone context.

Institutional bias is partly formed from the root of local justice systems, which are primarily organised to promote social conformity (sometimes generously called 'harmony') and to promote social cohesion. This can have significant benefits in environments where social cohesion has been destroyed, and in activities that require some form of social development following trauma, such as peacebuilding.

However, there is an issue here of how to treat those who do not conform, who do not look, act or think like the elders of a community, and who may digress from social rules. In practice, these are people who are effectively alienated from the benefits of those communities and are isolated from political participation and justice. It is here that there may be a clash with international ideas of human rights, partly because international law tends to try individuals for those crimes that are held to hold some degree of individual responsibility, whereas most local systems are really about social conformity, part of which is to uphold the power of those in control.

This leads to a dilemma for international support in the justice sector. Whilst some argue that international support should forget formal,

Western justice and support the local systems, it is clear that there are considerable issues here, and abuse of customary systems may have significantly contributed to conflict in the first place. For the powerless, this means that they have no effective access to justice, whilst justice is accessible for those from the indigene kinship group or for those who can afford suitable recompense.

The core issue, then, must be to encourage external support that empowers people to access justice within the legal frameworks within which they operate. In other words, there has to be an acknowledgement that a formal legal framework lacks hegemony and is unlikely to be available to every community in rural West Africa. In addition, it should also be acknowledged that formal legal systems may also be subject to political abuse. This does not mean that people within those communities should be just subject to the whims of local political elites or the biases of the chiefs. The international community needs to expand the formal legal system, particularly in overcoming barriers to access including knowledge and finance, and institutional issues within that legal system, such as capacity.

In the end, the analysis of power at the local level raises questions about who actually exercises ownership, since the implication of hybridity is that some local owners can be incorporated into broader reform processes, but these will tend to be elites who are able to control local power systems rather than those who are excluded from those systems. In the short term, this may be acceptable – indeed it may be the only choice – but the question for international donors must be how far they are willing to provide support for those who navigate these systems locally, particularly those who are excluded, as opposed to engaging with elite agents who may be able to exist in and use the formal system on one level and also to control a traditional system on another. The question of who resists and why is partly answered by looking at local elites who are both in a position to resist and who also have a reason: the question for the international community is really whether the maintenance of local elites constitutes legitimate resistance.

Notes

1 See e.g. the OECD/DAC *Guidelines on Security Sector Reform*, 2004, which are deliberately technical in approach and form the current 'orthodoxy' on security and justice interventions.
2 Pierre Englebert (2002) *State Legitimacy and Development in Africa* (Boulder, CO: Lynne Rienner); Lars Buur and Helene M. Kyed (2005) *State Recognition of Traditional Authority in Mozambique: The Nexus of Community Representation and State Assistance*, Discussion Paper 28, Uppsala: Nordic Africa Institute; Donald I. Ray and P. S. Reddy (eds) (2003) *Grassroots Governance? Chiefs in Africa and the Afro-Caribbean* (Calgary: University of Calgary Press).
3 Charles Piot (1999) *Remotely Global: Village Modernity in West Africa* (Chicago, IL: University of Chicago Press).

4 Paul Jackson (2007) 'Reshuffling the Deck? The Politics of Decentralisation in Sierra Leone', *African Affairs* 106: 95–111; Bruce Baker (2008) 'Beyond the Tarmac Road: Local Forms of Policing in Sierra Leone and Rwanda', *Review of African Political Economy* 35(118): 555–70; Ryann E. Manning (2009) 'The Landscape of Local Authority in Sierra Leone: How "Traditional" and "Modern" Justice Systems Interact', in Yongmei Zhou (ed.), *Decentralization, Democracy and Development: Recent Experience from Sierra Leone*, World Bank Country Study (Washington, DC: World Bank), 110–37.

5 Bruce Baker and Eric Scheye (2009) 'Access to Justice in a Post-Conflict State: Donor-Supported Multidimensional Peacekeeping in Southern Sudan', *International Peacekeeping* 16(2): 171–85.

6 Homi K. Bhabha (1994) *The Location of Culture* (London: Routledge).

7 Roger Mac Ginty (2010) 'Hybrid Peace: The Interaction between Top-Down and Bottom-Up Peace', *Security Dialogue* 41(4): 391–412; Oliver P. Richmond (2011) *A Post-Liberal Peace* (London: Routledge); Volker Boege, Anne Brown, Kevin P. Clements and Anna Nolan (2008) *On Hybrid Political Orders and Emerging States: State Formation in the Context of 'Fragility'* (Berlin: Berghof Research Center for Constructive Conflict Management).

8 Roger Mac Ginty and Oliver P. Richmond (2013) 'The Local Turn in Peace Building: A Critical Agenda for Peace', *Third World Quarterly* 34(5): 763–83.

9 See e.g. Peter Albrecht and Paul Jackson (2009) *Security System Transformation in Sierra Leone 1997–2007*, Global Facilitation Network for Security Sector Reform (GFN-SSR), http://epapers.bham.ac.uk/1529 (accessed May 2016); Bruce Baker (2006) 'The African Post-Conflict Policing Agenda in Sierra Leone', *Conflict, Security and Development* 6(1): 25–50; Baker, 'Beyond the Tarmac Road'; Peter Albrecht and Lars Buur (2009) 'An Uneasy Marriage: Non-State Actors and Police Reform', *Policing and Society* 19(4): 390–405.

10 There is a burgeoning literature that contests the modernist interpretation of Weber and sees him as a father of interpretive sociology. This was a development of Weberian thought by the German emigrant Alfred Schutz but rejected/ignored by Parsons. See Peter Kivisto and William H. Swatos, Jr. (1990) 'Weber and Interpretive Sociology in America', *Sociological Quarterly* 31(1): 149–63; Philipp Lottholz and Nicolas Lemay-Hébert (2016) 'Re-Reading Weber, Re-Conceptualising Statebuilding: From Neo-Weberian to Post-Weberian Approaches to State, Legitimacy and Statebuilding', *Cambridge Review of International Affairs*, ahead-of-print.

11 Quoted in Kevin P. Clements, Volker Boege, Anne Brown, Wendy Foley and Anna Nolan (2007) 'State Building Reconsidered: The Role of Hybridity in the Formation of Political Order', *Political Science* 59(1): 45–56, 46, their addition.

12 Mac Ginty, 'Hybrid Peace', 398.

13 Michel Foucault (2007) *Security, Territory, Population: Lectures at the College de France 1977–78*, ed. Michel Senellart (Basingstoke: Palgrave Macmillan).

14 United Nations Economic Commission for Africa (UN ECA) (2007) *Relevance of African Traditional Institutions of Governance*, Governance and Public Administration Division (GPAD) of the United Nations Economic Commission for Africa (ECA), http://repository.uneca.org/bitstream/handle/10855/3086/bib.%2025702_I.pdf?sequence=1 (accessed May 2016), 8.

15 Paul Jackson (2005) 'Chiefs, Money and Politicians: Rebuilding Local Government in Sierra Leone', *Public Administration and Development* 25: 49–58; Jackson, 'Reshuffling the Deck?'; Paul Jackson (2011) 'Decentralised Authorities, Decentralised Power and Who Gets Access to Justice in Sierra Leone', *Journal of Legal Pluralism* 63: 207–31; Richard C. Crook, Kojo Asante and Victor Brobbey

(2010) *Popular Concepts of Justice and Fairness in Ghana: Testing the Legitimacy of New or Hybrid Forms of State Justice*, APPP Working Paper 14 (London: Africa Power and Politics Programme); Richard C. Crook (1987) 'Legitimacy, Authority and the Transfer of Power in Ghana', *Political Studies* 35(4): 552–72; Bruce Baker (2011) 'Justice and Security Architecture in Africa: The Plans, the Bricks, the Purse and the Builder', *Journal of Legal Pluralism and Unofficial Law* 43(63): 25–47.
16 Baker, 'Justice and Security Architecture'; Piot, *Remotely Global*.
17 UN ECA, *Relevance of African Traditional Institutions*.
18 Piot, *Remotely Global*.
19 Ibid.
20 E.g. see Jackson, 'Chiefs, Money and Politicians', and Jackson, 'Decentralised Authorities, Decentralised Power'.
21 Jackson, 'Reshuffling the Deck?'
22 Stephen C. Lubkemann, Deborah H. Isser and Philip A. Z. Banks (2011) 'Unintended Consequences: Constraint of Customary Justice in Post-Conflict Liberia', in Deborah H. Isser (ed.), *Customary Justice and the Rule of Law in War-Torn Societies* (Washington, DC: USIP Press), 193–238, 217.
23 Stephen Lukes (2005) *Power: A Radical View*, 2nd edn (Basingstoke: Palgrave Macmillan).
24 Ibid. 27.
25 The *poro* and the *sande* are, respectively, male and female secret societies that historically met in sacred groves in the forest across West Africa, but most notably in Liberia and Sierra Leone. They have strong similarities to other secret societies more broadly such as leopard and crocodile societies. Chiefs are secular leaders only, and ritual power is in the hands of the *poro* secret society. Membership of *poro* is necessary for anyone in a position of authority, particularly those who enforce traditional law. In addition, the *sande* and *poro* and other secret societies educate boys and girls, regulate sexual conduct and social hierarchy, and concern themselves with agricultural fertility and military training normally connected with hunter militias. Paul Richards (2003) 'The Social Assessment Study: Community-Driven Development and Social Capital in Post-War Sierra Leone', unpublished paper commissioned by the Community-Driven Development Group of the World Bank for the National Commission for Social Action of the Government of Sierra Leone; Richard Fanthorpe (2006) 'On the Limits of the Liberal Peace: Chiefs and Democratic Decentralization in Sierra Leone', *African Affairs* 105: 27–49; Jackson, 'Reshuffling the Deck?'
26 George W. Harley (1950) *Masks as Agents of Social Control in Northeast Liberia*, Papers of the Peabody Museum of American Archaeology and Ethnology, 32(2) (Cambridge, MA: Harvard University); Harley (1941) *Notes on the Poro in Liberia*, Papers of the Peabody Museum of American Archaeology and Ethnology, 19(2) (Cambridge, MA: Harvard University).
27 Jackson, 'Chiefs, Money and Politicians'; Jackson, 'Reshuffling the Deck?'; Jackson, 'Decentralised Authorities, Decentralised Power'.
28 *Popular Concepts of Justice and Fairness in Ghana*.
29 Ibid.
30 Clare Castillejo (2009) *Building Accountable Justice in Sierra Leone*, FRIDE Working Paper 76 (Madrid: FRIDE).
31 This is partly where the secret societies come in since they perform a regulatory function in society, including influencing the chief.
32 Richards, 'The Social Assessment Study'; Fanthorpe, 'Limits of the Liberal Peace'; Paul Richards (2006) 'To Fight or to Farm? Agrarian Dimensions of the Mano River Conflicts in Liberia and Sierra Leone', *African Affairs* 104: 571–90; Castillejo, *Building Accountable Justice*.

33 Richard Fanthorpe (2001) 'Neither Citizen Nor Subject? Lumpen Agency and the Legacy of Native Administration in Sierra Leone', *African Affairs* 100: 363–86.
34 Ibid. Stephen D.K. Ellis (1999) *The Mask of Anarchy: The Destruction of Liberia and the Religious Dimension of an African Civil War* (London: Hurst).
35 Castillejo, *Building Accountable Justice.*
36 This is known locally, and in court records, as 'women trouble'.
37 Castillejo, *Building Accountable Justice.*
38 Richard Fanthorpe, Alice Jay and Victor Kamara (2002) 'A Review of the Chiefdom Governance Reform Programme, Incorporating an Analysis of Chiefdom Administration in Sierra Leone', unpublished DfID report, 31.
39 Ibid.
40 Castillejo, *Building Accountable Justice.*

Chapter 16

Hybridity as a tool for deconstruction

The case of child witches

Sam Fowles

Introduction

Homi K. Bhabha used the concept of hybridity to describe the product of cultural resistance in a postcolonial context.[1] Hybridity is a creature of conflict; it emanates from the resistance of a subaltern culture against a dominant culture.[2] Bhabha conceives hybridity as existing within the 'third space'; between two opposed cultures, being a part of neither of them but a child of both.[3] Jon Yorke's biological metaphor in this volume offers a useful means of understanding hybridity. Just as a hybrid organism is created from a (deliberate or coincidental) combination of other organisms (such as taking a cutting from plants or in the case of cross-breeding of animals), in the social sciences hybridity refers to phenomena which are created as combinations of other phenomena. Hybridity, in the social science sense, differs from hybridity in the biological sense because it is traditionally believed to have the added ingredient of resistance. A useful example in the West is *Negritude* scholarship. Aime Ceasare describes how black residents of Paris in the mid-twentieth century resisted the metropolitan French culture by attempting to reclaim a 'traditional' African culture[4], which had, in fact, never existed (at least not in the way that it was reclaimed).[5] Under the dominant pressure of French cultural hegemony, the African community in metropolitan France created new cultural phenomena based on an imagined history.[6] *Negritude* was neither French nor African yet it was the product of the interaction of both French and African imaginaries. Negritude demonstrates that hybrid phenomena are more than the sum of their parts. While Negritude was the product of cultural resistance, it developed into an independent entity and body of knowledge.

Hybridity is a useful descriptor because it 'underscores the fluidity of human societies'.[7] In choosing examples of hybridity it is important to remember that hybridity is a constant process not a discrete incident. As such it can be applied to more than just culture and has been applied in, *inter alia*, international relations, development studies, history and law.[8] As Jackson argues in this volume, hybridity is useful because it often represents 'the actual lived experience of people on the ground'. Yet, applied simply as a descriptor, hybridity is in danger of describing too much. From the historian's perspective the concept of hybridity is not new, just a different term for a process of dialectic development first postulated in the nineteenth century.[9] There is a danger of using hybridity as a catch-all term and creating the situation where 'everything is the result of hybridity, everything is a hybrid, there can be no certainty, and all discussions must be smothered in caveats'.[10] It is for this reason that there is utility in a discussion of the practical application of the concept of hybridity.

This chapter will posit hybridity as a tool for deconstruction of human rights abuses. Lawyers often work in a particular paradigm: events are seen on a case-by-case basis, a discrete victim is matched with a discrete perpetrator. This can also lead, however, to an under-representation of the structural causes of human rights abuses.[11] Discussion of human rights must include the structural as well as individual reasons for violations but reports from international human rights bodies are often methodologically inappropriate to consider these effectively.[12] Hybridity can be used as a tool to deconstruct all the elements of a particular abuse, with the eventual goal of eliminating the structures which facilitate the abuse rather than simply attempting to solve the results of structural issues on a case-by-case basis.

In this chapter I apply this method to the abuse of children accused of witchcraft in southern and central Africa. The last thirty years have seen an increase in the belief in witchcraft, with children believed to be the principal perpetrators.[13] Social scientists have attributed this increased susceptibility to belief in the occult to complex combinations of factors including poverty, deprivation, lack of political leadership, war and famine.[14] Anthropologists have focused on the anatomy of the beliefs themselves, describing how elements of different cultures come together to form new structures of belief.[15] However, there has yet to be a conceptual link drawn between the two approaches. It will be argued here that the belief in and abuse of 'child witches' is more than simply a perverted religiosity facilitated by poverty. It is a cultural hybrid combining Christianity with traditional African beliefs in the occult, which is developing against the backdrop of neoliberal economic reforms and a conception of aggressive evangelical and quasi-commercial religiosity exported to Africa from the United States.

The argument will progress in six stages. I shall begin by arguing that it is important to understand the structural causes of human rights abuses. I shall then examine the content of the belief in child witches and a number of posited explanations for the belief. Next, I will analyse the belief in 'child witches' first as a hybrid of Christian and traditional African beliefs, then as the product of a structural hybridity created by the growth of charismatic churches in West Africa with a strong commercial outlook. I will conclude by identifying the manner in which this case study demonstrates the utility of hybridity as a lens through which to analyse the structural causes of human rights abuses.

The structural causes of human rights abuses

Susan Marks argues that the study of human rights abuses often focuses on the abuses themselves to the exclusion of their causes. Although, in recent years, international organisations such as UNICEF or Save The Children have increased their focus on the 'root causes' of human rights abuses, their reports and other studies often fail to explore the 'root' (or structural) causes in sufficient depth. Marks argues that investigation of causes is often halted too soon, effects can be treated as though they were causes and when causes are successfully identified they are too often regarded as problems that are insurmountable and sidelined in favour of issues that do not require structural change.[16]

The result is that, while immediate causes of human rights abuses may be effectively identified, structural causes are often ignored. In particular, the political nature of structural violence is under-represented in studies of discrete abuses.[17] This is rarely deliberate, but a function of the institutions which investigate human rights abuses.[18] Nevertheless, the result is a less than complete picture of the abuse in question. Too often the limited nature of the methodology leads to a focus on the actions (or failure to act) of states at the expense of more in-depth consideration of the impacts of transnational phenomena.[19]

The cumulative impact of these limitations is that human rights abuses are seen as the results of 'bad people doing bad things'. While this is almost certainly accurate, it is not a complete picture. Human rights abuses are also caused by structures and systems which both facilitate and necessitate the abuse of human rights. As Marks puts it:

> Despite or rather, because of attempts to explain them, human rights violations are made to seem random, accidental or arbitrary. And if human rights violations are random, accidental or arbitrary, then the prospects of putting them to an end become as remote as though they belonged to the order of nature. They come to appear necessary, not just in the (false contingency) sense of historical necessity, but in the (false necessity) sense of 'natural' necessity.[20]

The danger in this analysis is that it makes human rights abuses seem inevitable. Yet we can control the structures which facilitate, and in some cases necessitate, these acts. As such, analysis of human rights abuses must look beyond 'who suffers?' and ask 'who benefits?' But it must also ask why a structure exists which necessitates the violence against some for the benefit of others.

Naomi Klein identifies how the application of the 'Chicago Doctrine' of radical neoliberal policies to Chile under General Pinochet 'necessitated' human rights abuses.[21] She argues that the human rights abuses which took place under Pinochet (including forced disappearances, imprisonment without trial, summary execution and torture) were the inevitable result of the attempt to apply this fundamentalist doctrine because without such abuses the population could never have been compelled to comply with such a socially destructive economic agenda.[22] Put another way, the structures imposed by Pinochet required wide-scale abuses of human rights in order to function. Without brutal repression, poverty and deprivation, the system could not survive.[23] This serves as an example of how the abuse of human rights is not simply caused by certain structures but *required* by them.

Hybridity can be used to dissect the structural basis of the belief in 'child witches' in a similar way. The belief has roots in contrasting religious ideas, but is also the product of social organisation and an attempt to rationalise a collective encounter with global economic forces which many cannot understand.

The belief in 'child witches'

Despite its medieval connotations the belief in 'child witches' is a recent phenomenon.[24] Although witches feature in African folk culture dating back thousands of years, the association with children is estimated to be approximately thirty years old.[25] Belief in 'child witches' has been recorded throughout southern and western Africa.[26] Although often associated with the area of the Congo basin (Republic of the Congo, the Democratic Republic of Congo and Gabon) it has also been recorded in South Africa, Nigeria, Liberia and Sierra Leone, Botswana, Cameroon, Ghana, Namibia and Tanzania.[27] The belief in 'child witches' is most common in urban areas, which distinguishes it from traditional African beliefs in the occult, which tend to be predominantly found in rural areas.[28]

In the past thirty years reports of human rights abuses related to witchcraft have increased significantly. Between 1985 and 1995 UNICEF estimates that 389 people were killed as punishment for 'witchcraft'.[29] Between 1996 and 2001 UNICEF estimates that over 600 were murdered in just one province.[30] But the belief in 'child witches' amounts to a more complex phenomenon than a large number individual murders or, respectively, human rights abuses. It is a widely held conviction throughout central and south western African society. The central African writer Pierre Sammy Mackfoy describes the change in recent years: 'Before it [witchcraft] was taboo. No one wanted to hear talk of witches . . . Yet now it has become almost commonplace. People talk about it all the time.'[31] The philosopher Achille Mbembe goes further, arguing that belief in the occult is so extensive in west Africa that the existence of the paranormal has become an accepted part of daily life: '[T]he greatest epistemological rupture – and thereby social – is not between what one sees and what one reads, but between what one sees [the visible] and what one does not see [the invisible].'[32] In Malawi, for example,

75 per cent of people believe that there are witches practising in their community, which includes such activities as cursing their enemies with disease, financial woes or bad luck.[33]

Traditionally African beliefs in witchcraft have been dualistic. The invisible world is construed as a balance between light and dark, and the occult is associated as much with 'witchdoctors' who protect and heal, as with those who seek to harm. By contrast 'child witches' are unambiguously seen as forces of evil.[34] Witchcraft is now a harmful and wicked force from which Africa must deliver itself.[35] Those accused of witchcraft vary in age from infant to adolescent and include both girls and boys.[36] But those accused are often children who can be identified as in some way different from the 'norm'. This has included learning difficulties or physical disabilities, but also bedwetting, 'bad behaviour', lying, stealing, eating too much without the expected accompanying physical development or fighting with other children.[37] But the identifying features of witchcraft can also be entirely external to the child accused. Children accused of witchcraft are often those who are unrelated to the rest of the nuclear family, possibly a child from another marriage or one who has come to live with relatives.[38] What unites all victims is that they lack the means to resist the accusations and the violence that often follows.[39] Those accused of witchcraft are those who are most easily isolated and, typically (as will become apparent) those most vulnerable.[40]

The nature of the alleged 'witchcraft' varies. Some iterations involve the belief that the child has been possessed by spirits, often in the form of animals. In others certain animals themselves are believed to be controlling the child. In South Africa there are reports of baboons executed by necklacing for the crime of witchcraft.[41] In many versions of the belief the child itself is at fault. Most versions involve the belief that the child has in some way betrayed their family, either by selling them for occult power or causing 'bad luck' such as miscarriages and crop failures.[42]

The belief in 'child witches' is often described as centring on Pentecostal churches. However not all churches which perpetuate the belief in 'child witches' are members of the official Pentecostal Church. A better description of the type of church that tends to promote the belief in 'child witches' would be 'charismatic churches'. As will be described below these churches are rigorously evangelical, with fast-growing congregations and their roots in American 'missions' of the mid-twentieth century.[43] They are generally led by charismatic pastors who claim special sight as a gift from God, which allows them to identify 'witches'.[44] These pastors are also the primary performers of 'exorcisms'.[45] A notable distinction is that the belief in 'child witches' tends to be limited to Christian communities. It has been suggested that this is because Islamic preachers have found it harder (or perhaps less necessary) to merge Islamic beliefs with traditional African beliefs because the Quran cannot be read in anything but Arabic.[46] This has allowed the international Muslim authorities to keep greater control over interpretations of Islam. By contrast Christian missionaries enthusiastically translated the Bible into local languages, which facilitated a greater range of interpretations.

'Exorcisms' can take place in churches or in the family home, although the former is more common. So-called 'exorcisms' are generally violent and many cause lasting harm. Children may be starved of both water and food for more than a week at a time, beaten (and forced to beat each other), forced to sleep outside during winter, deprived of sleep, spun in circles until they can no longer stand, burned, cut, have teeth and nails pulled out, beaten with switches, whips, bats and chains, scalded, have chillies rubbed into their eyes and genitals, be forced to ingest substances and be sexually abused.[47] Many children accused of witchcraft are forced out of the family home to live on the streets. In Kinshasa (Democratic Republic of Congo) alone it is estimated that there are more than 100,000 street children, 50 per cent of whom have been accused of witchcraft.[48] In summary, human rights abuses related to the belief in child witches are not isolated phenomena. They are justified by a widely held belief in the occult, promoted by charismatic churches. The victims of these abuses tend to be those with little social power, who are unable to resist accusations or 'exorcisms'.

Explanations for the belief in 'child witches'

A number of explanations have been offered for the belief in 'child witches'. It is argued that the changing nature of African societies has led to a renewed belief in the occult as people feel more vulnerable and less able to rely on traditional social structures. Ballet, Dumbai and Lallau argue that the change from rural to urban lifestyle has undermined the traditional foundations of social authority, which means that individuals who could previously have exercised legitimate authority as a parent or village elder now find themselves without a social role to play. Similarly, those who would previously have looked for direction from such authorities find themselves without guidance.[49] In Molina's words the 'transfer to urban modernity' has left people looking for an explanation for 'difference, individuality and abnormality'.[50] In addition the development of modern globalised economies has changed the nature of childhood. Parents are no longer able to provide for the needs of their children because those needs have changed (the levels of education required for employment, for example, have leapt forward in the space of a generation). At the mercy of economic and political decisions made in boardrooms and cabinet chambers and involving forces of which they have no conception, people feel like the events that define their lives are increasingly beyond their control. It is argued that this social breakdown and feeling of powerlessness leads people to turn to those offering explanations for their troubles; lacking the means to explain economics, science and international relations, these individuals turn to the occult.[51]

For others the reason for the development of the belief lies in the changing role of children in society. Aleksandra Cimpric suggests that in African society children represent an investment. Education is often the single largest expense for the average family in the Congo Basin and so each child educated represents and investment. This means that the expectations placed upon children are increasing as well, a problem compounded by economic developments that make finding the sort of work necessary to maintain a family ever more difficult. The result is that children fail to live up to expectations, to pay off their 'community debt', which breaks the bonds of trust between parents and children.[52] In addition, changing cultural norms have increased the vulnerability of certain children. As Naomi Cahn argues, urban families are increasingly polygamous and many children live in families with only one parent.[53] The 'new wife' often accuses the child of the old wife of witchcraft so she can get them out of the house.[54] De Boeck argues that it is the combination of these factors which has led to the prevalence of belief in 'child witches'. He describes the 'multi-crisis' of increased urbanisation, including the conversion to paid (rather than subsistence) employment, consumerism, and financial pressure.[55] An emerging individualism has caused a crisis in traditional family structures and other social relationships, presenting a challenge to the solidarity of African society. People are more disposed to fear 'the other'.[56]

While all of these explanations add something to our understanding of the belief in 'child witches', they focus on the social and economic conditions for the belief in the occult. They do not explain why it is that *this particular belief* which has developed. This is an important distinction. While the belief in 'child witches' may be facilitated by social and economic deprivation (which are harmful in their own right), the belief itself leads to harm. The explanations offered by De Boeck *et al.* explain why *a belief* in the occult might occur, not why *this particular belief* has occurred. It is here that hybridity can become a valuable lens because it can be used to deconstruct not only the social context of the belief but the structural causes behind the belief itself. In this sense, the pressures caused by global economic forces have not just created the conditions for the belief in child witches to flourish, they have contributed to the paradigm of belief which creates 'child witches' itself.

A mix of Christianity with traditional beliefs

Prima facie the belief in 'child witches' may be construed as a hybrid of Christian and traditional African beliefs in the occult. The idea of witchcraft or sorcery is not new to African cultures.[57] African folk culture includes different types of 'witches' or sorcerers including *thakathi* or *umthakathi* (in Zulu), malevolent mixers of potions, *sangoma*, who are thought to be diviners or seers, and *inyanga* or 'witchdoctors' who use magic to heal and protect. Traditionally beliefs in the occult also included a range of spirits taking different forms including birds and animals, which could be both harmful and benevolent. These spirits can sometimes possess a human through ingestion.[58]

The Christian influence comes from a particularly pentecostal or charismatic form of Christianity in which the believer must actively fight against evil in their daily lives.[59] Christian doctrine personifies evil in the form of Satan or demons.[60] The hybrid belief in 'child witches' includes the DNA of both Christian and African beliefs. Children accused of witchcraft are often associated with animals or accused of casting curses or spells similar to those associated with *thakathi* or are believed to be 'possessed'. But rather than by spirits the possession is the result of demonic activity and witches are agents of Satanic power.[61]

The so-called 'exorcisms' or 'deliverances' are also informed by a mix of Christian and folk belief.[62] The use of chillies or other natural substances is reminiscent or the remedies practised by *inyanga* and the starving of children accused or witchcraft reflects the folk idea of spirit possession because the exorcist claims he is starving the possessor not the child.[63] But the setting, a church, and the use of 'laying on of hands', burning or drowning reflect Christian ideas.[64]

The belief in child witches also reflects Bhabha's dominant/subaltern paradigm of hybridity. The Christian tradition may dominate, as Christian churches are generally the focus points of the 'fight against witchcraft' and pastors claim the exclusive power to 'deliver' those accused (and in many cases identify them) as a gift from God given only to them. But this dominant tradition has embraced many aspects of the subaltern folk traditions. The result is something that is neither 'Christian' (witchcraft has not been an aspect of mainstream Christian doctrine for nearly a century) nor traditionally African (*thakathi* were rarely conceived as children prior to the 1980s) yet contains elements of both. This is an excellent example of a hybrid phenomenon in which the competing cultural strands, from which it has developed, remain discernible.

The American model

The American model of evangelical churches is predicated on those churches growing continuously. Evangelisation is the fundamental purpose of charismatic Christianity: it exists to convert non-believers.[65] In order to achieve this the churches must turn to ever more excessive means to attract and retain audiences. The belief in 'child witches' helps churches attract and retain congregations because it acts as a self-fulfilling statement. A pastor claims that witches exist, 'proves' it by performing exorcisms and then blames witches when the other things he has promised his congregation do not happen, necessitating more exorcisms. Thus exorcisms and the belief are mutually reinforcing.[66] Overall the American model of charismatic

Christianity in Africa contributes to the development of hybrid structures that requires the torture of children.

Marks argues that any analysis of the root causes of human rights abuses should consider not just the victims but those who benefit from the abuse.[67] In the case of the belief in 'child witches' the most significant beneficiaries of the abuse are the pastors who carry out the exorcisms. Churches such as the N and M Church, Originale Spirituelle Prophétique, and Assemblée d'Israël- Ministère de combat contre la sorcellerie charge between $35 and $200 for an exorcism, often supplemented with payment in kind such as work on the church building. In addition, parents generally must pay for their child's upkeep whilst at the church for the period of the exorcism.[68] But the benefits pastors gain from the belief in 'child witches' are more extensive than the simply financial. Pastors gain fame and social standing. The most successful are featured on billboards, television and radio throughout their country and mix with the political and business elite. At a lower level pastors achieve high status within the local community.[69] Local authorities often welcome, officially or unofficially, the social control which churches can provide as well as the money they contribute in taxes and bribes.[70]

Charismatic Christianity is not an indigenous African phenomenon. It was introduced to Africa by foreign evangelists such as T. S. Osborn in the 1970s. These 'missionaries' generally came from the United States, although some, such as R. Boonke, were based in Western Europe.[71] *Prima facie* it may seem that this brand of American charismatic Christianity is another situational cause, as suggested by De Boeck's idea of 'multi-crisis', but when one dissects the belief in 'child witches' using the lens of hybridity it appears that the American model of charismatic Christianity not only causes the belief in 'child witches' but contributes to a framework that, in fact, necessitates it. The belief in 'child witches' and the patterns of behaviour accompanying it are intimately entwined. Their connection is more complex than mere cause and effect. Exorcisms are necessitated by the belief in witchcraft: Witchcraft is an evil and exorcisms are the cure. But exorcisms also validate the belief. Witchcraft must be 'real' because people in positions of authority are taking practical steps to counter it. But, conversely, those people also owe their authority to the belief in witchcraft. Action begets belief as much as belief begets action. As Tonda describes: 'The More God's servants fight against witchcraft . . . the more they extend the resources of witchcraft'.[72]

In this sense, American charismatic model does not merely facilitate the belief in 'child witches', it also necessitates such a belief. Evangelism is the fundamental logic of American charismatic Christianity.[73] Missionary churches like Osborn's were founded with the specific goal of exponential growth.[74] This logic has been replicated in the African charismatic churches. In Ghana a church is not considered established until it is running an effective Bible school (a common institution of conversion).[75] The theatre of church services is an essential part of achieving the goal of exponential growth. In both Africa and the United States healing, visions, confession and accusation form an essential part of charismatic church services.[76] Religion is more than an observance, it is a way of life. Congregations meet three or four times every week for services which can last in excess of three hours.[77]

This brand of religiosity requires a significant commitment from members of the congregation. A sense of theatre which goes beyond the church service plays an important role in maintaining this commitment.[78] Charismatic churches create a worldview in which the spiritual world is as real as the physical world. Religion is integral to every part of life.[79] The belief in 'child witches' is a part of this. The personification of evil grounded in African folk beliefs creates an ever-present spiritual danger. 'Exorcisms' and 'deliverances' both expand the theatre of the church and validate the pastor's warnings of the spiritual danger. This gives members of the congregation a reason to make the commitment necessary for the charismatic brand of religiosity to survive and the motivation to participate in the expansion which is so fundamental to its existence.

I have used the term 'brand' in reference to this specific type of religiosity quite deliberately. In American charismatic Christianity marketing and religion are one and the same.[80] Charismatic churches exist to convert and so must continuously attract new members to justify their existence. Growth is their raison d'être. The lens of hybridity can be used to demonstrate how this plays a fundamental part in the belief in 'child witches'.

The prosperity gospel

The influence of the American charismatic brand extends beyond patterns of behaviour. In Ghana, for example, African Christian works on demonology are rejected in favour of American works, with pastors preferring texts by Lester Sumrall, Kenneth Hagin and Gordon Lindsay which offer a more Western iteration of the belief in witchcraft.[81]

But the more interesting aspect is the way in which American ideological structures contribute to the belief in 'child witches'. Comaroff and Comaroff explain the belief in 'child witches' as a consequence of a combination of globalisation and political and economic liberalisation. Taking South Africa as their example, they argue that, with political liberalisation, the majority population were promised an escape from the grinding poverty which had defined their lives. But the corresponding economic liberalisation and globalisation had the opposite effect, concentrating wealth in the hands of just a few and appropriating resources offshore. Unable to understand why they had fought for independence and worked hard to provide for their families ever since, and have yet become poorer rather than richer, people turn to occult explanations.[82] In South Africa there is a belief that witches turn people into zombies and force them to work in slavery to provide the witch with riches.[83] In Congo it is believed that witches betray their family for personal financial and powerful gain.[84]

The direction of this aspect of the belief in 'child witches' relates to the American model of charismatic religiosity. Charismatic churches in both Africa and the United States preach a 'prosperity doctrine' in which the teachings of the gospel are a path to wealth and success. In this sense, the belief in 'child witches' is both expressions of a capitalist worldview and the explanation for the failure of its promise. Charismatic churches may promise prosperity but the economic structures (which they are part of) ensure that such a promise is unlikely to be fulfilled.[85] The failure of the pastor's promises of wealth can be blamed on interference by demonic agents in the form of 'child witches', whose motivations are explained in overtly capitalist terms; the acquisition of wealth and power. It is a horrible irony that the abuse of children as a result of the belief in 'child witches' is ensuring the wealth and power of the pastors who are, in turn, promising wealth and power to their congregation and justifying its absence by torturing those same children. The American religio-capitalist model thus does not merely contribute to the abuse of children through the belief in 'child witches' but also necessitates this very abuse. Without 'child witches' the doctrine preached by charismatic churches would all too easily be exposed as inconsistent.

Conclusions

Why is hybridity useful as a theoretical lens? It has been my contention that hybridity facilitates a different quality of analysis when studying the root causes of human rights abuses. Marks identifies a methodological gap in the study of human rights abuses. She posits that the structural causes of human rights abuses are often overlooked because the perspective of the investigators conditions them to focus on a case-by-case basis.[86] I have argued that hybridity can be used to fill this methodological gap. Hybridity can be used as a lens to deconstruct abuses of human rights in order to understand their structural causes.

This argument has been illustrated with an examination of the torture of children accused of witchcraft. The lens of hybridity has facilitated an analysis which looks beyond the situational causes of the belief in 'child witches' such as economic hardship,[87] social upheaval[88] or the combination of all of these in a 'multi-crisis'.[89] These create the context for such a belief to evolve but do not explain why this particular belief is the result.

The belief in 'child witches' is a complex iteration of Bhabha's first conception of dichotic hybridity (in which the resistance of a subaltern culture to a dominant culture creates a new cultural phenomenon)[90] but nevertheless a hybrid analysis allows the structural causes to be deconstructed. The simple dichotomy of Christianity with African folk beliefs is made more complex by the influence of a particularly American brand of capitalist religiosity. The belief in 'child witches' and the behaviour associated with this belief (the practice of parents paying for the torture of their children in exorcisms and the social and financial status which the perpetrators gain as a result) are analytically inseparable because they are mutually reinforcing. But hybridity allows us to examine their roots.

Charismatic churches must grow because conversion is their fundamental purpose. This is achieved by cultivating a particularly devoted following for whom religion is a way of life (and who will, consequently, embrace the mission of conversion). Their devotion is achieved and maintained with a particular spectacular and theatrical mode of worship and the promise of prosperity through Christ. The belief in witchcraft draws on African folk beliefs in the occult and folds them into the Christian paradigm of clearly personified evil. The motivations of witches are described in the same capitalist terms that motivate the congregation to attend church. Regular 'exorcisms' or 'deliverances' validate the belief in 'child witches' and contribute to the spectacle. As such the phenomenon is self-perpetuating. The structures of this brand of religiosity necessitate extreme beliefs, the belief 'child witches' bears the DNA of the 'prosperity gospel', traditional Christianity and African folk beliefs but, once established, it also creates a demand for the structures of charismatic Christianity.

The belief in 'child witches' is a hybrid with multiple inputs. It bears the DNA of Christianity, African folk traditions, American charismatic Christianity and capitalism, yet it does not entirely resemble any of these in their pure forms. It is the product of more than resistance between cultures; as such Bhabha's thesis underestimates the impact of human opportunism. Yet it could not exist without its cultural inputs. The lens of hybridity allows us to see the belief in 'child witches' for what it is: a necessary function of the accumulation of wealth and power within a culture which venerates such things. It shows that the solution is not case by case and it is about changing more than beliefs, it is about changing the structures which make those beliefs necessary.

Notes

1 Homi K. Bhabha (1994) *The Location of Culture* (London: Routledge), 1–28.
2 Jenny H. Peterson (2012) 'A Conceptual Unpacking of Hybridity: Accounting for Notions of Power, Politics and Progress in Analyses of Aid-Driven Interfaces', *Journal of Peacebuilding and Development* 7(2): 9–22, 12.
3 Bhabha, *Location of Culture*, 4–5.
4 Cf. Aime Césaire (1948) *Les armes miraculeuses* [The miraculous weapons] (Paris: Gallimard); (1945) *Notebook of a Return to the Native Land*, tr. Clayton Eshleman and Annette Smith (Middletown: Wesleyan University Press), 66.

5 Gary Wilder (2004) 'Race, Reason, Impasse: Cesaire, Fanon and the Legacy of Emancipation', *Radical History Review* 90(1): 31–61, 58.
6 Dominick LaCapra (2001) *Writing History, Writing Trauma* (Baltimore, MD: Johns Hopkins University Press), 20–4.
7 Roger Mac Ginty (2010) 'Hybrid Peace: The interaction between Top-Down and Bottom-Up Peace', *Security Dialogue* 41(4): 291–412.
8 E.g. respectively, Mac Ginty, 'Hybrid Peace', 391–412; Kevin P. Clements, Volker Boege, Anne Brown, Wendy Foley and Anna Nolan (2007) 'State Building Reconsidered: The Role of Hybridity in the Formation of Political Order', *Political Science* 59(1): 45–56; Catherine Hall (2007) 'History and Hybridity', *Journal of Victorian Culture* 2(1): 122–9; Olga Martin-Ortega and Johanna Herman (2011) 'Hybrid Tribunals: Interaction and Resistance in Bosnia and Herzegovina and Cambodia', in Oliver P. Richmond and Audra Mitchell (eds), *Hybrid Forms of Peace: From the 'Everyday' to Post-Liberalism* (Basingstoke: Palgrave Macmillan), 73–87.
9 Cf. Max Weber (2005 [1905]) *The Protestant Ethic and the Spirit of Capitalism*, tr. Talcott Parsons, 2nd edn (London: Routledge) and Karl Marx (2009 [1867]) *Das Kapital: A Critique of Political Economy* (Washington, DC: Regenery Publishing).
10 Peterson, 'Conceptual Unpacking', 44–8.
11 Susan Marks (2011) 'Human Rights and Root Causes', *Modern Law Review* 74(1): 57–78.
12 Ibid.
13 Aleksandra Cimpric (2010) *Children Accused of Witchcraft: An Anthropological Study of Contemporary Practices in Africa*, Report for UNICEF, WCARO, http://www.unicef.org/wcaro/wcaro_children-accused-of-witchcraft-in-Africa.pdf (accessed June 2016).
14 Cf. Filip de Boeck and Jean-Pierre Jacquemin (2000) 'Le "deuxième monde" et les "enfants sorciers"' [The Second World and child witches], *Politique Africaine* 80(4): 32–57.
15 E.g. Jean Comaroff and John L. Comaroff (1999) 'Occult Economies and the Violence of Abstraction: Notes from the South African Postcolony', *American Ethnologist* 26(2): 279–303.
16 Marks, 'Human Rights', 57–78.
17 Tobias Kelly (2009) 'The UN Committee Against Torture: Human Rights Monitoring and the Legal Recognition of Cruelty', *Human Rights Quarterly* 31(3): 798–99.
18 Neve Gordon, Jacinda Swanson and Joseph Buttigeig (2000) 'Is the Struggle for Human Rights a Struggle for Emancipation?', *Rethinking Marxism* 12(3): 1–22, 1.
19 Chidi Odinkalu recounts how human rights language is viewed with scepticism by African activists because it often serves to obscure rather than elucidate the transnational and structural causes of, so-called 'human rights abuses'. Chidi Odinkalu (1999) 'Why More Africans Don't Use Human Rights Language', *Human Rights Dialogue* 2(1): 1.
20 Marks, 'Human Rights', 57–78.
21 Naomi Klein (2009) *The Shock Doctrine* (Ottawa: Knopf), 512.
22 Ibid. 509.
23 Klein's case rests on two premises. (1) The Chilean population would not have accepted Chicago School measures if they had not been imposed by repressive means. (2) The economic systems imposed on Chile require extreme poverty in order to concentrate resources within a certain class. As such, the system itself requires deprivation.

24 Javier Aguilar Molina (2005) 'The Invention of Witchcraft in the Democratic Republic of Congo: Social Cleansing, Religious Commerce and the Difficulties of Being a Parent in an Urban Culture', Summary of research carried out on behalf of Save The Children, 2003–5, http://www.crin.org/docs/The_Invention_of_Child_Witches.pdf (accessed June 2016).
25 Cimpric, 'Children Accused of Witchcraft', 50.
26 Henrietta L. Moore and Todd Sanders (2003) *Magical Interpretations, Material Realities: Modernity, Witchcraft and the Occult in Postcolonial Africa* (London: Routledge), 105.
27 Ibid.
28 Florence Bernault (2006) 'Body, Power and Sacrifice in Equatorial Africa', *Journal of African History* 47(2): 207–39.
29 Isak Niehaus (2003) 'Witchcraft in the New South Africa: From Colonial Superstition to Postcolonial Reality?', in Moore and Sanders, *Magical Interpretations*, 184–225.
30 Gerrie ter Haar (ed.) (2007) *Imagining Evil: Witchcraft Beliefs and Accusations in Contemporary Africa* (Trenton, IL: Africa World Press), 5.
31 Cimpric, 'Children Accused of Witchcraft', 6.
32 Achille Mbembe (1996) 'La "chose" et ses doubles dans la caricature camerounaise' [The 'thing' and its double in Cameroonian caricature] *Cahiers d'Études Africaines* 36(141): 143–70.
33 Jill Filipovic and Ty McCormick (2012) 'Angels and Demons', *Foreign Policy*, 20 Dec., http://www.foreignpolicy.com/articles/2013/12/20/Angels_and_ Demons_Africa_Malawi_witches_HIV (accessed June 2016).
34 Naomi Cahn (2005–6) 'Poor Children: Child "Witches" and Child Soldiers in Sub-Saharan Africa', *Ohio State Journal of Criminal Law* 3: 413.
35 Peter Geschiere (1995) *Sorcellerie et politique en Afrique : La viande des autres* [Witchcraft and policy in Africa] (Paris: Karthala), 68.
36 Molina, 'Invention of Witchcraft', 40.
37 Ibid.
38 Aurore d'Haeyer (2004) *The Causes and Prevalence of Accusations of Witchcraft among Children in Akwa Ibom State* (New York: UNICEF), 24.
39 Rebecca Bannor-Addae (2009) 'Scapegoating the Most Vulnerable in the Central African Republic', UNICEF Central African Republic, 12 May, http://www.unicef.org/protection/car_49658.html (accessed May 2016).
40 De Boeck and Jacquemin, 'Le 'deuxième monde", 22.
41 Comaroff and Comaroff, 'Occult economies', 285–287.
42 Joseph Tonda (2000) 'Capital sorcier et travail de Dieu' [Capital sorcerer and the work of God], *Politique Africaine* 79: 48–65.
43 Paul Gifford (1994) 'Ghana's Charismatic Churches', *Journal of Religion in Africa* 24(3): 241–65, 253.
44 André Corten and André Mary (eds) (1990) *Imaginaires politiques et pentecôtisme: Afrique/Amérique* [Political imaginaries and pentecostalism: Africa and America] (Paris: Karthala), 102.
45 Joseph Tonda (2002) *La guérison divine en Afrique centrale (Congo, Gabon)* [Divine healing in Central Africa (Congo, Gabon)] (Paris: Karthala), 70–81.
46 Cimpric, 'Children accused of witchcraft', 15.
47 Mensah Adinkrah (2011) 'Child Witch Hunts in Contemporary Ghana', *Child Abuse and Neglect* 35(1): 741–752.
48 Richard Dowden (2006) 'The Small Witches of Kinshasa', *Guardian*, 3 Mar., http://www.theguardian.com/world/2006/mar/03/outlook.development (accessed June 2016).

49 Jérôme Ballet, Claudine Dumbi and Benoît Lallau (2007) 'Enfants sorciers à Kinshasa (RD Congo): De la décomposition à la marchandisation' [Child witches in Kinshasa (DRC): From decomposition to commercialisation], paper presented at the Seventh Conference of the HDCA: 'Ideas changing history', 17–20 Sept., New School, New York City.
50 Molina, 'Invention of Witchcraft', 19.
51 Ferdinand Ezembe (2009) *L'enfant africain et ses univers* [The African child and its universes] (Paris: Karthala), 91.
52 Cimpric, 'Children Accused of Witchcraft', 12–24.
53 Cahn, 'Poor Children', 413.
54 Ibid.
55 De Boeck and Jacquemin, 'Le "deuxième monde"', 38–40.
56 Filip de Boeck and Marie-Françoise Plissart (2004) *Kinshasa: Tales of the Invisible City* (Ghent: Ludion), 288.
57 Cahn, 'Poor Children', 420.
58 Filipovic and McCormick, 'Angels and Demons'.
59 Gifford, 'Ghana's Charismatic Churches', 20.
60 John H. Leith (1982) *Creeds of the Churches: A Reader in Christian Doctrine from the Bible to the Present* (Westminster: John Knox Press), 615.
61 Adinkrah, 'Child Witch Hunts', 750.
62 Filipovic and McCormick, 'Angels and Demons'.
63 Adam Ashforth (2005) *Witchcraft, Violence and Democracy in South Africa* (Chicago, IL: University of Chicago Press), 53.
64 Filipovic and McCormick, 'Angels and Demons'.
65 Mark A. Noll (2001) *American Evangelical Christianity: An Introduction* (Oxford: Blackwell), 54–67.
66 Tonda, *La guérison divine*, 44.
67 Marks, 'Human Rights', 70–5.
68 Molina, 'Child Witches', 27–30.
69 Ruth Marshall-Fratani, 'Prosperité miraculeuse: Les pasteurs pentecôtistes et l'argent de Dieu au Nigeria' [Miraculous prosperity: pentecostal pastors and God's money in Nigeria], *Politique Africaine* 83: 24–44.
70 Samuel Zalinga (2010) 'Religion, Economic Development and Cultural Change: The Contradictory Role of Pentecostal Christianity in Sub-Saharan Africa', *Journal of Third World Studies* 7(1): 43–62, 50.
71 Joel E. Tishkin and Andreas Heuser (2015) 'Africa Always Brings us Something New: A Historiography of African Zionist and Pentecostal Christianities', *Religion* 45(2): 153–73.
72 Tonda, *La guérison divine*, 36.
73 Jeanne H. Kilde (2002) *When Church Became Theatre: The Transformation of Evangelical Worship and Architecture in 19th Century America* (Oxford: Oxford University Press).
74 Douglas A. Sweeney (2005) *The American Evangelical Story: A History of the Movement* (New York: Baker), 55.
75 Gifford, 'Charismatic Churches': 19.
76 Sweeney, *American Evangelical Story*, 80.
77 Filipovic and McCormick, 'Angels and Demons'.
78 Tonda, *Divine Healing*, 108–10.
79 Mbembe, 'The Thing', 143–70.
80 Sweeney, *American Evangelical Story*, 72.
81 Gifford, 'Ghana's Charismatic Churches', 3.
82 Comaroff and Comaroff, 'Occult Economies', 279–303.

83 Sipke Shaughnessey (2013) 'The Modern Magic in Africa's Witchcraft Industry', Think Africa Press, 13 Jan., http://thinkafricapress.com/society/african-witchcraft-modern-reality (accessed Feb. 2014).
84 Diane Ciekawy and Peter Geschiere (1998) 'Containing Witchcraft: Conflicting Scenarios in Post-Colonial Africa', *African Studies Review* 41(3): 1–14.
85 Ibid.
86 Marks, 'Human Rights', 57–78.
87 Ciekawy and Geschiere, 'Containing Witchcraft', 1–14.
88 Cimpric, 'Children Accused of Witchcraft', 9–15.
89 De Boeck and Jacquemin, 'Le "deuxième monde"', 32–57.
90 Bhabha, *Location of Culture*, 3–19.

Chapter 17

The view from law and new governance

A critical appraisal of hybridity in peace and development studies

George Wilson

Introduction

In legal scholarship, hybridity is known in a variety of different fields and is used to describe a variety of different situations. In comparative constitutional law, hybridity is used refer to 'mixity' i.e. the coexistence of diverse, discrete, state legal traditions within a single jurisdiction or, less typically, the coexistence of state law and non-state norms.[1] Conversely, for regulationists, hybridity is used to refer to the combination of governance instruments with different origins.[2] A common example is private law tendering and contracting for services of public interest. More recently, hybridity has also been explored in relation to international human rights law.[3]

Somewhat underappreciated is the use of hybridity when investigating the relationship between law and 'new' governance. New approaches to governance are characterised by their departure from command-and-control regulation, the involvement of actors other than those formally tied to governments, and the absence of a traditional, overarching legal framework.[4] As such, new governance is 'less rigid, less prescriptive, less committed to uniform outcomes, and less hierarchical in nature'[5] than old(er) approaches to governance. Thus, law is not concerned exclusively with the achievement of specific outcomes; rather it can be understood as underpinning and encouraging autonomous modes of adjustment.

In the European Union (EU), the 'Open Method of Coordination' (OMC) is arguably the most prominent example of new governance. The OMC provides a framework for Member States to coordinate their national policies towards achieving common goals, in policy areas including employment, social inclusion and social protection. In similarity with other new governance processes, the OMC is based upon jointly identified and defined objectives, jointly established measurement instruments, and a comparison of performance and exchange of best practice between Member States. The OMC is frequently described as a 'soft' law instrument.[6] Unlike 'hard' EU law directives, regulations and decisions, the OMC is non-binding and non-justiciable. Often debates about the desirability of the OMC are framed in terms of the positives and negatives of soft law versus those of hard law. This distinction can be understood as turning on the issue of power; hard law attaches stronger sanctions and is more readily enforceable than soft law. Although challenged,[7] such a focus remains useful, especially when comparing hybridity between disciplines.

In the field of peace and development studies, a significant body of research on hybridity has developed in a relatively short period of time.[8] In similarity with literature on law and new governance, power is often the main focus of investigation, e.g. between the hegemon and subaltern.[9] Indeed, hybridity has challenged traditional understandings of power in both fields. This contribution explores the synergies between hybridity as understood in literature on law and new governance, and in peace and development studies. The view of hybridity from law and new governance is employed as a backdrop against which to critically appraise hybridity in peace and development studies. Consequently, a more nuanced understanding of hybridity is presented, that rejects inclusivity in favour of greater specificity. Hybridity is forwarded as a concept capable of accounting for change beyond the initial combination of modes of governance, to their progressive development together. This understanding is argued to hold the promise of improving legal regulation and the design of international peace interventions.

In what follows, the conceptual underpinnings of hybridity are considered first. Literature from postcolonial theory and peace and development studies is argued to present an ambiguous understanding of hybridity. Second, Trubek and Trubek's framework for describing the relationship between law and new governance is used as a basis upon which to evaluate hybridity in peace and development studies. Examples of EU law and United Nations (UN) interventions are employed to illustrate each of Trubek and Trubek's varieties of 'coexistence', with particular attention paid to 'transformative hybridity'. Third, the idea of 'programmatic development' is presented as a way of explaining the emergence of unplanned hybrids, with each of Trubek and Trubek's varieties of coexistence linked as stages in their development.

The conceptual underpinnings of hybridity

As Kraidy recognises, 'hybridity has entered many academic arenas, ranging from traditional disciplines like literature, anthropology, and sociology to interdisciplinary venues such as post-colonial theory and performance studies'.[10] The conceptual underpinnings of hybridity are most clearly articulated in postcolonial theory, in particular, postcolonial cultural theory, with regard to modern cultural, social and political relationships.[11] Peterson explains that the appropriation and development of the term in postcolonial cultural theory has 'found increasing currency in the analysis of externally driven peace and development interventions'.[12] Indeed, in *Hybrid Forms of Peace: From Everyday Agency to Post-Liberalism*, Richmond and Mitchell describe how the process of 'hybridisation' occurs at the 'site' where international peace interventions meet 'the every-day activities, needs, interests and experiences of local groups'.[13] This conceptualisation – of hybridity occurring between different entities or groups, unequal in terms of power – is most commonly associated with the work of Homi Bhabha.

For Bhabha, hybridity occurs within a 'third space', between the dominant and subaltern.[14] It results from an 'immanent difference, distortion and fracture'[15] *within* identities, that creates a 'contact zone'[16] for relationships *between* identities. This is said to allow both influence over each another and,[17] as claimed by Bhabha, for 'the possibility of a cultural hybrid that entertains difference without an assumed or imposed hierarchy'.[18] Freedman suggests that Bhabha's contact zone may be a metaphorical or a physical space,[19] in the case of the latter, enabling his work to be extended along structural/functionalist lines to hybrid norms and institutions. However, this development is still premised upon an implicit understanding of hybridity as a process of combination.

In response to concerns that Bhabha's conceptualisation of hybridity leads to 'in-betweenness' or liminality, contemporary accounts have suggested that hybridity should be viewed as a process that gives rise to new transcultural forms.[20] As such, the allure of hybridity appears to lie in its perceived ability to transcend absolutes (Western versus non-Western, modern versus traditional, universal versus particular) and, in doing so, uncovering and acknowledging the complexity or 'messiness' of reality. Surprisingly, given the myriad ways in which hybridity has been conceptualised, ideas regarding 'the series of iterations and in-betweens'[21] that lead to the creation of hybrids have remained somewhat underdeveloped. The division between hybridity as in-betweenness and hybridity as a process is apparent in literature on peace and development studies.[22] The work of Richmond and Mac Ginty, respectively, provide examples of these configurations. Richmond's 'local-liberal hybridity' describes the relationship between 'the local' and 'the international', where both coexist, rather than assimilate or dominate.[23] Although scope is provided for local resistance, modification and adaptation to the liberal peace, 'local-liberal' hybridity is said to represent a combination of different political practices.[24] Mac Ginty's 'hybrid peace' considers the role of agency and structure in the process of hybridisation, including the power of liberal agents to enforce and incentivise compliance and local actors to resist and maintain alternatives.[25] These processes are presented as taking place against a background of conflict and disparities in power between liberal agents and local actors.[26]

As Freedman recognises, hybridity can thus be understood in multiple ways: either as a theory, as a process and/or as an entity.[27] The result is a trade-off: as hybridity becomes more conceptually inclusive, its explanatory potential is diminished. Kraidy's challenge for scholars to develop 'tools to tackle [this] vexing ambiguity'[28] must be accepted. Literature from law and new governance and peace and development studies considers hybrid entities as outputs but approaches the inputs of theory and process in different ways.[29] The comparison of examples from both disciplines illustrates the competing understandings of hybridity common to each. Whereas research has often focused upon hybridity as a process of combination, little work has been undertaken on the transformative potential of hybridisation.

Hybridity, law and new governance

The publication in 2002 of Scott and Trubek's article *Mind the Gap: Law and New Approaches to Governance in the European Union* gave rise to a new area of research in the field of European law and legal studies.[30] In the time that has since passed, academic lawyers, political scientists and sociologists have investigated the 'phenomena' of new governance and its relationship to law.[31] This is described in various ways but increasingly with reference to hybridity. The framework presented below is developed from this literature and is employed as a basis against which hybridity – as understood in peace and development studies – is critically appraised.

When investigating the relationship between law and new governance, de Burca and Scott suggest that law may be blind to new governance (the 'gap' thesis), that law and new governance may coexist and engage with each other (the 'hybridity' thesis) or that new governance has demanded, and will increasingly demand, a reconceptualisation of our understanding of law (the 'transformation' thesis).[32]

With regard to the hybridity thesis, de Burca and Scott distinguish between three types of hybridity: (1) fundamental/baseline hybridity; (2) instrumental/developmental hybridity; and (3) default hybridity (or governance in the shadow of law).[33] To varying degrees, each explores different ways of securing constructive interaction between law and new governance. For de Burca and Scott, law and new governance are mutually independent and mutually sustaining, with the potential to play off each other's strengths and weaknesses.[34] Furthermore, de Burca and Scott suggest that hybridity may be viewed either as a long-term phenomenon or as a transition from a regime of formal legal ordering to a wholehearted embrace of new governance.[35]

When de Burca and Scott's types of hybridity are considered more closely, each implies a different understanding of the respective roles of law and new governance. First, for fundamental/baseline hybridity, law acts as a framework for new governance.[36] New governance is complementary to, but not a replacement for, law. Second, for instrumental/developmental hybridity, law's role as a framework for new governance is conceived as being dynamic not static; through interaction new governance processes can aid in the application and development of legal norms.[37] Third, for default hybridity, legal rules represent penalties to be paid for not participating in new governance processes.[38]

De Burca and Scott's account of hybridity is rearticulated by Trubek and Trubek but with a specific focus on 'situations of real integration and mutual dependence'.[39] Trubek and Trubek refer to situations of complementarity and rivalry between law and new governance as varieties of 'coexistence', whilst reserving the label hybridity for transformative relationships where law and new governance develop together. This categorisation of complementarity, rivalry and transformation can also be applied to international peace interventions and their reception by local actors. Parallels can be drawn between law and international peace interventions and new governance and local actors, specifically, in terms of disparities in power; centralisation is pitted against decentralisation, singular against multilevel authority, and relative stability against flexibility, etc. Ter Haar and Copeland suggest that Trubek and Trubek's framework can be refined to better reflect these differences;[40] considering law and new governance as specific types of governance allows their framework to be applied to scenarios beyond those particular to EU law, i.e. international peace interventions, like EU law, are specific modes of governance. Trubek and Trubek's framework is useful for categorising examples from peace and development studies in support of a more transformative understanding of hybridity. Below, EU law and UN interventions are considered as examples of complementarity (non-discrimination and Sierra Leone); rivalry (industrial relations and Liberia); and transformation (the environment and East Timor).

Complementarity

Situations of complementarity are described by Trubek and Trubek as occurring between law and new governance when both are used to pursue similar goals.[41] Complementarity is often employed where complex problems require a variety of different forms of intervention in order to secure successful political outcomes.[42]

The efforts of the EU to combat discrimination against women in the workplace exhibit complementarity between law and new governance. Legal instruments including Treaty articles and Directives, new governance processes that coordinate policies between Member States, and financial support schemes underwritten by the European Structural Funds, are directed to achieve equality between the sexes. Legal rights protect workers from discrimination on the grounds of gender in the workplace, whilst the 'European Employment Strategy' attempts to influence national policies and challenge discriminatory behaviour through guidelines, reporting, surveillance and facilitating the exchange of best practice between Member States.

Trubek and Trubek describe complementarity as a variety of coexistence rather than hybridity based upon the limited interaction between law and new governance. Instruments such as Directives and the European Employment Strategy operate independently of one another, rather than together, in furtherance of gender equality. Complementarity in this form is visible in the attempts of the UN to promote formal over informal political institutions after the civil war of 1991–2002 in Sierra Leone. Instead of falling into disuse, non-state institutions, such as religious leaders, village elders and secret societies have continued to exist alongside state institutions.[43] These informal institutions are increasingly seen as complements to formal institutions such as parliament in the search for a sustainable and lasting peace.[44] However, unlike situations of rivalry, these different modes of governance are not considered as alternatives to each other; religious leaders perform functions within local communities that cannot effectively be performed by parliament and vice versa, e.g. the punishment of less serious crimes and the provision of adequate sanitation.

Rivalry

Trubek and Trubek suggest that situations of rivalry are possible where legal and new governance processes both exist as alternative routes to the same outcome.[45] A conscious decision may be made to offer a new governance process as a substitute for a legal instrument where it is considered desirable or where a new governance process is viewed as a preferred approach to a particular issue.[46]

The European Social Dialogue (ESD) is a formal EU industrial relations process, allowing representatives of management and labour (known as 'social partners') to enter into agreements on behalf of their members. Two strands to the ESD can be identified: the first is a tripartite process, involving social partners and EU institutions, and results in binding EU law by way of Directives; the second is a bipartite process, involving social partners independently of EU institutions, and results in non-binding agreements that can later be transposed by Directives. Representatives of management favour the second route as the limited involvement of institutions such as the European Commission until the transposition of an agreement mean they have greater influence over its potential content and form.

The UN Mission in Liberia was established in 2003 to support the implementation of the ceasefire agreement reached at the end of the second civil war of 1999–2003. The mission protects UN staff and facilities, provides assistance for humanitarian and human rights activities and has assisted in the reform of security services (including the training of a new police force). Liberia's new police force is still heavily dependent upon the UN police for support.[47] In the provision of local security, competition has emerged between the police and neighbourhood watch groups. Liberians consider the police the legal but not the legitimate providers of security.[48] Consequently, disputes are common over who holds ultimate responsibility for the investigation and preparation for prosecution of less serious crimes such as theft.

Such interaction between modes of governance is a feature of situations of rivalry. However, this interaction is often negative. Drawing upon the example of the ESD, representatives of management are keen to utilise the second route discussed, whereas those of labour prefer the first as support from the European Commission addresses their inequality in bargaining power. Conflict between the social partners over which route of the ESD is used has been a feature since its inception. Conversely, positive interaction, that is supportive rather than disruptive of the relationship between modes of governance, forms the basis of transformation. Through positive interaction between modes of governance a new entity is created that is distinct from its component parts. Comparisons can be drawn with symbiosis: as the close and long-term interaction between two different biological species with an emphasis on cooperation and dependency. Trubek and Trubek's categorisation of only transformation – and not complementarity or rivalry – as hybridity can be read as an attempt to emphasise this uniqueness.

Transformation

Trubek and Trubek describe four different ways in which transformation may occur.[49] That which best matches the positive interaction, cooperation and dependency characteristic of hybridity detailed above, is when law is used to set general norms and new governance processes are designed to elaborate and concretise their form.

This relationship between law and new governance forms the basis against which Trubek and Trubek investigate transformation. Environmental protection is widely considered to be the first policy area in which such experimental forms of governance have been prioritised at EU level.[50] The Water Framework Directive[51] (WFD) is cited by Trubek and Trubek as an important example of hybridity and is suggested by Sabel and Zeitlin as pre-empting the future transformation of EU law.[52] The WFD regulates water quality by setting open-ended standards at EU level that are further developed at Member State level. Terms such as 'good ecological status' and 'good water quality' are defined in different ways between Member States.[53] Through a 'Common Implementation Strategy' (CIS), new governance processes are used to feed back Member State standards to an EU-level working group that adjusts the WFD to reflect new shared understandings. This method of standard production is dependent upon continued interaction between the WFD and the CIS for success; both modes of governance work together to ensure standards remain up to date.

The 'Commission for Reception, Truth and Reconciliation' in East Timor was established by the UN Transitional Administration in 2002 and sought to address violations of human rights and international humanitarian law between 1974 and 1999 (beginning with the departure of the colonial Portuguese and ending with independence from the invading Indonesians). The UN-led Commission combined 'Special Panels for Serious Crimes' with a 'Community Reconciliation Programme'. Known as CRPs, Community Reconciliation Programmes sought to include indigenous restorative justice processes within the formal UN Commission system.[54] The engagement of the Commission with traditional justice processes resonates with hybrid understandings of peacebuilding.[55] However, this literature neglects the progressive development of the relationship between the Commission and the CRPs that is characteristic of a more transformative understanding of hybridisation. Experience with the limited uptake of the CRPs led to the restructuring of the Commission system in order to encourage greater engagement with the CRPs. Here, interaction between modes of governance improved their joint operation and furthered the development of a 'governance architecture' supportive of hybridity.[56]

Programmatic development

This contribution has sought to forward a more specific understanding of hybridity, differentiating situations of complementarity and rivalry between modes of governance from those of transformation; with a focus upon positive interaction, dependency and progressive development. However, the utility of exploring varieties of coexistence extends beyond outlining the contours of what hybridity actually is. Trubek and Trubek's varieties of coexistence can be linked as stages in the development of unplanned hybrids, suggesting a theory of hybridity as a process; beginning with complementarity, undergoing rivalry and ending with transformation. This development can be read as a response to Peterson's observation that ideas regarding how unplanned hybrids develop have been neglected by scholarship.[57]

Programmatic development provides an alternative lens through which to view the joint operation of modes of governance, specifically, in terms of the potential for progression from situations of complementarity or rivalry to transformation.[58] Moreover, this nascent theory of hybridity as a process holds the potential of being able to inform the design of EU law and UN interventions in order to encourage the development of situations of transformation. Implicit in this suggestion is the opinion that hybridity is a positive phenomenon and can improve methods of governing.[59] Below, preliminary observations are made regarding the conditions under which progress between the stages of complementarity, rivalry and transformation occurs. These are presented with the intention of providing a basis for future research on programmatic development and, in particular, its application to real-world problems.

The role of conflict in the development of unplanned hybrids is recognised both in literature on law and new governance and peace and development studies.[60] Conflict can occur at multiple levels e.g. personal, relational, structural and cultural, and has been described as relating to 'immediate problems as well as underlying causes in the development of hybrids'.[61] Furthermore, conflict is often strategic, with actors competing over 'short-term gains as well as long-term perspectives'.[62] Progress towards hybridity is dependent upon productive use being made of conflict; situations of rivalry challenge held perceptions and require compromised be reached in order for the cooperative relationships characteristic of transformation to develop. Sociological insights stress the importance of this process for inducing self-reflection and the ability of competing actors to better understand one another's positions.

For productive use to be made of conflict, space must be provided for deliberation. As an example, standards set by Member States under the WFD are subject to peer review through the process of 'intercalibration'.[63] Member States evaluate one another's standards with the aim of developing universally applicable regulations. Similarly, truth and reconciliation commissions also provide spaces for deliberation. Participants from both sides of conflict engage with each other in special fora (e.g. public hearings) with the aim of creating authoritative reports of past events. However, deliberative processes have limited success if they fail to adequately represent the views and opinions of the actors they seek to reconcile.

Transformation requires that those involved in governing are representative of the constituencies from which they are drawn. Ensuring effective representation contributes towards creating a sense of ownership over decision-making processes. The revision of the commission system in East Timor led to a greater uptake of CRPs and a sense amongst local actors that their contributions were taken seriously. More sophisticated forms of actor representation are possible with progression from situations of rivalry towards transformation. The WFD experiments with involving civic society actors in the definition of standards (an area of competence until recently the sole preserve of Member States). Moreover, actors are consulted at 'test-sites' as opposed to across the EU-28. Facilitating transformation may require more rigid forms of representation but, once reached, allows for greater flexibility.

Conclusion

It is testament to the appeal of hybridity across disciplinary boundaries that its influence has developed so quickly. With regard to hybridity in legal scholarship, specific understandings have developed in fields including constitutional law, regulatory governance and human rights. As with peace and development studies, these legal approaches suffer from what Kraidy describes as 'vexing ambiguity'.[64] Contributions in this volume evidence this; hybridity is used to refer to the combination of generations of human rights and to situations of legal pluralism.[65] This contribution has sought to forward a more specific understanding of hybridity that emphasises its transformative potential; combination may be the first step in the process of hybridisation between entities but – through interaction and cooperation – a relationship of dependency develops that gives rise to new structural forms.

This understanding is developed from Trubek and Trubek's work on the relationship between law and new governance in the EU. Comparing examples from EU law with UN interventions illustrates the competing understandings common to each and allows situations of transformation, and thus hybridity, between modes of governance to be more clearly differentiated from those of coexistence and rivalry. Directing the focus of Trubek and Trubek's framework towards modes of governance allows it to be applied to UN interventions (both liberal agents and local actors govern using their own specific methods). This serves as a basis against which to critically appraise understandings of hybridity in peace and development studies. Although different modalities of hybridity have been explored in this literature before, such systemisation has not been undertaken.

Aside from conceptual rigour and providing a more accurate description of hybridity, this approach has important implications for UN interventions as well as EU law. Although considerably different fields of study, by better understanding hybridity, legal regulation and peacebuilding programmes can be more effectively designed. Investigating hybridity as a process casts light upon the dynamics required in order for the operationalisation of transformation. The introduction of programmatic development highlights the importance of making productive use of conflict, providing adequate space for deliberation and ensuring the effective representation of actors involved in governance processes. Further research should be directed towards the development of this theory and its application to real-world problems. Existing UN interventions could be improved by creating the conditions necessary for progress from conflict between liberal actors and local agents to cooperation. Although this contribution is perhaps unusual, given the disciplines that are its focus, only by challenging our existing understandings can the growing appeal of hybridity across disciplinary boundaries be justified.

Notes

1 Consequently, a division can be made between legal and normative forms of pluralism; see Louisa Riches's contribution in Ch. 10 of this volume.
2 Michiel A. Heldeweg (2013) 'Hybrid Regulation as a Legal Design Challenge', in Aurelia A. L. Colombi Ciacchi, Michiel A. Heldeweg, Bernd M. J. van der

Meulen and Richard Neerhof (eds), *Law and Governance: Beyond the Public-Private Law Divide?* (The Hague: Eleven International Publishing), 105–38, 105.

3 Rosa Freedman (2013) "Third Generation' Rights: Is there Room for Hybrid Constructs within International Human Rights Law?', *Cambridge Journal of International and Comparative Law* 2(4): 935–59, 935.

4 Gráinne de Búrca and Joanne Scott (2006) 'Introduction: New Governance, Law and Constitutionalism', in Gráinne de Búrca and Joanne Scott (eds), *Law and New Governance in the EU and US* (Oxford: Hart), 1–14, 2.

5 Ibid.

6 See David M. Trubek, Patrick Cottrell and Mark Nance (2006) '"Soft Law", "Hard Law" and EU Integration', in de Búrca and Scott, *Law and New Governance,* 65–96.

7 See Mark Dawson (2014) 'Soft Law and the Rule of Law in the European Union: Revision or Redundancy?', in Antoine Vauchez and Bruno de Witte (eds), *Lawyering Europe: European Law as a Transnational Social Field* (Oxford: Hart), 221–42.

8 For a prominent, early example from peace and conflict studies, see Kevin P. Clements, Volker Boege, Anne Brown, Wendy Foley and Anna Nolan (2007) 'State Building Reconsidered: The Role of Hybridity in the Formation of Political Order', *Political Science* 59(1): 45–56.

9 Jan Nederveen Pieterse, 'Hybridity, So What? The Anti-Hybridity Backlash and the Riddles of Recognition', *Theory, Culture and Society* 18(2–3): 219–45, 224.

10 Marwan M. Kraidy (2005) *Hybridity, or the Cultural Logic of Globalization* (Philadelphia, PA: Temple University Press), 2.

11 Jenny H. Peterson (2012) 'A Conceptual Unpacking of Hybridity: Accounting for Notions of Power, Politics and Progress in Analyses of Aid-Driven Interfaces', *Journal of Peacebuilding and Development* 7(2): 9–22, 9, 11.

12 Ibid.; whereas Peterson's focus on hybridity is analytical, Richmond and Mitchell's is empirical.

13 Oliver P. Richmond and Audra Mitchell (2011) 'Introduction – Towards a Post-Liberal Peace: Exploring Hybridity via Everyday Forms of Resistance, Agency and Autonomy', in Richmond and Mitchell (eds), *Hybrid Forms of Peace: From Everyday Agency to Post Liberalism* (Basingstoke: Palgrave Macmillan), 1–38, 1.

14 Homi K. Bhabha (1994) *The Location of Culture* (London: Routledge), 52–6.

15 Gëzim Visoka (2012) 'Three Levels of Hybridisation Practices in Post-Conflict Kosovo', *Journal of Peacebuilding and Development* 7(2): 23–36, 25.

16 Bill Ashcroft, Gareth Griffiths and Helen Tiffin (2000) *Post-Colonial Studies: The Key Concepts* (London: Routledge), 118.

17 Visoka, 'Three Levels', 25.

18 Bhabha, *Location of Culture,* 4.

19 Freedman, '"Third Generation" Rights', 941.

20 Ashcroft *et al., Post-Colonial Studies,* 118.

21 Peterson, 'Conceptual Unpacking', 12.

22 Visoka, 'Three Levels', 25.

23 Oliver P. Richmond (2010) 'Resistance and the Post-Liberal Peace', *Millennium: Journal of International Studies* 38(3): 665–92, 687.

24 Oliver P. Richmond (2011) *A Post-Liberal Peace* (London: Routledge), 189.

25 Roger Mac Ginty (2011) *International Peacebuilding and Local Resistance: Hybrid Forms of Peace* (Basingstoke: Palgrave Macmillan), 69.

26 Ibid.

27 Freedman, '"Third Generation" Rights', 940–2.

28 Kraidy, *Hybridity,* 70.

29 Hybridity as understood in terms of inputs and outputs is developed in Freedman, '"Third Generation" Rights', 940–1.

30 Joanne Scott and David M. Trubek (2002) 'Mind the Gap: Law and New Approaches to Governance in the European Union', *European Law Journal* 8(1): 1–18, 1.
31 Respectively, important contributions include Mark Dawson (2011) *New Governance and the Transformation of European Law: Coordinating EU Social Law and Policy* (Cambridge: Cambridge University Press); Adrienne Héritier and Martin Rhodes (eds) (2011) *New Modes of Governance in Europe: Governing in the Shadow of Hierarchy* (Basingstoke: Palgrave Macmillan); and Jonathan Zeitlin and David M. Trubek (eds) (2003) *Governing Work and Welfare in a New Economy: European and American Experiments* (Oxford: Oxford University Press).
32 De Búrca and Scott, 'Introduction', 4–10.
33 Ibid. 6–9.
34 Ibid. 6.
35 Ibid.
36 Ibid. 7.
37 Ibid. 8.
38 Ibid. 9.
39 David M. Trubek and Louise G. Trubek (2007) '*New Governance and Legal Regulation: Complementarity, Rivalry, and Transformation*, University of Wisconsin Law School Legal Studies Research Paper Series 1047 (Madison, WI: University of Wisconsin), 1, 5. This quote accompanies the text with n. 10.
40 Beryl ter Haar and Paul Copeland, 'EU Youth Policy: A Waterfall of Softness', 12th Biennial EUSA Conference, Boston, MA, 3–5 Mar., http://www.euce.org/eusa/2011/papers/11l_terhaar.pdf (accessed Apr. 2016), 1, 3. This point is reiterated by Kenneth A. Armstrong (2012) 'EU Social Policy and the Governance Architecture of Europe 2020', *Transfer: European Review of Labour and Research* 18(3): 285–300, 285.
41 Trubek and Trubek, *New Governance*, 6.
42 Ibid.
43 Patrick Tom (2013) 'In Search of Emancipatory Hybridity: The Case of Post-War Sierra Leone', *Peacebuilding* 1(2): 239–55, 247.
44 Ibid.
45 Trubek and Trubek, *New Governance*, 9.
46 Ibid.
47 Volker Boege (2014) 'Shaping Peace in Liberia and the Solomon Islands – the Role of "Illiberal" Actors', *Pax in Nuce*, 10 Oct., http://paxinnuce.com/2014/10/10/shaping-peace-in-liberia-and-the-solomon-islands-the-role-of-illiberal-actors (accessed Apr. 2016).
48 Ibid.
49 Trubek and Trubek also suggest that transformation may occur when law is used to set parameters for the operation of new governance processes; when law is used as a 'safety net' in the event that new governance processes prove ineffective; or when law is used to set minimum standards and new governance processes are made available to those who meet them. See Trubek and Trubek, *New Governance*, 11.
50 Charles F. Sabel and Jonathan Zeitlin (2008) 'Learning from Difference: The New Architecture of Experimentalist Governance in the EU', *European Law Journal* 14(3): 271–327, 309.
51 Directive 2000/60/EC of the European Parliament and of the Council 23 October 2000 establishing a framework for Community action in the field of water policy [2000] OJ L327/1.
52 Sabel and Zeitlin, 'Learning from Difference', 309–10.

53 See Articles 2 and 4 of the WFD, respectively.
54 Simon Robins (2012) 'Challenging the Therapeutic Ethic: A Victim-Centered Evaluation of Transitional Justice Process in Timor-Leste', *International Journal of Transitional Justice* 6(1): 83–105.
55 See Mac Ginty, *International Peacebuilding*.
56 The phrase 'governance architecture' is used to refer to the operation of distinct modes of governance together in pursuit of the same goal, e.g. the promotion of justice process in East Timor.
57 Peterson, 'Conceptual Unpacking', 12.
58 An event is said to be programmatic if it occurs in an iterative or step-by-step way.
59 Here, governing is used to refer to the act of governance, inclusive of different modalities.
60 See Trubek and Trubek, *New Governance*, and Richmond and Mitchell, 'Introduction'.
61 Paul Gready and Simon Robins (2014) 'From Transitional to Transformative Justice: A New Agenda for Practice', *International Journal of Transitional Justice* 8(3): 339–61, 351.
62 Ibid.
63 Trubek and Trubek, *New Governance*, 19.
64 Kraidy, *Hybridity*, 70.
65 See Ben Warwick's and Louisa Riches's contributions in Chapters 12 and 10 of this volume.

Conclusion

Chapter 18

After hybridity?

Gëzim Visoka

Introduction

The contributions in this edited volume have explored hybridity from an inter-disciplinary perspective, which indicates its conceptual importance and potential applicability across different epistemological fields. Across different disciplines, renewed interest in hybridity has come to signify the interweaving processes between different distinct social entities permitting collusion and complementarity as well as transformation. While some of the chapters have found hybridity useful to examine a wide range of topics, there is a general scepticism on the conceptual viability and empirical validity of hybridity when applied across different fields. Rather than summarising the contributions of this edited volume, this concluding chapter provides a more nuanced examination of the merits and drawbacks of hybridity in the specific context of peace and conflict studies and offers new research avenues for addressing some of the fallacies and criticism. Hybridity in peace and conflict studies has come to represent both the limits of liberal peace interventions and the transition towards post-liberal forms of peace that take into account local agency and context when designing peace interventions. Critical scholars of peacebuilding consider hybridity as a useful analytical device to reveal fundamental problems of externally imposed and top-down interventions in the area of statebuilding, reconciliation, peace-making and development, and highlight the power of local resistance and indigenous forms of governance, justice and welfare. Thus, hybridity has also a performative and emancipatory function, as the acts of resistance and coexistence can open space for transformation of power relations, increase equality, address claims for justice and welfare, and liberate the local subjects from domination. Nevertheless, hybridity in peace and conflict studies has been criticised for conceptual inappropriateness in accounting for post-conflict situations and the empirical inaccuracy of emancipatory power of hybrid forms of peace.

Undoubtedly, hybridity is an important concept which is alighted with the postmodern commitment to break the solidity and supremacy of certain concepts that do not hold much empirical accuracy, thus opening up the debate to more plural forms of knowledge and agency. In general, hybrid peace is situated amid postmodern ontologies because it avoids singular and universal truths; promotes plurality of divergence perspectives; pursues uncertainty; and recognises particularities. However, hybridity as an approach that explains fusion of different entities with distinct identities and power ratios has the tendency both to reinforce existing binaries and create new hybrid entities, which risk undergoing conceptual enclosure and solidifying in turn. The normative aspects of hybrid peace risk being affiliated with positivist prescriptive assertions and thus throw up the important question as to how to rescue hybrid approaches in peace and conflict studies from such an affiliation with positivism, modernity, solidity and certainty. This chapter charts a preliminary proposal for expanding the conceptual avenues of hybridity. It proposes three alternative conceptual frameworks – liquidity, assemblage and figuration – to decouple hybridity from prescriptive and normative assertions and restore its explanatory potential as an analytical device. These three alternative concepts supplement hybridity by highlighting the spatio-temporality of relations, processes and agencies that shape peace and contribute to reconceptualising the epistemological understanding of hybrid peace as an unintended figuration of liquid assemblages.

This chapter is organised as follows. Arguments in favour of hybridity in peace and conflict studies are first discussed to examine the analytical power of hybrid peace and disentangle its multi-faceted dimensions. Some of the contributions in this book that are in favour of hybridity are examined to reveal the contribution they make to broader debates. Following this, the criticism of hybridity is discussed to unpack some of the key disagreements that challenge the conceptual viability and empirical reliability of hybridity. Some of the contributions in this book are situated here to explore the limitations of hybridity across different disciplines. The second part of the chapter explores ways in which Bauman's liquidity, Deleuze's assemblage and Elias's figuration could complement and supplement hybridity debates. The chapter concludes with a brief discussion of what an expanded new research agenda on hybridity would look like.

In defence of hybridity

In the past five years, hybridity in peacebuilding and development has emerged as another 'trendy' concept which seeks to invigorate debates on how to understand and build peace and states after violent conflict. It is symptomatic of the limits of liberal peace interventions and failure of externally imposed statebuilding, peacebuilding and development programmes. The early critiques of peacebuilding were entrenched in the ontological commitment not to produce problem-solving knowledge, and thus avoided providing any alternative solution to 'liberal peace'.[1]

In response, proponents of liberal peace have argued that the critique of liberal peace is inappropriate and incongruent with reality on the ground. They highlighted that, regardless of its shortcomings, there is no better alternative replacing liberal peacebuilding. Hence, hybrid approaches to peacebuilding have emerged inductively from analysing the limits of liberal peacebuilding in practice, which signified that peace intervention encountered hybridisation *with* rather than a liberalisation *of* local societies.[2] As the problem of peacebuilding for critical scholars has been the ineffectiveness of hegemonic, top-town interventionism, they have suggested as an alternative a contextualised and hybridised peace which would be more 'locally sustainable, resilient, and legitimate' compared to existing praxis.[3] One of the first uses of hybrid peace was in Richmond's work as early as 2005, where he notices certain epistemological potentials and the empirical traces of hybrid forms of peace.[4] However, the concept of hybridity started to become more popular in the work of Volker Boege *et al.* who used 'hybrid political orders' to describe the inability of external statebuilding to monopolise the use of control over the whole of society and the resilience of transitional and indigenous institutions that have governed historically societies that are different from the normalised understanding of the modern state.[5] In this context, hybrid political orders started to be used as an effort to break away from a Western and static measurement of contemporary statehood, which categorises other forms of statehood as fragile and weak states, stressing 'the positive potential rather than negative features of so-called fragile states'.[6] They argue that hybrid political orders are optimal outcomes of the collusion between external intervention and local agency and as such often are more likely to provide stability, effectiveness and legitimacy.

In peacebuilding studies, Oliver P. Richmond was one of the first to invoke hybridity as tool for developing 'an ontology that is not exclusive but is open to difference'.[7] He uses hybridity solely as a transitory concept for a more emancipatory peace, or in his words, to 'make liberal states, institutionalism, and governance viable in everyday liberal and non-liberal contexts'.[8] Later he elaborated his understanding of hybridity as 'local-liberal hybridity' to describe the interaction between 'the local' and 'the international', where both coexist rather than assimilate or dominate and where the locals resist, modify or adapt to the liberal peace.[9] For Richmond hybridity represents 'a transmutation of both the liberal and the local discourses of peace, even in view of their relatively unequal material relations and of course, their differences and similarities'.[10] He further makes a normative distinction between positive and negative hybrid peace. Positive hybrid peace is defined as 'complementary practices related to democracy, self-determination, agency, autonomy, solidarity, human rights and needs, and a rule of law, with customary social support networks, customary forms of governance and political order'.[11] Nevertheless, he does not exclude the possibility of a negative hybrid peace which he sees as being 'rigorously determined liberal institutionalism and market development solutions with patriarchal, feudal, communal, or sexist, practices'.[12]

From an early stage, debates on hybrid peace have been more sympathetic to the notion of hybridisation than hybridity, which tried to highlight the processual aspects of hybrid peace and avoid reproduction of static binaries. Roger Mac Ginty has conceptualised hybridity as a process focusing more systematically on conceptualising hybrid peace by exploring the interactions between top-down and external actors with bottom-up and local actors in the context of post-conflict peacebuilding and statebuilding. According to Mac Ginty, hybrid peace is:

> The result of the interplay of the following factors: the ability of liberal peace agents, networks and structures to enforce compliance with their will; the incentivising powers of liberal peace agents, networks and structures; the ability of local actors to resist, ignore, or adapt liberal peace interventions; and the ability of local actors, networks and structures to present and maintain alternative forms of peacemaking.[13]

For Mac Ginty, the hybrid peace framework seeks to 'capture and explain the process through which hybridization is perpetuated'.[14] Hybrid peace is a realist theory explaining the process and outcome of peacebuilding; realist not in the narrow meaning as often used in IR theories, but as used more broadly in political and social theory, which entails capturing the agencies, structures and relations that are temporal and contextual in nature. Mac Ginty and Richmond admit that hybridity is shifting towards 'more generous, and realistic, categories of institutions that can transcend strictly Weberian notions of the state and liberal institutionalism'.[15] Hybridity highlights the lack of autonomy among peacebuilding actors as well as pointing to the mixing and distorting processes that shape peace after conflict. Mac Ginty is well aware that binary combinations 'risk projecting oversimplified notions of human societies that are divided into discrete compartmentalized units'.[16] However, he insists that '[r]ather than a static model, the hybrid peace can be conceived as one of constant dynamism', whereby '[d]ifferent factors prevail in different contexts, on different issues, at different times'.[17] He further argues that 'notions of hybridism and peace encourage us to note how actors and institutions are capable of change, and become adept at managing change'.[18] In other words, hybridity is used instrumentally to open the space for potential emancipation, justice and equality in conflict-affected societies and utilised as 'a critical vehicle that allows us to look at alternatives'.[19]

The work of Oliver P. Richmond and Roger Mac Ginty on hybrid peace has also a political and practical dimension. One of the purposes of hybridity is to reveal the structural weaknesses of liberal peace and gradually promote an alternative peacebuilding agenda, which dedicates more resources and attention to local needs and culture beyond formal institutional interactions with local elites. Through the lens of hybridity, they seek to expose the hierarchical order of Western political agencies, cultures and modes of knowledge and show how in practice they interact and are mutually constitutive and affective to local, transitional and non-Western knowledge and practices. Richmond argues that '[c]alls to engage with the local or local-local, in the context of a hybrid outcome of the mediated encounter between the international and the local, imply a decolonisation of knowledge and a disaggregation of power'.[20]

Despite conceptual limitations and extensive scope for criticism, hybridity in peace and development interventions has served as an entry point for shaping broader debates on global governance, security studies and area studies. One particular spill-over area from the early debates on hybrid peace is the area of governance. In the context of governance, Anna K. Jarstad and Roberto Belloni define hybridity as 'a condition where liberal and illiberal norms, institutions, and actors coexist, interact, and even clash'.[21] Belloni argues that '[i]n hybrid peace governance, liberal elements coexist, and sometimes clash, with illiberal norms and practices'.[22] Hybridity-as-coexistence highlights the persistence of a gap between international and local agendas for peacebuilding. Nevertheless, Belloni is sympathetic to hybrid peace governance because for him it 'presents important advantages vis-à-vis the ideal-typical version of liberal peacebuilding', especially in providing political stability and grounded legitimacy to the very slow process of statebuilding and recovery after conflict.[23] As echoed by Belloni, hybridity 'suggests the need to move beyond the ontological and methodological dominance of Western actors and approaches and to engage with bottom-up, local views of politics and society'.[24]

The literature in support of hybrid peace has gradually grown to provide compelling evidence from different post-conflict case studies, and illustrate empirically the coexistence between external intervention and local indigenous mechanisms that operate as a local infrastructure for peace in the area of justice, community participation, dispute resolution and conflict prevention.[25] The author's own work on hybrid peace has focused on the institutional, public and hidden levels of hybridisation to understand better 'the figuration, articulation and impact of local agency in post-conflict societies'.[26] Laura McLeod has tried to develop a feminist approach to hybridity.[27] However, a 'hybrid turn' is not only evident within peace and conflict studies. Hybridity has become a trendy concept in security studies to describe hybrid nature of threats and responses to contemporary transnational security challenges.[28] Hybrid wars are defined as those conflicts which break down the 'classic distinctions between public and private, government/regular and rebel/irregular, and internal and external'.[29] The UN has launched several hybrid peace operations in partnership with regional organisations. The conflict in Ukraine and regional crisis in the Middle East have pushed security analysts to refer to these conflicts as 'hybrid wars', which signifies the merging of conventional military and unconventional civilian means of warfare, including irregular tactics, distortion of political institutions and criminal disorder. Unpacking this new understanding of warfare, two other concepts are being used: 'hybrid threats', to signify physical and unconventional threats, and 'hybrid security', which signifies merging the responses of regional security bodies to tackle hybrid nature of threats and warfare.

Some of the chapters in this volume have illustrated that hybridity can be applied across different disciplines to explain the interaction between different modes of knowledge, practices and social institutions. Ruth Houghton uses hybridity to explore the interaction between global civil society and international governmental organisations. She argues that hybridity provides a convincing conceptual framework to question state-centric understandings of decision-making in world politics, and thus illustrate empirically how NGOs shape international institutions to produce hybrid outcomes. The hybrid constituency of international organisations consisting of state and non-state actors highlights the hybrid nature of global governance, especially in the area of human rights. In other words, the multiple and multi-layered transactions in shaping global covenants reveals that the UN and other global and regional organisations who are often portrayed as liberal actors are actually hybrid products. While it is important to emphasise that global civil society can shape the global policy agenda, its power is not solid and varies from one situation to another. What is worth taking from this chapter is the necessity of expanding the analysis of hybridity not only in the context of the interactions between international and local actors within the peacebuilding, development and diplomacy frameworks, but also to disentangle the prior hybridisation practices within these global and regional organisations to understand how prior hybridisations are concealed and presented as ahistorical and solid blueprints for intervention in turbulent societies.

Similarly, Fiona de Londras's discussion of counter-terrorism strategies from the prism of hybridity in this book reveals the usefulness of the concept to expand the horizons for studying contemporary terrorism and political violence. Sam Fowles's chapter applies hybridity as a useful tool to deconstruct human rights abuses in African societies and unearth the structural causes of violence against children labelled as 'child witches', which are product of cultural hybridity of native African beliefs with external models of aggressive religiosity. He thus considers the added value of hybridity in serving as an entry point for understanding structural factors behind human rights abuses and broadening the base for investigating human rights in underdeveloped societies. Likewise, George Wilson's chapter examines hybridity in the context of law and new governance theories to illustrate conceptual and empirical similarities and differences with the typologies of hybridity in the context of peace and development studies. Building on the legal literature, Wilson concludes that hybridity more often than not leads to transformation and formation of new entities rather than complementarity, coexistence and revelry. The hybridity literature in peacebuilding studies, but also across different disciplines, should be seen as a transitional epistemological journey towards alternative possibilities for explaining and understanding intertwined social affairs. However, as with any other analytical frameworks, hybridity recently has been in the spotlight of academic criticism, which deserves specific examination and serious consideration regarding the future direction of hybridity debates.

Against hybridity

Hybridity has been subject to extensive criticism in postcolonial studies and social theory. The postcolonial critique highlights the hegemonic nature of hybridity, especially in failing to account for uneven power relations within groups and hierarchies of subordination among the local population.[30] The critique of hybridity in peacebuilding and wider international studies considers hybridity as a disguised form of interventionism, a problem-solving tool that reproduces hierarchical orders of liberal peace, and an escape route after failed statebuilding. David Chandler argues that the critique of liberal peace tends to come to a consensual conclusion that the problem with international interventions is the 'relationship between the liberal West and the non-liberal Other'.[31] Through an imprecise reading, Suthaharan Nadarajah and David Rampton argue that hybrid peace approach is 'a problem-solving tool' which 'reproduces the liberal peace's logics of inclusion and exclusion, and through a reconfiguration of the international interface with resistant "local" orders, intensifies the governmental and biopolitical reach of liberal peace for their containment, transformation, and assimilation'.[32] Despite the fact that the scholars who use hybrid peace as conceptual lens are aware of the risk of essentialising and re-entrenching binaries between the local and the international, the liberal and traditional, John Heathershaw argues that they remain 'entrapped by the terms of the liberal peace debate where liberals compete against locals', thus maintain 'the myth that they are naturally oppositional'.[33] Meera Sabaratnam considers these binaries between the local and international as symptomatic to a Eurocentric critique of liberal peace[34] and suggests decolonising the critique of liberal peace by problematising what Eurocentric thinking discounts, through a repoliticisation of post-conflict fields and promoting positional critique, and by bringing up the materiality and material impact of peacebuilding processes.[35]

Nadarajah and Rampton point out that hybrid peace contains descriptive aspects which account for how the peacebuilding process unfolds, as well as prescriptive aspects which relate to possibility for local emancipation through hybridity.[36] Coming from a policy-minded approach, Dominik Zaum questions the descriptive power of hybrid peace approach, arguing that is 'stating the obvious and should not come as a surprise to political scientists. It is difficult to think of a peace that is not a hybrid peace.'[37] Gearoid Millar labels the work of Richmond and Mac Ginty on hybrid peace as 'prescriptive hybridity', which according to him 'assumes that administering hybrid institutions will foster predictable peace-promoting experiences among local people'.[38] He argues that 'internationally planned and administered hybrid institutions will not result in predictable experiences and may even result in negative or conflict-promoting experiences'.[39] Questioning the prescriptive power of hybrid peace, Shahar Hameiri argues that interactions between international and local actors may not result in producing hybrid peace but rather in 'new forms of political rule and statehood'.[40] Zaum contends that diverse and incompatible reasons and motives among peacebuilding organisations which sometimes fall outside the realm of liberal peace can contribute to hybrid outcomes more than being products of local resistance against international actors.[41] Despite their futile polemical function, it remains unclear where the conceptual innovation and added value are of these critics of the critics.

In response, Richmond and Mac Ginty (2015: 175) argue that these arguments 'somewhat miss the point' because '[h]ybridity has been adopted as tool precisely to interrogate categories and combat lazy dichotomies often used by policymakers and mainstream theorists, as well as to understand political tensions/resistance over peacebuilding'.[42] In defence of hybridity as a conceptual tool, they argue that '[t]he non-acceptance of established political categories allows us to reassess boundaries and identify the connections, networks and co-constitutive elements that comprise the context for contemporary peace-support intervention'.[43] Scholars of hybrid peace consider hybridity a useful concept to focus on relations rather than static affairs, to conceive social processes in terms of their fluidity rather than solidity, to decentre analyses from elites and institutions to non-elite entities and the field of everyday practices, and to finally trace dynamic changes and transformations.[44] What critics consider as prescriptive aspects of hybrid peace represent a normative commitment to an emancipatory peace for Richmond and Mac Ginty, which is more an aspiration than an empirical certainty, an immanent quest than a solid end result. Nadarajah and Rampton interpret the emancipatory prescriptive potential of hybrid peace as resonating similarities with liberal peace.[45] However, they fail to acknowledge that Richmond has never denied sympathy to the emancipatory wing of liberal peace affiliated with civil peace and peaceful civil society, which in practice is often disregarded by peacebuilding organisations. Richmond argued that there are some 'emancipatory forms of human security, associated with individual emancipation and social values, that offer a significant opportunity to enhance the process of building peace in postconflict states'.[46] Furthermore, Nadarajah and Rampton conflate hybrid peace with post-liberal peace.[47] For Richmond, hybrid peace is only one of many other components of post-liberal peace,[48] which, as he recently made clear, 'should not be confused with postliberal governance or hybrid forms of politics emerging from the clash between Northern and Southern epistemologies'.[49]

Some of the chapters in this book were critical of the emancipatory potential of hybridity, while others questioned its conceptual viability across different disciplines. Paul Jackson's chapter in this volume convincingly criticises hybridity for reinforcing local structures and legitimating local authoritarian elites and their traditional and inherited rule over more subordinated social groups. Jackson deconstructs the nature of power of local indigenous structures which are more about exercising power than serving justice as fairness, recognition and retribution; he further points to the local fluid hierarchies of power which are in themselves local hybrids before encountering external modernity. By looking at how identity, social reconstruction and transitional justice were administered in post-genocide Rwanda, Danielle Beswick's chapter concludes that hybridity has served the purpose of national elites to reconcile the divided society and strengthen their popular legitimacy and political authority. Despite the fact that hybrid governance in Rwanda contained undemocratic and illiberal aspects, it was tolerated internationally due to the persistence of guilt for failure to prevent the 1994 genocide and the discursive entanglement of hybridity with local ownership and participatory peacebuilding. Similarly, Louisa Riches questions whether hybridity is a suitable concept to explain the tensions between universalist and particularist understandings of human rights regimes and practices. She argues that hybridity is a homogenising concept posited closer to universalist understandings of human rights. Instead, she argues that normative pluralism could hold more explanatory power than hybridity when explaining the causal power of international human rights regimes and the interaction between sovereign states and international human rights organisations. According to Riches, normative pluralism emphasises the possibility for the transfer, transplantation and translation of human rights discourses and mechanisms to different contexts without denying universal human rights principles, but permitting cultural specificity to shape the promotion and protection of human rights.

Various chapters in this volume have used hybridity as a conceptual lens to break away from universal, uniform and solid understandings of social practices in a wide range of contexts, including peace, development, law and culture. For some scholars hybridity in peace, development and cultural studies is suggested as a response to the intellectual and social uniformities, as 'a way of questioning the fixity of categories and boundaries'.[50] There are other scholars do not see any added value of hybridity approach, considering it a fabrication of the very subject of critique it intends to interrogate. More nuanced views of hybridity consider it a useful lens to capture one episode or fragment of interaction that may lead to heterogenisation (through resistance and persistence of indigeneity) or homogenisation (through coercive and incentivising power of certain actors over the other) of distinct entities, actors and political and socio-legal institutions. As discussed in this section, the critique of hybridity reveals that theories that are perceived as having prescriptive aspects; even if such claims are normative in nature, seeking to advance emancipation, justice and equality, they will become a target of criticism, often misplaced and inadequate, and subject to epistemic delegitimisation. The reason why normative commitments of hybrid peace are being labelled as prescriptive has to do more with Popperian logic of falsification than with evaluating its empirical validity. This generates the need to expand the conceptual lens to understanding social processes refered to as hybrid in nature. The remainder of this chapter will explore three possible alternatives for expanding the epistemological perspectives on hybridity.

After hybridity? Liquidity, assemblage, and figuration

The hybrid approaches to peacebuilding originate in the desire of a group of critical scholars to offer alternative perspectives on why international interventions after violent conflicts fail to reach their intended goals. However, despite these attempts, as illustrated in this book, hybridity runs the risk of becoming another encapsulating concept, especially in side-lining uneven power relations within groups and ignoring hierarchies of subordination within distinct entities, be they individuals or collective institutions. One way of rescuing hybridity in peace and development studies is to engage in more systematic analysis and find empirical evidence of the positive impact of hybridity. This entails strengthening the empirical validity of the descriptive, normative and prescriptive claims of hybrid peace and resolving some of the dilemmas raised by the critics.[51] Currently, there is evidence of work undertaken in this direction by scholars of hybrid forms of peace who are broadening the scope of case studies where post-liberal peace transitions are occurring,[52] and widening and diversifying the methodological tools for tracing hybrid and everyday indicators of peace.[53] While this is a promising avenue in the project of developing a more consolidated research programme, any further advancement will make hybridity more vulnerable to new ways of criticism and epistemic delegitimisation.

Another potential avenue for rescuing hybridity in peace and development studies would be to modify some of its conceptual basis, avoid prescriptive claims, and improve the descriptive scope. Recent work by Mac Ginty and Richmond tries to rescue hybridity from being institutionalised as a policy receipt to handle complex post-conflict processes.[54] In defence of hybridity they argue that it is not a prescriptive theory because it is a process deeply rooted on contextual dynamics of negotiation, co-optation, domination, resistance, assimilation and coexistence. Most importantly, Mac Ginty and Richmond see hybridity as 'an analytical device . . . a way of seeing the world and capture change and lack of fixity between categories'.[55] This reappraisal of hybridity is encouraging as it rightly reinforces the necessity for developing better accounts that capture the relationships between complex processes and fluid outcomes in a spirit of deliberate imprecision and epistemic contingency.[56] Similarly, Philipp Lottholz argues that 'the problems of hybridity approaches, both in theory and practice, seem to lie in insufficient and uncritical conceptualization', claiming that 'hybridity can be a useful lens when used in combination with a critical, reflexive approach to research'.[57] The remainder of this chapter offers a preliminary proposal for expanding the conceptual basis of hybridity. Three well-known concepts – liquidity, assemblage and figuration – could hold the key to rescuing hybridity. Although these three concepts come from different authors and are part of different branches of sociology and philosophy, they are all postmodern ways of reading social life, and they operate on the logic of epistemological anti-foundationalism and methodological relationism.

Bauman's liquidity

If one of the problem with hybridity is its affiliation with conceptual solidity and policy prescription, then perhaps one useful avenue to overcome such conceptual entrapment and enclosure would be Zygmunt Bauman's work on liquidity. Liquid modernity is a sociological theory of Bauman which illustrates the fluid forms of governing contemporary social, political and economic affairs.[58] In its original meaning, Bauman's work through the notion of 'liquid modernity' tries to explain the 'increased transience, uncertainty, and insecurity of all social forms'.[59] Liquidity describes conditions of disintegration, individualisation and disengagement of collective agencies and the persistence of fluidity and ambivalence as new forms of invincibility.[60] Liquidity has come as a response to the scientific certainty and foundationalism has resulted 'into a brutal reality of material and symbolic domination'.[61] Liquidity is the antithesis of solidity, and does not see social relations and power as static and solid, but fluid, decentred, optimal, temporary and disguised. It is a post-Marxist understanding of social life against absolute truths. Liquidity operates on the premises of temporality, contingency, ambivalence, precariousness, which could capture the ever-changing dynamics of social life.[62] It signifies that social structures, identities, agencies and relationships are 'constantly being made, undone and remade'.[63] Bauman perceives society as a network rather than a structure, which consists of 'a matrix of random connections and disconnections and of an essentially infinite volume of possible permutations'.[64] Although Bauman's work is a critique of Western social life, some of the core theoretical propositions can apply to different societies, especially those affected by violent conflicts.[65]

Regardless of contextual nuances, ontologically a hybrid understanding of society is based on solid identities, actors with static ideologies, collective agencies and fixed material relations. Without some conceptual or empirical solidity, the case for hybridity is impossible. It is this implicit solidity which is the basis for fusion with other solids to produce hybrid forms of identities, both in temporary or more permanent basis. Bauman finds hybrids problematic because categorising 'third elements' or those entities that come in-between existing solids for him is an attempt to lay 'orderliness of the world and particularly in the ordering capacity of knowledge'.[66] Therefore, liquidity might hold the key to avoiding uniformity-hybridity entrapment as it has the potential to avoid both essentialism and relativism, which in the case of hybridity are fused together. Liquidity could be more useful than hybridity in explaining contemporary social practices, the fluid nature of identity, disembodied individual and collective agency, and unpredictable patterns of social interactions. In a liquid understanding of social life, ruling forces do not seek singularities of identity, power and economic gains; they rather govern through difference and pluralism. The pursuit of difference and pluralism was the very idea of why hybridity was brought to peace and conflict studies by Richmond and Mac Ginty. Thus, liquid accounts of peace, development or social formations would avoid making universal and general truth claims. The focus would instead be in exploring the 'shape-shifting quality' and the 'permanent transition' of the contemporary world.[67]

Bauman describes liquid modernity as a process of becoming without a solid beginning and end, where living 'seems to possess no sense of privileged direction, expanding instead sideways, upwards and backwards, with the same frequency and without detectable regularity which would enable a prediction of the next move. New stems arise in spots impossible to predict in advance.'[68] Although liquidity does not preclude the possibility for hybridisation, the imprecise and precarious nature of social life makes difficult solidification and normalisation of what may be perceived as 'hybrid' entities. Hence, liquidity helps us to see social and political interactions, identities and power relations as open and performative processes subject to constant change. Whereas research on hybridity often favours cultural relativism, and develops fairly linear narratives about indigenous identities, practices and relations, liquid modernity sees social interactions as contingent performances with demarcared boundaries. Hybridity assumes that agents are shaped by their interactions, but also are embedded in their own habitus, be it a traditional, local order or institutional bureaucracy of international organisations. On the contrary, liquidity considers habitus as insufficient to explain individual and collective identities. Here, Bauman prefers to speak of spaces of indeterminacy and mobility, which at best can only shape an agent's 'perpetual disembedding and re-embedding' of beings.[69] Communities are nothing more than ambivalent relationships that constantly change. Through the notion of the local and everyday, the hybrid peace theory tries to unearth subaltern and critical forms of local agency. This process in academic discourses often unintentionally discounts individual agencies where the local is presented as collective agency. Liquidity theory is better suited to make space for individual agency and structured autonomy in an environment of constant ontological and material insecurity.

How would peace look like from the perspective of liquidity theory? In a liquid understanding of peace, the declared intentions of actors constantly change, and forms of intervention are fluid, hidden and often circumvented. From a liquid, postmodern perspective, the agency of individuals and collective entities should be seen as contingent and adjusting rapidly to different contexts, fluid identities in permanent state of flux, plural selves with multiple social roles and complex interactions, contradictory yet knowledgeable with practical, discursive, reflexive and intuitive.[70] Even hybrid entities and hybridisation processes do not last, they are temporary. Hence, any claim about hybridity is about capturing empirically a temporary moment of hybridisation. Outcomes are not predetermined and thus any prescriptive claim or any effort for generalisation is related to a sequence or moment of hybridisation, which is not representative of other cases or moments within a particular society or across different societies. Traces of emancipation, progress and justice can be interpreted retrospectively and not *a priori* prescribed and predicted. One of the methods of proponents of hybridity is the development of alternative everyday peace indicators which seek to move away from universal measurements of peace. However, as long as the alternative everyday and bottom-up indicators are codified they risk being solidified, thus failing to capture change and new temporary manifestation of local agency. Most importantly, the risk is prevalent that policy-makers will start using everyday indicators to hide their failure and defuse their impact. Bauman argues 'means successfully tested in the past need to be constantly inspected and revised since they may prove useless or downright counterproductive once circumstances change'.[71] At best such general frameworks of analysis cannot have prescriptive function, only descriptive role to (re)produce contingent historicism. He further argues that '[a] swift and thorough forgetting or outdated information and fast ageing habits can be more important for the next success than the memorization of past moves and the building of strategies on a foundation laid by previous learning'.[72]

Time as becoming has been widely ignored in peacebuilding studies, namely the spatio-temporalities of identities, power, intentions and relations.[73]

Despite the fact that hybridity favours relativism, it tends to ignore the relevance of time. Conversely, liquidity cherishes time as a key ingredient that shapes social life.[74] Hence, Bauman refers to those spatio-temporalities as liquid times, consisting of 'a readiness to change tactics and style at short notice, to abandon commitments and loyalties without regret – to pursue opportunities according to their current availability, rather than following one's own established preferences'.[75] This liquid understanding of time could be also helpful in capturing the fluid nature of international interventions. For instance, remote interventions through drones and cyber attacks are anti-hybridity situations; they do not require engagement with local subjects.[76] The only engagement is surveillance over the local, through drones, big data and other means of remote extracting knowledge without having to interact, thus hybridise, with the other. Therefore, what liquid theory would contribute to hybridity is rethinking the role of agency, networks and structures as well as the meaning of peace, forms of actions and potential outcomes as fluid, ambivalent and disembodied phenomena.

Deleuze's assemblage

The second conceptual framework which would help overcome some of the problems but also complement hybridity is Deleuze's concept of assemblage. Assemblages are temporary groupings of expressive and material heterogenic components that do not form a seamless whole, but appear as contingent constitutive parts that are already detached or are components of another assemblage with different dynamics of interaction.[77] As Jason Skeet argues, 'assemblages are not predesigned by anyone, they are not brought about through a blueprint predetermining their makeup or what it is they can produce. In fact, assemblages have to be considered more along the lines of self-organizing entities.'[78] They represent multiplication of connections which constantly change. Skeet argues that '[f]or Deleuze, it is process rather than form that is primary, and every form is the effect of a process of becoming'.[79] Through the concept of territorialisation, Deleuze speaks of the process of homogeneity of an assemblage, whereas deterritorialisation signifies the process of heterogeneity of an assemblage. Assemblage theory has recently taken more prominence in security studies, but within hybridity studies it is still under-researched.[80]

There are several areas where assemblage theory could complement hybridity theory. A Deleuzian reading of hybrid peace or hybrid political orders would consider them as assemblages of multiple components with the potential of territorialising, homogenising or heterogenising different entities. Perceiving hybrid peace or hybrid political orders as assemblages of practices enables unpacking better the multiplicity of material and discursive agencies that constitute the local resistance, co-option, assimilation, and coexistence in their spatio-temporalities in conflict-affected societies.

While we know a great deal about local critical agency that plays a crucial role in the development of positive and negative hybrid peace, we still do not know how local agency is assembled, what are its components and how they constantly change. While the everyday is already recognised as an important site of local agency, we still don't know the material and expressive elements of everyday peace and interaction between insider and outsider agents. Similarly, international governance seen from the assemblage point of view would help unpack the role of military presence, diplomacy, hidden agendas which permits their fluid coexistence with local political orders and enables hybridisation practices. Therefore, assemblages would perceive hybridisation as a process of momentary interaction and interference of different agents with different agencies, both in their material and express as well as individual and collective appearances. In this context, hybridity would come to be understood as assemblages of heterogeneous entities. Moreover, hybridity as assemblage would enable exploring the contextual formation of peace and understanding what elements enable peace and what break peace and how such dynamics shape peace in the long run.

Seen from the perspective of assemblage theory, peace can be conceptualised as a temporary assemblage of agents with different intentions, organisational networks, power basis, discourses and material strengths. In this regard, scholarship on actor-network could be helpful in complementing hybridity studies.[81] These agents can be from same or different geographical approximation, political and cultural affiliation, which are not only organised around their 'inside-ness' or 'outside-ness' towards a particular assemblage, but also on their capacities and performative functions across different assemblages. Although the hybridity theory expands the scope for agency for the subaltern and marginalised, it is the assemblage theory which has clearer scope for locating agency and tracing how their capacities and interactions limit, enable and shape their assemblage as well as other assemblages.[82] Assemblage theory recognises the agency of individuals and larger social assemblages, which can be networks of individuals, organisations and broader communities.[83] In this regard, assemblage theory would be more adequate to account for multiple assemblages between individual and the state.

Assemblage is more complex than hybridity in its conceptual ability to account for more complex social formations situated horizontally and vertically. Hybridity theory in peace and development studies mainly accounts for the interactions between local and international actors, networks, and structures. The analyses mainly look at the institutional hybridisations, though there are also other studies that look at other sectors of societies. This runs the risk of reproducing binaries and does not account for different levels of hybridisation within and between temporary groupings. Unpacking hybridity as assemblage enables exploring that hybridisation practices are a conglomeration of institutional, public and everyday assemblages of resistance and co-optation.[84] Furthermore, assemblage theory can account for both basic and larger assemblages of 'multiscaled social reality'.[85] It is possible to account for the assemblages of material and expressive between different actors, networks and organisations involved in peacebuilding and development assistance. Hybridity has not engaged so far in exploring the formation of temporary material and expressive assemblages, which are crucial for making sense of social actions and emergent features. Assemblages as entities of becoming and spaces of possibilities do not permit predictability of outcome. Hence, hybridity as assemblage more adequately decouples it from the normative and prescriptive attributes, which has been the key criticism directed against hybridity in peacebuilding studies. Hybridity theory does not spell out the possibility of a reversal process of 'dehybridisation'. Assemblage theory provides a better conceptualisation of the decomposition of assemblages. Existing theories of hybridity in peace and conflict studies mainly look at the macro-level and collective entities of hybridisation. On the other hand, assemblage provides the possibility to make individuals aware of the constant process of precariousness and deterritorialisation.[86] Accordingly, the issues explored here and are many other points of encounter speak of the usefulness of assemblage theory in complementing existing accounts of hybridity.

Elias's figuration

The third suitable intellectual avenue for expanding the conceptual frontiers of hybridity is Norbert Elias's concept of figuration. In Elias's work, the notion of figuration signifies the zone where social structures, practices and facts interweave with the networks of relationships between human beings. Elias defined society as 'the processes and structures of interweaving, the figuration formed by the actions of interdependent people'.[87] Elias considers figurations to be temporary, changing by nature and full of tensions, highlighting thus the presence of figurational sequences and changes in social relations as a result of figuration changes.[88] The main reason why Elias preferred the notion of figuration over other concepts such as systems, structures and agency, was to illustrate the interdependent and interconnected nature of individual and society, agency and structure, power and resistance, rationality and blindness, without having to reduce these notions to static states of being, detached from their dynamic and ever-changing character. Elias's figurational sociology long before Bauman's liquidity and Deleuze's assemblage highlights processes and temporalities as core attributes of social life. Eric Dunning and Jason Hughes maintain that figurations direct 'attention towards shifting patterns, regularities, direction of change, tendencies and counter-tendencies, in webs of human relationships that are always changing over time'.[89]

Until recently, Elias's figurational theory has been widely ignored in international relations and peace and conflict studies. The author's own work has tried to bring figurational sociology to peacebuilding studies when studying the long-term impact of liberal peacebuilding.[90] A figurational view of peace and development processes provides an account of how certain peace intentions are translated into practice and utilised by different agents, and mediated via socially constructed events, which produce various outcomes that may be unintended, unanticipated and unprevented consequences of human interdependencies and interactions.[91] Elias argued that intentional actions of human interactions most often lead to unplanned and unintended outcomes, maintaining that social life is constituted of interweaving of intentional human actions, which produce unplanned and unintended outcomes.[92] Seen from the perspective of figurational sociology, hybrid peace is not a desired state of affairs or an intended outcome, rather it is an unintended and unplanned outcome of multiple actors, networks and structures who shape the outcomes but do not control it.[93] This would evade the criticism that hybrid peace receives, especially concerning its perceptive aspects. Figuration theory would be able to trace the process and mechanism which impede, shape, deviate and transform actors, networks and structures in new unexpected directions.

Elias's figurational sociology is 'against any form of normative, teleological, and metaphysical interpretation of historical development and social life',[94] favouring an empirical interpretation where relationality and contingency of social formation, such as identity, power, and institutions are explored. A post-philosophical view of hybridity as offered by figurational theory would facilitate removing unnecessary overloading normative, ideological and philosophical lenses for studying post-conflict societies and transformations. A figurational view of hybridity would not seek to mediate knowledge about various actors and structures, or to undertake social re-engineering by intervening to change the existing relations, structures and networks. Contrary to this, using Bruno Latour's expressions, a figurational view of hybridity could serve as an intermediary body of knowledge between the occurrence of acts and their normative interpretation in a complex, both associative and dissociative manner, to present the complex figuration of peace by looking at the intentions, events and consequences in a particular post-conflict place and time.[95] Therefore, peace figuration does not try to impose a special ontological order on post-conflict societies, but only explicate and interpret it by disentangling the figuration of multi-layered intentions, agencies and structures, events and consequences.

A figurational view of the hybridisation process is essential in order to highlight that the identity of foreign interveners and local actors is not static, but determined by the social functions they perform and their relation to a particular place in its spatial temporality.[96] The location of power would move from legal-institutional frameworks to networks of relations and interactions of a multitude of assemblages of agents. State institutions would not be considered static, but as a 'powerful, metaphysical effect of practices that make such structures appear to exist'.[97] Figuration theory sees power not as solid or powerful, but as temporary, relational and divided. It would bring to forefront agential pluralities, multiple interdependencies and various ways that post-conflict subjects manage to shape the peacebuilding process. Figurational theory is against reducing social relations to states, objects or things. This is relevant to the hybridity approach as it has started to be perceived and invoked as states or static conditions, thus cloaking its relational and processual aspects.[98] For instance, Elias favoured using processual notions such as 'developmentalisation' rather than development. In the context of hybridity, there is clear evidence of the usage of hybridisation, but it is still overshadowed by the prevalence of notions such as hybridity, hybrid peace or hybrid forms of peace.[99]

The discussion so far has revealed that liquidity, assemblage and figuration provide some scope for supplementing the existing debates on hybridity and overcoming some of its conceptual and empirical anomalies. Going backwards, Elias's figuration is similar to Deleuze's assemblage in the sense of perceiving social formations as temporary groupings of individuals where interactions determine the identity and behaviour of those contingent entities which operate in a larger web of other similar and different formations that constantly shift capacities, functions, intentions and relations. While assemblage provides a good basis to map the complex social and material networks, figuration is better suited to capture the fluid and processual establishment and disintegration of social formations as well as trace long-term patterns and outcomes of social figurations. Liquidity in a sense is narrower than assemblage and figuration, yet it appears to be a much larger depiction of contemporary social life. It is narrower when describing the fluid nature of micro-social processes, agencies, networks and structures, but also much broader in describing global social trends across different social, political and economic fields. Hybridity it seems is much narrower then all these three concepts. Hybridity can represent only one component or dimension of figuration, assemblage and liquidity. In a liquid world, all entities are hybrid because they are not fixed entities, they have displaced identities and are products of multiple political and cultural compositions. In the context of assemblage, hybridity can signify the placement of individuals in multiple different assemblages which have delineated identities. Finally, hybridity in the context of figurations represents the dynamics of social interactions and emerges as unplanned outcome.

Conclusion

The research on hybridity is still in the consolidation stage. However, since its emergence it has been subject to both criticism and well-intended efforts to expand the frontiers of this research agenda.[100] This chapter has charted new possible conceptual avenues that would rescue hybridity from the perceived policy-prescriptive positivism and critical-emancipatory normativism. By way of conclusion, an outline for an expanded research agenda on hybridity is presented. Conceptually, definitions of hybridity should expand and account not only the actors, forms of interactions and outcomes but also the complex lineages, assemblages and figuration of processes that shape peace after violent conflict. This entails expanding the vocabulary of hybridity studies to account for the liquid nature of practices, to disentangle the assemblage, interruption and cessation of socio-material connections, as well as to explore the temporalities of intentions, forms of agency, power relations and contingent resemblance of consequences.

So far, debates on hybridity have either reinforced existing identities of agents in post-conflict societies when perceiving hybridity as coexistence or come up with new identities when perceiving hybridity as in-betweenness. Bauman's work on liquid identities provides a good basis upon which more fluid understandings of agents' identity could be constructed in post-conflict societies. For instance, one person can have multiple identities that change depending on their social functions (practices) or closeness or distance towards a particular place. The author's work on the geo-ontological positioning of agents of peace has revealed that beyond local–international dichotomies or other hybrid identities, agents of peacebuilding have fluid identities, for instance in relation to a particular place they can be insiders or outsiders, or depending on their social functions they can be labelled differently.[101] Such spatio-temporal performances show that no singular event or articulation of agency can be reducible to another event or agency 'for such occurrences are singular and unrepeatable'.[102] This certainly has implications for any research which seeks to capture patterns, deviations, regularities and irregularities in post-conflict societies. One area where hybridity studies have not engaged so far is the politics of affection in conflict-affected societies. Affect helps capture the movement of our ideas, beliefs, body and cognition, which holds the key to our social behaviour and change.[103] Such acts of becoming are affected by interactions and as such result in fluidity of our identity and practices. In understanding the psychological aspects of post-conflict societies, politics of affect help explain the role of humiliation, empathy, fear and revenge in shaping the collective identity and practices of peace agents as well as help explain the impact of political experience in peacebuilding and peace-breaking processes.[104] In other words, it is important to investigate in the future how emotions as interwoven mind-body experiences are involved in constituting hybrid forms of peace.

Debates on hybridity have mainly explored institutional and public forms of hybridisation. This is largely due to the availability of tangible, transferable and understandable knowledge for scholars. Even ethnographic studies of hybridity have excavated and observed only obvious practices of interaction between local and international actors.[105] Capturing the complex assemblages and their discursive and material aspects requires expanding the catalogue of methodological possibilities as well as more profound engagement with uncommon sites of knowledge.[106] In making claims about hybridity, it is important to avoid conceptual and empirical fixity and instead promote processual analysis. If hybridity is perceived as assemblage, it is important to expand the role of materiality, emotions, micropolitics, virtuality and technology in shaping peace intentions, events and outcomes. Similarly, debates on hybridity should pay more attention not only to the process of formations, construction, consolidation of things in peacebuilding context, but also to the reversal processes, dissemblance, agential dissolution and peace-breaking dynamics.[107] One particular area which needs further examination is the social and political spaces where different identities, ideologies, actors and representations form their meaning and connote power.

Finally, studies on hybridity have largely explored hybridity as contextual process yet in the realm of the interactions of rational actors motivated by claims to power, justice, entitlements and welfare. Hybridity studies need to expand and make sense of complex peace figurations as unintended outcomes of multiple interactions of actors, networks and processes connected across different temporary assemblages. A figurational view of hybridity would require moving beyond positivism and normativity when interrogating peace processes. Understandably such modes of knowing might run against politics of epistemic responsibility and thrust for social change. However, every new precise and solid form of knowledge risks being institutionalised and utilised by power-holders. As discussed in this chapter, hybridity has been also affected by such tendencies.[108] Hence, it is crucial to develop fluid knowledge it is in the domain of describing peace processes rather than becoming complicit in generating policy-relevant knowledge. Therefore, expanding the research agenda on hybridity across these three alternative concepts not only could save hybridity for its criticism, but also contribute in generate new fertile knowledge which would expand the scope for understanding the messiness of peacebuilding in conflict-affected places.

Notes

The author is grateful for insights and comments from Nicolas Lemay-Hébert, Roger Mac Ginty, and Philipp Lottholz.

1 See David Chandler (2006) Empire in Denial: The Politics of State-Building (London: Pluto Press); Shahrbanou Tadjbakhsh (ed.) (2011) Rethinking the Liberal Peace: External Models and Local Alternatives (Abington: Routledge).
2 Roger Mac Ginty (2010) 'Hybrid Peace: The Interaction between Top-Down and Bottom-Up Peace', *Security Dialogue* 41(4): 391–412; Oliver P. Richmond and

Audra Mitchell (eds) (2012) *Hybrid Forms of Peace: From Everyday Agency to Post-Liberalism* (Basingstoke: Palgrave Macmillan).
3 Oliver P. Richmond (2009) 'A Post-Liberal Peace: Eirenism and the Everyday', *Review of International Studies* 35(3): 572.
4 Oliver P. Richmond (2005) *The Transformation of Peace* (Basingstoke: Palgrave Macmillan), 198.
5 Volker Boege *et al.* (2009) 'Building Peace and Political Community in Hybrid Political Orders', *International Peacekeeping* 16(5): 599–615.
6 Ibid. 611.
7 Richmond, 'A Post-Liberal Peace', 565.
8 Ibid. 566.
9 Oliver P. Richmond (2010) 'Resistance and the Post-Liberal Peace', *Millennium* 38(3): 687.
10 Oliver P. Richmond (2011) *A Post-Liberal Peace* (Abington: Routledge), 151.
11 Richmond, 'A Post-Liberal Peace', 19.
12 Ibid. 18.
13 Roger Mac Ginty (2011) *International Peacebuilding and Local Resistance* (Basingstoke: Palgrave Macmillan), 69.
14 Mac Ginty, 'Hybrid Peace', 404.
15 Roger Mac Ginty and Oliver P. Richmond (2016) 'The Fallacy of Constructing Hybrid Political Orders: A Reappraisal of the Hybrid Turn in Peacebuilding', *International Peacekeeping* 23(2): 219–39.
16 Mac Ginty, 'Hybrid Peace', 398.
17 Ibid. 404.
18 Ibid. 408.
19 Oliver P. Richmond and Roger Mac Ginty (2015) 'Where Now for the Critique of the Liberal Peace?', *Cooperation and Conflict* 50(2): 177.
20 David Chandler and Oliver P. Richmond (2015) 'Contesting Postliberalism: Governmentality or Emancipation?', *Journal of Development and International Relations* 18(1): 1–24.
21 Anna K. Jarstad and Roberto Belloni (2012) 'Introducing Hybrid Peace Governance: Impact and Prospects of Liberal Peacebuilding', *Global Governance* 18(1): 1.
22 Roberto Belloni (2012) 'Hybrid Peace Governance: Its Emergence and Significance', *Global Governance* 18(1): 22.
23 Ibid. 24.
24 Ibid. 34.
25 Chetan Kumar and Jos De la Haye (2012) 'Hybrid Peacemaking: Building National "Infrastructure for Peace"', *Global Governance* 18(1): 13–20; Stefanie Kappler and Nicolas Lemay-Hébert (2015) 'Hybrid Local Ownership in Bosnia-Herzegovina and Kosovo: From Discursive to Material Aspects of Ownership', in Sung Yong Lee and Alpasan Özerdem (eds), *Local Ownership in International Peacebuilding: Key Theoretical and Practical Issues* (Abington: Routledge).
26 Gëzim Visoka (2012) 'Three Levels of Hybridisation Practices in Post-Conflict Kosovo', *Journal of Peacebuilding and Development* 7(2): 24.
27 Laura McLeod (2015) 'A Feminist Approach to Hybridity: Understanding Local and International Interactions in Producing Post-Conflict Gender Security', *Journal of Intervention and Statebuilding* 9(1): 48–69.
28 Jana Hönke (2013) *Transnational Companies and Security Governance: Hybrid Practices in a Postcolonial World* (Abington: Routledge).
29 Human Security Study Group (2016) *From Hybrid Peace to Human Security: Rethinking EU Strategy towards Conflict* (Brussels: Human Security Study Group), http://www.securityintransition.org/wp-content/uploads/2016/02/HSSGReport.pdf, 4.

30 Anjali Prabhu (2007) *Hybridity: Limits, Transformations, Prospects* (Albany, NY: SUNY Press).
31 David Chandler (2010) 'The Uncritical Critique of "Liberal Peace"', *Review of International Studies* 36(S1): 146.
32 Suthaharan Nadarajah and David Rampton (2015) 'The Limits of Hybridity and the Crisis of Liberal Peace', *Review of International Studies* 41(1): 50.
33 John Heathershaw (2014) 'Towards Better Theories of Peacebuilding: Beyond the Liberal Peace Debate', *Peacebuilding* 1(2): 277, 280.
34 Meera Sabaratnam (2013) 'Avatars of Eurocentrism in the Critique of the Liberal Peace', *Security Dialogue* 44(3): 259–78.
35 Ibid.
36 Nadarajah and Rampton, 'Limits of hybridity', 59–60.
37 Dominik Zaum (2012) 'Beyond the "Liberal Peace"', *Global Governance* 18(1): 124.
38 Gerard Millar (2014) 'Disaggregating Hybridity: Why Hybrid Institutions Do Not Produce Predictable Experiences of Peace', *Journal of Peace Research* 51(4): 501.
39 Ibid.
40 Shahar Hameiri (2011) 'A Reality Check for the Critique of Liberal Peace', in Susan Campbell, David Chandler and Meera Sabrantnam (eds), *A Liberal Peace? The Problems and Practices of Peacebuilding* (London: Zed Books), 197.
41 Zaum, 'Beyond the "Liberal Peace"', 125.
42 Richmond and Mac Ginty, 'Where Now for the Critique of the Liberal Peace?', 175.
43 Ibid. 180.
44 Roger Mac Ginty and Gurchathen Sanghera (2012) 'Hybridity in Peacebuilding and Development: An Introduction', *Journal of Peacebuilding and Development* 7(2): 3–4.
45 Nadarajah and Rampton, 'Limits of Hybridity'.
46 Oliver P. Richmond (2007) 'Emancipatory Forms of Human Security and Liberal Peacebuilding', *International Journal* 62(3): 459.
47 Nadarajah and Rampton, 'Limits of Hybridity', 53.
48 Richmond, 'A Post-Liberal Peace', 577. Richmond, *A Post-Liberal Peace*, 147.
49 Chandler and Richmond, 'Contesting Postliberalism', 11.
50 Richmond and Mac Ginty, 'Where Now?', 184.
51 See Richmond and Mitchell, *Hybrid Forms of Peace*.
52 Oliver P. Richmond and Sandra Pogodda (eds) (2016) *Post-Liberal Peace Transitions: Between Peace Formation and State Formation* (Edinburgh: Edinburgh University Press).
53 Roger Mac Ginty (ed.) (2014) *Alternative and Bottom-Up Peace Indicators* (Abington: Routledge).
54 Mac Ginty and Richmond, 'Fallacy', 2.
55 Ibid. 6.
56 John Law (2004) *After Method: Mess in Social Science Research* (Abington: Routledge).
57 Philipp Lottholz (2016) 'Exploring the Boundaries of Knowledge via Hybridity', *Journal of Intervention and Statebuilding* 10(1): 1.
58 Zygmunt Bauman (2000) *Liquid Modernity* (Cambridge: Polity).
59 Nicholas Gane (2004) *The Future of Social Theory* (London: Continuum), 9.
60 Bauman, *Liquid Modernity*, 14.
61 Simon Susen (2015) *The 'Postmodern Turn' in the Social Sciences* (Basingstoke: Palgrave Macmillan), 45.
62 Bauman, *Liquid Modernity*.
63 Tony Blackshaw (2005) *Zygmunt Bauman* (Abington: Routledge), 48.
64 Zygmunt Bauman (2007) *Liquid Times: Living in an Age of Uncertainty* (Cambridge: Polity), 3.

65 Zygmunt Bauman *et al.*, (2014) 'After Snowden: Rethinking the Impact of Surveillance', *International Political Sociology* 8(2): 121–44.
66 Zygmunt Bauman (1991) *Modernity and Ambivalence* (Cambridge: Polity Press), 59.
67 Blackshaw, *Zygmunt Bauman,* 64.
68 Zygmunt Bauman (1992) *Intimations of Postmodernity* (London, Routledge), 27.
69 Blackshaw, *Zygmunt Bauman,* 93.
70 Susen, *Postmodern Turn,* 36.
71 Bauman, *Liquid Times,* 3.
72 Ibid.
73 William E. Connolly (2011) *A World of Becoming* (Durham, NC: Duke University Press), 22.
74 Bauman, *Liquid Modernity.*
75 Bauman, *Liquid Times,* 4.
76 See M. Duffield (2015) 'The Digital Development-Security Nexus: Linking Cyber-Humanitarianism and Drone Warfare', in Paul Jackson (ed.), *Handbook of International Security and Development* (London: Edward Elgar), 80–94.
77 Gilles Deleuze and Félix Guattari (1987) *A Thousand Plateaus: Capitalism and Schizophrenia* (Minneapolis, MN: University of Minnesota Press).
78 Jason Skeet (2014) 'On the Flyleaves of Modernism: Deleuze and Guattari's *Kafka*', in Paul Ardoin, S. E. Gontarski and Laci Mattison (eds), *Understanding Deleuze, Understanding Modernism* (New York: Bloomsbury), 65.
79 Jason Skeet (2014) 'Becoming', in Ardoin *et al.*, *Understanding Deleuze,* 253.
80 Michele Acuto and Simon Curtis (eds) (2014) *Reassembling International Theory: Assemblage Thinking and International Relations* (Basingstoke, Palgrave Macmillan); Marc C. Doucet, (2015) 'Global Assemblages of Security Governance and Contemporary International Intervention', *Journal of Intervention and Statebuilding* 10(1): 116–32.
81 Bruno Latour (2005) *Reassembling the Social: An Introduction to Actor-Network Theory* (Oxford: Oxford University Press).
82 Justin Litaker (2014) 'Assemblage', in Ardoin *et al.*, *Understanding Deleuze,* 252.
83 Manuel DeLanda (2006) *A New Philosophy of Science: Assemblage Theory and Social Complexity* (London: Continuum), 36.
84 Visoka, 'Three Levels'.
85 DeLanda, *New Philosophy of Science,* 34.
86 Ibid. 28.
87 Norbert Elias (1994) *The Civilizing Process: Sociogenetic and Psychogenetic Investigations,* tr. E. Jephott (Maiden, MA: Blackwell Publishing), 213–14.
88 Norbert Elias (2012) *What is Sociology?,* tr. G. Morrissey, S. Mennell and E. Jephcott (Dublin: UCD Press), 127.
89 Eric Dunning and Jason Hughes (2013) *Norbert Elias and Modern Sociology: Knowledge, Interdependence, Power, Process* (London: Bloomsbury Academic), 52.
90 Gëzim Visoka (2016) *Peace Figuration After International Intervention: Intentions, Events and Consequences of Liberal Peacebuilding* (Abington: Routledge). Gëzim Visoka (forthcoming), 'Norbert Elias and Statebuilding after Violent Conflict', in Tatiana S. Landini and Francois Depelteau (eds), *Norbert Elias and Violence* (Basingstoke: Palgrave Macmillan).
91 Visoka, *Peace Figuration.*
92 Norbert Elias (1997) 'Towards a Theory of Social Processes: A Translation', *British Journal of Sociology* 48(3): 355–83.
93 Visoka, 'Three Levels', 33.
94 Charalambos Tsekeris (2013) 'Norbert Elias on Relations: Insights and Perspectives', in *Conceptualising Relational Sociology: Ontological and Theoretical Issue,* eds. Chrisopher Power and François Dépelteau (New York: Palgrave Macmillan), 88.

95 Visoka, *Peace Figuration.*
96 Visoka, 'Norbert Elias and Statebuilding after Violent Conflict'.
97 Timothy Mitchell (1991) 'The Limits of the State: Beyond Statist Approaches and Their Critics', *American Political Science Review* 85(1): 94.
98 Visoka, *Peace Figuration.*
99 Mac Ginty, *International Peacebuilding;* Richmond and Mitchell, *Hybrid Forms of Peace;* Visoka, 'Three Levels'.
100 Nicolas Lemay-Hébert and Florian Kühn (2015 'Letter from the Editors: Taking the Hybridity Agenda Further', *Journal of Intervention and Statebuilding* 9(1): 1–3.
101 Gëzim Visoka (2017) 'Agents of Peace: Place, Identity and Peacebuilding', in Christine Agius and Dean Keep (eds), *Identity Making, Displacement and Rupture: Performing Discourses of Belonging, Place and Being,* ed. (Manchester: Manchester University Press).
102 Susen, *The 'Postmodern Turn', 165.*
103 Ty Solomon and Brent J. Steele (2016) 'Micro-moves in International Relations theory', *European Journal of International Relations,* Early view, doi: 10.1177/1354066116634442.; See also: Nicolas Lemay-Hébert and Stefanie Kappler (2016) 'What attachment to peace? Exploring the normative and material dimensions of local ownership in peacebuilding' *Review of International Studies.*
104 Emma Hutchison (2016) *Affective Communities in World Politics: Collective Emotions After Trauma* (Cambridge: Cambridge University Press).
105 Millar, 'Disaggregating hybridity'.
106 Claudia Aradau, et al.(eds) (2015) *Critical Security Methods: New frameworks for analysis* (Abington: Routledge).
107 Visoka, *Peace Figuration after International Intervention.*
108 Mac Ginty and Richmond, 'Fallacys'.

Index

www.ingramcontent.com/pod-product-compliance
Ingram Content Group UK Ltd.
Pitfield, Milton Keynes, MK11 3LW, UK
UKHW022009180926
475701UK00003B/273
* 9 7 8 1 1 3 8 3 3 3 5 9 8 *